FULL CIRCLE

FULL CIRCLE

How the Classical World
Came Back to Us

FERDINAND MOUNT

SIMON &
SCHUSTER

London · New York · Sydney · Toronto

A CBS COMPANY

First published in Great Britain by Simon & Schuster UK Ltd, 2010
A CBS COMPANY

3 5 7 9 10 8 6 4 2

Simon & Schuster UK Ltd
1st Floor
222 Gray's Inn Road
London WC1X 8HB

www.simonandschuster.co.uk

Simon & Schuster Australia
Sydney

A CIP catalogue record for this book is available
from the British Library.

ISBN: 978-1-84737-798-2

Typeset by M Rules
Printed in the UK by CPI Mackays, Chatham ME5 8TD

For Harry Mount

Explorator viae

The world's great age begins anew,
　　The golden years return . . .

A loftier Hellas rears its mountains
　　From waves serener far . . .
　　　　　Shelley, *Hellas*

'There's a frightful great fountain, too, in front of
the steps, all rocks and sort of carved animals. You
never saw such a thing.'
　　　'Yes, Hooper, I did. I've been here before . . .'
　　　I had been there before. I knew all about it.
　　　　　Evelyn Waugh, *Brideshead Revisited*

CONTENTS

INTRODUCTION

God's long funeral is over, and we are back where we started. Two thousand years of history have melted into the back story, which nobody reads any more. We have returned to Year Zero, AD 0, or rather 0 CE, because we are in the Common Era now, the Years of Our Lord having expired.

So much about the society that is now emerging bears an astonishing resemblance to the most prominent features of what we call the classical world – its institutions, its priorities, its recreations, its physics, its sexual morality, its food, its politics, even its religion. Often without our being in the least aware of it, the ways in which we live our rich and varied lives correspond, almost eerily so, to the ways in which the Greeks and Romans lived theirs. Whether we are eating and drinking, bathing or exercising or making love, pondering, admiring or enquiring, our habits of thought and action, our diversions and concentrations recall theirs. It is as though the 1,500 years after the fall of Rome had been time out from traditional ways of being human.

These similarities do not arise out of conscious imitation of Greek and Roman models, as they did in the Renaissance when artists and architects and philosophers actively sought to revive the best of the ancient world. Today's 'classical revival' seems to have arisen naturally, out of our new situation, for the most part without our noticing. Now and then, it is true, we have an inkling that we are engaged in some activity in a style that recalls the way the Greeks or the Romans did it, but we do not perceive how systematic the resemblance is or how deep it goes.

Let me pause for a moment and try to make clear what this book is about. Most people are aware of the right answer to the question that John Cleese asks in *The Life of Brian*: 'What have the Romans ever done for us?' Like the Galilean peasants in the film, we murmur hesitantly, 'Well, there's the aqueducts . . . and the drains and the roads and the underfloor heating . . . and medicine and education . . . oh and the wine.' If we include the contribution of the Greeks too, then we must acknowledge that we owe half our vocabulary to their dead languages, that their doctors identified and named most of our organs and the diseases which afflict them – arthritis, bronchitis, cancer – that their philosophers invented the language which philosophers have used ever since, that their builders devised the orders of architecture which are still around us today. Our classical inheritance is visible whenever we choose to look down into a book or up at the skyline of Trafalgar Square, or the Place de la Concorde or downtown Washington DC. However hard we try to shake ourselves free and proclaim that we are uniquely independent, freshly minted, unprecedentedly modern, our debt to the achievements of Greece and Rome remains with us.

But that is not what I am talking about in this book. That debt, that inheritance has been staring us in the face for two millennia. It is not a new discovery. What I am suggesting here is something quite different and of much more recent origin. What I want to focus on is the way we live now. By 'now' I mean any period from the past five years to the past half-century, depending on the context. By 'we' I mean especially 'we in Britain' but also more generally 'we in Europe and North America'. And what I want to argue is that our present habits, our enthusiasms, our preoccupations and our world-view don't just carry in them some interesting traces of the civilization that crumbled when Rome crumbled. In a weird but exact way, they often *reproduce* the mindsets of Rome under the early emperors and – more weirdly still – of the Greek colonies scattered across the Eastern Aegean between, roughly, 550 and 250 BC. The questions I want to explore are not about how much we owe to the Greeks and the Romans, but about how much we are like them, how in so many ways, large and small, trivial and profound, we *are* them and they are us.

In fact, the vogue for films and books showing what the Romans did for us suggests that, half-consciously, we are groping towards an understanding of what we are, a perception of some deeper closeness to the classical world. And this is a far more unsettling thing than merely listing the devices we have inherited from our ingenious ancestors. We are not just making an inventory, we are reaching out across an abyss.

This is unnerving in the same way it is unnerving when you go into a strange room or see a strange view through a gap in the hedge and think, 'I have been here before.' We pride ourselves, after all, on the uniqueness of our perspective. We are the heirs of all the ages. We know so much more than our fathers and forefathers. This is not because we are cleverer. It is because we enjoy the advantages of their achievements. As Sir Isaac Newton said, 'If I have seen further, it is by standing on the shoulders of giants.' For that reason, we tend to regard our modernity as a culmination. There has been nothing like it in history before and, whisper it gently, nothing to match it. All human history has been tending towards Us.

Now this is not how earlier generations have always regarded themselves. On the contrary, they often thought of themselves as having fallen away from previous ages, of having become decadent, in their art, or in their morality, or their religion or their politics, or even in the wit and style of their society. The best they could hope for, the most they could aspire to was to try to restart the motors, to midwife some laborious rebirth of the old glories, to stage a 'renaissance'.

This idea of 'renaissance' makes moderns decidedly uncomfort-able. How can we claim to be so unprecedentedly *new* if we spend time and effort on reviving and recreating defunct patterns of life?

Modern professors and commentators dislike the idea so much that they have tried to prove that there was never any such thing.[1] The New Historicist school of historians, led by the charismatic Stephen Greenblatt, have persuaded most of their colleagues to say as little as possible about 'the Renaissance'. Much better to call that period by a quite different name: 'the early modern period'.

This term 'early modern' is now all but universal among today's historians. Yet if you stop to think about it, the phrase is a rather queer one. How peculiar it is to examine a large slice of history, three centuries and more, predominantly in the light of how its tendencies foreshadow and enable the emergence of Us. All historians operate to some extent within the preconceptions and preoccupations of their own time. But has there ever been a generation before which has proclaimed so proudly and loudly that the birth of the modern is the only birth that counts?

But the awkward fact remains that cultural leaders in those 'early modern' years believed that what they were seeing around them and were themselves helping to create was a rebirth of the old learning and the old art. In his *Lives of the Painters*, published in 1550 and immensely popular then and ever since, Giorgio Vasari used the term '*Rinascimento*' in precisely this sense, perhaps for the first time ever. He argues the case with simplicity and clarity: the arts had reached perfection under the Greeks, then went downhill under the Romans.[2] Only after nearly 1,000 years of barbarous darkness and philistine destruction did the process of recovery and rebirth begin. For Vasari, there was nothing mysterious about 'the process by which art has been reborn and achieved perfection in our own times'. It was a deliberately engineered Renaissance, achieved by consulting the best classical models that had survived.

Not all the moderns of the sixteenth and seventeenth centuries were so confident that they had managed to equal, let alone surpass, the achievements of the ancient world. The France of Louis XIV was the first nation state to dominate European culture and politics in a way that recalled the magnificent dominance of ancient Rome. The

Sun King's reign from 1643 to 1715 came to be thought of as a glittering century, *le grand siècle*, great in its military prowess, in the splendour of its court, in the energy and brilliance of its art and literature. Yet it was this same Great Century, stretching over the second half of the seventeenth century and into the first quarter of the eighteenth, that was dogged by a nagging self-doubt: for all their wealth and splendour, were they really as great as the ancients on whom they so carefully modelled themselves? The *querelle des anciens et des modernes* raged on up to the last years of the Sun King's reign. On one side of the quarrel were those who believed that imitation of the giants of Greece and Rome was the first duty of modern writers and artists but that they could not hope to surpass their models. La Fontaine did not dare to assert that his fables were any match for those he had borrowed from Aesop, despite the fact that, according to tradition, Aesop had been a mere slave living in the sixth century BC. La Bruyère felt equally inferior to Theophrastus, the sketchwriter of the third century BC, whose work he had translated and also heavily borrowed from for his own acute and delightful pen portraits.

Others, though, believed that the French could and would reach heights never before achieved, if only they applied Reason and drew on the glorious traditions of their own nation. The advances of modern science were a sure indication that the modern era was destined not only to surpass the ancients but to continue an avenue of progress leading on far beyond their own horizon and out of sight.[3]

The controversy flared up again in the early years of the next century. And it was only gradually over the following decades that the idea of human progress finally gained a secure grip on European minds, a grip which, despite the most appalling setbacks, it was never again to lose. Ironically, the most untroubled rhapsody on the subject was written at the height of the Terror by one of the Revolution's most ardent supporters, the mathematician Condorcet, while he was on the run from Robespierre's Red Guards.

Condorcet's *Esquisse d'un tableau historique des progrès de l'esprit humain* (1793–4) did just what it said on the tin. The book described ten epochs in which mankind progressed, stage by stage, from primitive society through the classical era to the invention of modern technologies such as printing and modern ideals such as the rights of man, leading to the ultimate liberation of mankind from tyranny and the triumph of reason, toleration and humanity. It was published posthumously after Condorcet died in mysterious circumstances, probably by taking poison, after he had been arrested and was almost certainly about to be guillotined.

But ultimately Condorcet triumphed. We are now hard-wired to expect history to deliver progress, jerky, flawed progress marred by horrors usually of our own making, but progress nonetheless. We look back primarily in order to see how far we have moved on. And one central element in that ever-growing sense of self-confidence was the gradual exclusion of religion from the picture. Man had wriggled free of the divine plan. We were no longer the creation of the mind of God but the product of natural development.

This wriggling-free was not accomplished without pain or regret. To extricate ourselves from religious belief was a slow and often agonizing process which left many heads muzzy with grief, disoriented in a universe that was suddenly without purpose or pathways. In such a time, only the most confident ideologues of progress could remain confident that they knew exactly where they were heading.

What none of them would have dreamed of saying was that we might be retracing our steps. That would have been a deeply uncongenial thought. For part of the ideology of modernity is that we are moving forward and that we are going somewhere new. It is our novelty that comforts us. We are travellers who are thrilled to be told that we have reached the trackless quarter of the desert. Besides, it is better not to think too hard about what we have left behind.

Our sense of newness is very precious to us now. It feels like the throb of life. We agonize whenever our social arteries look in danger of becoming sclerotic. We are terrified of seizing up. Anything that is even ten years old is pigeonholed as 'retro'. The success of the TV series *Life on Mars* was that it recreated the 1970s as an unimaginably remote period. Chopping periods of time into smaller and smaller slices flatters our sense of movement. This 'decadeitis' is really quite recent. I can find no evidence before the Victorians that people referred even to centuries as possessing an aroma of their own. The first decade that was thought of in this way was the 1890s, the naughty *fin de siècle* of absinthe and Oscar Wilde. Now every decade, however recent, is diagnosed to have its own tang. So the last thing we wish to be told is that we have fallen back into ways pungently reminiscent, not of the 1920s or the 1820s but of the 20s AD or even the 420s BC. The lifestyle and mindset that we are re-enacting are those not of Noel Coward or the Prince Regent but of the contemporaries of Tiberius and Socrates.

This book argues that, on the contrary, we have been on a round trip. We have sailed round the harbour and seen the glimmering, misty, limitless sea, and now after nearly 2,000 years we are back at the jetty we embarked from. It is the assumption behind this mini-odyssey through modernity that we can properly understand what we are seeing and experiencing only if we first understand that we have been here before. As we begin to explore some striking and concrete instances of our return to the world of the Greeks and Romans, I would like to apologize for disturbing the conventional faith in our unique and unprecedented novelty. And I can only apologize again when I reveal that this mini-odyssey is to begin in Swindon.

One final warning. I am an unsteady guide to this new world. Sometimes I feel like a bewildered stranger in it, a character left over from an earlier epoch who struggles to find his way around, an unwilling passenger on a time machine he never took a ticket for. At other moments I am a creature of the times I was born into and as comfortable in my skin as anyone else around. There are times when I experience a surge of elation at being alive now, while still being startled at what 'now' is like. This journey has taken me from

Harrogate and Leamington Spa to Paris and Rome, from the crags of western Turkey to the mountains of North Wales, from the banks of the River Shournagh in Co. Cork to the shores of the Nile, from Queen Victoria Street to the Baths of Caracalla. In all these inconstant moods and all these wanderings, what never leaves me is the feeling that, like it or not, we have come full circle.

BODY

I

THE BATH

A Bigger Splash

As a boy, I supported Swindon Town, 'the Robins' after their red-breasted shirts, but only because it was the nearest place that had a team in the Football League. Swindon was never anyone's mecca, not the sort of place that you would actually choose to start an odyssey from. Yet if you are looking for somewhere to represent modern Britain, it is an appropriate spot. Swindon, after all, lies in the middle of the Golden Rectangle, or Golden Coffin as more lugubrious observers like to call it, that stretches from London to Bristol, reaching as far as Milton Keynes and Basingstoke at its northern and southern elbows, the heartland of new towns and new industries girdled by medium-rise office blocks and roundabouts and spotted laurels. A prosperous place, at least before the credit crunch, but nobody boasts of living there. It is in Swindon that Ricky Gervais sets his comedy of modern office life.

Swindon has been modern for a long time, ever since that day in 1840 when Isambard Kingdom Brunel and his chief engineer Daniel Gooch threw a pebble, or according to another version a sandwich, from their picnic, to decide the exact site on the large-scale map where they would build the new engine works for the Great Western Railway. The pebble or sandwich fell next to the small market town of Swindon. Actually this story may be a legend. The pebble method was supposedly chosen, in times long pre-dating the invention of the sandwich, to fix the site of New Sarum, the modern Salisbury. That may be a legend too. The stone-throwing was probably first used to fix the site of Stonehenge.

New Swindon soon dwarfed the unpretentious old town which had the misfortune to find itself at the junction of the Bristol and Cheltenham lines. Brunel and Gooch built not only the engines there but the carriages and the rails too. By the turn of the century there were more than 10,000 workers on site. But New Swindon was never a slum. In no time, Gooch, now Sir Daniel, was building model cottages for his workers. He used the creamy Bath stone that had been carved out of the excavations for Brunel's famous Box Tunnel near by, then the longest railway tunnel in the world.[1]

The GWR built a church too for its workers, paid for by the directors and several wealthy parishioners at the end of the line in Bristol. Only five years after Brunel and Gooch had fixed the site of the new works, there stood St Mark's, Swindon, near the station on the Bristol side, a stone building all spikes and prickles, designed by the young Gilbert Scott who was to go on to design St Pancras.[2]

But the GWR was as concerned for the body as for the soul of its workers. It is here at Swindon that you perceive the beginnings of the crucial transition in public welfare – from cleansing the soul to cleansing the body. The Great Western leads the Great Switch in official concern from the spiritual to the physical health of its workers. And in this department Gooch's achievements were not only remarkable but wholly original and, to me, amazing. The GWR lost no time in setting up its own little private welfare state. There was the GWR Medical Fund which provided doctors and surgeons, an eye dispensary, a dentist's practice, free artificial legs for employees who had been injured in railway accidents, and free funerals with the company's own horse and hearse if all else failed. Then there was the Mechanics Institute with its eight baths and its dining room and lecture hall and reading room, all designed for 'disseminating useful knowledge and encouraging rational amusement amongst all classes of people employed by the Company at Swindon'.

Sir Daniel soon came to the conclusion that the baths inside the Institute were too poky for his ever-growing workforce, and so in the early 1860s he had a more splendid bath complex built across the road, which covers a whole modern city block and now includes, as well as a dozen baths for washing in, an Olympic-sized swimming pool with high windows filled with stained glass and iron arches swooping across the water like the great arches at Paddington Station. And finally inside this palace of splash Sir Daniel's men installed something rare and wonderful, unheard of in Wiltshire for 1,500 years: Turkish baths.

Well, we call them Turkish baths, and that is what is carved over the entrance: 'WASHING & TURKISH BATHS', but of course they are really Roman baths. When the Roman Empire split into two, the Western Empire let its baths fall into ruin, but the Eastern Empire carried on bathing into the reign of the Prophet. The capital of the Eastern Empire being Constantinople, it is in present-day Turkey that the tradition of public bathing continued most conspicuously much as the Romans had left it. In Disraeli's novel *Coningsby*

(1844), the mysterious omniscient stranger, later revealed to be Sidonia, says: 'The East is the land of the bath. Moses and Mahomet made cleanliness a religion.' But that is a misunderstanding of history, though a common one. It was Greek and Roman civilization – what we think of as the West – which put public bathing at the centre of its social life. The Turkish hammam is simply the surviving fraction of the Roman imperial tradition. This is no sentimental myth like the Brunel pebble/sandwich. The great historian of the bath, Fikret Yegül, says firmly in his masterly *Baths and Bathing in Classical Antiquity* (1992) that: 'Turkish baths are the direct and only descendant of this long line of baths and bathing cultures.'

So when Sir Daniel insisted on installing these unheard-of Turkish baths for his workers, he was doing so in more or less direct imitation of those Roman emperors who competed as to which of them could build the largest and most splendid baths for the populace. His idea of rational amusement for the lower orders was exactly the same as that of Diocletian and Hadrian and Caracalla. '*Mens sana in corpore sano*'. A clean and healthy mind in a clean and healthy body. '*Ariston men hudor*'. Water is best – the Greek slogan still inscribed over the entrance to the Roman baths at Bath, though inscribed by the Georgians rather than the Romans.

The Romans even built baths specifically intended for the work-force. At Ostia, the port of Rome, in its heyday a thriving cosmopolitan town of 100,000 inhabitants and the transport hub of the empire, the authorities built a set of baths for the cart-drivers, the *cisiarii*, just next to the road along the Tiber. Their mosaics, still beautifully preserved, show cart-drivers working up quite a sweat as they drive their horses on down to the harbour which is thronged with prancing dolphins. Swindon is Victorian Britain's answer to Roman Ostia.

Though quite unsung, the Turkish baths here are the first true Roman baths built in Wessex since the ones the Romans themselves built. They are among the first ever built in mainland Britain by the British (in Ireland they were a little quicker off the mark, for reasons we shall discover). True, in London so-called bagnios – not many, perhaps four or five – had briefly flourished under the Restoration. These were sometimes described as Turkish baths, but they were really more like the old Irish sweating-houses, places to sweat off some plague or ague, though they had the incidental virtue of melting off the extra pounds. See Congreve in *Love for Love* (1695), act one, scene xiv: 'I have a beau in a bagnio, cupping for a complexion and sweating for a shape.' These establishments soon became little better than bawdy-houses, and by the beginning of the eighteenth century the word 'bagnio' meant a one-night-stand hotel, as in Hogarth's 'The Bagnio' in his 'Marriage à la Mode' series. In Bath itself under the Plantagenets and Tudors, sufferers from the gout, the ague and other ailments had bathed their limbs in the medieval King's Bath but for strictly medical reasons. You can still see the rings on the walls donated by grateful patients for their successors to hang their garments on. But the true Turkish bath, with its succession of dry-heat rooms dedicated to pleasure and well-being, was something entirely different. And for that we had to wait until the middle of the nineteenth century.

Today Swindon's Turkish baths are the oldest surviving Roman baths still in use in the British Isles. There is no other institution still functioning in the twenty-first century that the Roman-British inhabitants of the second century would recognize so readily and find so little changed – except, I suppose, for Stonehenge.

It is a foggy morning in North Wilts and it might be nicer to be shopping under cover in the bright lights of the Brunel Centre or sitting in a warm office in one of the spanking office blocks near the station listening to a PowerPoint presentation by someone from Human Resources. There is nobody about in the streets of the Railway Town, which is now a Heritage site, and nobody much inside the Turkish baths (£7.50 to non-members). The cooling room is painted a sickly hospital green and the lounging chairs look as if they have been lounged on once too often. The pot plant on the ledge is withered. Is it an aspidistra? If it is, it certainly isn't the biggest in the world. Just the marble table in the anteroom and the handsome Victorian pipes running round the walls remind you of the GWR in its heyday. The only other customer present, an elderly gent who is stowing his battered kitbag in the locker, looks askance at me as I lower my trousers to change into my swimming trunks. On the website it says with a barely suppressed note of panic: 'Please note that swimwear MUST be worn at ALL times (this includes single-gender sessions).' The notorious excesses of the bagnio are not to be repeated in Swindon.

'Excuse me.' He clears his throat and comes a step or two nearer. For one wild moment I imagine that I am about to become the last man on earth to be picked up in the Turkish Baths at Swindon. 'There's a changing room next door, you know.'

I pull my trousers up again, which is just as well, because at that moment in comes a tiny elderly woman carrying her shopping. She tells us that the fog on the M4 last night was something terrible. The man with the kitbag says he wouldn't go out in it if you paid him.

Somehow this is not quite how I imagined the whole experience. But then I push open the heavy door into the actual baths and I am transported. As I sit under the great silver pipes of the steam bath and watch the sweat drops creeping out of my pores, I imagine that I am an engine driver who has just finished his shift and slid his huge snorting beast into Sir Matthew Digby Wyatt's majestic train sheds at the end of the street and come down to Sir Daniel's baths to raise his own head of steam. Then I pad through the narrow door labelled '*Tepidarium*' for a warm-down before graduating to the *caldarium* and the final reheating in the *sudatorium*. As I sit on the stone bench and feel the merciless dry heat invading me from below until it becomes unbearable, the whole place at last becomes as marvellous and mysterious as I had thought it would be. I am no longer a GWR train driver coming off shift but a Roman legionary who has just finished a patrol on the Bath Road and wants to clean the mud off and dream of blue skies and olive groves. *Tepidarium*, *caldarium*, *sudatorium* – and all in Milton Road, Swindon.

As I plunge into the cold pool next to the elderly lady who is now wearing a garish swimsuit and tells me she used to come on Tuesdays because you have the place to yourself and Tesco's isn't so crowded, I think again, Why Swindon? What made the fashion for Turkish baths sweep mid-Victorian Britain? And why did it seem so natural, even morally obligatory, to provide them for the workers first? Because it is a remarkable fact that the earliest ones built in the late 1850s and early 1860s were mostly built in or near industrial towns in the North and North Midlands. And even when the first Turkish baths were built in London a year or so later, they tended to be built near railway stations, on the Euston Road and in Bell Street, Paddington.

The mystery remains. What inspired the Victorians, after a gap of 1,500 years, to start building Turkish baths with that relentless energy which characterizes everything they did? The immediate answer is to be found in the life and enthusiasms of one extraordinary Irishman, Dr Richard Barter.

Dr Barter and the Rediscovery of the Bath

The early life of Richard Barter was as odd as the rest of it. He was born at his family's farm Cooldaniel, Co. Cork, in 1802, into a moderately well-off clan of merchants and farmers. They were partly descended from the sober and energetic Huguenots who had settled in Cork and soon dominated the place. Richard's father died when he was a child. His mother was frightened by the unrest and violence which was sweeping the rural West of Ireland at the time, and she left Cooldaniel, a long low farmhouse in the wild hills beyond the River Lee, for the shelter of Cork City. She took her favoured elder son with her but left Richard behind to look after himself. A strange abandoning, with the notorious Whiteboys in their white smocks roaming the country at night on their shaggy ponies under their mythical leader Captain Moonlight. Even today, when Cooldaniel is a steeplechase stud, it still seems a remote and desolate spot, keeping some of the old ramshackle Irishness with mud all over the place and heather growing out of the gutters. But Richard was obviously a resilient lad. Then in his early teens, he often joined the Whiteboys in their midnight scampers, he later said for the sheer hell of it, heedless of the danger of being hanged or transported if he were caught. After passing one such night in the open air, he woke to find the sun shining and the birds twittering and all nature rejoicing in the freshness of the morning and immediately resolved to abandon these dangerous habits and devote himself to the study of medicine. He retained from his abandonment only a bitterness against his mother, often a handy impetus for success in later life.

After qualifying as a doctor in London, he was appointed dispensary doctor in Inniscarra, Co. Cork, and was treating his dirt-poor patients there when one of the periodic epidemics of cholera hit the area. At that time, medical orthodoxy was still in the grip of the mistaken belief that cholera was an airborne infection arising out of the stench of the slums where the outbreaks were so often concentrated. One day a woman was brought to his hospital who had been reported as having symptoms of the advanced and fatal stage of the disease. Yet examining her on her arrival, he found no such symptoms; her skin was soft, her colour natural. Richard asked the man who had brought her in on a cart what she had done since she left home. Nothing but drink water. How much? Oh I don't know, but every time she put the cup to her lips she never let it down till she drained it. Hospital orders, however, were to deny the patients water and instead to put them in a bed heated with hot tins. 'If you do not give me water, I shall be dead by morning!' the woman cried. 'I dare not disobey orders.' 'Then I must die!' And she did.

Barter then evaded the hospital rules by going out to patients who had refused to come into hospital and giving them fresh water. In a few days they melted away cured into the country. He himself then decamped to Dublin and on to Edinburgh, in order to gain a hearing for his belief that rehydration was the answer. But by then this particular outbreak was fading everywhere and nobody was much interested in the pamphlet he wrote. It was another fifteen years and several thousand corpses later that Dr John Snow achieved immortality with his monograph expounding the water-borne theory, 'On the Mode and Communication of Cholera'. Barter's pioneering work does not earn so much as a footnote in modern accounts of how cholera was defeated.

This whole episode left Barter with a fierce and lasting disrespect for his fellow doctors and their stubbornly held orthodoxies. His disrespect buoyed him up during his later struggles with the medical profession. This wilful, largely self-educated, idealistic man never hesitated to follow his own instincts. He had been right once and he would be right again.

The other conviction that the cholera experience implanted in him was a lasting belief in the therapeutic properties of water. A lecture given in Cork by Captain Claridge, the tireless advocate of Vincent Preissnitz's water cure, inspired him to travel to Malvern and Ilkley where the new cure was being promoted and then to found his own hydropathic establishment at St Anne's Hill, outside Blarney in his native county. It is a delightful neighbourhood set among woods and orchards, not far from the holy spring of St Anne from which he drew his water supply by a small wooden aqueduct.

Here Barter installed a Russian steam bath, hot vapour being much in vogue then. The bath was housed in a little beehive-shaped thatched building, bearing a perhaps coincidental resemblance to the traditional Irish sweating-house. The doctors of Co. Cork ridiculed this vapour establishment, but after a few technical hiccups, the baths began to attract a gratifying number of desperate patients, and soon Barter was building on to the beehive, experimenting with different arrangements of pipes to improve the circulation of the steam. But his restless mind never stayed content for long. In 1856 he was bowled over by *The Pillars of Hercules*, a travelogue written by the diplomat David Urquhart (1805–77), himself a restless, mercurial figure. Urquhart had fought for the Greeks in their war of independence, served as secretary of the embassy in Constantinople, been arrested by the Russians for leading a foray in a British schooner into Circassia, founded the first magazine dedicated to diplomacy, *The Portfolio*, and back at home stirred up opposition to the Crimean War, rather as retired diplomats today have stirred up opposition to the Iraq War and on much the same grounds. In the course of his travels around the Mediterranean, Urquhart had formed a passion for the classic, dry-heat Turkish bath, and in his book he gives the most precise, vivid and idyllic account of visiting the typical hammam.

In the process, he gives us an unrivalled descripion of a tradition and practice which had been carried over, virtually unchanged, from the late Roman Empire. More important still, *The Pillars of Hercules* was to prove an immensely influential blueprint for the revival of that tradition.

Urquhart raises the curtain which covers the entrance to the street and takes you through into the separate world of the hammam. In the domed hall, where the fountain plays, the *apodyterium* of the Romans (Urquhart uses both Latin and Arabic terms as he goes along, to remind us of the shared origins of the bath), you undress and are wrapped in three towels, one folded round the head into a turban, one thrown over the shoulder and the third acting as a loin-cloth. You are also given wooden sandals to protect the feet against the hot floor and then conducted into the *tepidarium* where you recline on your personal mattress and wait for the attendant to bring coffee and pipes. A boy chafes your feet and taps you all over your body to work up the sweat. When the bathman, the Tellak of the Turks, the Tractator of the Romans, is satisfied with the state of your skin, he ushers you into the *adytum*, 'a space such as the centre dome of a cathedral, filled not with dull and heavy steam but with gauzy and mottled vapour, through which the spectre-like inhabitants appear'. This misty realm is not a quiet place. Apart from the splashing and the clanking of the brass vessels, there is the sound of sides being slapped and occasional shouting and even singing too.

Then you lie down on the marble slabs under the dome and the Tellak begins to manipulate you, vigorously pummelling your ribs and thighs and digging his knee into your neck. He puts on a glove made of camel's hair and starts to scrape your skin, coaxing off rolls of dead matter which 'fall right and left as if spilt from a dish of macaroni' – the operation performed in ancient Rome by the instrument known as the strigil. After this, the bather is lathered and not just shaved but thoroughly depilated all over (Urquhart says that Europeans don't do this bit).

Finally the skinned and shorn customer moves on to the couches of repose. These are in the form of a letter M spread out, so that as you rest your weight is everywhere directly supported and every tendon, every muscle is relaxed. Groups of these couches are divided by low balustrades into little enclaves where families sit and eat and gossip and have their nails manicured. More coffee, sherbet, watermelons and other fruit are brought. You can even send out for kebabs. The scene somehow suggests a row of bathing huts at a British seaside resort.

But what British seaside resort ever matched the sensations of well-being conferred by the hammam?

> The body has come forth shining like alabaster, fragrant as the cistus, sleek as satin and soft as velvet. The touch of your own skin is electric . . . There is an intoxication or dream that lifts you out of the flesh, and yet a sense of life and consciousness that spreads through every member . . . those who experience these effects and vicissitudes for the first time exclaim 'I feel as if I could leap over the moon' . . . you walk forth a king from the gates which you had entered a beggar.[3]

Even today this tour de force leaves one tingling. The whole hammam process includes pretty well every service offered in the most luxurious of modern spas. At the hammam, all is *luxe, calme et volupté*, in that famous phrase of Baudelaire's which Urquhart seems to have anticipated by roughly a decade. This is pampering on a heroic scale.

After reading *The Pillars of Hercules* and perhaps echoing Urquhart himself saying that at the end of it all the touch of your own skin is electric, Barter said simply: 'I was electrified.' As always with him, this meant being electrified into action. He immediately invited Urquhart over to St Anne's Hill, offering in his expansive entrepreneurial style to put 'men, materials and money' at his new friend's disposal. He also republished Urquhart's chapters on the Turkish bath in a little book by that title, 'for the benefit of my own patients and others'. The two men wholeheartedly agreed that it was the hot air as distinguished from hot vapour that gave the Turkish bath its peculiar excellence – and Urquhart said so in a brief postscript to the new publication.

They set about building a bath right there in rural Co. Cork, the first to be erected in Western Europe since the Romans. Urquhart was delighted: 'For twenty years I have looked in vain for a man to make this experiment.' The first hot-air bath was heated by underground pipes on the lines of the Roman hypocaust, though it was scarcely on the scale of Caracalla, being a small, low-roofed circular building, largely made of turf.

Again, there were technical hiccups, but by 1858 they were ready to conquer the world. First, they conquered Ireland. By 1868 there were fourteen Turkish baths in Co. Cork alone, including a People's Bath in Cork City erected by public subscription for the use of the poor. There were two opened in Dublin, one 'the Saracenic edifice' in Lincoln Place which reminded Leopold Bloom in *Ulysses* of a mosque, although the bath he paid 1s 6d for was taken at the other premises, the Turkish and Warm Baths at nearby 11 Leinster Street.

In London, Urquhart advised on the building of the famous baths in Jermyn Street, where my father used to go after a heavy night to lose a few pounds to make the weight in a steeplechase the following day. Perhaps it was these same Jermyn Street warm baths that Mr Merdle in *Little Dorrit* (1855–7) cut his throat in, with the tortoiseshell penknife he had borrowed from his daughter-in-law that same evening.

Turkish baths were soon added to the amenities of every self-respecting spa: Leamington, Cheltenham, Harrogate, Bath itself. In Leamington beside the bubbling waters of the River Leam, behind the calm grey classical pillars of the pump room there still stand the dear little baths of 1863, perhaps the earliest surviving set in England, though now serving as part of the town's museum. Its Moorish arches of good Warwickshire brick are a fiery orange, and stained-glass windows of a lurid azure blot out the sullen Midlands sky. How pleasant to think of the Brummie manufacturers, all aglow after the *tepidarium*, putting their frock coats back on and repairing next door to the Assembly Rooms to take a cup of Mr Twining's tea and dance a polka with their wives.

In Cambridge, the newly floated Roman Bath Company com-missioned Sir Matthew Digby Wyatt to erect a pretty set of baths in Jesus Lane, unusually, perhaps uniquely in the classical style, the Company's claim being that the Roman bath was superior to the Turkish hammam (although, as we have seen, they were basically the same thing). No doubt it was thought that the classical approach would appeal more to the swarms of Cambridge dons who were to patronize them. These were, after all, the first avowedly Roman baths to be built in England since the fall of Rome. Alas, the aca-demic community was slow to respond, and the venture was a total flop. Within two years, the baths had folded, and the Roman Bath Company had been broken up. Wyatt himself took on the ownership of the building and let it off to the Pitt Club, the recently established watering hole for rich undergraduates. On the upper floor, the Fenland squires drink deep to this day. On the pediment of the façade, there is a round plaster relief of Pitt the Younger, with that incredibly pointed nose. Downstairs you can still see what was once the swimming pool with its stout iron pillars, like a miniature version of the railway stations Sir Matthew was famous for. Now it is the dining room of a branch of Pizza Express. And the only Roman thing about it is the succulent cheese-and-tomato topping of the Pizza Romana.

The failure of the Cambridge Roman baths is, I think, significant and not so surprising. After all, half their proposed academic clientele were at that date still in holy orders. They were the last people you would expect to be converted to the cause of self-pampering. They were professionally trained to resist the cult of the body. The Company could scarcely have chosen a less suitable town for what was its first venture.

In the big cities, with their grime and soot, the story was different. Every rising industrial centre was proud of its new baths, which usually turned a decent profit: Glasgow, Edinburgh, Aberdeen, Newcastle, Birmingham, Barnsley, Blackburn, Bradford, Leeds, Liverpool, Manchester – and among the very earliest, Swindon. For it was above all the working classes who needed to have the impurities sweated out of them.

Some of these premises are sumptuous kasbahs in local pastiches of the Moorish style, such as the baths at Harrogate which are still in business today. Others, like Swindon, are plain and functional, but even the most modest set of baths required quite an outlay with their three or four rooms to be heated to different temperatures plus the attendant cold plunge and cooling room. Soon the craze spread to the Continent, where the baths were known, more accurately, as Roman-Irish baths – the Irish in that hyphenated term being Barter's lasting personal memorial.

Almost as famous in London as the Jermyn Street baths was the establishment in Northumberland Avenue, visited by Sherlock Holmes and Dr Watson in one of the last Holmes stories, 'The Adventure of the Illustrious Client': 'Both Holmes and I had a weakness for the Turkish bath. It was over a smoke in the pleasant lassitude of the drying-room that I have found him less reticent and more human than anywhere else.' What a delightful picture the passage conjures up: the two friends lying side by side smoking with the bath sheets wrapped round them and several hours of idleness before them. For the note from the Illustrious Client which Holmes fishes out of his pocket suggests a rendezvous at 4.30 that afternoon, and after Watson has read it, Holmes says, 'Until then we can put the matter out of our heads.' There is no mention of refreshment being available such as Urquhart describes – the sherbet and the choice of watermelons, let alone the kebabs. But there are certainly refreshments as well as tobacco on the go in the Russian steam baths in Chicago visited by the narrator in Saul Bellow's novel *Humboldt's Gift* (1975), where the brawny patrons consume huge quantities of schnapps, salt herring and meat-and-potato pancakes.[4]

Bellow's Russian steam baths bring back the sweaty, boozy life of the old Roman baths. You can still recapture something of that atmosphere at the Turkish baths in Harrogate on the Yorkshire moors. You duck down the little flight of steps under the great dome of the Royal Baths which dominates the spa town and can be seen for miles across the rolling hills. All at once you are in an oriental palace the splendour of which startled its first visitors in the 1890s and startles me now. Here came (though not all at the same time) Elgar, Neville Chamberlain and Agatha Christie during her mysterious fugue from her first husband. Now on a wet Friday afternoon session (gentlemen only) it is thronged with sturdy Yorkshire businessmen. Through the Moorish keyhole squints, I glimpse rosy Yorkshire buttocks swaggering towards the *tepidarium*. Under pointed arches picked out in orange, jade and magenta strut mighty Northern paunches with their hairy scrota swinging beneath as proud as sporrans. In the silent inner sanctum of the steam room, plump Yorkshire cheeks are sweating off last night's pints of John Smith. Outside in the cooling room, gravelly chuckles recall how someone lost it at the cricket club dinner and someone else was done for doing 75 down Ripon Road in the rush hour. Now and then the patrons have to raise their voices to make themselves heard above the splashing from the plunge bath next door. On the wooden arch leading to the plunge, there is a big Victorian clock flanked by the crescents of Islam. As the dripping bathers come through the arch, each one twists on his heel, like a nude dancer in a modern ballet, to look back up at the clock. For outside this cheerful refuge from time where the busiest executive can frolic naked and watchless, there are accountants and appraisals waiting.

The women's baths in Nell Dunn's play *Steaming* (1981) (also a 1985 film by Joseph Losey starring Vanessa Redgrave and Sarah Miles with Diana Dors as the bath attendant, her last film as it was Losey's) offer a female equivalent to Saul Bellow's Russian baths: a place where hard-pressed men or women can escape from the strains of work and family and express themselves in a steamy atmosphere of relaxation. In Nell Dunn as in Conan Doyle and Bellow, the pleasure element is uppermost. But Dunn makes it a morality play too. Her bath-house is a democracy, in which the successful female attorney, the promiscuous floozie and the working-class bath attendant discover that they are sisters under the skin. Strip off your clothes and unveil your problems and you will realize how much you have in common.

Dr Barter too had a moral mission. In describing the Barter Sanatorium of the future, he said: 'Our great object is to prove that in whatever way we consider our project, either from the medical point of view or as a great moral agent; as a shield against intemperance; a means of educating our people in cleanliness and self-respect; or as affording the best, the most certain and the safest mode of cure it is unequalled.' That is a high Victorian sort of prospectus, exuding moral seriousness at every pore and not much hint of fun. Yet Barter was electrified by Urquhart's hammam, which promised such an exquisitely fused amalgam of pleasure, well-being and beautification. If the hammam made you a better person, it was because it made you feel good. It was impossible to disentangle the moral benefit from the physical well-being. In any case, Barter was anxious that his new baths should not be taken over by his fellow medicos. He issued stern instructions that doctors should play no part in administering the baths and that people should come and use them quite freely without any need for medical recommendation. Nobody who had enjoyed Urquhart's book and his company as much as Richard Barter had could be in any doubt that pleasure was an integral part of the equation.

In its heyday, St Anne's Hydro was a truly magnificent sight with its grand long irregular façade standing high on the hill facing Blarney Castle, with its gardens and terraces and its unrivalled range of Turkish baths, or Roman-Irish baths as the more patriotic patrons insisted on calling them. It had its own post office and its own railway station in the valley below. For almost a century under the management of a succession of Richard Barters, the water bubbled up from St Anne's Well and the customers poured in from all over the country. But by the time the Barters sold the establishment to their manager Dr Quigley after the Second World War, the fashion for this sort of hydro had passed, and in any case nobody in Ireland had any money. Dr Quigley boarded every window and nailed every door, but this did not prevent the locals from getting in and stripping the place of every usable piece of wood, lead and stone. We shall meet this universal local custom elsewhere, amid the scant vestiges of Greek Miletus in western Turkey and the rubble of Antinoopolis in the middle Nile Valley, but nowhere has the site been more thoroughly cleared than by the twentieth-century looters of the Blarney district. Dr Quigley's sparkling daughters still perch on the hill – Olwen keeps a small country hotel, and Zwena has turned Hydro Farm into allotments. But of the hydro itself only the odd ivy-crusted heap of stones remains. Well, at least I could pay homage to St Anne's Well, the source of the first Roman bath since the Romans. 'I can give you the directions, but you'll get soaked and you'll never find it,' Zwena said merrily.

The moment I left her, her instructions fled out of my head, and I took the first available wrong turning which petered out in a field of waist-high sodden corn. To get out of the field, I tried to leap an evil ditch and caught my foot in a loop of bramble and fell smack against the opposite bank with a rib-shattering thump. After taking a few minutes' injury time, I retraced my steps and found another path deep into the woods. The path led over a stream and up a steep slope through interminable brambles and dripping Himalayan balsam. I stumbled up and down the boggy hillside, now and then catching sight of the bubbling waters of the River Shournagh below me. I saw a fox, a hare, even a starved-looking grey pony tethered to a tree, but never a sign of a well. In a way, I was rather pleased by my failure. The best quests are often the hopeless ones.

The only trace of Dr Barter himself in the area is the stained glass his children put up to him in the east window in Inniscarra Church, a sweet, grey Gothicky building beautifully kept by a surprisingly active Church of Ireland congregation, many of whom still boast of their Huguenot ancestry. The window depicts the parable of the Good Samaritan, which is a brilliant choice, not just because the Samaritan bound up the wounds of the victim of the roadside mugging and poured oil and wine into them (Dr Barter would have advised water), but because the Samaritans were an unpopular minority community of settlers like the Huguenot Protestants, and this particular Samaritan was obviously an independent-minded, not to say stroppy, and successful man of business (which was no doubt why Mrs Thatcher chose to praise him in her notorious sermon on Edinburgh Mound) – very much a Barter sort of person.

What lives on of Richard Barter is the this-worldly, unashamed enjoyment of physical health and physical pleasure. His teachings have swum out from the therapeutic controversies of the nineteenth century into the mindset of the modern world.

The Grandeur that Was Rome

We have traced a rough line of descent from the Roman bath through the delights of the Muslim hammam by way of the Victorian rediscovery of the bath to the modern spa. But how do our modern re-creations compare with the original? What were the real Roman baths like and what was it like to bathe in them? There are

few more dramatic sights in Rome itself or in the great cities of the
Roman world than those soaring salmon-pink vaults and arches,
dwarfing even in their broken, crumbling state everything else in
sight, their domes reaching as high as the invading pines and
cypresses which have grown up around them. The Baths of
Diocletian, Caracalla and Hadrian are among the largest buildings
that we know of in the ancient world. The Baths of Caracalla, covering 25 acres, are bigger than the biggest opera house in the world.
I have heard *La Traviata* performed there, and even on a calm
summer's evening only the faintest echoes of the voices of Alfredo
and Violetta reached me from the stage erected at the far end of the
auditorium, which must have been a good 200 yards away. Even the
colonial offshoots were of magnificent size. The baths at Aquae Sulis,
our own Bath Spa, were the largest north of the Alps, certainly the
largest surviving. It has taken nearly two centuries to excavate their
full extent. The remains of the baths in what is now the museum of
Cluny in Paris were so huge that the Franks and later the French
could not believe that they were merely baths and up to the nineteenth century called them the Palace of the Emperor Julian. The
origin of this misnomer was that Julian had actually spent the icy
winter of 357–8 living in the *frigidarium* because, being well insu-
lated, it was warmer than anywhere else in Paris.

The building and staffing of these complexes was such a consuming enterprise that it is reckoned that the baths employed more
people than any other institution except the Roman Army. Nor
were the huge imperial baths the only place to go for a splash. By the
end of the fourth century it is calculated that there were 856 smaller
baths in Rome. Constantinople had 150. Some of these were built
and maintained by private citizens for their own pleasure. Cicero in
his letter to his friends was always fretting about the plumbing in his
bath. Martial gushed over the beauties of the baths of his friend
Claudius Etruscus. Some baths were run for profit by businessmen;
others were financed by whip-rounds among plutocrats. Pliny the
Younger gave nearly a million sesterces to his native town of Como

to build, maintain and decorate a public bath. In times of crisis, having somewhere to go for a wash and a splash was a high priority. After the Sardis earthquake in AD 17, the Emperor Trajan gave 6 million sesterces to lay out a monumental bath, gymnasium and colonnaded avenue.

These buildings were not only immense in size. They were, aesthetically and technologically, at the cutting edge. Their breathtaking height and daring curves produced unheard-of shapes and new visual effects. The massive buttresses and flying ribs, their broad façades punctuated by tall arched windows, are the forerunners of the medieval cathedrals. In the same way, the surrounding colonnades lined with shops and places to eat and drink pointed the way to the architecture of medieval markets and modern shopping malls. The technology too was demanding and generated its own beauties. The smaller baths could recycle the water from cisterns and reservoirs. But the larger baths needed aqueducts, themselves a wonderful sight as they lope from hill to hill. By Trajan's time, Rome was served by nine colossal aqueducts bringing in a million cubic metres per day.

When we are taught about ancient Rome, we are rightly invited to admire the system of hypocaust heating which channelled hot air through underground pipes supported on bricks. This had been devised as early as the second century BC. An entrepreneur called Sergius Orata claimed the credit. Like many entrepreneurs, he had not actually invented the system but he marketed it brilliantly, having first successfully experimented with hypocausts to heat his fishponds and oyster beds in the Gulf of Baiae, the most luxurious resort of the imperial age.

The hypocaust was indeed a technological marvel. But what seems to me rather more marvellous, not to say mysterious, is the impulse which led the Romans and the Greeks before them to devote such huge resources to these baths, so that they were more splendid in size and decoration than their palaces and temples. By the time of the reign of Antoninus Pius so many new baths were being

built at public expense that the Emperor forbade any new ones to be
built, and ordered that all investment should go into the maintenance
of existing baths, which didn't stop the upwardly mobile Ephesians
from constructing their fourth colossal bath-gym complex. In
Pompeii, at the time of the fatal eruption, the authorities were building the largest set of baths that the city had yet seen.

What is particularly striking is the public-spirited motive behind
both the building and the administration of the baths. The entrance
fee to any of these baths was trifling, a quadrans or quarter of an as.
The first great bath complex was specifically built by Agrippa for the
free use of the people. Even the poorest citizens regarded it as both a
pleasure and a duty to take an afternoon bath. There was little or no
class distinction. You might meet anyone in the baths up to and
including the Emperor. During a visit to the baths, King Antiochus
Epiphanes (c. 175 BC), a Seleucid ruler of Syria, had a large jar of
costly perfumed oil poured over a poor man who had said how grateful he was to be bathing with a king. The poor man then slipped and
cracked his head on the oily floor, causing much royal mirth.

Some bathing pools were reserved for men, but others seem to
have permitted mixed bathing – always a controversial practice and
one later banned by the Emperor Hadrian. Juvenal mocked women
who took exercise in the baths, although he didn't object to a little
ladylike swimming. Women were certainly allowed to use the baths
of Trajan. Clement of Alexandria claimed that one could see ladies
of noble birth bathing naked, not just prostitutes who were bath-
haunters because the baths were a convenient pick-up point.
Elagabalus (Emperor AD 218–22) rounded up the prostitutes in the
baths and gave them a lecture on sex, rather in the style of Mr
Gladstone. Not surprisingly with these assorted perils, there were
some ladies who were too modest to venture to the baths. Martial
professes himself amazed that certain women refuse to bathe with
him, although some of his other verses suggest possible reasons why,
for example, 'If you hear applause in the baths, it is probably in
response to the appearance of Maro's member.'

The atmosphere was democratic, sometimes rowdy. That immortal grump, the philosopher Seneca, frequently complained about the ghastly racket coming from the baths next door to his house. He attributed the growing softness and effeminacy he saw around him to the luxury and excess of the bath, although he himself regarded a brisk plunge as a therapeutic essential. He looked back with nostalgia to the dark old baths like the Stabian or Forum Baths in Pompeii: 'Our ancestors did not think that one could have a hot bath except in darkness . . . nowadays, however, people regard baths as fit only for moths if they have not been so arranged that they receive the sun all day long through the widest of windows, if men cannot bathe and get a tan at the same time, and if they cannot look out from their bathtubs over stretches of land and sea.'

There was night bathing too, though this was frowned on, as much because of the cost of lighting as because of the moral hazards. But the Baths of Zeuxippus in Constantinople were artificially lit at public expense.

Drinking shops were often found near baths, for example at Pompeii, where the changing rooms of the suburban baths are full of erotic frescoes and graffiti: 'Apelles, chamberlain of the Emperor, had lunch here most pleasantly [*jucundissime*] and fucked at the same time.' The changing rooms were rife with thieves. Archaeologists found a huge haul of curse tablets when excavating Bath, for example: 'Solinus to the goddess Sulis Minerva. I give to your divinity and majesty my bathing tunic and cloak. Do not allow sleep or health to him who has done me wrong, whether man or woman, whether slave or free, unless he reveals himself and brings these goods to your temple.' The idea was that the goddess would do the detective work and find the thief if you first transferred the ownership of the clothes to her.

But these prayers to the goddess were exceptional. In general, there was nothing the least bit godly about the baths. They were an utterly secular institution. It has always been a temptation for posterity to assume that because these baths were built on such a heroic scale they must have had some religious and ritual significance associated with them. But as far as we can see, there was none at all.[5]

There was no ceremony as you entered the baths, no mysteries of initiation or rites of purification, nothing to hold up your pleasant amble from the changing room or *apodyterium* to the *tepidarium*, then the *caldarium* and then the rigours of the sweating-room, the *laconicum*. The hot baths were open as soon as the *tintinnabulum* rang and, if you met a friend on the way in, there was no elaborate salutation: merely a grunt of *'Bene lava!'* – Have a good bath – and on the way out *'Salve latus!'* – Hi, thou washed-one – both no more than the equivalent of 'Cheers!'

The whole business slotted naturally into a civilized Roman day. Work finished by noon, a light lunch, short siesta, then a visit to the baths – Martial suggest that 2 p.m. was the best time. But you might also take an aperitif or a light meal in the baths – lettuce, eggs, eels.

Well-to-do Romans going to the baths would be preceded by slaves carrying their towels, exercise robe, sandals and toilet box, the *cista*, a cylindrical metal box containing their oils, strigils or scrapers and sponge, all the gear which is today provided in-house at any decent spa. In the *Satyricon* of Petronius, Trimalchio is carried out of the baths on a litter wrapped in soft blankets and surrounded by slaves and hangers-on.

The baths were a social centre. Martial describes the characters who haunted them, the club bores of the ancient world. Selius would scour all the baths, even the darkest and dingiest, in search of a dinner invitation. Menogenes the flatterer would try every ploy to persuade you to ask him home for a meal: allow you to win a point in the ball game, retrieve the ball for you, fetch you a drink, wipe the sweat from your brow, admire your hair and your towels. The ball game in question has been identified as a primitive form of tennis (*sphairistike* or 'sticky' as Major Wingfield was to christen its modern form), but it sounds to me more like one of those soppy games people play on beaches with a brightly coloured plastic ball.

The classical bath complexes included pretty well all the facilities that are on offer in modern spas and leisure centres. In fact, they were more hospitable to the innocent pleasures of life than their present-day equivalent, which strictly forbid smoking on the premises, and often drinking and eating too.

What, I think, has now and then confused people into imagining that these ancient baths might have some deeper spiritual significance was a very different type of place: the natural springs and the thermo-mineral baths attached to them. Cold and hot springs were attributed magical properties and a divine origin. To seek a cure in such a holy place, you paid homage to the local nymphs and tutelary deities. The gods who might be invoked here were prayed to because of their association with health – Aesculapius, Hygeia, Hermes, Hercules, Aphrodite. And a temple might be erected where worshippers would bring gifts and votive objets. There are sacred springs with modest temples attached all over the Roman world, at Baiae, for example, and Nîmes, where the water sanctuary is dedicated to the spring-god Nemausius.

But the best example is in faraway Britain: where the sanctuary and temple of Sulis Minerva adjoin the great Roman baths. It is at Bath that you can see most clearly the distinction between the sacred and the profane.

The city of Bath began where its centre still is today: nestling in a hairpin bend of the River Avon, guarded on all sides by the steepling limestone escarpment of the southern end of the Cotswolds. Within 100 yards of each other, three natural springs have forced their way to the surface through the clay outcrop. The springs all produce a constant flow of hot water. The Hot Bath is the hottest – 49°C – the King's Bath the most copious, nearly a third of a million gallons a day. To the ancients, this bubbling abundance of hot water seemed miraculous. It seems miraculous today, as you see the steaming water gush out of the lead conduit into the open channel which leads to the Great Bath. If anything in this world is worth giving thanks for to whatever gods may be, the hot springs of Bath surely are. They were famous throughout the Roman world. As early as the second century AD, the geographer Ptolemy calls Bath 'Aquae Calidae'. But there is archaeological evidence that, long before the Romans came, the ancient Britons had driven a causeway across the swampy flood plain of the Avon towards the centre of the springs so that they could make their devotions to Sulis, the goddess of the spring.

The Romans in their usual way elided the local goddess with their own and built a temple to Sulis Minerva next to the spring. It was a modest, handsome, orthodox building with a nicely curved pediment and four Corinthian columns in front. Much of the stone was preserved in the Avon mud which engulfed it in the Dark Ages. Also marvellously preserved and discovered in 1790 was the glowering Gorgon's head that was set into the middle of the pediment: Barry Cunliffe, who led the more recent excavations, describes it as one of the most dramatic pieces of sculpture from the whole of Roman Britain. Although the Gorgon is normally a female in classical mythology, here in Bath he is shown like a Celtic god with moustaches and beetling brows and his fierce upstanding hair sprouting into wings and serpents. This dazzling figure is surrounded by the owl and the dolphin, attributes of Minerva, in a glorious melange of classical and Celtic. The whole effect does honour to the spring itself which bubbles up in a more or less circular pool only a few yards away.

Beyond the pool, on the secular side, the spectacular remains of the bath complex are still being excavated. They are several times the size of the temple and utterly distinct from it. This is the first major leisure centre to be built in our islands and on a spectacular scale which has hardly been equalled since. As you came into the hall, the *apodyterium*, you could choose either to turn right to the great bathing pool and the other hot pools beyond it, or left to the dry ('Turkish') baths with their familiar sequence of *frigidarium*, *tepidarium*, *caldarium* and *laconicum* plus a cold plunge to finish off. All told, the establishment has a dozen pools and chambers. There was, as we have said, nothing like it north of the Alps. But it was strictly secular. The only contact with the divine was at the large windows at the

far end of the *frigidarium* through which the devout could toss coins
and other offerings into the spring – a quantity of jugs, bowls,
brooches, even a rattle, often of silver and gold, have been found.

In Praise of Dirt

You have hardly ceased wondering at this spectacular survival from
the ancient world when a second question suggests itself: why on
earth did such a handsome and useful establishment fall into decay, to
such an extent that, although the former existence of the baths never
quite disappeared from the memory, there was not a scrap of them to
be seen above ground? And why did the same fate overtake baths all
over the Roman Empire? Why was the tradition of public bathing
obliterated almost as completely as the magnificent buildings in
which these essential rituals of the ancient world had been performed with such pleasure for so many centuries?

In the case of Bath, the first cause was the rise in the sea-level
during the third and fourth centuries AD and a consequent rise in the
inland water-table. There were increasingly severe floods, not from
the springs but from the River Avon curling round the site. The
hypocausts were flooded. The Romans raised the level of the base-
ment floors, but the new floors too were flooded and covered with
thick layers of black and grey mud. As the empire declined, so its
officers lost the entrepreneurial zest to clean out the baths when the
flood waters receded. Other baths suffered from a similar mixture of
natural decay and human inertia. The smaller baths developed leaks
in their reservoirs and cisterns. The aqueducts which fed the larger
baths needed constant maintenance, which the imperial power, men-
aced by chaos and invasion, could no longer provide. In some cases,
such as the Baths of Diocletian, the aqueduct was actually destroyed
by the invading Ostrogoths. The empire no longer had enough men
like Dr Richard Barter. When the little wooden aqueduct that
brought the water to his hydropathic establishment from St Anne's

Well silted up, Barter and his friends and relations took their spades and they dug it out themselves.

But the worst enemy of the bath was not nature or human incompetence. It was the new faith. Christians used water for baptism, not for bathing. *Baptisma*, in Latin as in Greek, meant a 'dipping into', and the dipping was a consecration. A bath might be used but only for God's purposes, and not for the purposes of hygiene and certainly not for pleasure. Cleanliness was not next to godliness. It was irrelevant, if not actually harmful.

St Jerome said: 'He who has once bathed in Christ has no need of a second bath.' St John Chrysostom did not object to his followers baptizing new members of their church in the great bath in Constantinople, but he deplored the vanity of mothers who spoiled their daughters with luxuries and refinements, such as baths. Some churches owned and operated baths commercially, but only after the baths had been purified. Pope Leo I (390–461) made the Christian view clear when he had inscribed over the fountain in the atrium of San Paolo Fuori le Mura (where St Paul was buried after his execution): 'Water removes dirt from the body, but faith, purer than any spring, cleanses sin and washes souls.' Gregory the Great (540–604) permitted baths for the needs of the body but 'not for the titillation of the mind and for sensuous pleasure'. If the doctor prescribed a weekly bath for some medical condition, well and good. But bathing for pleasure stirred up lustful thoughts and practices. Jerome and Augustine denounced the notorious libertinism of Baiae. The devil set his snares wherever men and women bathed together.

Christian ascetics went a step further and praised *alousia*, 'the state of being unwashed'. The hermit father Julian forbade his followers to wash at all. St Anthony boasted that he had never washed his feet in his life.

No new baths to speak of were built after the seventh and eighth centuries. The Byzantine emperors built churches instead. And the existing baths were left to fall into ruin or put to new purposes, such as barracks or storerooms, or their stones were pillaged by the local inhabitants as top-grade building material.

Gibbon describes in a famous passage in his autobiography how he came to write his great work: 'It was at Rome, on the 15th October 1764, as I sat musing amidst the ruins of the Capitol, while the barefoot friars were singing vespers in the Temple of Jupiter, that the idea of writing the decline and fall of the city first started to my mind.' It would have been just as appropriate, perhaps more so, if he had sat musing in the ruins of one of the baths of Rome, more splendid in their size and architectural daring than most of Rome's temples except the Pantheon. He could have imitated Shelley, who tells us in the Preface to *Prometheus Unbound* that 'This Poem was chiefly written upon the mountainous ruins of the Baths of Caracalla, among the flowery glades and thickets of odoriferous blossoming trees, which are extended in ever winding labyrinths upon its immense platforms and dizzy arches suspended in the air.' Perhaps the most evocative site of all to reflect on the decline and fall of the baths of Rome would have been under the great transept of Santa Maria degli Angeli. For this marvellous baroque church, remodelled by Michelangelo himself, arose out of the ruins of the Baths of Diocletian, the largest and most beautiful of all the baths of Rome. The site covers 32 acres and, according to tradition, was built between AD 295 and 305 by 40,000 Christians condemned to forced labour. Twelve centuries later, the Christians took their revenge when Pope Pius IV had the central block of the baths, which happily followed the form of a Greek cross, converted into a church and charterhouse. Michelangelo, by then 86 years old, was put in charge and kept closely to the architecture of the original baths. What is now the church's vestibule was the *tepidarium*, the transept was the central hall and the chancel was the *frigidarium*.

This whole magnificent conversion job had its original impetus not from the architectural megalomania of the Pope but from a rather obscure Venetian artist called Antonio del Duca who had a vision in which he saw a cloud of angels rising from the Baths of

Diocletian. From then on, he never stopped badgering the Pope to build a church on the site of the baths. Del Duca's picture of the Virgin surrounded by adoring angels still hangs behind the high altar, much venerated today and a potent reminder of the Christian vendetta against baths in particular, and the cult of the body in general.

The Baths of Caracalla lie in the green lee of the Celian Hill, their soaring broken domes and arches left to moulder undisturbed through the Christian centuries. But Diocletian's baths have been invaded and overgrown by the city of the Popes and the motor car, making it hard to grasp just how enormously they once sprawled from what is now the Via Parigi to the bus station in front of the railway station, roughly a quarter of a mile in every direction. Those main halls of the bath complex which have not been incorporated into Santa Maria degli Angeli are still being restored to serve as museums of antique sculpture. Hundreds of yards away to the left there is another part of the baths converted to a church, the pretty little San Bernardo with its chaste dome and lemon-yellow baroque exterior. Behind the pink mass of Santa Maria degli Angeli there is a beautiful cool white cloister probably designed by the ancient Michelangelo for the new Carthusian monastery. Then to the left again on the next street corner there is a large octagonal domed hall, formerly used as a planetarium, and now another sculpture museum. All these churches, museums and transport links now occupy the space that Diocletian had given over to one purpose only: bathing. For the Emperor and the citizens of Rome alike, the cult of the body came first, before the cult of the soul or the aesthetic sensibilities or the commercial priorities of a great city.

The startling thing is how suddenly it all crumbled to nothing, to be replaced by its exact opposite, an equally intense vendetta against the culture of the body. This vendetta continued through a millennium and more. When the pious Holy Roman Emperor Charles V attempted to convert the Moors of Granada, one of his first instructions was that they should cease their repellent practice of bathing.

His son, Philip II of Spain, went one step further and destroyed all the baths in Granada. Thus the last vestiges of the Roman bathing tradition were extinguished in Western Europe.

In the modern era, the rebirth of the public bath and spa has closely paralleled the decline of Christianity. Though spas began to become fashionable in the eighteenth century, the medical pretext remained the driving force behind 'taking the waters'. Those 'waters' were mostly taken at mineral springs and taken through the mouth. And the sulphurous taste usually made the experience anything but a pleasure. They were also supposedly taken for some complaint certified by one's doctor, some digestive or muscular malady that had refused to yield to the ordinary remedies.

Shangri-spa

Today in the twenty-first century well-being and pleasure go hand in hand, enjoying total legitimacy and public approval. How happy Dr Barter would be to see a double-page advertisement in a colour supplement with the headline 'Ireland wishes you good health', announcing a new Spa Categorization Scheme which will see Ireland's spas divided into four main categories: Destination Spa, Resort Spa, Hotel Spa and Specialized Retreat. Ireland is no longer the land of saints and scholars, it is Shangri-spa:

> With air soft as a lover's kiss, water so pure they bottle it and where misty mountains sweep down to unspoilt golden sand, Ireland provides the perfect backdrop for the ultimate spa experience. The Irish, renowned for their warmth and friendliness (as well as their wonderful complexions) have a Celtic inheritance of healing in their blood.
>
> The very climate of this laid-back land, with its inspiring sense of history and great sense of fun, bathes the skin in a perfect caress and irons out the stresses of modern life.[6]

And in Bath itself, you can enjoy a pretty ultimate spa experience at the new Thermal Bath Spa. This glamorous project, lubricated with a £7.78 million Lottery grant from the Millennium Commission, occupies a handsome Georgian block next to the Roman baths. It was formerly occupied by the Hot and Cross Baths, but it draws its waters from all three hot springs, a million litres of mineral-rich water every day at a heart-thumping temperature. Its opening in August 2006 was an occasion for celebration. For thirty years there had been no bathing at all in these miraculous waters. As for Turkish baths, the last one in Bath had closed in 1961. And now here it is reborn, all white and crystalline inside the Georgian shell. A couple of stops down Brunel's line from its modest beginnings in Swindon, and a century and a half later, the tradition of public bathing is flourishing again. Compared to the Turkish baths in Swindon, this is like the great bath in Constantinople beside a village hammam. But the message is the same: the bath is for pleasure and there is no more delicious pleasure than the bath.

Yet I cannot conceal from myself a sense of apprehension, even dread, as I insert my credit card and take the white robe and fluffy slippers from the attendant with her not-quite-smile. There is a hospital feel to the glistening bare stairs and passageways. In the changing room, other customers all in the white towelling dressing gowns drift by with the same half-smile on their faces as though they were doing their best to look cheerful under the circumstances. Down in the steamy-green Minerva Pool, middle-aged couples with a few nervous-looking single women in their thirties are wading and half-floating, keeping their voices down like well-behaved children. Even the women on the loungers are reclining rather stiffly as though just about to be photographed. The whole scene seems somehow artificial, like one of those tableaux organised by modern artists who persuade thousands of strangers to lie down naked in the street. Isn't there something a bit odd about coming all this way and paying £80 to wallow decorously in a hottish bath when you can do the same at home for nothing? The English are famous for taking their pleasures sadly, I know, but this doesn't seem much like a pleasure at all, and I wonder if anyone else is thinking this but doesn't quite like to say so because it is all supposed to be such a liberating experience.

Far from inducing the advertised calm and serenity, the surroundings are making me a little panicky, not to say irritable, more so when I climb some bare stairs to the huge steam room, because the whole place has no windows and I begin to wonder whether I am ever going to get out, a sensation which only intensifies as I pad into the misty gloom. The room has three or four bell-shaped enclosures, ranging from tepid to scalding. On the circular bench inside each bell, shadowy shapes sit expressionless, scarcely moving, some with their knees up to their chins. This is a scene, not out of some region of hell as we fancied, but from one of the dimmer sections of purgatory reserved for people who haven't done anything very bad. All this silent reverence begins to annoy me. What's so great about raising a sweat? I do it every time I cycle to the post office and then at least I come back with some postage stamps. What's become of the famous old comradeship of the baths? Why aren't people eating chicken legs, or hunks of salami, like in the Russian baths in Bellow's Chicago, or smoking a pipe of tobacco or something stronger, like Holmes and Watson, or exchanging hard-luck stories of their love-life like in Nell Dunn's local baths? Where are the songs and shouting and clapping of Urquhart's hammam? Anything rather than this vacuous, worshipful hush.

It is clear that this new faith, like so many old faiths before it, has gone through a reformation. The old indulgences, the popular feasts and customs, the genial encrustations of time and human weakness, have all been swept away, and a new purity and austerity reign in their stead.

I escape to the circular open-air bath on the roof. It is a spectacular place. The water-level is at the rim of the parapet so that you fear if you splash too hard the water might cascade down onto the citizens of Bath below. I have seen this ingenious effect in pictures of fancy villas where the pool appears to brim over into the azure sea beyond. But here several storeys up in a wonderful Georgian city the effect is even more remarkable. All around are the limestone combes with the creamy classical terraces curling up their steep sides. Below us is the Roman bath and beyond the tower and pinnacles of the Abbey, the last glorious gasp of the English Perpendicular tradition, the stone blanched and dazzling in the winter sunshine. All our history is around and below: the rough Celtic causeway of stakes and stones taking worshippers across the swamp to the shrine of Sulis, the huge Roman bath-complex with its Rasta-haired Gorgon glowering down from the temple pediment, then the first simple church rising to obliterate the Romans and, fifteen centuries on, the last and greatest church soaring as high as the Roman baths had sprawled.

And what is everyone doing in this extraordinary spot? Floating semi-upright with blue rubber rings to support their necks. It is like a therapeutic centre for victims of serious spinal accidents, a Stoke Mandeville in the sky. Nobody is looking at the amazing view. In fact, most people aren't looking at anything because they are in this semi-upright position with their faces turned to the sky and their eyes tight shut against the sun.

This is the supreme moment. It is the worship of the body's equivalent to the Elevation of the Host. All guilt and anxiety fled, the brain emptied of thought, the body weightless and effortless, existing only in the moment, just floating. And suddenly I think of Seneca again, the first grumpy old man, decrying the spoilt and empty-headed Romans for insisting on being able to get a tan while they bathed and on having a spectacular view to gawp at as they lolled in the water.

There is, it seems, nothing left in life more central and meaningful than to watch the beads of sweat prickle up across your chest or very slowly to float across steaming water with a rubber ring propping up your head.

The spas are not as grandiose today as the baths were in the later days of Rome, but they are just as numerous and widespread. Every time a church and chapel closes in Swindon or any other town in

Britain, a spa or fitness centre opens. In Swindon alone, the customer can choose from Curves of Cromby Street, St Tropez at 137 Victoria Road, Halls of Fitness in Fleet Street, the Nightingale Hotel and Leisure Club with its Heaven Sent Spa, the De Vere Shaw Ridge, not to mention the dear old public washing and Turkish baths, now far eclipsed by their deluxe state-of-the-art modern successors.

Every country-house hotel, every conference centre, every beauty salon, every leisure centre has a spa attached, offering every kind of massage and therapy: sauna and steam room, aromatic moor, mud wraps, goat's milk and waterbeds and macadamia, luxury caviar facial, Pevonia de luxe pedicure, Pantai Luar, peat bath and body scrub. I could go on for ever but the message is always the same: relax, and all will be well, your body will heal your mind, no worries, calm is balm, feel good and feel good about yourself, go ahead, pamper yourself, you've earned it.

How alien such thoughts would have been to the vast majority of people in Western Europe for the preceding 1,500 years and more. The delicate pampering of the body, far from being a duty that you owe yourself, would have been thought a sinful vanity and a pernicious distraction from God's work. Indifference to bodily imperfections and malfunctions, as to all material hardships, would have been regarded as highly commendable. Christianity always had an element of Stoic tradition in it, and even when Christianity declined, Stoicism continued to be regarded as an important component of the good life, not the only one perhaps but certainly a conspicuous ingredient in the make-up of men and women we admired.

Now the body has become a god, whose every whim must be humoured and every complaint attended to without delay. There is no ghost in the machine, there is only the machine. And our first duty is to keep the machine oiled.

As for the churches and chapels now surplus to requirements, what happens to them? Well, they are often transformed into apartments, new floors slicing the airy vault of the nave into cosy living-space. Sometimes they become bingo halls, or casinos, or restaurants – the money-changers coming back into the temple with a vengeance. Or they can become offices, like the charming late-eighteenth-century chapel of St James Pentonville down the hill from us, where Grimaldi the clown is buried in the graveyard, and which is now rebuilt as the HQ of a marketing firm. Such conversions recall, in reverse, the conversion of royal office blocks, 'basilicas' (kingly things), into the first great churches after the Emperor Constantine was himself converted. The less prepossessing Nonconformist chapels in poor areas like the heads of the Welsh valleys are turned into warehouses and junk stores. But a select few former places of worship have qualified for the most upmarket, state-of-the-art change of use that the twenty-first century can imagine.

My last port of call in this chapter is to a venue if possible even less glamorous than Swindon. Our destination lies to the east of London, in the overgrown Essex suburb of Chigwell. On a bluff above the River Roding still stands the white Georgian mansion of Claybury Hall with its grounds laid out by Humphry Repton who praised its 'profusely beautiful situation'. A century later, that beauty was swamped by the building of the enormous Middlesex county asylum, by George Thomas Hine, the asylum specialist. Hine entered every architectural competition for these new model mental hospitals and won five of them. For most of the twentieth century, these colossal complexes with their castellated water towers and carefully segregated buildings dominated the skyline on the hills round London – the great Italianate palazzo of Colney Hatch, for once not by Hine but by Samuel Daukes, being the most famous. For nearly 100 years, the physically infirm and mentally distressed of the Home Counties were shovelled into these vast hilltop institutions. But then in the second half of the twentieth century, reported cases of neglect and brutality in the mental hospitals began to afflict the public conscience. Radical thinkers began openly to question whether so many vulnerable people needed to be institutionalized in this way. The

places became known as 'snakepits', and one by one they closed, and
their inmates were released into the inattentive arms of Care in the
Community. Claybury shut its doors in 1996, and like so many of
the others the buildings were converted to private homes to meet the
insatiable appetite for housing in and around London. As well as the
existing residential blocks, the spacious grounds provided intensely
valuable land for building on, and little clumps and crescents of new
houses were added to Hine's massive blocks. But what was to be
done with his Grand Recreational Hall with its superb barrel vaulting and ornate proscenium arch topped by a bust of Shakespeare?
What, above all, was to be done with Hine's adjoining chapel with
its sturdy Early English nave and ribbed apse, its splendid cruck ceiling and delicate brick clerestory?

There could only be one answer – a health club and spa. At a cost
of £3.6 million, Esporta Health and Fitness had the hall and chapel
converted to the designs of Goodwin Austin Johnson into a superb
gymnasium and swimming pool. Now you may loll in the azure
chlorine and gaze on George Thomas Hine's Gothic pillars and
canted apse and reflect on all the thousands of mental patients who
over the years mumbled their quavering prayers just above your
head.

What a delight it is to swim slowly up the aisle between these
sturdy round pillars so creamy in the light splashing through the
stained glass. Where the high altar used to stand, rejuvenation is
now provided by the jets of the spa bath bubbling up from below
rather than by the Holy Spirit descending from above. To the right,
the old Lady Chapel conceals a handy sauna to sweat out one's physical impurities, where once the supplicant in private prayer sought to
wash away her spiritual shortcomings. Most glorious of all, round the
apse are blazoned the three emblems of Esporta: the beaming sun,
the ripples and the wine glass. As I stumble still steaming from the
sauna, in a moment of vision I see that these are the three modern
sacraments: sun, sea and sangria, as it used to say in the old advertisements for Spanish tourism. For the first time, it comes to me too

how closely they mirror the emblems of the older faith: the sun, the waters of baptism and the communion cup. Why, that is the smiling image of Sulis Minerva, the obverse of the glaring Rasta-locked god of Roman Bath.

Claybury is not the only one of Hine's piles which has been thus converted. The chapel at his Netherne Hospital in the Surrey hills, not far from Epsom racecourse, is now a splendid pool for the use of members of the Netherne Management Company. Perhaps the same thing will eventually happen not just to all Hine's chapels but to other redundant churches too. One Sunday morning in the foreseeable future, the Gibbon of the day may perform a leisurely backstroke up the nave of some great cathedral – Winchester for preference, it has the longest nave in Europe – gazing at the magnificent ceiling and reflecting how odd it is that this soaring edifice was originally built as a house for men to offer up their prayers to a God whom they could not hear or touch or see.

England is not the only country where churches have been converted into swimming pools. At the height of the official Communist campaign against religion in Soviet Russia, Khrushchev had the Lutheran Cathedral in St Petersburg converted into an Olympic-sized indoor pool. More dramatically, in 1931 Stalin demolished the enormous Cathedral of Christ the Saviour in Moscow, and Khrushchev later had the site turned over to the construction of the largest swimming pool in the world, this one being outdoors.

But the difference is that in no-longer-Soviet Russia the cathedrals have now been reconverted, just as Leningrad became St Petersburg again. The Lutheran Cathedral was reconsecrated in 1997. In Moscow, the Cathedral of Christ the Saviour was entirely rebuilt by Yeltsin. The chances of the chapels at Claybury and Netherne returning to their original use must be rather slimmer.

For in Western Europe we have come full circle. From bath to church, then from chapel to bath, from the Baths of Diocletian to Santa Maria degli Angeli and San Bernardo, and now from Claybury Hospital chapel to the Repton Park Esporta Spa swimming pool.

From Diocletian to Michelangelo, from George Thomas Hine to Goodwin Austin Johnson. The icon of our age is not the Baptism of Our Lord but A Bigger Splash.

Once salvation only took a few drops of water sprinkled over a baby's head. Now it requires a state-of-the-art leisure complex pumping millions of gallons for our delight. It seems a bit unkind to enquire: which offers the more intense experience?

But why should the history of public bathing – its rise and fall and rise again – play such a prominent part in the history of the Western world? Why has such a relatively trivial activity – whether we do it for hygiene or purely for pleasure – consumed such huge quantities of time and money in some societies and virtually none at all in others? From everything we have seen so far, what drives it all is an obsessive religion of the body, a cult which in some centuries came to overshadow religion of the traditional sort. How and why did men and women come to worship at the shrine of their own flesh?

II

THE GYM

Bodies Beautiful

'For FATBURN programme press ENTER!' Gingerly I press, and suddenly the LCD is a blaze of numbers like a fruit machine when you are getting lucky. So far I have been pedalling easily enough, my feet sitting snugly in the straps, the posture vaguely pre-op as though in a blink the surgeon will tilt me backwards and start an intimate examination. Above me on the big television there

is a house-sale show and a bald, nervous man is being shown round
a limestone farmhouse on some bleak northern escarpment. But
nobody else is watching the screen, and nor am I as the pedals suddenly turn nasty and it feels like cycling through porridge. I wonder
whether my neighbours have chosen 'FATBURN' too and are now
regretting it, but it seems nosy to look over and see what they have
on their LCDs. One thing you can say for the Aquaterra Leisure
Fitness Centre in Market Road is going in there doesn't make you
feel too inferior, because the other exercisers average 30 lbs over-
weight and the men all look as if they had a load on last night. The
portly razorhead on the treadmill is jogging for two. I saw him
through the window on my way in and later I see him through the
window on my way out, still remorselessly trotting nowhere and staring straight ahead, but without evident distress despite carrying
enough weight to stop a Gold Cup horse in its tracks.

Actually, staring is not quite the word, that suggests a desperate,
strained look. What everyone in the gym has is not a strained look at
all, but rather a contained, empty gaze. The big television screens are
a waste of space; nobody in that absorbed state could possibly grasp
the latest twist of *Neighbours* or take any interest in this elderly lady's
toby jug – there's an antiques show on now – anyone who has ever
watched daytime television knows that's all there ever is on, so the
meditators on the treadmill aren't missing anything. It's more their
solitary vacant stare that strikes me, as though there was nobody else
in the gym, perhaps nobody else in the greater London area, except
each of them pounding on. Though we are only 9 inches apart, we
are utterly spaced out. In the gym everyone is a solipsist. At first I had
taken it as a sort of delicacy, the etiquette of the gym, that nobody
looks at anyone else. After all, we are most of us not a pretty sight,
with our oily bottoms wobbling inside our tracksuit bottoms and the
sweat gradually invading our T-shirts. And the stuff we do there is
not for the most part elegant, designed to fortify the sinew, not to
show off the figure. All those squats and pull-ups and shoulder-
presses and ball-crunches and Bulgarian splits and stiff-leg dead-lifts

are anything but balletic. But now I see that we are beyond curiosity. Each of us lost in his bubble of self-improvement like people in church, the only person we talk to is God, the God who bestows muscular tone and takes away the flab and defines our abs and pecs and glutes. We are a congregation without a priest to insist on the sign of peace.

This is, after all, the new divine service, the proper faith for those who are serious about being modern. And it is an explosive phenomenon of the last twenty years. According to the Fitness Industry Association (already there is an association), there now are more than 5,700 public and private gyms in the UK. Fred Turok, chairman of the FIA and chief executive of LA Fitness, says that in the 1990s 'every time we opened a club it was full six months later'. Mintel, the market research company, reckons all those gyms between them coin £2.3 billion a year. Not a penny of this vast sum comes from me, because Islington Council regards my state of fitness in my old age as such a top priority that my IZZ card allows me to use all these beautiful expensive machines free for ever. At present around 12 per cent of the adult population uses a gym of some sort. Both the private gym operators and the Department of Health think of this as *only* 12 per cent and are scratching their heads as to how to entice, badger and chivvy the remaining 88 per cent of us into joining up. No old-style evangelists were ever more insistent and importunate. Insurance companies are offering 75 per cent discounts to customers who join a gym and work out twice a week. No Brave New World could be keener to monitor our personal physical regimes. Even the government has been suggesting that the NHS should think twice about treating patients who refuse to lose weight or give up smoking.

This might then seem to be a joyful time for the missionaries of the body beautiful. Not a bit. As with missionaries of the soul, any growth in one's congregation is also a cause for anxiety, especially when it is this rapid. For the flesh is as weak as ever. The spectre of backsliding looms. Across the industry, between 50 per cent and

60 per cent of gym-goers slip silently off the register each year. At
the Tottenham Court Road branch of Fitness First, they reckon to
lose 4.5 per cent of their members each month. It is a constant
struggle to replace them, a case of running very hard to stay in the
same place – in fact, a treadmill.

For the truth is that working out is, for many – perhaps most –
people, a desolate and joyless occupation. Its satisfactions are hard
won over a depressingly long period, or often not won at all, as the
pounds so painfully shed somehow slink back on again. If you want
a suitable emblem from classical mythology to represent the average
member of a gym club, I would suggest the figure of Sisyphus in hell
rolling his stone uphill and watching it fall back down again to the
end of time.[1]

It is not surprising that the better-off seekers after fitness should
lighten the burden of their solitude by employing a personal trainer.
This is a profession even more shiny-new than the gym itself and, to
those celebrities and wannabes who can afford their services, even
more irresistible. How better can you hope to obliterate the pain of
every creaking muscle than by listening to their words of encouragement and advice? The mere presence of this godlike figure
matching your every stride makes you feel better. Some of his or her
own glowing, vibrant physical tone must surely rub off on you.
With the personal trainer at your side, failure is not an option.

Thus our age has reinvented the Father Confessor, that indispensable figure who allayed the angst and dispelled the boredom of
high-born ladies of the past. It is not surprising that the most popular confessors were drawn from the Jesuit Fathers, famous for their
charm, tact and subtlety, for all these qualities were needed to detect
signs of spiritual progress in the most unpromising cases and to reas-
sure their fretful patrons.

But it would be unkind to the Jesuits to accept the popular carica-
ture of them as worldly and social-climbing. In overseas missionary
work, they endured hardship and often martyrdom. Their founder,
Ignatius Loyola, had originally been a rather dissolute soldier but

after being badly wounded at the siege of Pamplona decided to become a Soldier of Christ. And there was undeniably a military flavour to the discipline he instilled into his order and to the Spiritual Exercises which he prescribed for his followers and which are still widely practised on religious retreats to this day.

They are written in the form of a handbook, to help the exerciser understand the will of God and give him the energy and courage to follow that will. For the first week, he is to meditate on sin and its consequences; for the second on Christ's life on earth, the third on his Passion and the last week on Christ Risen. Ignatius laid down that in the full version these exercises should be performed once or twice only, but in a shortened version they might be made once a year over three or four days. This is, so to speak, the sort of refresher course which thousands of modern Christians undergo when they go on religious retreats.

But of course you can just as well perform these spiritual exercises on your own, once you have got the hang of them. The same goes for physical exercises. Another threat to the prosperity of the gym is the possibility of continuing an equally strenuous regime by yourself, entirely free of charge in the privacy of your own home. A press-up on the bedroom carpet is just as good as a press-up on the gym floor. And these private regimes too mimic the discipline of military training. For years, the most popular set of exercises were those prescribed for the Royal Canadian Air Force – indeed, it is the only thing anyone knows about the Canadian Air Force.

In 2008, the *Guardian* newspaper ushered in the New Year by folding into each day's issue for a whole week a booklet setting out the 'Official British Army Fitness Programme', as though there might also exist some unofficial programme containing dodgy exercises which would do irreparable damage to your spine. These little pamphlets are each bound in military beige or khaki and adorned with the crown and crossed swords of the British Army. It shows the unquestioning character of the new faith in personal fitness that these militaria should be slipped in between the pages of Britain's most famous liberal-pacific newspaper. One almost expected the following week's issues to contain further official Army instruction manuals: for parade-ground drill perhaps, or bayonet practice or how to interrogate enemy suspects. This week-long feature not surprisingly attracted the attention of *Guardian* letter-writers, especially from indignant pacifists, prompting the relevant editor to explain that the paper was promoting fitness, not fighting, but other correspondents were more concerned about the demanding nature of the exercises being unsuitable for older readers. No one dreamed of objecting that to devote so many pages to a fitness regime was wasteful or disproportionate.

The quest for personal fitness now invades the most unlikely places. Under the tag line 'Muscular Christianity', the Roman Catholic website Universalis promotes the practice of going to the gym and praying while using the rowing machine. 'At the rate of one word per stroke, rowing one mile on the machine takes me one Our Father and two Hail Marys.' Respondents eagerly endorsed this suggestion. Tim Heywood says: 'I have done the same sort of thing with Stations of the Cross.' Rachel Romains reports that 'a university chaplain I know prays the Office on his exercise bike'. Others say they pray while jogging or doing aerobics or during the rest breaks in their karate classes. In the old days, especially in Ireland, the parish priest was often a slow-moving, corpulent fellow whose principal forms of exercise were lifting the occasional glass of whisky or moving from the rails to the bookie's. Now, it seems, he is expected to be as lean as the greyhounds he used to race.

For most of the Christian era, all this would have been unthinkable, or at any rate unthought of. Physical exercise on this intensive, purposive, organized – and often compulsory – scale was simply not on the agenda for the overwhelming majority of men, and not at all for women. There was military training, of course, which included many sports still practised today, such as fencing, archery, equitation and shooting. The modern pentathlon derives partly from that tradition of military training, and the medals often go to serving officers in the armed forces. But for ordinary civilians, PE was to be endured by children only, if at all, and certainly not to be continued into adult life.

Noble and Nude and Antique

We have to go back to the Greeks and Romans to find physical jerks practised at this sort of level and frequency. In our minds there is indeed a vague image of naked Greek youths wrestling in the palaestra or the gymnasium. In fact the similarities, if studied a little more closely, are striking. It was central to the Greek view of education that the body must be trained and exercised as thoroughly as the mind. From the ages of 8 to 12, Greek boys were put through it in the palaestra by the *paidotribes* or trainer. The palaestra was a low building with a central courtyard with a sand floor surrounded by changing rooms and baths. It was usually part of the gymnasium, a sports centre set outside the city walls which was a public institution and open to all. It would normally contain a running track, a jumping pit, discus and javelin ranges, a boxing room with assorted punch balls and a room for ball games. The ball games were remarkably varied and worth a word or two. Though the evidence is scanty, we cannot miss some modern resemblances. The balls themselves ranged in size from the smallest, the Greek *harpaston*, a hard ball stuffed with hair, comparable perhaps to a modern cricket ball, up to the largest, the Roman *follis*, which may have been filled with air like a modern football. The games played ranged from simple games of catch, through complicated variants of pig-in-the-middle, to more competitive pastimes like smacking the ball against a wall with one's hand and counting the strokes, the ancestor of fives, pelota and squash.

According to Galen, the great physician of the second century AD, in the most strenuous form of ball game the players form a scrimmage round the player in the middle and try to prevent him getting

the ball, tackling him by the neck or body and using all the holds of
the wrestling ring. Galen tells us that the game was originally called
phaininda, or feinting, deceiving an opponent by pretending to throw
to one player and throwing it to another. *Harpastum* — the Latin
name for both the ball and the game — means snatching or inter-
cepting. The rougher and more devious tricks of rugby seem to
have come as naturally to the ancients as they did to nineteenth-
century schoolboys. The first dummy was sold long before the birth
of Christ. There was another game known as *episkyros* or *epikoinos*,
the team game, according to Pollux, who compiled a sort of
encyclopedia in the second century AD. *Epikoinos* was played
between two teams of equal numbers with a white line chalked
between them in the centre of the ground. Each team tried to catch
the ball and throw it back over and beyond their opponents until one
side or the other was forced back over the goal line. Here we have
even louder echoes of modern rugby, and of American football too.

Stone reliefs found at Athens dating from the late sixth century BC
show these sports in progress and also another in which players with
curved sticks are hooking a ball very much in the manner of a
hockey bully. In late Hellenistic times, there were ball-game coaches,
the *sphairistes*, who taught the techniques of *sphairistike*, which, as I
have mentioned, was the name borrowed by Major Wingfield for the
game of outdoor or lawn tennis which he devised in the 1870s.

Nor is it only the ball games of ancient Greece and Rome which
seem quite familiar to us. I leave aside the sports of throwing, jumping and running, which, like those of boxing and wrestling, were
deliberately revived and codified for the modern Olympiad. In these
the similarities between ancient and modern are obvious. Less well-
known perhaps are the physical exercises carried out by the youths of
between 14 and 20. In ancient Greece, these seem to have been fairly
free and spontaneous. In the fifth century BC, at any rate, there
seems to have been little system or science of physical culture. But
600 years later, by the time of Galen, there was a detailed programme mapped out. Galen's own treatise distinguishes between

exercises for the legs, the arms and the trunk, between slow and rapid and between exercises to tone up the muscles without violent movement and those designed to improve speed and strength. Many of these are to be seen in any modern gym: raising the legs alternately backwards and forwards, rolling on the ground, swinging the arms, exercising the biceps with or without dumb-bells, or *halteres* as they were called.

All these exercises, like what little we know of ancient ball games, might well have developed seamlessly into the sports and games that we play today. No doubt the rules would have been elaborated and codified over the years, the equipment modernized. But all the basic elements were in place before the birth of Christ: the desire for fitness, the competitive instinct, sheer human playfulness.

The decline and fall of the Roman Empire meant the gradual eclipse of the whole apparatus of physical education, athletic competition and organized games. Like the Roman baths, the gymnasium and the palaestra fell into disuse across the whole empire; weeds covered their sandy floors – 'arena' only means sand. Their stones were pillaged for building material by the local inhabitants.

No doubt the collapse of order and classical culture was partly to blame. These institutions were, after all, the fruits of a long civilization of self-improvement and civic order and could not be expected to survive their ruin.

But there was another reason, no less powerful and in the long run more decisive. The gymnasium didn't merely fall into decay, it was wilfully destroyed. And the initial provocation for that destruction lay in one simple circumstance: that the athletes exercised naked. *Gymnos*, after all, means naked. Greek youths exercised in the nude quite naturally as an expression of freedom and delight in the physical world, the sunshine on their backs, the warm breeze rustling through the olive groves which surrounded the gymnasium, the sparkling water from the nearby spring, for gymnasiums were often situated near a sacred grove or spring. Their nudity was not simply a matter of a benign climate, it was a cultural lack of inhibition – and one which was soon to disappear. Already in the Roman Republic nudity began to be viewed as unseemly and likely to lead to disorderly conduct. Cicero agreed with the poet Ennius that 'the beginning of shameful acts is to strip the body naked amongst other men'.[2] Compulsory PE dropped out of the curriculum, although young men continued to exercise in large numbers in the palaestrae, now often situated as part of the enormous new bath complexes.

It was not simply that the Roman sense of modesty was shocked by public nudity. The old easy-going homosexual antics of the Greek gym seemed to them a blot on Greek civilization. In any case, they regarded non-military sports as useless for the training of soldiers. As for competitive athletic games, they were introduced into Rome in 186 BC by the philhellenic senator Fulvius Nobilior, but most of the competitors came from the Greek colonies, and in any case the Romans quickly came to prefer the more sensational amusements of gladiators and wild beasts.

The poet Martial told a youth that it would be better to till the vineyard than to waste strength on the silly dumb-bells. Before the Battle of Pharsalus, Caesar allegedly told his troops, 'Don't worry. Pompey's army is full of levies from the Greek gym, trained in wrestling and athletics but hardly able to carry a full weight of arms and armour, let alone use them.'

Juvenal was contemptuous of a Roman woman who said how much she admired athletes, and the dyspeptic Seneca lamented: 'How many men, I say to myself, train their bodies and how few train their minds. What crowds flock to the games, spurious as they are and arranged merely for pastime — and what solitude reigns where the good arts are taught! How feather-brained are the athletes whose muscles and shoulders we admire!' Yet just as Seneca did take an occasional plunge in the baths, so he also believed in keeping fit.

Some emperors, anxious to occupy their restless youth, did attempt to revive PE. Augustus established the *juventus*, compulsory physical jerks for young men on the Campus Martius. Domitian established the Capitoline games and set up the first purpose-built permanent stadium in Rome, now the Piazza Navona. Only in the fourth century AD did gym culture begin to decline. At Sardis, the south wing of the palaestra was given over to the Jews, later to be reconstructed as the largest synagogue of the ancient world.

The Revolt Against the Body

But the gymnasium had a more convinced and passionate enemy than the Romans. In the long run, it was the revulsion of the early Christians that secured the virtual obliteration of the gym culture for more than 1,000 years. The two institutions that were central to classical culture – the bath and the gym – were those that provoked most sharply the disgust and condemnation of the new faith.[3] Never again until our own times were bathing and physical exercise so closely associated with each other and with psychic as well as physical health.

Even in the East, where the baths continued under the Ottoman Empire pretty much as they had been under the Romans, the tradition of physical exercise disappeared. Fikret Yegül says emphatically: 'Like the Byzantine and early Islamic baths, Turkish baths don't have palaestrae. The notion of exercise connected with bathing is entirely absent. In fact, the suggestion to a conservative Turk of exercise in connection with bathing would be nothing short of absurd.'

Under the Empire, the Romans themselves had become notorious couch potatoes. They flocked to the circus for all-day-long spectaculars. The only exercise they took was the early start to secure a decent seat. Crowds of 400,000 sat there from dawn to dusk, watching gladiators, chariot races and the butchery of large mammals, as utterly absorbed and inert as addicts of modern reality TV, the only difference being that the unluckier entrants might suffer death rather than mere humiliation or ejection from the Big Brother House. The expense of these amazing shows may remind us of the spiralling cost of the 2012 London Olympics, up to £12 billion at the time of writing from an original estimate of less than

£4 billion (*Guardian*, 15 November 2007). But today's Olympics are a miserable spectacle in comparison. Who would willingly watch a gaggle of ill-featured scrawny athletes in unbecoming vest and knickers running round an unadorned arena when, to take only the displays in the Roman circus under Carinus, one might see a forest of trees transplanted bodily into the arena of the Colosseum to be immediately filled with 1,000 ostriches, 1,000 stags and 1,000 wild boar to be butchered at the pleasure of the multitude; to be followed the next day by the slaughter of 200 lions and lionesses, 200 leopards and 300 bears, not to mention 20 zebras from Madagascar and 10 camels from Ethiopia, a rhinoceros and a hippopotamus and 32 elephants?

It is not surprising that, even when they were not being slaughtered themselves, Christians should deplore the extravagance and cruelty of these displays and the idle voyeurism that they encouraged. But there was a further and deeper reason for the loathing of the early Christians for all the common pleasures of Rome, especially those centred on the bath and the gymnasium. For Christians, the cult of the body – both as an object of pleasure to be caressed and pampered and as a source of pride to be toned and exercised to a pitch of muscular perfection – represented an ongoing sin against the spirit. The weakness of the flesh was never more manifest than when the flesh was flexed and oiled and powdered in an ecstasy of self-love. In *The Body and Society* (1988), his great study of sexual renunciation in early Christianity, Peter Brown places full weight on the traditions of continence and sobriety which those early Christians inherited from the late classical world, but his principal aim is to show how wholly different both in kind and degree the Christian attitude to sex was to be, how sharp and dangerous and novel were the teachings of St Paul: 'For I know that nothing good dwells in me, that is, in my flesh . . . I see in my members another law at war with the law in my mind . . . wretched man that I am! Who will deliver me from this body of death?'[4] From the sinful nature of sexual activity, except when properly controlled and sanctioned, Paul deduced the irremediable sinfulness of the body as a whole. The sexual part, so to speak, represented the whole, a corporeal synecdoche which overwhelmed the Church for nearly two millennia.

Some apologists have argued that the Early Fathers were not as unrelenting towards the body and its sports as this would suggest. Surely they admired the striving and self-denial of serious athletes. The title of 'athleta Christi' was accorded to such early soldier martyrs as St Sebastian, as it was later by popes to men who had led military campaigns to defend Christianity, such as those medieval kings of Hungary, Albania and Moldavia who fended off the invading Turkish infidels. But this title was a metaphorical one, like 'Soldier of Christ', designed to appropriate those virtues of courage and steadfastness for their proper spiritual object, not in any serious sense an accommodation of athletics but rather an attempt to commandeer its aura of popular heroism. The seventeenth-century hymn 'Athleta Christi Nobilis' is the Catholic equivalent of 'Onward, Christian Soldiers'.

In the Italian Renaissance and again in the wider neo-classical movement at the end of the eighteenth century, painters and sculptors attempted to undermine and break away from this suspicion of the body. Saints being martyred are no longer decently draped. Instead, they exhibit swelling thighs and biceps, their flesh shines with manly vigour, even as they are being peppered with arrows or disembowelled. Goddesses and female martyrs show off lustrous breasts and bottoms. Yet what had become permissible in art – and indeed widely admired – had not percolated through to church and society at large.

It is only in the middle of the nineteenth century that the conflict between faith and body at last erupts and comes to resolution. At about the same time as David Urquhart and Richard Barter are preaching the delights of the Turkish bath, a new movement begins to stir within the Church of England. This movement became derided by its opponents as 'Muscular Christianity'. And the moving spirit in it was an eccentric obsessive who to posterity is known mainly for his improving children's story, *The Water-Babies* (1863).

Yet if one single man is to be identified as the maker of the modern world in one of its most crucial aspects – the cult of the body – I would unhesitatingly nominate the Revd. Charles Kingsley.

Muscles and Christians

The 1850s were a period of intellectual turmoil in England unequalled in its violence and intensity since the religious quarrels of the seventeenth century, in fact more disturbing and agonizing to those involved since the war was being fought on three fronts, often by the same intellectuals and divines. We have tended to study these three battlefronts separately, yet they were all in essence part of the same wars, even if not all the combatants were on the same side in each of them.

The first front was the conflict between the theory of evolution and what we would now call creationism, the theory that God created the world in six days, probably at some relatively recent date (4004 BC, according to Archbishop Ussher's somewhat hazardous guesstimate). The 1850s saw the long march of evolutionary theory culminate in the publication in 1859 of Darwin's *Origin of Species*. The following year, in the hot summer of 1860, there took place in Oxford the famous meeting of the British Association for the Advancement of Science at which the Bishop of Oxford, Samuel Wilberforce, made an immortal fool of himself. Soapy Sam, as he was called because of his oily manner and slippery mode of argument, egged on by his massed clergy, derided the speculations of the Darwinists and, as a parting gag, politely enquired of Thomas Henry Huxley, the uncompromising promulgator of Darwinism, the Richard Dawkins of his day (he was known as 'Darwin's Bulldog'), 'was it through his grandfather or his grandmother that he claimed descent from a monkey?' Huxley rose and minced Wilberforce into shreds from which his reputation never recovered.

But Soapy Sam was also heavily involved on the second front in the mind wars of the 1850s, the conflict between the claims of the Church of England and those of the Church of Rome. As Bishop of Oxford, he was responsible for the teeming ranks of young clergymen and theological students who were aglow with a zeal to revive the ascetic purity of the early Church and to bring back to the Church of England the gorgeous rituals of Rome, which they saw as the rightful inheritance of the Church of England as much as of the Roman Catholic Church. These so-called Tractarians, led by John Keble, John Henry Newman and Edward Pusey, wanted to rescue the Church of England from what they saw as its indolent liberalism and defend it as divinely ordained and its clergymen as true inheritors of Christ's mission through the Apostolic succession. This was all very well, and certainly defensible on the historical evidence. The trouble was that the defenders of the ecclesiastical status quo angrily protested that some of the Tractarians' claims were heretical and took to the Church courts to have this proved. This naturally led some of the Tractarians to think, Well, if we aren't welcome here, why should we not submit to Rome where our views will be quite acceptable, indeed orthodox? Why settle for the substitute when you can have the real thing? The Pope, was, after all, St Peter's undoubted heir. Doubts about the claims of the Church of England began to afflict them. Perhaps the idea of a middle way, a *via media*, between Rome and the excesses of Protestantism, was a fantasy after all. That was the view taken by Newman, who in 1843 resigned as Vicar of St Mary's Oxford and two years later became a Catholic. He was followed to Rome through the 1850s by a steady trickle of Anglican clergymen, often accompanied by their wives, including several members of Soapy Sam's own family. Wilberforce was himself a High Churchman, and he began to be blamed for these defections, since so many of them occurred within his own diocese. He was an energetic organizer as well as a fluent speaker, and to set the Church of England back on the right road he instituted a training college for theological students at the nearby village of Cuddesdon. Alas, here too the Romish tendencies crept in like the damp rising from the River Thames. Worse still, the students began to affect an unappealing camp manner. Wilberforce wrote to a friend in 1858:

> Our men are too peculiar – some at least of our best men . . . I consider it a heavy affliction that they should wear neckcloths of peculiar construction, coats of peculiar cut, whiskers of peculiar dimensions, that they should walk with a peculiar step, carry their heads at a peculiar angle to the body, and read in a peculiar tone. First, because it implies to me a want of vigour, virility and self-expressing vitality of the religious life in the young men . . . Secondly because it greatly limits their usefulness and ours by the natural prejudice which it excites.[5]

No one would have agreed with these sentiments more heartily – and heartily is the word – than the Revd. Charles Kingsley (1819–75), who had become Vicar of Eversley, Hampshire (where he was to stay for the rest of his life), at about the same time that Newman was becoming a Catholic. As a student, Kingsley had himself been enthused by the Tractarian spirit, but he had swiftly revolted against all ascetic and Romish practices, especially the cult of the Virgin Mary. He wrote to a priest who was about to become a Catholic: 'If by holiness you mean "saintliness" I quite agree that Rome is the place to get *that* – and a poor pitiful thing it is when it is got – not God's ideal of a man, but an effeminate shaveling's ideal.' The artificial separation between the flesh and the spirit cultivated an unmanly 'fastidious, maundering, die-away effeminacy' and turned out 'prayer-mongering eunuchs' rather than upstanding Englishmen.[6]

Kingsley was himself a model of manly vigour. The son of a well-to-do country vicar, he was adept at all country sports. He thought nothing of walking 10 miles to a favoured fishing spot and 10 miles back. He once walked the 52 miles from Cambridge to London inside a day. Like his friend Thomas Hughes, the author of *Tom Brown's Schooldays* (1857) and *Tom Brown at Oxford* (1861) who was a boxing coach, he was especially fond of a scrap. In his novel, *Two Years Ago* (1857), published two years after the Crimean War which had caused such public anguish, he commends warfare as the way to regenerate sick souls.

It was in a review of *Two Years Ago*, in the *Saturday Review*, that we find the first recorded mention of 'Muscular Christianity':

> We all know by this time what is the task that Mr Kingsley has made specially his own – it is that of spreading the knowledge and fostering the love of a muscular Christianity. His ideal is a man who fears God and can walk a thousand miles in a thousand hours – who in the language which Mr Kingsley has made popular breathes God's free air on God's rich earth, and at the same time can hit a woodcock, doctor a horse and twist a poker round his fingers.

Physical strength, religious certainty and the ability to shape and control the world came together in the Muscular Christian. He made his own luck, forged his own physical and spiritual armour-plating to withstand the world.[7]

Christian socialists, like secular socialists and indeed social reformers in all parties, were concerned with sanitation, housing and the relief of poverty. A concern for the physical fitness of the poor arose naturally out of this mission. It would be absurd, after all, to strive to equalize the social conditions of our fellow citizens without striving also to equalize their physical health and robustness. Gyms and swimming baths were just as much part of the new Jerusalem as drains and schools. And so were Turkish baths for the railwaymen of Swindon.

This then is the third front in the mind wars of the 1850s, the war between those Christians who regarded the flesh and spirit as inseparable parts of 'the whole manhood' and those who regarded the flesh as a source of temptation and weakness to the spirit – the Manicheans as Kingsley called them, after a heresy supposedly promulgated by the third-century preacher Manes who based his ascetic faith on a primeval conflict between light and darkness. And by 'the whole manhood' Kingsley meant, primarily, bluntly and whole-heartedly, sex.

It is possible to read some accounts of the famous quarrel between Kingsley and Newman – as notorious in its day as the dust-up between Huxley and Wilberforce – and come across scarcely any mention of sex. For the immediate provocation for the quarrel was not sexuality but mendacity. In his review in *Macmillan's Magazine* of Froude's *History of England*, Kingsley had said in his breezy, bluster-ing way: 'Truth for its own sake has never been a virtue of the Roman clergy. Father Newman informs us that it need not, and on the whole ought not to be, that cunning is the weapon which Heaven has given to the saints wherewith to withstand the brute male force of the wicked world which marries and is given in mar-riage.'[8] In a subsequently published pamphlet, Kingsley imprudently added to the original insult, by declaring: 'Yes, Dr Newman is a very economical person, teaching in the words of St Clement that, in cer-tain cases, a lie is the nearest approach to the truth' – an early appearance in print of 'economical with the truth'.

Newman exploded. Where had he ever said such a thing? Where had the Church ever recommended or sanctified lying? Of course Kingsley had not bothered to establish chapter and verse – he seldom bothered to research a subject minutely before he sailed into the attack with guns blazing. Newman had him on toast, and both in his immediate response and his *Apologia Pro Vita Sua*, one of the most eloquent essays in self-defence in the English language, he established to his own satisfaction and that of his co-religionists that the One True Church had never ever recommended lying, nor had he him-self.

But lying was only the immediate provocation. What Newman did not defend himself against was Kingsley's underlying charge, that by distorting the true tradition of the Church the Oxford Tractarians had 'struck at the roots of our wedded bliss'.[9] The fact was that Newman saw the celibate life as superior. He did not care at all for the company of women, except his sisters. He lived all his life, whether Anglican or Roman Catholic, in the company of celibate men, preferably younger men. Every time his friends got married he threw a hissy fit.[10]

So perhaps Kingsley's accusations were ultimately not so far off the mark. But his blundering, blustering rhetoric had lost him the argument. The non-believing George Eliot described his pamphlet as 'thoroughly vicious . . . a mixture of arrogance, coarse impertinence and unscrupulousness with real intellectual incompetence'.[11] Newman had not said what Kingsley had claimed he said. And what he had said about the honoured place of monastic life and ascetic behaviour in Christian tradition was perfectly true. St Paul would have recognized every word of it.

Kingsley had lost the battle, but had he lost the war? His attitude towards sex, that intercourse between a married couple was not only lawful but sacred, corresponded much more closely to the attitudes of the average Victorian couple than Newman's asceticism, let alone Newman's disgust. Despite being so thoroughly floored by Newman in the eyes of the intellectual world, Kingsley remained highly popular with the general public. Parents continued to christen their sons Kingsley well into the twentieth century. Kingsley Martin, editor of the *New Statesman* in the 1930s, and Kingsley Amis are only two of many. Charles Kingsley's novels glorifying manly struggle continued to win audiences, even if the characters were mostly made of cardboard. And his active involvement in bettering the lot of the poor was much more congenial to the public than Newman's praise of withdrawal and contemplation.

Yet there is no gainsaying that Kingsley was a very odd fish: awkward and gangling, scrawny, hatchet-faced, with straggling grey whiskers and liable to strange facial contortions when he spoke in his surprisingly rough, uncouth manner. And though his attitude towards sex may sound healthy and uninhibited, it arose out of the extraordinary turmoil that he underwent before his marriage to Fanny Grenfell. 'Matter is holy,' he told her, 'awful glorious matter.

Let us never use those words *animal* and *brutal* in a degrading sense. Our animal enjoyments must be religious ceremonies.'[12] His instructions were as precise as they were weird: 'At a quarter past eleven lie down, clasp your arms and every limb round me, and with me repeat the Te Deum.' But these ceremonies were not simply a matter of praising the Lord. There was mortification and purification to be undergone too. He demanded that Fanny go on vigorous fasts. In one letter he enclosed instructions for the manufacture of a couple of hair shirts (in fact, to be made of canvas). Flagellation too. He drew the line at whipping her himself. 'Your own hands or your maid's must give the stripes. I will kneel outside the door and pray.'[13] Marriage was for all eternity, so it would not matter if they delayed its delights for a month: this would purify and prolong their bliss, so that when they reached heaven, they could go on for ever without interruption: 'Will not these thoughts give us more perfect delight when we lie naked in each other's arms, clasped together with each other's limbs, buried in each other's bodies, struggling, panting, dying for a moment? Shall we not feel, even then, that there is more in store for us, that those thrilling writhings are but dim shadows of a union which shall be perfect?'

After such a build-up, not unnaturally Kingsley feared disappointment. But there was none. His passion for Fanny only increased after they were married, though it did perhaps settle down into a more secular style. After more than seven years of marriage he wrote to her while on a steamer to Germany: 'Oh that I were with you, or rather you with me here. The beds are so small that we should be forced to lie inside each other, and the weather is so hot that you might walk about naked all day – cela va sans dire! Oh, those naked nights at Chelsea! When will they come again? I kiss both locks of hair every time I open my desk – but the little curly one seems to bring me nearer to you.'[14]

Had any ordained clergyman of the Church of England before him ever said that he preferred his wife's pubic hair to the hair on her head?

And it is Kingsley who represents the values of the future. Long before *Lady Chatterley's Lover,* he exalts sex as sacred. Long before the revival of the gym, he exalts physical fitness. In this respect he scored a decisive victory in the battle. Between 1860 and 1880, every major English public school made games compulsory. Football and cricket clubs were formed in the new industrial towns, often under the patronage of the local clergy and given official approval. Sports clubs and associations gained royal patrons and royal prefixes. If Kingsley was the ancestor of D.H. Lawrence, he was also the ancestor of Lord Baden-Powell. *Scouting for Boys* (1908) is Kingsley's manly fiction turned into an educational programme. Sir William Alexander Smith founded the Boys' Brigade in Glasgow on the basis of sports and military drill to strengthen Christian manly character. It was he who asked Baden-Powell to rewrite his *Aids to Scouting* (1899) as a handbook for the Brigade. Baden-Powell was then a war hero, famous for his exploits against the Boers. *Scouting for Boys* thus emerged from a confluence of the military and the Christian. Even those Church organizations which had originally neglected physical activity were now compelled to take account of it. At its inception in 1844, the Young Men's Christian Association had concentrated on Bible study, prayer and education and had frowned upon games and athletics as an undesirable distraction from the Christian mission. But they found it difficult to retain members who would rather be out on the playing field. Kingsley's gospel of manliness came to the rescue, and the YMCA gym became one of its most prominent features – to become, alas, in recent times one of the most notorious pick-up locations.

Perhaps most spectacular of all, British Muscular Christianity provided the spark that lit, or relit, the Olympic torch. Baron Pierre de Coubertin (1863–1937) was educated by the Jesuits, but could not swallow all the dogma of the Church and instead adopted 'the religion of humanity'. He read a French translation of *Tom Brown's Schooldays* and visited Rugby School. He saw the traditions of the English public school as a means of rebuilding the character of the

French people after the humiliation of the Franco-Prussian war. And how better to spread those ideals wider, indeed to all humanity, than by reviving those Olympic Games which had finally petered out 1,000 years earlier. He regarded the sports arena as 'a laboratory for manliness'. The Churches soon realized that they had to jump on the wagon and show themselves eager to be part of this great experiment. Within a few decades, the Catholic Church was just as sport-crazed as the rest of society, and Catholic schools like Ampleforth put out the most ferocious rugby teams. Cardinal Basil Hume, whose happiest days had been spent teaching at Ampleforth, would really light up as he began to discuss the prospects of the 1st XV that year. Pope John Paul II, in his youth a fine swimmer, skier and climber, told the National Olympic Committee in Rome in 1979 that 'the Church has always been interested in sport, because she prizes everything that contributes constructively to the harmonious and complete development of man, body and soul.' There is now an Office for Sport within the Pontifical Council for the Laity, whose mission is to foster 'a culture of sport' as 'an instrument of peace and brotherhood among peoples'.

This is all rewriting history in a big way. As we have seen, it is not true that the Church has always been interested in sport, to put it mildly. It is not even true of the YMCA. But the comeback of the body has proved irresistible. For once, bearing in mind the previous examples of Lazarus and Jesus, the word 'resurrection' is neither exaggerated nor inappropriate.

We have concentrated so far on the revival of the body cult within the Churches, since they were the institutions which had initially repressed it with such self-righteous vigour. But that revival can be seen just as vividly displayed in the secular sphere and among individuals who had nothing to do with Christianity or were actively hostile to it. The revival of the Olympic Games in 1896 did not owe its success primarily to religious pressures. The Churches were merely supporting players in a cast of politicians and educationists who had come to regard sport as a benign and civilizing influence within and between nations. But the most intense pressure came from the popularity of sport with the general public. To promote sport in one way or another was a way for officialdom to seem more in touch and in sympathy with public opinion. Over the course of the twentieth century, what became increasingly remarkable was the willingness of governments to expend large sums of money, first on securing the Olympics for one of their major cities and then on hosting the games, despite the ever-growing certainty that they were very unlikely to see any of that money again and were more likely to be saddled with debts for years to come. When the cult of the body returned, so did bread and circuses. In the modern era, it has taken even more bread to pay for the circuses than it did under the later Roman emperors.

As an example of how the body cult had colonized non-religious fields, the growth of gymnastics in Germany stands out. *Das Turnen* or *Die Leibesübungen* have played a larger part in German history and culture than gymnastics ever have in Britain. The father of gymnastics in Germany, Friedrich Ludwig Jahn, 'Turnvater Jahn' (1778–1852) was a Prussian teacher who, like Kingsley after the Crimean War and like Coubertin after the Franco-Prussian war, wanted to rebuild the morale of his people after their humiliation by Napoleon. He opened his first *Turnplatz*, or open-air gym, in Berlin in 1811, and soon a gym union or *Turnverein* was flourishing in every German city. The *Turnverein* movement spread rapidly, crossing the Atlantic with German immigrants to the USA and Canada, where *Turnvereine* still prosper, especially in the Midwest. In Germany the movement swiftly developed a thirst for national liberation to go with the firmer biceps. Jahn himself was not merely a fierce Prussian nationalist but an ill-humoured xenophobe and anti-Semite, who organized public book-burnings – a medieval custom which the Nazis were also later to take a fancy to. But from the general standpoint of the day, Jahn was regarded as a progressive character. We should remember him more specifically as the inventor of the parallel bars, the balance beam,

the vaulting horse and the horizontal bar, for some of us instruments
of torture, for others lighting the path to well-being.

During the restoration of the anciens régimes after Waterloo, gymnastics was regarded as a subversive activity. The *Turnvereine* were
banned by Metternich, and Jahn himself was locked up for six years
and then prohibited from teaching or gymnastic work after his release.
In the more liberal 1840s, the *Turnsperre* (gym ban) was lifted and the
Turnvereine took a leading part in the revolution of 1848, by now
recruiting women, children and many Jews among their leaders. The
movement took on the characteristics of a left-wing organization,
even to the extent of having a split between the All-German Gym
Association and the more radical Democratic Gymnastic Union.

In the following century, the Nazis were equally quick to realize
the potential of PE for mobilizing and militarizing the population,
especially the young. This does not mean that we should draw a
direct line of descent from the left-wing gymnasts of the 1840s to the
gymnasts of the 1930s. The reality rather is that gymnastics had
become part of the German way of life. Any regime which wanted
to mobilize its population would naturally deploy it as a weapon.
The beauty of PE for the would-be dictator is that it suffuses with
the innocent glow of physical culture activities which would otherwise appear alarmingly close to military drill. The movement was
not restricted to any class. The aristocracy began to be just as infected
by the idea as left-wing university students from humble homes.
The Empress Elizabeth shocked the Viennese court in the 1880s by
doing her Swedish gymnastic exercises every morning. Her aim was
to reinforce the strict dietary regimes which she followed in order to
keep her 20-inch waist.

The Nazis, like Jahn and Kingsley and Coubertin, were anxious to
find a means of reviving the spirits of a nation depressed by military
humiliation. From the start, in their 25-point programme of 1920,
they placed a high priority on outdoor physical exercise, especially
gymnastics and swimming. Other Nazi organizations not directly
responsible for sport and gymnastics stressed the importance of these

activities. The League of German Maidens' rulebook laid down: 'A German woman does not use make-up, a German woman does not smoke, a German woman has a duty to keep herself fit and healthy.' German youth was not to 'sit in stuffy rooms and develop crooked backs and weak eyes'.

The Nazis also infused the sacred German woods, the ultimate residence of the German soul, with the spirit of physical culture. To this day, beside the well-marked ramblers' paths in every great German forest, you will often see rings and parallel bars and balance beams and other of Dr Jahn's useful inventions set out at intervals with instructions for carrying out a sequence of exercises. In the woods outside a dozen German cities, you may also come upon a more sinister relic of those terrible years, the *Thing*. This is the same as our own English word, but in German it has kept only its original meaning of 'gathering-place for the German people'. As part of his Blood and Soil programme, in 1933 Goebbels' Propaganda Ministry began building outdoor amphitheatres in picturesque surroundings – rocks, woods, water, hills. 1,200 of these *Thingplätze* were planned, but only about forty were built, because they proved unpopular, not so much because of the propaganda plays and displays performed there, as because of the beastly cold and damp German weather. It is hard to build an ugly amphitheatre, but Goebbels managed it. Today these are deeply sinister places, defacing barren hillsides or hidden away in dank and dripping firs with weeds growing between the stained and cracked concrete blocks. To walk up the Philosophers' Way where Hölderlin and Eichendorff once gazed down upon Heidelberg the other side of the river and come upon the overgrown local *Thing* is to experience the utter degradation of the German spirit. The *Thingplätze* that are still in use work well enough as venues for rock concerts, pagan revels of a sort unlikely to appeal to Dr Goebbels.

Pagan revivals in general, and the cult of the body in particular, were certainly not confined to officialdom, whether evil or well-meaning. What is so striking is that body cult took a powerful hold,

not merely of the Christian educational establishment but of dissi-
dents, outsiders and artists, particularly those who hated Christianity
in all its forms.

For the poet Swinburne, the world had been drained of life and
beauty the moment that the Christian faith was proclaimed in Rome
and the Emperor Julian said as he was dying: '*Vicisti, Galilaee*' –
'Thou hast conquered, O Galilean!' Swinburne's 'Before a Crucifix'
is the most savage indictment of the life-denying, body-hating new
religion, 'the poison of the Crucifix'. Yet Swinburne asserts in
'Hymn to Proserpine' that nothing lasts for ever and Christianity too
will fade: 'Yet thy kingdom shall pass, Galilean, thy dead shall go
down to thee dead.'

Algernon Charles Swinburne (1837–1909) was a tiny man with an
embarrassing squeaky voice and a huge head covered with bright-red
hair. For all his excited praise of sexual pleasures, especially flagellation, it is doubtful how much actual experience of them he enjoyed.
In his later years he was deaf, drunk and so distressed that he seldom
ventured far from his home at No. 2 The Pines, Putney, at least not
without his faithful but ponderous companion, Theodore Watts-
Dunton.

There is a poignant comparison to be made between Swinburne
and his contemporary Friedrich Nietzsche (1844–1900). Both men
were gentle and unprepossessing in person, and their praise of violence and physical strength and beauty seems infused with sad
personal longing. Nietzsche too spent his last years in a state of
extreme distress, his mental illness and physical paralysis apparently
precipitated by the syphilis he had caught in a brothel years earlier.
The signs of his own decline were already becoming apparent in
1886–7 when he added a fifth and final section to *The Gay Science*,
the treatise in which he first proclaimed in so many words that God
was dead. He repeats in this last section: '*Wir Furchtlosen*' – we fearless ones – 'we have outgrown Christianity.' But just as their
forefathers had been uncompromising in their integrity and ready to
sacrifice anything for their Christian beliefs, so too would the New

Fearless Ones lead lives of hardship and sacrifice, not just for their unbelief but for 'the hidden Yea' in them, which was 'stronger than all the Nays and Perhaps of which you and your age are sick'.[15]

And what is this 'Yea', this new faith, this position outside of conventional morality, beyond good and evil, or at any rate beyond *our* good and evil? Well, as with other prophets of heavenly kingdoms, Nietzsche is light on specifics. Indeed, it is part of his message that the New Man must travel light, not weighed down with the old baggage, he must wander freely and be able to soar above the tired muddy conventional world. But one vital thing the New Man must have: physical health. In this, his near-enough final rhapsody, Nietzsche tells us: 'We, the new, the nameless, the hard-to-understand, we firstlings of a yet untried future – we require for a new end also a new means, namely, a new healthiness, stronger, sharper, tougher, bolder and merrier than any healthiness hitherto.'[16]

In all our voyages to the dangerous edge of things, we Argonauts of the Ideal have one supreme duty, to get fit – and stay fit, for Nietzsche like any personal trainer knows that you cannot put fitness in the bank, it must be constantly renewed. The one place we cannot avoid in all our free-souled roaming is the gym. For it is no good trying to pretend that this fitness can be merely a mental thing. This separation between body and soul was the great mistake the Christians made. Our body must be as hard and glowing as our mind.

Not for the first or only time in his life, Nietzsche proved to be a potent prophet – but also a hopelessly misunderstood one. For no single thing is more striking about men and women in the modern world than their obsessive concern for their physical well-being and flourishing. There is a limitless appetite for miracle medicines, cures for the incurable, sure-fire routes to spectacular weight loss, life-changing therapies, surgical breakthroughs and diagnostic techniques that solve all medical mysteries. At the founding of the British National Health Service in 1948, it was assumed that the demand for its services would be finite and that accordingly the bounds of its budget could be more or less foreseen. But in no time hospitals, clinics and surgeries were swamped and the costs were spiralling out of control. After two years, the prime creator of the NHS, Nye Bevan, was moaning, 'I shudder to think of the ceaseless cascade of medicine which is pouring down British throats at this time.'

But at the outset, patients were relatively reluctant to make excessive demands on the service. It is only in much more recent years that the clamour to be well has reached an almost hysterical level. In the newspapers, the columns and supplements devoted to health matters keep on swelling, while the space devoted to religion and politics shrinks, to vanishing point in the case of the former. It is amazing how often even *The Times* and the *Daily Telegraph* splash on their front pages a story about some new health scare or some new medical breakthrough, usually under thrilling headlines such as 'Doctor Blazing a Trail to Stamp Out Genetic Cancer' (*The Times*, 10 January 2009). The scare, if there is any substance in it at all, often turns out to involve a fractionally increased risk of dying early from some rare disease. And the breakthrough is often sketchy and premature, involving speculative research, whether into cancer or the common cold, which may be years away from undergoing clinical trials.

Most conspicuously frenzied is the quest to resist the effects of ageing: to hold back the advance of wrinkles and double chins and grey hair and cellulite and flabby bottoms; to retain physical agility into old age and a healthy heart and the lung capacity of an athlete; to keep mentally alert and prevent memory loss. If the important thing about life is that 'it is not a rehearsal', then we need to be fit to play our part at all times, because it is also the case that we have no understudies.

Tragically, the corollary of all these efforts is that life without health has come to seem hardly worth living. For those suffering the most painful incurable or terminal diseases, we tend to believe that it may not be worth living at all. They should have the right to put themselves out of their misery, with state help if need be. Opinion polls record large and steady majorities in favour of euthanasia and of the right to make a 'living will' to the effect that if the patient suffers irrecoverable loss of his faculties, then he would wish either not to be resuscitated or to have his life terminated. Religious objections based on the sanctity of life are dismissed as lacking in compassion. What holds back the legalization of euthanasia is primarily the qualms of doctors who have been rigorously trained to save life rather than to destroy it.

Yet I do not think that if Friedrich Nietzsche were alive today, he would be pleased to see all this, any more than he would have been pleased to see what his Nazi fans did with his doctrine of the Superman. For there is little that seems 'bold' or 'merry' about our obsession with keeping in shape. On the contrary, it seems a somewhat timorous and joyless pastime, a sign of our fear of death rather than of our readiness to confront life. Secretly or not so secretly, we have a sneaking admiration for those who don't give a toss about the condition of their own carcasses: the Dylan Thomases and Brendan Behans, the Kurt Cobains and Amy Winehouses. It is an uncomfortable thought that they, the reckless cokeheads and the insatiable piss artists, may be the true Nietzscheans.

Sitting in Croydon public library twenty-five years later, D.H. Lawrence (1885–1930) discovered the intoxications of Nietzsche and was never quite the same again. He thrilled to Nietzsche's message, that 'behind thy thoughts and feelings, my brother, there is a mighty lord, an unknown sage – it is called self; it dwelleth in thy body, it is thy body. There is more rationality in thy body than in thy best wisdom . . . Of all that is written, I love only what a person hath written with his blood. Write with blood, and thou wilt find that blood is spirit.' That, in a nutshell, is the message of all Lawrence's novels, but most particularly of *Lady Chatterley*. The passage comes from Thomas Common's 1906 translation of *Thus Spake Zarathustra*.[17] Croydon Library held that book and four other of Nietzsche's principal works in translation – showing how far the gospel of the body had already penetrated into the English suburbs by 1910.

It is no less poignant to think of Lawrence, a skinny rufous starveling already afflicted with the first signs of the TB that was to kill him, rhapsodizing the splendours of the healthy body when he himself was closer to the condition of Sir Clifford Chatterley than that of Mellors. Lawrence, Swinburne and Nietzsche make a strange trio – so passionate and so nearly impotent, so violent in their praise of violence and yet in some ways so gentle, so lyrical in their praise of the health they themselves lacked. Well, they knew at least what they were missing. And although each of them had a reputation for preaching wild and dangerous things, at the same time they were things that a good many of the public wanted to hear.

The sculptor Auguste Rodin (1840–1917) was also a contemporary of Nietzsche's, though he seemed to have become a Nietzschean before he had actually read any of the master's works. And it is hard not to see in his most famous statue, the one that was to become known as *The Thinker*, a monumental representation of Nietzsche's ideal man. Originally Rodin had intended *The Thinker* to represent Dante thinking about his great poem. But he soon came to the conclusion that the New Thinker could not be portrayed as a pallid ascetic crowned with a laurel wreath and concealing his skinny limbs beneath a green ankle-length robe, which is how Dante was portrayed in the frescoes of his native Florence by Giotto, Raphael and Orcagna. The New Thinker had to be physically as well as mentally strong. And so *Le Penseur* became a muscle man with huge fists and a craggy, almost brutish head. Even his pensive posture reminds us of a standard bodybuilder's pose showing off his biceps and triceps, his right elbow perched on the opposite knee and the right fist crunched into his teeth like an uppercut.

Le Penseur was an instant hit in its own time, especially on the Left. This was a Thinker for the people, not an etiolated airy-fairy aesthete who seldom stirred from his ivory tower, but a tough character whose hands had done a hard day's work, one who dwelt in the here and now, whose speculations were rooted in the material world. One socialist reviewer, Pierre Baudin, said: 'He is not an intellectual whose energy is sapped by heredity . . . He is a strong, muscular, well-balanced, calm individual who is afraid neither of his solitude nor his nothingness.'[18] The whole purpose of Rodin's enterprise is to suggest the ability to dominate and make sense of the world. Man has at last learnt to trust in his own powers and to accept his own fate. He must think with his body because his body is all he has got. *Le Penseur* is Nietzsche's music frozen into stone, and it is the background music to the modern world.

The body is not only 'a mighty lord', it is also 'an unknown sage', Nietzsche tells us. You must listen to its voice, for there is more *rationality* in your body than in all your wizened old thinkers. And nowhere does your body talk more sense than when it comes to what might be called its special subject, the ever-interesting topic.

III

THE BEDROOM

It Is Not a Moral Issue

I'm sure I'm not the only person who hides such a guilty secret, and I'm equally sure that anyone in my position would guard it as ferociously as I do.

Once, sometimes twice, a month I meet up with Justin, a 36-year-old divorcee. We go out for a meal and maybe to a club before spending the night in a hotel. I am a divorced mum and work part-time to spend as much time as I can with my four children. Justin also has four children. But what differentiates our dates from the norm is that I pay for Justin's company, including having sex with him.

This arrangement has worked very well for me for the past three years and I hope it continues. My ex-husband and I get on pretty well, but I don't want all the complications involved in getting into a relationship – I want to be able to concentrate on my children, my job and my life without introducing a man who might well walk out at some point, thus upsetting the children. Although I know I could go out a couple of times a month and find someone for sex I don't have the time or energy for a series of one-night stands – I want to know exactly what's going to happen without any worries about the next day.

My ex-husband and I had a great sex life, so when our marriage ended, I decided to go online and see if anyone out there could fill the gap. I found a huge number of websites and adverts offering a wide range of services. In the end I found Justin. He costs £200 for an hour, £270 for three hours and £600 for overnight – and every penny is well spent . . .

This way I'm very satisfied sexually, which makes me a much calmer and happier person, and I do like the secrecy element of this arrangement. I keep both lives totally separate and Justin does-n't know where I live, what I do or even my real surname. I get a real buzz out of my elegant, controlled image and the fact that no one knows I've got a secret side – one that would shock everyone.

I came across this anonymous *cri de coeur* – well, more of a boast really – in the regular 'Family Secrets' feature in *The Times* for 5 December 2007. At the end of it, the paper asked, as it does every week in this slot: 'Do you have advice for this writer?' More than 150 replies were posted on *The Times* website and half a dozen printed in the following week's 'Family Secrets'. These responses are even more striking than the original contribution from Justin's occasional partner.

'Sounds great, what's his number? Only joking, can't afford it,' says Pav of London. 'Hey, if this works for her, then more power to her,' says Anonymous from Miami. 'It's fantastic that women are at last standing up and taking control of their lives,' exults Justin Darling, Edinburgh. 'You can have me for free, on the first night,' says Jeff of Manchester. 'I went out for dinner with some female friends last week . . . We agreed that if we found ourselves in *exactly* the situation that the author describes (children, divorced, the love of her life gone) then using the services of a male prostitute would be very much an option. There is much to be said for getting it exactly the way you want it, when you want it,' ruminated another anonymous blogger, although she did hazard a guess that after three years of being Justined the writer might be getting emotionally attached to him.

This little caveat aside, the only other anxieties expressed by respondents were that her children might not thank her for spending so much money on Justin which could have been better spent on their upbringing. Any note of moral distaste or disapproval, let alone disgust, was entirely absent. Of course, the bloggers are a self-selecting sample. It may be that only the more jocular and libertine of *Times* readers respond to 'Family Secrets'. But there was no hint of moral anxiety anywhere else in the paper. In the old days when a newspaper was about to publish something which the editor feared might offend some of his readers, there would be a portentous comment piece alongside in that day's issue, saying: 'We are well aware that many of our readers may find this material shocking, but we feel it our duty to bring to public attention . . . etc., etc.' None of that these days.

How far off now seems that *Times* first leader at the height of the Profumo affair in 1963 when the editor Sir William Haley thundered: 'IT *IS* A MORAL ISSUE. Everyone has been so busy assuring the public that the affair is not one of morals that it is time to assert that it is.' The revelation that the Secretary of State for War had been committing adultery with Miss Christine Keeler showed

that 'eleven years of Conservative rule have brought the nation psy-
chologically and spiritually to a low ebb'.[1] Just because a Cabinet
minister was having a bit on the side, as Cabinet ministers have had
since the beginning of time? These days it would be Sir William that
human resources would send for sexual counselling. Why bring
morality into it?

Besides, why should there be a single eyebrow raised by Justin's
moonlighting? Dr Thomas Stuttaford, formerly a Tory MP and the
Times doctor for many years, has recently been writing in tandem
with Suzi Godson, the author and sex therapist, a page in the 'Body
& Soul' section entitled 'Agony & Ecstasy' which boldly confronts
every sexual dilemma you can think of. For example, on 10
November 2007: 'My husband of five years masturbates to internet
porn. He doesn't seem to fancy me and won't touch me. Is it the end
of our physical relationship?'

Dr Stuttaford wants to know more: 'What is it that keeps him
glued to the screen that he finds so exciting? Is he watching men and
women together, men and men, women and women, men and children or beasts? Is sadomasochism his line? Does he have any fetishes,
a predilection possibly for rubber, shoes, underwear or uniforms?'
These eager questions rather build up our hopes that, depending on
the answers given to his questions, the good doctor will have the
exact prescription for restoring marital harmony. Alas, in practice all he
can suggest is that she consult her GP or a 'detached sex therapist'. Ms
Godson is even less encouraging: 'It might be the end of your relationship, period.' The only consolation she offers is that everyone else
is at it: 'A 2001 study of 7,037 adults in the US found that 75 per cent
of the respondents admitted masturbating while online.' Presumably
not much hope for their marriages either, especially when, as Ms
Godson glumly reports: 'In July 2003 there were 260 million pages of
porn online, an increase of 1,800 per cent since 1998' – a lot to
plough through before the wife is likely to get a look-in.

Dr Stuttaford offers more positive advice when faced with a correspondent who cries: 'Help! I am a 50-year-old divorced female

who fakes her orgasms.'[2] 'I would recommend a vibrator,' he says unhesitatingly. 'I am told that with a vibrator which has adjustable speeds, the very intense sensation usually ensures a rapid orgasm.' Note the 'I am told' which makes it clear, in lofty doctorspeak, that he has not himself actually been anywhere near one of those infallible devices. Three years later,[3] he is gamely understanding when a reader reports that her husband has acquired an artificial vulva – sauce for the goose, sauce for the gander. Ms Godson is, however, less tolerant. She is, for example, ready to act as shoppers' guide, warning her readers off the goods on display at the Festival of Erotica at Olympia as mostly overpriced and unreliable in their claims to transform your sex life. Worse still, the Festival of Erotica is deplorably tacky: 'The show feels like a retrospective of the tawdry sex industry that existed in Britain ten years ago. Sadly it also stands as a snapshot of the tawdry present.' She recommends instead several manufacturers who are not displaying at Olympia: 'In the past couple of years companies such as Myla, Coco de Mer and Emotional Bliss have revolutionized the sex-toy market. By creating beautifully designed, well-produced and innovative products, they have broken the mould of the wobbling pink plastic penis.'[4]

What was wrong then with the British sex-toy industry was that it was end-of-the-pier naff, intolerably kitsch. The wobbling pink plastic penis was the equivalent of the joggling furry dice in the car window, the china ducks on the wall, the garden gnome. Now that the sex industry's answer to Sir Terence Conran has improved its standards of style and taste, one may safely patronize its retail outlets when seeking to follow Dr Stuttaford's advice.

These sex columns are themselves the equivalents of the other weekend lifestyle columns which advise us on cooking, fashion and gardening. Sex products represent merely another branch of retail therapy. Even if one does not feel inclined to purchase, one browses and licks one's lips.

In the same way, sex advice is merely another branch of medical counselling. 'How to give your wife or anybody else an orgasm' is just as much a question for the doctor as how to cope with piles or acne or insomnia. The problematic aspects of sexual relations have been medicalized, removed from the hands of the priest and the novelist and relocated to the cool dispassionate atmosphere of the doctor's surgery.

It is not simply that these problems have been de-moralized, they have been routinized, reduced to a matter-of-fact level where the difficulties are technical or economic, questions of blood flow and gymnastic expertise, rather than of passion, morality and spiritual fulfilment.

The first achievement of this mechanization is to drain the sump of any poisonous residues of guilt. Sex relationships are officially de-consecrated and emptied of moral content; there need be no sense of shame if one changes partners, even quite abruptly. It is sometimes argued by up-to-the-minute philosophers that if you have any duty at all, it is to the truth of your emotions. It ought to be your goal to live an authentic life, and that is impossible if you continue to live a lie. 'Faking it' is a sin against the modern gospel, not just when it comes to orgasms but in any protestation of eternal love which is not sincerely felt. Indeed, it may be better to enter into a new relationship without making any such protestations, but rather on a down-to-earth basis of mutual physical attraction.

Until recently, such a plain and emotionally unadorned arrangement was hard to find. Erica Jong in her famous best-seller *Fear of Flying* (1973) described a sexual encounter for its own sake without emotional involvement or commitment and between two previously unacquainted persons as 'a zipless fuck' and said that it was 'rarer than the unicorn'. Now, according to the writer Angela Levin in a three-part series in the *Daily Telegraph*, such encounters are available at the click of a mouse. Here is a typical advert posted by a 44-year-old IT manager on a popular website:

Been left parked in the garage of marriage too long, battery getting flat and needs somebody to give it a spark of life, full tank and ready to go. Present owner does not like going for a ride any more but am not up for sale. Seeking discreet lady mechanic, preferably married, to enjoy some NSA run-outs together.

This website is patronized by men, and increasingly by women too, who are looking for a No-Strings-Attached relationship. At the bespoke end of the market, David Miller, a former producer of TV commercials, runs an internet dating site, lovinglinks.com, which he claims has 23,000 members, all allegedly married men and women who are looking for him to introduce them to a trouble-free NSA relationship.

At the end of the Angela Levin series, each part of which occupies a full page of the newspaper, there is a modest box offering banal advice on how to stop your spouse having an affair. But this is merely a gesture to the old proprieties, no more than a fig leaf. The real purpose of the series is to excite the readers with the thought of this zipless fucking churning away on such a vast scale, without a speck of guilt to gum up the works. Perhaps the picture is an exaggerated one. Is it really the case that, as a recent survey found, eight out of ten couples will, at some time in their marriage, be unfaithful? My concern here, though, is not with statistical accuracy but with what is publicly acceptable: what the respondents are unashamed to say to Angela Levin, their claims of untroubled consciences, the amount of space the *Daily Telegraph* is prepared to give her findings without any purpose except how to sell more copies.

The deadening of moral shock, the flattening of affect, seems to operate right through the whole process, from the customers' cheerful logging on through all the supporting network to the actual fucking, the post-match interviews and the final publication. Zipless from start to finish, apparently.

In practice, the whole adventure may not always run so smoothly. There may be tears after bedtime, violent recriminations, crippling divorce settlements, agonizing bursts of remorse, none the less painful for being camouflaged. My concern remains not so much with what actually happens as with the emerging public orthodoxy: that the NSA relationship is a legitimate option. There have of course been societies in the past where that was true – the court at Versailles in the days of Louis XV, for example. Eighteenth-century society in England was equally unbuttoned. Field Marshal Ligonier, the hero of every English victory from Blenheim to Fontenoy, at the age of nearly 80 gave it as his opinion that 'no woman past 14 is worth pursuing' – not a sentiment that would go down well today. But until now NSA relationships have never been on the official menu in respectable bourgeois society. And of course such escapades cannot be entirely string-free even today, because even in an NSA relationship, there is likely to be a third party whose rights and feelings have to be considered: the betrayed husband or wife. He or she has been 'cheated on' – an interesting recent replacement for the old language of adultery. Today adultery, if it is an offence at all, is the equivalent of a tort or civil wrong, rather than the sinful breach of a moral duty. It is not a wicked act in itself, but deplorable and actionable only because it hurts the betrayed party. That wrong may be put right in the divorce courts – 40 per cent of divorce suits are still on grounds of infidelity. But it is noticeable, even in that once unforgiving tribunal, how the rights of the new couple grow in importance, how the new truth of the heart trumps the old marriage contract. The wronged spouse may keep the marital home and be compensated with a large slice of the ex's earnings, but seldom does the court feel justified in standing in the way of the second marriage. The straying partner has the right to 'get on with his or her life', to make a fresh start.

In the divorce courts, the sexual union has undergone a gradual dethronement. It used to be regarded as the essential core in marriage, one which had at all costs to be maintained inviolate. A breach of the marriage vow to 'forsake all other' was a serious, near-criminal act. Infidelity still remains a ground for divorce, but the court must now take into account all sorts of other things – financial arrangements, social compatibility, non-sexual behaviour in public and private.

The law has certainly not become easy-going in everything to do with sexual relations. Yes, where those relations are between freely consenting adults, anything goes, and a modern-minded person takes it for granted that there must be no legal prohibition of any sort. But where one of the partners is not adult or is not to be regarded as freely consenting, then we are sterner than ever. Sex of any description with persons under the age of consent is regarded as the most disgusting crime and punished with the utmost severity. So is rape, in theory, although juries still hesitate to convict.

And the rules of professional decorum have grown sterner, not laxer. A 35-year-old lecturer puts his job at risk if he makes advances to a 21-year-old student, though he may make love to a 16-year-old shop assistant with impunity. A doctor or dentist who falls in love with his patient will be struck off. A teacher who strokes his pupils will be sacked; a teacher who seduces his sister-in-law is professionally in the clear. Progressive MPs and commentators are united in wishing to lower the age of consent for homosexual behaviour and at the same time to stiffen the penalties for pae-dophilia. The law has simultaneously enthroned childhood and dethroned sex.

This legal dethronement parallels the general routinization and demystification of sex which we have already mentioned. To show oneself to be a modern person, one needs to be disdainful of the old romantic myths about love, especially love in marriage. As the columnist Charlotte Raven puts it: 'When our relationships frac-ture, the pain is ameliorated by the comforting assessment that we haven't fallen for the myth of "togetherness". More important than fulfilment is the thrill we get from knowing that we are the first people since the Renaissance with the balls to admit the bathetic truth about love.' Raven, herself the coolest of columnists, adds sharply: 'It seldom occurs to us that our lack of romanti-cism – our much vaunted "realism" – may look as weird in the future as Barbara Cartland's romantic effusions do to us.'[5] Sophisticated TV series such as *Sex and the City* and *Mistresses* toy with the ups and downs, the ons and offs of modern love, but the underlying theme is one of staying cool. The most important thing is to maintain a posture of ironic and un-illusioned distance, and to carry this off with the aplomb of a French courtier under the ancien régime.

Raven questions whether this new coolness is really as liberating for women as it is supposed to be. 'It's a funny world, where having sex with some dolt you don't really like or actually really fancy is seen as empowering. It seems not to matter because nothing does. Sex is just another activity, like shopping or making compilations for your iPod. The claims made for its significance in former times seem portentous and overblown.'[6]

As the title of Mark Ravenhill's play *Shopping and Fucking* (1996) suggests, this is the first generation in which sex and buying stuff are so publicly equated. And our language has to adjust, in order to show how blasé we are. We no longer woo, we are on the pull. If we score, we shag rather than make love. This casual, brutal style of talk has become de rigueur. To use the old soft, courtly terms would suggest that we had failed to see through the phoney packaging. Of course this is how men in pubs and clubs always talked. Rough echoes of it are to be heard as far back as the comedies of Shakespeare and Ben Jonson. But it was never the language of respectable society, or for the most part how most men and women talked to one another. Nothing shows better the low-voltage nature of modern sex than the verb 'to shag'. The older demotic words had a transgressive brutal punch to them: 'shaft', 'bang', 'poke', above all 'fuck'. But 'shag' has a lethargic, faintly comic sound. Partridge's *Dictionary of Slang* derives it from the obsolete verb 'to shag', to waggle or toss about. This verb in turn looks like a humorous derivative from 'shake', suggesting the absurd wiggling and jiggling involved in sexual intercourse, and reminiscent of the old English 'jig-a-jig' and its Hindi equivalent 'jiggy-jig'.

How did we get here, to this relaxed, downbeat, low-expectation view of love?

The Road to Sensible Sex

People today unthinkingly accept the time-frame set out by Philip Larkin in 'Annus Mirabilis' that sex began in 1963 after the end of the Chatterley ban, which, he claimed, was 'rather late for me'. It emerged after his death that Larkin was being a little disingenuous about his own personal experience. He had two or three long-term girlfriends who were attached to him by strings which did not include any expectation of marriage or 'wrangle for a ring' as he puts it in the poem. In that sense, he was a pioneer of the NSA affair.

At any rate, Larkin wholeheartedly welcomed the end of the 'shame that started at sixteen and spread to everything'. Suddenly sex had become normal and open. The morality had gone out of it, the burden had been lifted. The old prohibitions had collapsed, and sex had become 'a brilliant breaking of the bank, a quite unlosable game'. Overnight, it seemed, life and language had loosened up. Moral values had flipped with less trouble than the tossing of a pancake.

The explanation often given is that it was all a delayed reaction to the strains of the Second World War, or perhaps a reverberation of the general loosening up that happens in wartime when people find themselves thrown together with strangers and let rip sexually because they may not live to see tomorrow. Yet even such a cataclysm as a world war seems unlikely to destroy overnight and unaided those patterns of restraint and inhibition which had been integral to Western civilization for so many centuries.

In reality, the forces battering against the dam were many and various, and they had been gathering strength for most of the twentieth century and a fair bit of the nineteenth century too. We can, I think, identify four principal battering rams, separate but linked, which between them broke through so memorably in 1963 – if you want to choose a single date, that date will still do as well as any. The four forces which ultimately transformed our sexual mores, or at any rate our ways of talking about sex in public, could each fill a separate chapter, but for the purposes of the argument we need only mention each of them briefly here, for none of them is unfamiliar to us.

First there is what might be called *the kindness revolution*. Over the centuries, the Christian doctrine of sex had hardened into a set of legal and social rules and punishments which operated with extreme cruelty against those who strayed or fell from the standards demanded. As the humanitarian values of the Enlightenment gradually percolated through society, it began to seem intolerable that unmarried women should suffer such unrelenting ostracism if they conceived a child or that unhappily married women should be punished so harshly for having an affair. At times, it seems as if the nineteenth-century novel, particularly in the second half of the century, has no other theme but that of the woman who strays and the terrible fate that society inflicts on her. *Anna Karenina* (1873–7), *Middlemarch* (1871–2), *Tess of the D'Urbervilles* (1891), *Ann Veronica* (1909) are only the best-remembered of the novels which make us weep at the inhumanity of our social arrangements. It is more usual to group these and dozens of other novels on the same theme which have now been forgotten under the heading of 'the woman question', as the contribution of literature towards the growing movement for female equality, just as the suffragettes were the movers in the political sphere. And so indeed they are, but these novels are also part of a slow swelling intimation that society ought to be less rigid and more understanding in regulating sexual behaviour, for sex is, after all, only an expression of our natural instincts.

It was a long time before the same charitableness was to be extended from heterosexual to homosexual behaviour. That extension, in Britain signalled by the Wolfenden Report of 1957, also rested, at least in part, on an uneasy recognition of the variousness of nature. The birds and the bees were not always faithful to each other. Nor indeed was their repertoire of sexual behaviour always decently directed towards reproduction. On the contrary, they often fooled around with members of the same sex in the most flagrant and indelicate fashion.

Comparative studies of sexual behaviour across different species provide but one example of the *intrusion of science* upon sexual morality, which is the second transforming force. Just as much as the actual findings of biology, psychology and anthropology, it is the mere fact of the intrusion that is so upsetting. Sexual behaviour, it turns out, can be studied in just as cool and objective a manner as rock strata or the annual growth rings on trees. The independence of our moral choices, a belief in which we have invested so much over the centuries, turns out to be rather shaky. Daring theses, such as those advanced with great literary brilliance by Sigmund Freud, appear to undermine our free will altogether. If our behaviour in most things, but especially in sex, is dictated by instinctual drives which themselves are influenced by traumas long buried in our subconscious, who then is the 'I' who purports to be making these choices? For our purposes here, we don't need to try to assess what smidgeon of truth there may be in these theses. All we are concerned with is their impact on our moral self-confidence, an impact which reaches far beyond the analyst's couch to infect the press, politics and Hollywood. Every time the man in the white coat comes on screen and tells James Stewart: 'Your wife is suffering from what we call transferred personality syndrome,' the belief that we are the masters of our fate dies a little.

Science is perhaps even more numbing to our sense of free will when it lumps us all together in statistical analyses. There is a case for saying that the crucial date in our sexual liberation was not 1963 but 1948 or 1953, the dates when Alfred Kinsey published his *Sexual Behavior in the Human Male* and *Sexual Behavior in the Human Female* respectively. Confronted with his remorseless pages of statistics setting out the massive scale on which the actual behaviour of Americans diverged from what it was supposed to be, even the sternest moralist lost heart. There seemed to be no sexual practice that quite a bunch of Americans did not regularly indulge in. A tiny minority even did it with squirrels.

Kinsey (1894–1956), a professor of entomology and zoology, had rebelled against his strict Methodist parents to become a confirmed atheist. His early scientific career was spent in the study of gall wasps. He switched to humans only in 1933, becoming generally recognized as the father of the new discipline of sexology. He himself engaged energetically in a good few of the unorthodox sexual practices that he spent his later years logging. His wife, students and co-workers were co-opted into group sex in the Kinsey attic, often with a masochistic edge. Kinsey himself enjoyed filming the action. His biographer, James H. Jones, argues that Kinsey's own tastes and his rebellion against conventional sexual morality drove him to distort his research, prisoners and prostitutes being over-represented among his subjects.

Whatever his intention, his books did have the effect of undermining the conventions of sexual morality, since they appeared to prove that supposedly unheard-of behaviour was in fact quite common, which inevitably diminished the shock and horror one was supposed to feel.

Similarly, the introduction of formal sex education into schools blunted the edge of sexual fear. It was not precisely, as old-fashioned moralists argued, that sexual education actively encouraged pupils to go out and start experimenting. But familiarity with the mechanics and having them explained by figures in authority certainly reduced the dark mystery which itself was a deterrent to early sexual activity. This was part of the intention of the campaigners for sex education. They wanted to make sex a natural, unfrightening part of life, much as it was supposed to be on the South Sea Islands visited by Margaret Mead, one of the most highly influential and popular anthropologists of her day. A clear understanding would help children to adopt a mature attitude and reduce the incidence of teenage pregnancies. Here education was supposed to work hand-in-hand with technological advances in contraception, especially the pill. The dire consequences of sexual adventure would disappear. In fact, the more intense the programme of sex education, the more responsible adults would be.

So far results have been decidedly mixed. Campaigners for sex education insist that if teenagers are not being deterred from getting pregnant, it is only because the lessons have not been of the necessary quality or frequency. Schools must redouble their efforts. A report to the government by Chris Bryant MP now suggests that sex education should begin at the age of 9 or 10, with parents being sent an advice pack and at the same time lessons about sex and relationships being made compulsory in school.[7]

Thus a consensus now runs throughout officialdom that sex must be familiarized and routinized, with the old risks and alarms taken out of it. This all follows the lines predicted in Aldous Huxley's *Brave New World* (1932) where sex is deliciously recreational and free of guilt and danger. We have not perhaps progressed quite as far as Huxley's dystopia in which promiscuity was compulsory, in order to prevent the exclusive attachments of the disgusting and now forbidden institution of marriage. Nor do we exactly encourage happy fondling amongst teeny-boppers. Yet despite our horror of paedophilia, many boys and girls do seem to start experimenting at an age that Margaret Mead would have applauded. Above all, the contraceptive pill offers the opportunity to remove the practical hazards from underage sex as it does from fornication and adultery at any age. As Georgene Thorne says to her hesitant lover Piet Hanema in John Updike's *Couples* (1968), that ground-breaking saga of suburban swinging: 'Welcome to the Post-Pill Paradise.'[8]

Science and technology could not have made such swift inroads into traditional sexual morality without the assistance of a much greater openness in public discourse. The movement for *freer speech* – the third of our four transforming forces – is another of the slow-ripening fruits of the eighteenth-century Enlightenment. Willingness to speak in plain language about sex took a long time coming and was punctuated by fierce and usually absurd battles with the censor and the courts. Over the century between the prosecution of *Madame Bovary* (1857) and the prosecution of *Lady Chatterley's Lover* (1960), a guerrilla war raged unceasingly between writers and artists and publishers and producers on the one hand and the police, the courts, the Lord Chamberlain and the Hays Office on the other. Those tussles are well chronicled. What is less well evidenced is the gradual freeing-up of private speech which was going on behind the scenes and which gradually eroded the stiffness of public discourse too. We catch glimpses of it in literary circles, where the evidence more often survives. For example amongst the Bloomsbury Group. Virginia Woolf describes the famous scene on a spring evening in her family home in Gordon Square in 1908, her sister sewing, two of them gossiping idly:

> Suddenly the door opened and the long and sinister figure of Mr Lytton Strachey stood on the threshold. He pointed his finger at a stain on Vanessa's white dress.
>
> 'Semen?' he said.
>
> Can one really say it? I thought and we burst out laughing. With that one word all barriers of reticence and reserve went down. A flood of the sacred fluid seemed to overwhelm us. Sex permeated our conversation. The word bugger was never far from our lips. We discussed copulation with the same excitement and openness that we had discussed the nature of good. It is strange to think how reticent, how reserved we had been and for how long.[9]

It was about the same time that Virginia Woolf got to know a group of Cambridge friends led by Rupert Brooke. Here too freedom of speech rather self-consciously reigned. A month after he had first slept with Ka Cox, Brooke wrote to her exultantly: 'I remember the softness of your body: and your breasts and your thighs and your cunt. I remember you all naked lying to receive me; wonderful in beauty. I remember the agony and joy of it all: that pleasure's like a sea that drowns you wave by wave.'[10]

Brooke's description of his first full homosexual experience is a blow-by-blow account which spares us even fewer of the details.[11]

The correspondence of the whole circle is filled not only with the

naming of parts but with anxious, puzzled discussion of rival methods of birth control: irrigators, syringes, sponges, pessaries and
condoms litter the pages. All this was not simply a matter of practical importance; it was also part of a determination to be utterly
candid in everything to do with sex, including the mechanics as
well as the emotions.

Above all, there was to be no more shame. Their souls were to be
as naked as their bodies plunging into the pool at Grantchester.
Virginia (or was it Vanessa?) christened them the Neo-Pagans. In the
summer of 1908, Rupert Brooke announced that he was 'becoming
a wild rough elementalist. Walt Whitman is nothing to me.' It was
not only young poets like Brooke who were influenced by Edward
Carpenter's Neo-Pagan gospel. In *Civilisation: Its Cause and Cure*
(1889), Carpenter predicted the coming of a new post-Christian
man:

> The meaning of the old religions will come back to him. On the
> high tops once more gathering he will celebrate with naked
> dances the glory of the human form and the great processions of
> the stars, or greet the bright horn of the young moon which now
> after a hundred centuries comes back laden with such wondrous
> associations – all the yearnings and the dreams and the wonder-
> ment of the generations of mankind – the worship of Astarte and
> of Diana, of Isis or the Virgin Mary.[12]

This vision arises quite naturally out of the *cult of the body* which we
have already discussed and which provides the fourth and deciding
element in the assault on Christian and sexual morality. And it leads
equally naturally to the Neo-Pagan yearning for a return to the easy,
down-to-earth sexual life of the ancient world.

Lytton Strachey recorded in his diary for November 1896 how he
had been reading Plato's *Symposium* 'with a rush of mingled pleasure and pain . . . of surprise, relief, and fear to know that what I feel
now was felt 2,000 years ago in glorious Greece. Would I had lived

then, would I had sat at the feet of Socrates, seen Alcibiades, won-
drous Alcibiades, Alcibiades, the abused, but the great, felt with
them all!'[13]

First encounters with the sages of the ancient world were often
both startling and exhilarating. The novelist Simon Raven, dedicated
all his life to the classics and to cricket, describes his delight at what
he found on entering the classical sixth form at Charterhouse:

> Here was Horace, openly boasting of how he ran away from a
> battle. Tacitus, quietly equating enthusiasm with stupidity.
> Thucydides, grimly announcing that the only law of human affairs
> was 'Necessity'. Lucretius recommends regular one-night stands as
> a way of securing immunity from passion, which was simply the
> unwholesome and ridiculous produce of suppressed or thwarted
> lust. Catullus, advocating sex with women or sex with boys,
> whichever you fancy at the time, because there is no such thing as
> right and wrong in this context . . . *All* of them insistent that you
> take what pleasure you can from this world, because only super-
> stitious fools believe in the existence of the next.[14]

Bourgeois society was not, however, ready yet to strip off and abandon itself to the pursuit of pleasure. Penalties for infringement of the
old inhibitions and taboos remained harsh throughout the first sixty
years of the twentieth century. Renegades like Norman Douglas
and Simon Raven who wrote admiringly of the sensible matter-of-
fact attitudes of the ancient world were constantly running into
trouble in their personal lives. Raven was expelled from every institution he ever graced – Charterhouse, the army, the racecourse,
even the East India and Sports Club, admittedly more often for failure to pay his debts than for buggery. Raven was sentimentally
attached to all the institutions he passed through and did not repine
when he was thrown out of them. Theirs were the only rules he
respected, even if he was unable to abide by them.

Douglas had to live abroad because of his sexual exploits with underage boys and girls. Even in his civilized exile in Capri, he found himself in trouble with the authorities over his friendship with a 10-year-old girl. There was a class divide in these matters. The lower classes who were caught were sent to jail, the upper classes were sent abroad. Lord Beauchamp fled abroad to avoid prosecution and was dismissed as Lord Lieutenant of Worcestershire – one of the only two holders of the office ever to be sacked. It was only when a peer of the realm was not only caught in flagrante but was actually tried and sent to jail that the conscience of the elite was stirred and homosexual behaviour between consenting adults in private ceased to be a criminal offence. That may be a truncation of the process which led from the conviction of Lord Montagu of Beaulieu in 1954, via the Wolfenden Report of 1957 to the 1967 Sexual Offences Act. But I think it is a fair one.

So, not without pain and grief, the newer, freer sexual world came to birth. But were the Neo-Pagans right? Did the world they hoped to see really resemble the sexual world of the ancients? Did the sex life of the Greeks and Romans really have much in common with the sex life of Rupert Brooke and Ka Cox or Norman Douglas and Simon Raven? Or was that just a convenient myth, as sentimental in its way as the Victorian attitudes the renegades were out to shatter?

General Sophocles and Captain Raven

Until the past few decades, it was not easy to gain any reliable answer to such questions. Access to the sexual beliefs, practices and morals of the ancient Greeks and Romans was not exactly encouraged in schools and universities. In E.M. Forster's novel, *Maurice* (1971), not published in the author's lifetime because of its homosexual theme, when the undergraduates reach the part of Plato's *Phaedrus* where same-sex passion is described in poetic language, their tutor advises them in a dry toneless voice: 'Omit: a reference to the unspeakable vice of the Greeks.' School editions of the canonical authors would leave out sexually explicit material. In the Loeb Classical Library, where Greek texts faced English translations, the English right-hand page would switch to Latin when the text reached an indecent passage. In one old edition of Martial, the right-hand page switched over to Italian, as though any old modern language would do to protect innocent sensibilities from being corrupted.[15]

Classical teachers up till the 1960s were in a bind. On the one hand, they wished to introduce their pupils to the beauties and profundities of Greek and Latin literature; on the other hand, they wished to protect them from corrupting influences. In fact the dilemma was worse than that. They needed also to convince their classes that the wisdom of Athens and Rome was compatible with Christian teaching, and that the two sources of learning illuminated one another, indeed that Christianity was continuous with Greek and Latin philosophy. In *The Legacy of Greece* (1921), the book that my housemaster gave me when I left school, there is an essay on Greek religion by W.R. Inge, the famous Dean of St Paul's, better known as 'the Gloomy Dean', in which he argues, at length and rather desperately, that the religion of Greece was the natural precursor to Christianity. Inge declares: 'The Christian Church was the last great creative achievement of the classical culture . . . Catholicism preserved the idea of Roman imperialism, after the secular empire of the West had disappeared, and even kept the tradition of the secular empire alive.'[16]

Now this is all stirring stuff and helps to remind us, quite legitimately, how much, say, Thomas Aquinas owes to Plato and Aristotle. But as impish spirits like Simon Raven were not slow to notice, what about the great classical philosophers like Lucretius who regarded religion as a disaster which was responsible for so many evils: '*Tantum religio potuit suadere malorum*'? If there is such an unbroken continuity between the religious life of Greece and Rome and the Christian life, why were the Christians so vigorously persecuted by the later Roman emperors?

Above all, why did the Greeks in particular show such a complicated affection, amounting to obsession, for the sin that, in the

Christian era, dare not speak its name? In most of Christian Europe throughout the Christian era, sodomy was a serious criminal offence, punishable if not always actually punished by imprisonment, torture or even death. In classical Greece, under the right circumstances, sodomy could be not only permissible but commendable and romantic. Some discontinuity there surely.

Scholars continue to argue furiously about the precise boundaries of permissible homosexual behaviour among the Greeks, but all, I think, would agree that the Greeks do not make a huge fuss about the question, any more than they agonize over the boundaries of heterosexual behaviour.[17] The sexual appetite is one appetite among others and like the others needs to be mastered. As Martha Nussbaum and John Sihvola put it: 'The admirable person is one who does not get carried away by any pleasure, but who displays mastery and control of all his pleasures, pleasures of intercourse as well as pleasures of eating and drinking. None of these pleasures is inherently shameful, and all can be managed as elements in a life governed by manly self-control.'[18]

The Greeks do regard sex as more like eating and drinking than do Christianity and other cultures, which make a connection between sex and original sin. Of course there is an important difference. Sex involves other people.

> The sexual appetite can be a source of pleasure or displeasure, of kindness or cruelty . . . for the young man who is typically imagined as the recipient of the lover's desire. Thus the ethical questions posed in this area became far more complicated than the ethical questions posed in the area of food and drink. What is at stake in sex is not only one's self-mastery, but also the well-being, happiness, and ethical goodness of another.[19]

So you'll be very much mistaken if you approach the Greeks expecting them to be capering around in a carefree manner with erect penises as they are to be seen on the more erotic Greek vases.

Sexual desire was a powerful instinctual drive, and a necessary one. One Greek euphemism for the penis was the 'necessity'. But just because it was necessary, both for the purposes of reproduction and for the experience of pleasure, that did not mean that its operations did not have to be regulated and monitored. Certain actions were indecent and contrary to the public good, and right-thinking citizens ought to disapprove of those actions and those who committed them. But there is a gulf between this kind of regulatory framework and the idea of some kinds of sexual behaviour being inherently sinful and endangering our immortal soul. As big a gulf, one might say, as that between the laws regulating licensing hours and punishing public drunkenness and the view of Christian temperance campaigners that the Demon Drink was the devil's brew.

Laws and opinions relating to sex varied widely across the Greek world, between citizens of the same city, and over time. The way in which women were regarded, for instance, softened from brute patriarchy in the Archaic period to an acceptance that women were more or less human and that, even if marriages were originally based not on affection but on the need for legitimate procreation, husband and wife might naturally come to love one another. But at no time do sexuality and religion merge into one another.

The playwright Sophocles at one time served as a general and, when already in his mid-50s, shared command with Pericles during the Athenian expedition to suppress the revolt on Samos (440 BC). Pericles cared only for his second wife Aspasia and, unlike Sophocles, had no interest in boys. When Sophocles happened to praise the beauty of a certain youth, Pericles rebuked him saying, according to Plutarch in his *Life of Pericles*: 'A general, Sophocles, should refrain not only from soiling his hands but from contaminating his eyes.'[20] Superficially this might seem to resemble Jesus's pronouncement in the Sermon on the Mount: 'Whosoever looketh on a woman to lust after her hath committed adultery with her already in his heart.'[21]

Yet in reality the two pronouncements are far apart. Pericles is concerned with the public externals of conduct, Jesus with the inner movement of the heart. Pericles is merely reminding his colleague that it is beneath the dignity of a general to ogle a pretty youth. Jesus's words, according to a commentary on them by Pope John Paul II, go far deeper: they not only confirm the Ten Commandments (No. 7: Thou shalt not commit adultery and No. 10: Thou shalt not covet thy neighbour's wife), they 'express that knowledge of man which enables us to unite awareness of human sinfulness with the perspective of the redemption of the body. This knowledge lies at the basis of the new ethos which emerges from the Sermon on the Mount.'[22]

Sophocles, at any rate, was undeterred by the rebuke. Athenaeus, an Egyptian who lived around 200 AD, records him going out into the country with a handsome youth intending to take his pleasure with the lad. The boy laid his shabby cloak on the grass, and they covered themselves with the poet's own fine warm woollen cloak. Afterwards, the youth made off with Sophocles' cloak, leaving his own in its place. Sophocles was 65 at the time. This must be one of the earliest recorded examples of a fate which has since overcome many an elderly pederast.

This is the kind of episode that would have very much appealed to Captain Raven: the sex with a handsome lad in idyllic surroundings, perhaps recalling some eclogue or lyric by one of his favoured poets and then the sting in the tale – the boy making off with the high-quality cloak purchased from the Athenian equivalent of Cordings or Harrods.

But here too there were limits. The sexual assailant of a child, even the child of a slave, was to be charged and punished. Any Athenian citizen who prostituted himself was to be excluded from exercising any public function or even from speaking in the Assembly. Plutarch says of rent boys: 'Boys who voluntarily agree to act as accessories to debauchery of this kind are regarded as the most degraded of beings.'

Socrates condemned carnal passion because it disturbed the intelligence and by its violence drove out liberty and logic. This applied to homosexual as well as to heterosexual relationships. Love in the true sense was non-physical, or platonic as we have come to call it. In the *Phaedo*, Socrates (or Plato's version of him) places love as the highest form of ecstasy, making lovers the superiors of prophets and poets.

The Epicureans, by contrast, take a dim view of love. Epicurus himself says: 'Sexual intercourse never did anyone any good and one can think oneself lucky it doesn't do one harm. A wise man will neither marry nor have children. Nor will he yield to the passion of love.' On the other hand, his follower, the materialist Roman poet Lucretius, regards regular sexual intercourse as a legitimate and healthy pastime, while warning against the dangers of falling in love: 'To avoid the passion of love is not to deprive oneself of the joys of Venus but on the contrary to savour their delights without undergoing their exactions.'[23]

Aristotle, in the *Nicomachean Ethics*, takes a much more charitable view of sexual relationships, at least within marriage: 'Between husband and wife mutual affection (*philia*) seems to be an effect of nature. For human beings are more naturally inclined to live in couples than in urban society, all the more so since the family is older than the city, as well as more necessary, and also since reproduction is a faculty common to all mankind . . . Thus in this kind of affection the useful is combined with the agreeable.'[24]

Nowhere in any of these varied viewpoints is there any hint of sin. Sexual indulgence may be a foolish diversion which the would-be philosopher ought to steer clear of; or it may be an entirely natural part of married life, generating not only children but long-lasting affection. But sex has nothing to do with religion.

Rent boys are to be disapproved of. Whoremongers are to be ostracized. Child-molesters are to be severely punished, even if the victim is a slave-child. But these and other features of the social code are there to protect the vulnerable and to maintain public decency. They are not intended to designate certain sexual practices as intrinsically wrong.

Thus sex is not to be thought of as sinful in any of its manifestations. Nor is it capable of elevating our souls to a transcendental state.

Plato's swooning lovers have slipped the surly bonds of earth. Their passion is an out-of-body experience. But there is no sex in it.

Much of this is recognizable to us today. Except for a minority of religious fundamentalists, we are reluctant to condemn any specific sexual practice as wrong in itself. Only its social context may be deplorable: running a string of whores, using rent boys, having sex with your pupil or with someone who is underage. Between consenting adults in private, there are almost no limits. The English courts found it extremely difficult to say exactly why a group of consenting males were to be convicted for hammering nails into parts of each other's anatomies. What law was it precisely that they had broken?

The view of sexual pleasure that most people take today ranges between that of Aristotle and that of Lucretius: on the one hand, a natural and cementing part of a healthy relationship (still for the majority expressed in marriage) and, on the other, an equally healthy but emotionally undemanding form of physical exercise.

The Christian Surprise

Like the other great one-god religions, Christianity blew in out of the desert. Its intensity, its simplicity, its single-mindedness were utterly hostile to the sprawling easy-going affluence of the city. The Christian way of life was both a rebellion against and a merciless commentary on the slack, unfocused mores of the pagan world. The Dead Sea Scrolls, discovered in 1947 in a cave in the Judaean desert beside the Dead Sea, revealed one such community of believers who had vowed that 'they should seek God with a whole heart and soul'. They were to be pure and transparent towards God and towards one another. Some but not all of the community had vowed to live as celibates for an indefinite period. They were not alone. Pliny the Elder, a contemporary of Jesus of Nazareth, reported on the Essenes who were also settled beside the Dead Sea and who were 'remarkable among all other tribes in the whole world, as it has no women and has renounced all sexual desire'.[25] They had taken literally the commandment of Jesus to leave their families, and follow him, not even pausing to carry out any domestic duty such as burying one's father. There were even some who had made themselves eunuchs for the kingdom of heaven's sake.[26]

Thus ascetic tradition led to the most extreme instances of sexual renunciation and avoidance. An Egyptian monk of the fifth century dipped his cloak into the putrefying flesh of a dead woman so that the smell might banish thought about her.[27] Symeon of Emesa would go into the women's section of the public baths stark naked with his robe knotted into a turban on his head, in order to show how immune he was to temptation.[28] Sitting on their pillows or crouching in their caves, the men and women of the desert (for there were female hermits too) eventually achieved an amazing serenity, no longer tortured by the desires of the flesh even in their dreams.

For the Four Doctors of the Church – Ambrose, Augustine, Jerome, Gregory – sexuality was always saturated with original sin. According to Augustine, the Christian married couple ought to 'descend with a certain sadness' to the task of begetting children, for their very bodies must remind them of Adam's shame – an interesting reversal of the classical saying that every animal is sad *after* sex – *post coitum omne animal triste est*. For Ambrose, the loss of virginity was an irremediable pollution. The perpetual virginity of Mary was essential if our human bodies, 'scarred' by sexuality, were to be redeemed by Christ. For the cantankerous St Jerome, we were all in the same boat and all cursed: 'In silken robes or rags, the same kiss holds sway. Desire neither fears the Emperor's purple, nor keeps away from the beggar's filth.'

All this is so lurid and, to our way of thinking, so alien and alarming that it is easy to forget that it was never the whole picture. Indeed, in the long run it was probably not even the most important part of the picture. For my own part, I have been criminally slow to understand this, with the result that in retrospect what I wrote about the Christian view of marriage in *The Subversive Family* twenty-five years ago looks one-sided and misleading.

Yes, St Paul might be in no doubt that it was good for a man not to touch a woman and that 'nothing good dwells in me, that is, in my flesh'. If it was better to marry than to burn with unsatisfied desire, that was the best that could be said for marriage. The married person's heart could never be undivided as a true Christian's heart should be. Marriage was a second best, a compromise with the flesh, and one that was due to be swept away in the Great Transformation that was coming shortly.

But Jesus himself in Matthew 19 tells the Pharisees that God 'at the beginning made them male and female', that 'for this cause shall a man leave father and mother and cleave to his wife and they twain shall be one flesh' and 'what therefore God hath joined together, let not man put asunder'.[29] This has been clearly understood as an unequivocal prohibition of divorce, but it is an equally clear statement that not only sexual difference but marriage is both entirely natural and divinely ordained. Other parts of the New Law follow through the logical consequences of this view. For example, in the Epistle to the Ephesians, we are told: 'Husbands, love your wives, even as Christ also loved the church, and gave himself for it . . . So ought men to love their wives as their own bodies. He that loveth his wife, loveth himself.'[30] Ephesians (allegedly written by Paul in prison but said by some scholars not to be his own work, but rather one of the digests of his teachings put together to ginger up the scattered congregations of the New Faith) then goes on to repeat the 'one-flesh' passage from Matthew 19, showing that Jesus's words about marriage were already part of Christian teaching.

And there were voices too within the Church, though not the dominant ones, who were prepared to confront with approval the sexual side of marriage. Bishop Julian of Eclanum, the last and the most relentless of Augustine's critics, spoke warmly of sexual pleasure, the *calor genitalis*, as 'a drive in our bodies made by God' and 'the chosen instrument of any self-respecting marriage . . . acceptable in and of itself, and blameworthy only in its excesses.'

Even those Early Fathers who distrusted and condemned sexual pleasure could not help describing, often with a lyrical intensity, just how pleasurable it was. For St John Chrysostom, 'The woman receives the man's seed with rich pleasure, as if she were gold receiving the purest gold.' Tertullian holds nothing back in his description of orgasm: 'The whole human frame is shaken and foams with semen, as the damp humour of the body is joined to the hot substance of the spirit . . . in that last breaking wave of delight, do we not feel something of our very soul go out from us?'[31]

And, most famously of all, Augustine in his *Confessions* made the most reluctant farewell to sex, imploring God to make him chaste but not yet and describing how 'plucking at my garment, my flesh, these my past sweet joys softly murmured: "Are you dismissing us? . . . From this moment, will you never be allowed to do this, or to do that?" And, oh my God, what was it they suggested in those words, "this" and "that"?'[32]

And was marriage really a second-best description? Could an institution so plainly established by Jesus himself be anything less than sacred?

When the medieval Church formally declared the Seven Sacraments, from the end of the twelfth century onwards marriage was included among them. *The Catholic Encylopaedia* admits that 'it would be rash, of course, to infer immediately from the expression, "This is a great sacrament" that marriage is a sacrament of the New Law in the strict sense, for the meaning of the word sacrament is too indefinite.'[33] But if you take it together with the preceding words, the intention is pretty clear. Christian marriage is a copy and token of the union between Christ and the Church, which makes it a living sign of the life of grace, and as such fully worthy to be considered a sacrament. And the Council of Trent hammered home the dogma pronouncing anathema on anyone who claimed that 'matrimony is not truly and properly one of the Seven Sacraments of the

Evangelical Law, instituted by Christ our Lord, but was invented in the Church by men, and does not confer grace'.

This was a counter-attack against the Reformers who violently disagreed, and did so in coarse, contemptuous language. Calvin says in his *Institutions*: 'Lastly, there is matrimony, which all admit was instituted by God, though no one before the time of Gregory regarded it as a sacrament. What man in his sober senses could so regard it? God's ordinance is good and holy; so also are agriculture, architecture, shoemaking, hair-cutting legitimate ordinances of God, but they are not sacraments.'[34] Luther makes the same point in *Von den Ehesachen* (1530): 'No one indeed can deny that marriage is an external worldly thing like clothes and food, house and home, subject to worldly authority, as shown by so many imperial laws governing it.' Earlier, he had described the claims of marriage to be a sacrament as 'a mere jest' and 'the invention of men in the Church, arising from ignorance of the subject'.

This is, I think, a crucial cleavage. For the Catholics, marriage is an indissoluble sacrament. For thoroughgoing Protestants, it is a purely human contract, and the priest who blesses a marriage has no more claim to be administering a sacrament than Richard Rogers or Manolo Blahnik when they are plying their trades.

Theologically, we can see the arguments on both sides. Marriage is not like baptism or the Eucharist, a means of receiving God's grace which only an officiating priest can bring about. Marriage is an agreement between a man and a woman, the validity of which depends solely on their free consent and not on the presence of a priest, as the medieval Church courts readily agreed. On the other hand, even the Protestants concede that it is an institution blessed by God and one which is central to our being.

My concern here is not to offer any sort of theological judgement but rather to point out the huge impact of the Catholic view over the millennium and a half during which it reigned over Western civilization – and the equally huge impact of the rise of the Protestant view which has gradually superseded it.

This is what might be called the Christian surprise. A new religion which certainly had not set out with the prime aim of enthroning marriage as the sacred heart of our existence – anything but, as we have seen – ended up by doing so, never quite meaning to. A faith which was absorbed with chastity and celibacy and other ascetic ideals imported into marriage a spirituality which went far deeper than the social regulation and decent behaviour that were the important things about marriage in the pre-Christian world. The revulsion against sex and the consequent insistence on channelling sex into marriage, and marriage alone, gave sex inside marriage an intensity and centrality it had never had before. Until the beginning of the third century, Christians didn't even possess any sort of liturgy for celebrating marriage, but even then the couple thought of themselves as being united before Christ. In bas-reliefs of the period, Christ is represented as crowning the bride and joining the couple's hands. Even the bitter and ascetic Tertullian felt compelled to hymn the business: 'How can we describe the happiness of this marriage which the Church approves, which the oblation confirms, which the blessing seals, which the angels recognise, which the Father ratifies?'[35] In practical terms, the Church was merely taking over a good deal of the pagan marriage rites – the veil, the reading of the contract, the joining of the hands – while removing the bits it considered idolatrous: the sacrifices, the reading of horoscopes. But because the new religion purported to take possession of the depths of the human heart, the new ceremony had a far more intense meaning. To use the word we still use today, marriage was being *solemnized* – and so, willy-nilly, was sex.

Nobody in our own time has understood this better than D.H. Lawrence, although he was no friend of Christianity. In fact, he saw the reality so clearly just because he was in general so hostile to religion. In his remarkable essay *Apropos of Lady Chatterley's Lover*, sometimes printed as a preface to the novel, for example, in Heinemann's Phoenix edition, Lawrence argues that the survival of the Church and the survival of marriage are crucially linked: 'The marriage-tie, the marriage bond, take it which way you like, is the fundamental connecting link in Christian society. Break it, and you will have to go back to the overwhelming dominance of the State which existed before the Christian era.'[36]

Marriage, according to Lawrence, was the greatest contribution to the social life of man made by Christianity. Indeed, it was Christianity that had brought marriage as we know it into the world. This was a true freedom, because it was a true fulfilment, for men, women and children. The Church, Lawrence argued, 'created marriage by making it a sacrament, a sacrament of man and woman united in the sex communion, and never to be separated, except by death. And even when separated by death, still not freed from the marriage. Marriage, as far as the individual went, eternal.'[37]

By Church, he means here of course the Catholic Church. 'If we are to take the Nonconformist, Protestant idea of ourselves: that we are all isolated individual souls, and our supreme business is to save our own souls; then marriage is surely a hindrance.' What matters is the individual freedom to choose a partner and, if need be, to switch from one to another, just as you change from one hairdresser or shoe shop to another if your old supplier is not giving satisfaction. No sacrament, no deep mystery, just a nice, free contract which was dissoluble at will.

Anyway, what exactly is this sacrament, this mystery? Well, and here Lawrence becomes torrentially, unstoppably Lawrentian:

> But – and this *but* crashes through our hearts like a bullet – marriage is no marriage that is not basically and permanently phallic, and that is not linked up with the sun and the earth, the moon and the fixed stars and the planets, in the rhythm of days, in the rhythm of months, in the rhythm of quarters, of years, of decades and of centuries. Marriage is no marriage that is not a correspondence of blood. For the blood is the substance of the soul, and the deepest consciousness.[38]

This of course is what *Lady Chatterley's Lover* is all about. This is the real marriage between Connie and Mellors, as opposed to the counterfeit marriage between 'personalities', like Sir Clifford Chatterley before he was crippled or Connie's ghastly lover Michaelis, people who share the same tastes in furniture or books or sport but who are incapable of the warm blood-sex that establishes the living and revitalizing connection between man and woman, which Lawrence says we have to get back, 'for the bridge to the future is the phallus, and there's the end of it'. Fucking was the most serious thing in life, and it was the first step in understanding this to call it by its right name.

The trouble is that for us who live in what for poor, consumptive, dying Lawrence was the future he wasn't going to see, all this sounds like overblown nonsensical gush. This blood-talk makes us uneasy and embarrassed. We don't want it splashing all over us. We are glad to be free of the old restrictions on sex, but we don't want to be sucked instead into this steamy slush which sounds so sinister and even fascistic.

And even if we hose off Lawrence's rhetorical excesses, we aren't really comfortable with the sacramental idea at all. What is important for us in our 'relationships' – a word that would have made Lawrence explode – is precisely that they should be workable and in the last resort disposable. If the sacramental sort of marriage is Christianity's unique contribution to the life of man, then thanks, but no thanks. Our reason for wishing to be free of sexual inhibition is simply that we wish to be free, not to enable us to plunge into some gluey claustrophobic communion from which it is impossible to escape. Even if we like the idea of commitment, we want it to be a self-chosen commitment from which we can choose to exit as freely as we entered.

And so we are brought to a conclusion which we don't really want to admit in so many words: that the underlying message of *Lady Chatterley* is a message that we want to escape from, not one that we are running towards. There is no zipless fuck on offer here.

Worse still, it turns out that we cannot recover the sexual candour of the ancients without also recovering their relative indifference. We cannot enjoy the liberties they enjoyed without losing some of the potency of the Christian surprise. Desacralizing sex cannot help downgrading it a little, even if that is not our aim. *Apropos of Lady Chatterley's Lover* is for me one of the finest English essays of the twentieth century. Weird and overblown and rambling in parts, it is nevertheless devastatingly acute and touching in others. Yet ultimately it is a *cri de coeur* from the losing side. For Michaelis and Sir Clifford turn out to be the winners in the long run. For the twenty-first century is the century of recreational sex, gourmet sex, sex as lifestyle, sex as fulfilling relationship, anything but sex as sacrament.

Which brings us to an equally unpalatable irony: that if the publication of Lawrence's novel is the signal for anything to begin, it is the signal for a revaluation of sex in a direction that he would have hated. In the sense he meant, in the sense he so earnestly hoped for, it would, alas, be truer to say that sexual intercourse *ended* in 1963. The age of sacred fucking was over, and it was shagging time again. One dreads to think what Lawrence would have said if a woman had said to him after five minutes' acquaintance: 'Do you fancy a shag?' Theocritus or Catullus, on the other hand, would have been quite unmoved, and responded simply: 'Your place or mine?' For sex is as natural as eating and drinking. Why should anyone think twice about an invitation to a decent restaurant?

IV

THE KITCHEN

First Stuff Your Dormouse

If sex becomes more like eating and drinking, then eating and drinking become more like sex. Both are seen as entirely human preoccupations, to be savoured, rhapsodized, analysed, and argued and complained about. There is nothing sacred about them at all. They are of the earth, earthy and that's what we like about them. We fossick for their pleasures, and sometimes employ experts to fossick on our behalf, just as they train pigs in southern France to unearth truffles.

To our Christian forefathers, to think of these two sides of life in the same breath would have seemed swinish if not blasphemous. To our remoter classical ancestors, however, such an association would have seemed obvious, even commonplace. Eating, drinking and fornicating went together, whether you approved or disapproved of these pastimes. In the Greek world, it was Sicily that was famous, or notorious, for overindulgence in both departments. Plato speaks sourly of Sicily as a gluttonous place where men eat two banquets a day and never sleep alone at night and the inhabitants are obsessed by food.[1] But quality went with quantity. The Sicilians were gourmets as well as gourmands. Socrates commends 'these refinements of Sicilian cookery for which the tables of Syracuse are famous'.[2] Aristophanes gives Sicily a good write-up for travelling foodies.

The island was then the bread basket of Italy and the home of some of its finest wines. The climate was presumably less fierce than it is now. Sicily occupied the position of France today in enjoying the finest produce as well as the finest cooks.

By a natural progression, it also bred the first cookery writers. There are older recipes to be found elsewhere, for example on the Babylonian cuneiform tablets now at Yale. These tablets, dating from the seventeenth century BC, list ingredients for a bouillon to be made of various meats such as lamb and pigeon, for a duck stew and for some sort of porridge. But they offer only terse and practical advice. They do not constitute what we would call a cookery book. Cookery writing as we know it seems to have begun in Sicily in the fifth or fourth century BC. And what a lot of cookery writers there were, and the most celebrated of them were Sicilians: Heracleides of Syracuse, Dionysius of Syracuse, Hegesippus of Tarentum (admittedly on the heel of the mainland), Agis of Syracuse. All their works have perished, like those by Greek foodies from elsewhere. Where is the book on bread-making by Chrysippus of Tyana or the treatise on salt fish by Euthydemus of Athens?

One such work does survive, and that only in fragments, the *Gastronomia* by Archestratus of Gela or Syracuse (his birthplace is as uncertain as much else about him, though he was clearly a Sicilian). These fragments from a poem dated 330 BC are preserved in a much later compendium, the *Deipnosophistai*, or *Philosophers at Dinner*, put together by Athenaeus. While quoting chunks of Archestratus, often at length, Athenaeus never loses a chance to take a snipe at his predecessor. It is as though our only knowledge of *Mrs Beeton's Household Management* came from quotations scattered through a derisive anthology compiled by Clive James.

Archestratus was also the first galloping gourmet. The sixty-two fragments quoted by Athenaeus mention recipes and delicacies from every part of the world the Greeks knew, from the Ionian Sea to the Black Sea, from Thrace all the way down to Crete, stopping off at every city or island where the fish or the grapes or the cooking were worth noting. In all, 120 places are mentioned. Athenaeus says: 'This Archestratus, in his love of pleasures, travelled over every land and sea, in a desire, it seems to me, to review with care the things of the belly; and imitating the writers of geographical descriptions and voyages, his desire is to set forth everything precisely, wherever the best to eat and the best to drink are to be found.'[3]

Elsewhere Athenaeus is more unbuttoned about his predecessor, referring to 'Archestratus who sailed round the inhabited world for the sake of his belly and the parts beneath his belly'.[4] So we must think of Archestratus as rogering his way round the Mediterranean as well as browsing and sluicing in every taverna and fish market.

Athenaeus also quotes Klearchos, a student of Aristotle's who was never happier than when detailing other people's depravity, as criticizing 'those people nowadays who start conversations at parties like which sexual posture is the most enjoyable, or which fish, or how cooked; or which is in season now, or which is best to eat after Arcturus or after the Pleiades or after Sirius – this is typical of a man who is at home with the works of Philaenis and Archestratus.'[5] Philaenis was the author of the first known sex manual, discovered in the papyrus rolls of the Oxyrhynchus dust heap. So she was probably the first woman pornographer. Thus for the Greeks gourmet sex and food porn were inextricably entwined.

The market in chefs was already as developed as the market for cookery writers. The best chefs were highly sought after and were hired out to the smartest homes together with their train of sous-chefs. Then as now, they had a reputation for being bad-tempered and temperamental, and often appear as comic figures in Greek comedy. One may imagine hot competition for the supreme masters of their craft, not unlike the competition to lure away Anatole, the miraculous French chef employed by P.G. Wodehouse's Aunt Dahlia.

Greek chefs in the fourth century BC had strong views about the right and wrong ways to do things. Anaxippus of Athens, in his comedy *Behind the Veil*, has a cook make a speech about the rise of the *nouvelle cuisine*:

> Sophon of Acamania and Damoxenus of Rhodes were fellow pupils in the chef's art, and Labdacus of Sicily was their teacher. These two wiped away the clichéd old seasonings from the cook-books and did away with the mortar: no cumin, vinegar, silphium [a mysterious herb, said to be some variety of giant fennel, later extinct], cheese, coriander – seasonings which old Kronos used to have. They did away with all these and said the man who used them was only a tradesman. All they asked for were oil and a new pot and a fire that was hot and not blown too often. With such an arrangement every meal is straightforward.[6]

This fashion for conspicuous simplicity carried on into the Roman world. The Umbrian comic playwright Plautus in his *Pseudolus* (produced in 191 BC and like the rest of his output a free version of a lost Greek original) has a cook denouncing other cooks who serve up 'whole pickled meadows' in their stewpots, indiscriminately chucking in coriander, fennel, garlic and horse parsley, along with sorrel, cabbage, beet and asafoetida (possibly a substitute for the mysterious silphium) 'pounding up a wicked mustard which makes the pounder's eyes water'.[7]

Thus already we have the demand for simplicity and the reaction against crude and pungent flavours. These demands are advanced partly on health grounds, as reform movements in cookery often are. '*Faites simple*' was the watchword in the fourth century BC, as it was of Escoffier in the twentieth century AD. The elements of our present-day food snobbery are clearly detectable, as they are in Archestratus' remarks on how to cook fish:

> When you come to Miletus, get from the Gaeson Marsh a kephalos-type grey mullet and a sea bass, one of the children of the god. That is where they are best, such is the nature of the place. There are many other fatter ones, in famous Calydon, in wealth-bearing Ambracia and in Lake Bolbe, but they do not have the fragrant fat of the belly, or such pungent fat. The Milesian fish, my friend, are amazing in their excellence. Descale them and bake them well whole, until tender, in salt. When working on this delicacy do not let any Syracusan or Italian come near you, for they do not understand how to prepare good fish. They ruin them in a horrible way by 'cheesing' everything and sprinkling them with a flow of vinegar and silphium pickle.[8]

The ruins of ancient Miletus are now five miles from the sea. The marsh, which lies in the delta of the River Maeander, silted up in the Ottoman period, so the sea bass and grey mullet must have gone long before that. Only the shopping tips of Archestratus survive.

Goose and hare should be cooked simply, sprinkled with salt and not overdone, but taken from the spit while still undercooked. And you should not be distressed to see the divine *jus* dripping from the meat, but eat it up greedily: 'All other methods are mere sidelines to my mind, thick sauces poured over, cheese melted over, too much oil over – as if they were preparing a tasty dish of dogfish.'[9]

Like the more laid-back type of modern cookbook, Archestratus is often happy to leave the exact quantities and procedures to your own initiative. For example, for cooking small fry – sprats, whitebait and so on – he says: 'In fig leaves, with not too much oregano, is the way. No cheese, no fancy nonsense. Simply place it with care in the fig leaves and tie them with rush-cord from above. Then put into hot ashes and use your intelligence to work out the time when it will be roasted. Don't let it burn up.'[10]

Yet by the time we reach the imperial period, dishes were often swamped by fantastically complicated seasonings and sauces. For the Roman period, we do have a more or less whole cookbook, the *De Re Coquinaria* of M. Gaius Apicius. Even this, however, was compiled some centuries later, and while the majority of the recipes do come from Apicius, the compiler threw in recipes from other sources, such as a lost book on agriculture and domestic science by Apuleius, the author of *The Golden Ass*, another ancient writer whose work combined sexual and culinary sauce. Apicius himself flourished in the heyday of Augustus and Tiberius and was a noted gourmet and spendthrift. Seneca says that he spent 100 million sesterces on food, then found he had only 10 million sesterces left which would condemn him to starvation. So he poisoned himself.

Certainly Apicius' range of recipes is on the heroic scale. He mentions some 400 sauces, and his ingredients include twenty-seven types of fish, forty varieties of fruit and nuts, sixty of herbs, thirty-three of vegetables. Apart from the introductions from other continents – potatoes, tomatoes, rice, bananas – there are few ingredients that we use today that Apicius did not find several uses for. His *batterie de cuisine*, too, sounds not unlike the modern Le Creuset list, with the exception of the not yet invented fork.

He often gives us the standard version of a dish and then his own variant, the Apiciana or à l'Apicius. Some of his dishes, like the *Patina Apuana*, he himself claims are so full of complicated flavours that 'at table no one will know what he is eating' – '*ad mensam nemo agnoscet quid manducet*' – a sensation which is familiar today, especially in the more expensive restaurants, or would be if the menu did not elaborate the ingredients at enormous length, a trend of which Apicius would surely have approved. Apicius is also capable of giving precise technical instructions, as, for example, in his speciality *Patina Apiciana*:

> Make in the following way. Pieces of cooked sow's udder, fillets of fish, chicken meat, fig-peckers [the little *beccafico*, the Italian equivalent of our blackcap, was an esteemed delicacy because it fed on figs and grapes], cooked breasts of turtle dove, and whatever other good things you can think of [*et quaecumque optima fuerunt*]. Chop all this, apart from the fig-peckers, carefully. Then stir raw eggs into oil. Pound pepper, lovage, moisten with *liquamen* [a ubiquitous sauce in Roman cookery, see below], wine and *passum* [a sweet wine sauce, almost as ubiquitous as *liquamen*], put in a saucepan, heat and thicken with cornflour. But first add all the different meats and let them cook. When cooked, transfer with the sauce, using a ladle, into a pan in layers having added peppercorns and pine-kernels. Place under each layer as a base an oil-cake, and put on each oil-cake one ladleful of meat mixture. Finally pierce one oil-cake with a reed stalk and place this on top. Sprinkle with pepper. Before you put all these meats with the sauce into the saucepan, you should have bound them with eggs. What kind of metal pan you need is shown below [suggesting that the original version contained illustrations].[11]

Liquamen occurs in hundreds of recipes. It was the Roman equivalent of Worcester sauce, a compound of mashed sprats, anchovies and mackerel which was left to mature in the sun for a couple of months and then strained and mixed with old wine or vinegar. It was made in factories, according to various secret recipes. At Pompeii there was found a small jar inscribed: 'Best strained *liquamen*. From the factory of Umbricus Agathepus.' *Liquamen* could go off and smell horrible – Apicius also includes recipes to remove the odour from bad *liquamen*. The Romans not only liked strong flavours, but they had a taste for mixing sweet and savoury tastes equal to that of the most self-expressive modern cooks. Apicius boils pears in cumin, pepper and, of course, *liquamen*.

Now and then, though, his recipes seem straightforward enough and perfectly suitable for a present-day gastropub. For example, his forcemeat sausages in wine: 'Chop up meat and pound with white bread without crust which has been steeped in wine. At the same time pound pepper, *liquamen* and, if you like, seeded myrtle berry. Make little forcemeat balls, inserting pine kernels and peppercorns. Wrap in sausage skin and cook gently in sweet wine reduced by one third.' His celebrated recipe for stuffed dormouse would not, however, find favour with the RSPCA or the World Wildlife Fund: 'Stuff the dormice with minced pork, the mincemeat of whole dormice, pounded with pepper, pine kernels, asafoetida and *liquamen*. Sew up, place on tile and put in oven.'[12]

My reason for giving a selection of Apicius' recipes is not to argue that we would find them delicious or even eatable.[13] The point is that the appreciation of food and of the finer points of cooking were as much part of life in Greek and Roman cities as they are in ours. This was not the case throughout most of the Christian era, so that when the Renaissance attempted to revive the classical arts, for cooking they virtually had only Apicius to go on and *De Re Coquinaria* was reprinted several times.

The elevated place of cookery in Roman life is nowhere better shown than in the recipe for *placenta* in Cato the Elder's treatise *De Agri Cultura, On Agriculture*. '*Placenta*' simply meant a flat cake, especially one used in religious ceremonies; its shape led to the word being borrowed by the obstetricians. Cato was the epitome of austere conservative morality. When he was censor in 184 BC, he taxed luxury, cleaned up both the Senate and the sewage system. He treated the people and the nobility equally. His reputation for virtue and austerity has resounded down the centuries. His receipt may well be the most painstaking and comprehensive of any that has come down to us. It is certainly the first from a grade-one celebrity. It is as though Mr Gladstone had left us a three-page recipe for bread-and-butter pudding.[14]

It is a plain cake – flour, cheese and honey and the faintest whiff of bay leaves, suitable for the most austere statesman of the Republic, but made with infinite care. Here is a man who has made *placenta* with his own hands. You can tell by the adverbial solicitude – 'thoroughly', 'gradually', 'gently' – and the insistence on making each step absolutely clear. Amateur cooks – even the most busy and distinguished ones – took the business of cooking just as seriously as the professional prima donnas of the Roman kitchen.

A Naïve Domestic Falernian

We have detected two common forms of gastro snobbery in Archestratus, both exhibited in his remarks on grey mullet and sea bass: first, when he tells us that the only place to get the fish is from the swamp below Miletus on the Turkish coast, not exactly next door for the average Athenian or Thracian, and that the fish from other well-known sources is nowhere near as good; and second, when he claims that only he knows how to cook the fish and that other chefs from Syracuse and the Italian mainland spoil them with their vulgar sauces.

Can we also find in Archestratus, the third supreme mode of the gastro snob, not the geographical omniscience or the culinary sneer but the poetic effusion? Remarkably, even in the fragments that Athenaeus has preserved for us, there are several ripe examples of foodie gush. Here is Archestratus' riff on bread: 'Now the best to get hold of and the finest of all, cleanly bolted from barley with a good grain, is in Lesbos, in the wave-surrounded breast of famous Cresus. It is whiter than snow from the sky; if the gods eat barley groats, then Hermes must come and buy it for them from there. In seven-gated Thebes it is reasonably good, and in Thasos and some other cities, but it is like grape pips compared with Lesbian.'[15]

It is another Lesbian product, the wine, which provokes
Archestratus to his supreme dithyramb:

> You must drink an old wine with a really grey old head, its moist
> locks festooned with white flowers, born in Lesbos with the sea all
> around. I praise Bybline wine from Phoenicia, though it does not
> equal Lesbian. If you take a quick sip of it and are previously
> unacquainted, it will seem to you to be more fragrant than
> Lesbian, for this lasts for a very long time. When tasted thor-
> oughly though, it is very inferior, and the Lesbian will take on a
> rank not like wine but like ambrosia. If some scoff at me, brag-
> garts, purveyors of empty nonsense, saying that Phoenician has the
> sweetest nature of all, I pay no attention to them. Thasos also pro-
> duces a noble wine to drink, provided it is aged over many good
> seasons down the years. I know too of the shoots dripping with
> grape clusters in other cities . . . But the others are simply worth-
> less beside the Lesbian wine. Some people of course like to praise
> products of their own locality.[16]

Here we have all the techniques of the twenty-first century wine
connoisseur: the expertise displayed in the way he distinguishes
between the short-lived Bybline wines with their fragrant bouquet
and lack of 'finish', and the superior Lesbian wines which grow on
you; the surging to poetic heights after a draught of the *premier cru*;
the no-nonsense impatience with ignorant rivals, especially those
who blindly stick up for their own local products, just as French
vignerons today pooh-pooh wines from Australia and California
which in reality are often superior.

Ancient Greece clearly had plenty of genuine expertise in wine-
making. Indeed, ignorance of wine was generally considered the
mark of barbarians, such as the Scythians who lived in present-day
Crimea (where vines were planted centuries later). Greek writers
mentioned fifty varieties of grape. Some of these were continued in
Roman vineyards, such as those known by the Romans as the Greco

and the Grechetto. Theophrastus talks of matching grape varieties to different types of soil and climate. Hesiod, the first of Greek poets, recommends early September as the best time for harvest. The Greeks believed in additives such as honey, brine and herbs, the latter producing a sort of vermouth. Theophrastus was keen on blending, suggesting that the hard, aromatic wine from Heraclea did well when mixed with Erythraean, a softer, salty wine without much bouquet. Wines probably did not last very long in ancient Greece, though Theocritus speaks of drinking four-year-old wine, perhaps from Kos. And Peparethian was a well-known slow-developer, which took six years to reach maturity. But the alluring comparisons of the wine merchant were already a feature. The comic poet Hermippus talks of a mature wine 'smelling of violets, roses and hyacinths' and attributes a scent of apples to the wine from Thasos, to which, as we have seen, Archestratus awarded two stars, provided that it was properly aged.

The Romans took over all this paraphernalia and embroidered on it. Pliny thought that seawater 'enlivened a wine's smoothness',[17] but the great authority, Columella, in his *De Re Rustica* declared that 'the best wine is one that can be aged without any preservative; nothing must be mixed with it which might obscure its natural taste' – foreshadowing modern purists, and even the campaign for organically grown wine. The Romans began to produce long-lasting wines, such as the Falernian which became drinkable only after ten years and was at its best between fifteen and twenty years old. Wine from Sorrento only came into its own after twenty-five years. It was a strong thin white, which either Tiberius or Caligula is said to have dismissed as 'high-class vinegar'. Wines were endowed with stamina by 'maderization', that is, letting some air in to oxidize the wine and also heating it, which turned the wine a brownish colour. Cato himself recommended leaving some air in the amphora before sealing it.

The legendary Falernian was a deep amber colour, suggesting some degree of maderization. It was grown on the southern slopes of

Monte Massico in northern Campania. And here for the first time
we encounter distinct vineyards or *crus* within a wine-growing
region: Caucinian on the hilltops, Faustian on the slopes, and
Falernian proper at the edge of the plain. Falernian was expensive.
Horace in his *Odes* worries that he can't afford it any more. Pliny
worries, like many another wine-bibber after him, that quality is
being sacrificed to quantity, although Falernian seems to have stayed
in the top rank pretty much up to the fall of Rome. In Book 14 of
his *Natural History*, which is devoted to wine, Pliny ranks the wines
of Italy. Caecuban (later described by Galen as 'sinewy' and 'packing
a punch'), from a vineyard in the marshy region south of Terracina
on the west coast of central Italy where they trained the vines up
poplar trees, used to be the best, but now Falernian was number one,
followed by Setine, Alban and Surrentine with Mamertine from
Sicily in the third rank. Horace drinks a grand old Caecuban to celebrate the defeat of the monstrous Cleopatra. To celebrate the return
of Augustus, he drinks a wine that goes back to the Social War of
91–88 BC, twenty years before he was born. At the farm in the
Sabine hills which Maecenas gave him, he serves his patron a wine
that he had laid down in the year in which Maecenas had recovered
from a serious illness. For intimate occasions the poet suggests a
simple wine, reserving for honoured guests the wine from the year of
his birth.[18]

Clearly the idea of vintages is by now familiar, which it does not
seem to have been to the Greeks. Old wine under the Republic was
known by the name of the Consul for that year. The most famous was
Opimian, after Lucius Opimius who was Consul in the exceptionally
hot year of 121 BC. It became so famous in fact that 'opimian' became
an adjective denoting excellence in any wine, in English as well as
Latin. Opimian didn't last for ever. In 46 BC, Cicero says it is already
too old to drink.[19] Pliny says it's 'reduced to a kind of bitter honey',
but is still recognizably wine and still very expensive.[20]

By now, the nouveaux riches in Rome are slurping Opimian, or
from amphorae labelled Opimian, as if there was no tomorrow. The

nouves and their fancy vintages are an easy target for Martial's epigrams.[21] He even invents a wine that is so ancient that it hasn't got a Consular year because it was laid down before the Roman Republic was even founded. The reader needs to know which wines were good and which were not in order to get the point of the epigram, just as a writer in *The Times* or the *Spectator* today would be able to refer to Dom Pérignon and Château Pétrus on the one hand, and Prosecco or Algerian red on the other, to make a point about social habits and aspirations. By the end of the Roman Republic, the wine-drinking public is already divided into several classes: the ordinary folk who drink the rough local wine, which is usually no more than a year old; the nouves who despise the proles for drinking plonk and spend a fortune on the priciest vintages; and the connoisseurs who despise both. It cannot be said that we have moved on much.

The Fall and Rise of Gastronomy

By contrast, for the committed foodie, the Dark Ages really were dark. From the fall of Rome until the 14-year-old Catherine de Medici was brought over the Alps to marry Henri II in 1547, the cooking in most of Europe was atrocious and the civilized discussion of gastronomic matters was non-existent. The disapproval of gluttony, as of all other sensual overindulgence, ruled out not only overeating but any lubricious lingering on the quality of food. Perhaps the only bright spot for foodies was the wine which played a central role in the Eucharist and so was exempt from the disapproval of the Church. Monasteries prized their vineyards and behind the cloister walls brewed beer and mead and distilled their own sticky liqueurs, in whose names, alas, often lingers all that is left of that extraordinary monastic civilization – Benedictine, Chartreuse and so on. The medieval banqueter had to content himself with meat that was often roasted to a frazzle because the fire was too hot and not easy to damp down, the meat itself hung for too long, its vile aroma only half hidden by being doused in herbs and spices. The soups and stews were scalded, and fresh vegetables were a rarity in northern climes, and non-existent out of season.

Some monastic orders did of course become notorious for their guzzling. Friar Tuck was a key feature in the Robin Hood legend; Chaucer's wanton and merry Friar Hubbard 'knew the taverns well in every town' and preferred to deal with wealthy merchants and victuallers rather than the sick and the poor. St Thomas Aquinas (1225–74), the greatest theologian of the medieval Church, was known as 'the Dumb Ox'. He was so gloriously fat that a segment had to be carved out of the refectory table to accommodate his massive paunch. The miracle that earned him canonization was characteristic: on his deathbed near his ancestral home in southern Italy, he called for a dish of herring. His family explained that there were no herring in the Mediterranean. To everyone's amazement, the next consignment of sardines from the local fishmonger turned out to contain a load of herrings. The devil's advocates who were interrogating Thomas's claim to sainthood queried whether his untravelled relatives would have been able to tell a herring when they saw one. But Aquinas became St Thomas nonetheless.[22] The Miracle of the Herrings, representing as it does the Feeding of the One rather than the Five Thousand, must be regarded as the first foodie miracle.

Such stories brought the Church into disrepute for its gross betrayal of the ascetic ideals it taught. Gluttony was, after all, included among the Seven Deadly Sins, first formulated by Pope Gregory the Great in the sixth century and immortalized (if that is the right word) by Dante in *Il Purgatorio*. High on the programme of every Church reform movement up to and including the Reformation itself was to put an end to the greed of the monks in every sense. In an age with such priorities, gastronomy never stood a chance of becoming a courtly art.

Occasionally, new foods or new dishes can claim a medieval origin – Roquefort cheese, for example, first developing its stinging bouquet in some eleventh-century cave. Chefs sometimes did commit their recipes to paper. The first documented receipt for pasta comes from the eleventh-century *De arte coquinaria per vermicelli e macaroni siciliani* by Martino Corno, chef to the Matriarch of Aquileia. Books on household management of the late Middle Ages often include recipes. Elizabeth David (1913–92), the great high priestess of post-war cooking, approves of the complicated recipe for walnut mustard contained in the *Ménagier de Paris*, a treatise composed around 1393 by a middle-aged bourgeois for his young bride.[23] By the late sixteenth century, treatises on cooking are beginning to appear, such as Bartolomeo Scappi's *L'Arte del Cucinare* (1570). Elizabeth David recommends his receipts for galantine, quince mustard and walnut-and-garlic *agliata*.

Catherine brought with her some of the fresh vegetables and herbs that had continued to flourish in Italy and some of the dishes from farmhouse and monastery that were new to the barbarous north: parsley, artichokes, haricot beans, polenta, liqueurs. She even brought the fork, an ingenious Italian appliance not known in the north. By the end of the sixteenth century, fresh produce from the New World was beginning to appear: rice, avocados, chocolate, tomatoes, potatoes. Serious recipe books soon followed, Robert May's *The Accomplisht Cook* (1664), *The True Gentlewoman's Delight* (1687), possibly by the Countess of Kent, or possibly not, and *The Closet of Sir Kenelm Digby Opened* (1669). Traditions of how to cook are becoming well established, so that Elizabeth David in *An Omelette and a Glass of Wine* (1984) can give recipes for syllabub from English kitchens in each of the past four centuries: for the seventeenth century, from Robert May and Kenelm Digby; for the eighteenth century, from Elizabeth Raffald's *The Experienced English Housekeeper* (1769); for the nineteenth century, from Mistress Margaret Dods' *The Cook's and Housewife's Manual* (1819); for the twentieth century, her own. The instructions and ingredients are slightly different in each case, but not so different that any one of the cooks could not have happily borrowed any of the other mouth-watering receipts.[24]

Elizabeth David does the same service for *crême brûlée*, or burnt cream as honest English cookbooks call it, such as Maria Eliza Rundell's *New System of Domestic Cookery*, first published in 1806. By now cookery books were becoming big business. Mrs Rundell's book was reprinted for the sixty-eighth time as late as 1867. Back in 1819, John Murray had paid the huge sum of 2,000 guineas to buy the copyright. But to little avail. No fewer than five other publishers brought out pirated editions.[25]

By the middle of the eighteenth century, cooking has become a conspicuous preoccupation of the aristocracy. Louis XV began the practice of awarding a Cordon Bleu to the finest female chefs. Casanova, who liked to think he knew everything about every department of life as well as women – music, art, medicine, politics, the stage, literature, cards, magic – also fancied himself as a connoisseur of food and wine. When he is attempting to seduce the Burgomaster of Cologne's wife, he lays on a sumptuous breakfast at the chateau of Brühl:

> By the time the oysters were done, 24 bottles of champagne had been emptied [between 24 guests], so that when the actual break-fast commenced everybody began to talk at once. The meal might easily have passed for a splendid dinner and I was glad to see that not a drop of water was drunk, for the champagne, Rhine wine, Madeira, Malaga, Cyprus, Alicante and Cape wine would not allow it. Before dessert was brought on, an enormous dish of truf-fles was placed on the table. I advised my guests to take maraschino with it, and those ladies who appreciated the liqueur drank it as if it had been water.[26]

Not surprisingly the Burgomaster's wife surrendered.

Casanova can be disapproving of those who eat and drink too much, or too coarsely. He found it curious that the English ate so little bread and that in their taverns no soup was available, while boiled beef was regarded as fit only for dogs. Casanova himself is partial to *boeuf à la mode*, cold beef in jelly, as long as it is properly made. Among other dishes he consumes larks, mushrooms, *bécasse*, *coquillage*, *crostate*, eels' livers, smoked tongues, mortadella, *olla podrido*, as well the wines from all the countries he visited, many of them still familiar to us, such as Hermitage and Tokay. His was a cook's tour, as well as a seducer's odyssey. Occasionally as with the Burgomaster's wife, the two pursuits coincided. In Venice in 1754, he got to know not only the licentious Cardinal de Bernis but the Cardinal's cook, du Rosier. A Venetian lady found one of du Rosier's dishes so delicious that she claimed she would be unhappy for the rest of her days if she did not learn how to make it. Casanova got du Rosier to teach him the recipe and the lady was satisfied in every sense.[27]

The elite had begun once more to concentrate as it had in ancient Greece and Rome on the finer points of eating and drinking. But gastronomy in its modern form was still in its infancy. The word itself did not yet exist, being revived from the ancient Greek in 1800 in a third-rate epic by a provincial lawyer, Joseph Berchoux. *La Gastronomie: poème en quatre chants* pays homage to, among others, the Roman gourmand Lucullus, who apart from his lavish banquets was famous for bringing the cherry to Europe.[28] But Berchoux was eclipsed by a far more remarkable figure, Balthazar Grimod de la Reynière (1758–1838).

Grimod came from a line of gluttons and tax collectors. His grandfather died of a surfeit of *pâté de foie gras*, and his father inherited both the appetite and the lucrative office of *fermier général*. Grimod himself qualified as a lawyer but soon gave up the law to pursue actresses and give enormous banquets. When he was running out of cash and a tapeworm was discovered to be running around his stomach, Grimod's father had him locked up for a couple of years by the device of a *lettre de cachet*, that handy way of throwing inconvenient relatives in the slammer under the King's seal (Mirabeau was put inside by his father under the same procedure). On his release, Grimod was trampled underfoot by the Revolution and became a travelling salesman for a while, but he bobbed up under the

Directory and even more so under the Empire, during which he published eight volumes of his hugely successful *Almanach des Gourmands* (1803–12).

Grimod opens the introduction to the first volume by making a blatant commercial pitch in his habitual sardonic style: 'The upheaval in fortunes, brought about as a necessary consequence of the Revolution, having placed them in new hands, and the minds of almost all these overnight plutocrats turning above all towards the purely animal pleasures, I hoped to help them out by offering them a reliable and faithful guide in the most concrete region of their dearest affections.'[29]

Here we have the derisive manner of Martial two millennia earlier, combined with the lifestyle advice to be found two centuries later in Nigella Lawson's *How to Eat* (1998). The nouveaux riches are simultaneously patronized and told how to entertain in proper style. Grimod advises his readers on which restaurants to go to, on how to serve fish, meat and vegetables, on where and what and at which season to buy as well as on how to cook. Vol. I offers an *almanach* in the true sense of the word, with a rambling essay on each month plus seasonal tips. In the November section, for example, on how to cut up a turkey and whether it is more stylish to serve the legs separately on a bed of onions or with a sauce Robert. In October, we are told what to do with whiting, a fish which Grimod thinks insipid and in need of gingering up with a side dish. M. Rouget, he tells us, makes excellent hot pâtés with rolled fillets of whiting and also excellent quenelles.

Grimod will help you out with your shopping too. 'Let us descend the same rue Saint-Martin which during its length changes its name as often as a bankrupt fleeing his creditors', and we shall find M. Vaugeois at the Green Monkey, the leading *tabletier* of Paris (a *tabletier* was a purveyor of fancy items for the dining-room table – the nearest modern equivalent might be Tiffany's or Asprey's) who has ivory salad forks, boxwood salt-cellars in the latest taste, in which the salt is protected by the verdigris and which, unlike ones made of crystal, don't have the drawback of being fragile. 'We also find there ebony oil-holders, mahogany punch-bowls, rosewood egg-cups, to provide at modest cost a very elegant *ménage*.'[30]

But Grimod has another claim to fame. Apart from being the first shophound for foodies and other conspicuous consumers, he is also responsible for introducing high camp to the dinner table. Before his father had him locked up, Grimod gave a series of fantastic twice-weekly dinners, at which the diners had to observe bizarre rules written in gold letters on the walls of the dining room. The *Président* at each *déjeuner* was the first guest to swallow twenty-two cups of coffee. The most celebrated of these exhausting occasions was the 'funeral dinner' in 1783: the invitation was in the form of an obituary notice. Seventeen guests were invited, but there were also 300 spectators who were to watch from a balcony. The guests, who included his mistress Madame de Nozyl dressed as a man, were led into a completely dark room and then into a room dimly lit with tapers with a huge black catafalque in its midst; according to some accounts, there was a coffin behind each chair. After each course, Grimod said, 'Excellent pork [or whatever], it came direct from the butcher [or grocer], he's a cousin of my father's. His shop is at No. – in the rue – and I strongly recommend you buy from him in future.' Grimod was in part pursuing his campaign to tease his snobbish father, but also he had a precocious interest in commercial exploitation and may well have shored up his rocky finances with a few backhanders. The dinner menu is not preserved, but the idea was copied, one might almost say religiously, by J.K. Huysmans a century later in his celebrated decadent novel, *À Rebours* (*Against Nature*, 1884), where his hero gives a Black Dinner in memory of his lost virility, 'modelled on an eighteenth-century original':

> The dining-room, draped in black, opened out on to a garden metamorphosed for the occasion, the paths being strewn with charcoal, the ornamental pond edged with black basalt and filled with ink, and the shrubberies replanted with cypresses and pines.

The dinner itself was served on a black cloth adorned with baskets of violets and scabious; candelabra shed an eerie green light over the table and tapers flickered in the chandeliers.

While a hidden orchestra played funeral marches, the guests were waited on by naked negresses wearing only slippers and stockings in cloth of silver embroidered with tears.

Dining off black-bordered plates, the company had enjoyed turtle soup, Russian rye bread, ripe olives from Turkey, caviare, mullet botargo, black puddings from Frankfurt, game served in sauces the colour of liquorice and boot-polish, truffle jellies, chocolate creams, plum-puddings, nectarines, pears in grape-juice syrup, mulberries, and blackheart-cherries. From dark-tinted glasses they had drunk the wines of Limagne and Roussillon, of Tenedos, Valdepeñas, and Oporto. And after coffee and walnut cordial, they had rounded off the evening with kvass, porter and stout.[31]

Yet the 'eighteenth-century original' was not in fact original at all. Grimod's banquet had been closely modelled on the banquet given by the Emperor Domitian for Roman senators and knights in AD 89. The Emperor's dining room was entirely black, with black couches, crockery and food; even the naked serving boys had been painted black. Each guest's name was painted on a slab shaped like a tomb-stone, while Domitian himself discoursed on death to the silent and fearful company who thought that their last hour had come. Nothing of the sort. They were all sent home and the knock on the door that followed heralded not the imperial Gestapo but a going-home pres-ent: each guest's silver name-slab, the precious black dishes from which they had been served and their individual serving-boy now well scrubbed and nicely dressed.[32]

Thus Grimod reintroduces single-handedly pretty well all the ele-ments of Roman foodie culture which have now become so familiar to us in our own time: the ministering to the aspirations of the upwardly mobile, the playful, camp adornment of a basic human activity, the commercial sponsorship, even the business of cooking and eating before an audience, now familiar to us from a hundred TV programmes. In old age, prosperous again, he retired to the country where he continued to entertain lavishly and was kept company by a pig who had a seat of honour at the table, a mattress to sleep on, and its own valet. When he was dying, he would sit curled up in his arm-chair and talk wistfully of food: 'There has been a good deal of rain, there will be a fine quantity of mushrooms in the woods this autumn. Aren't ceps lovely. What a sweet perfume they have.' On his deathbed he called for a glass of water, saying 'At the moment of appearing before God, I would like to be reconciled to my most mortal enemy.' He drank it and died. In fact, Grimod was not a great wine-drinker. His real lasting allegiance was to food, and to style.[33]

It was in the first thirty years of the nineteenth century that France led the way in transforming cooking and dining into a culinary obsession. Not merely an art, but a quasi-religion and a science too, of sorts. Henrion de Pansy, a judge in Champagne famous for his wit and a favourite of Napoleon's, addressing three of France's most famous scientists, declared: 'I regard the discovery of a new dish, which sustains our appetite and prolongs our enjoyment, as an event of far greater interest than the discovery of a star; we can already see quite enough of those.'[34] This aphorism is often wrongly attributed to another judge, Jean-Anthelme Brillat-Savarin, who quotes it in his *Physiologie du Goût* (1825). Everything is an -ology or an -onomy now. Athenians had called Archestratus' tour his Gastrologia as well as his Gastronomia, so the modern revival could have followed either form. The year after Brillat-Savarin's *Physiologie*, Balzac published his *Physiology of Marriage*. These pseudo-scientific treatises become a respectable branch of literature. In Michaud's *Biographie Universelle*, Brillat-Savarin, who achieved nothing else apart from being an unimportant, rather reactionary judge who believed in capital pun-ishment and opposed the introduction of the jury system, receives a long obit from 'B – z – c' (the characteristic way of signing an entry). It is a delightful notice:

Brillat-Savarin is one of the rare exceptions to the rule which deprives men of high stature of any high intellectual faculties [Balzac himself was short and pudgy]; although his almost colossal frame gave him the look of the drum-major of the Appeal Court, he had a very fine mind. His writings are speckled with maxims, so brilliantly phrased that most of them immediately became proverbial sayings among gourmets and for many people take the place of original wit. Since Brillat's book came out, how many people have not rubbed their hands seeing a dessert without cheese and thought themselves witty by saying: 'A dessert without cheese is like a beauty without an eye.'[35]

The fraternity of connoisseurs whom Grimod two decades earlier was still describing as 'gourmands', the medieval word for glutton, now call themselves 'gourmets'. The history of 'gourmet' is worth noting. It probably derives from the same root as our 'groom', and gradually came to be applied to a wine merchant's clerk and, so, no doubt because of the clerk's patter, to a connoisseur of wine and eventually food.

Balzac himself was a foodie, of an eccentric obsessive kind, more like Grimod than Brillat. On one occasion, the meal he served his guests consisted entirely of onions: onion soup, onion purée, onion juice, onion fritters and onions with truffles. Two hours later, all his guests were sick.[36] He would sometimes miss out all the earlier part of the dinner and the demolish an entire pyramid of pears or peaches. When frantically writing, he would have the same meal every day: consommé, steak and salad and a glass of water, followed by enough cups of coffee to exhaust any branch of Starbucks.

But Balzac was capable of heroic trenchermanship, especially when someone else was paying. He once invited his publisher Werdet to Véry's famous restaurant in the Palais-Royal. Werdet, fearing that Balzac had chosen a place that was far too expensive, ordered only a bowl of soup and a chicken wing, but Balzac tucked into 100 Ostend oysters, twelve *pré-salé* mutton cutlets, a duckling with turnips, a brace of roast partridge, a *sole normande*, plus various entremets and a dozen pears, all washed down by the finest wines and liqueurs. Balzac: 'I'm afraid I haven't any cash. My dear fellow, could you help me out?' Werdet: 'I must have some 40 francs.' Balzac: 'That's not enough. Just give me 5 francs.' He then called for the bill, gave the 5 francs to the waiter, and scribbled something at the bottom of the bill, saying, 'This is for the lady at the *caisse*. Tell her it is from Honoré de Balzac.' The next day Werdet received a bill for 62 francs 50. However, he had the last laugh, deducting the entire sum from Balzac's royalties account, not forgetting the 5 francs.

By the time of Balzac's death in 1850, the science of gastronomy had recovered all its ancient dignity and added a few new frills which the Greeks and Romans would have applauded. All that remained was for the new science (or religion) to cross the Channel and bewitch the English-speaking world.

There was, after all, quite a gulf to be crossed. Talleyrand spent an hour every morning with his chef. The Duke of Wellington, on the other hand, could not hang onto his famous French chef Félix, who left in a rage, saying, 'I serve him a dinner which would make Udé or Francatelli burst with envy and he says nothing. I serve him a dinner badly dressed by the kitchenmaid and he says nothing. I cannot live with such a master, were he a hero a hundred times over.'[37]

Buffs and Buffers

Some time in the spring of 1931, Monsieur André Simon (1877–1970), a Frenchman who had become the doyen of the English wine trade, held a lunch in London for fellow wine-lovers. Among them was Sir Jack Squire, Georgian poet, cricketer and editor of *Punch*. Squire reported that Professor George Saintsbury was very ill at his home in Bath. The lunchers immediately resolved to send him a message of good wishes and to hold a dinner in his honour. At the dinner they decided to form a club in his honour.

The Saintsbury Club included among its early members the glitterati
of the day, Duff Cooper, Hilaire Belloc, A.P. Herbert, Sir Gerald du
Maurier, Sir Compton Mackenzie. Saintsbury himself never attended
a meeting and died two years later, but the club continues to this day,
as do various wine clubs and firms of wine merchants trading on his
memory.

Saintsbury (1845–1933) was one of the most influential English
academics of the late nineteenth and early twentieth century. He
wrote histories of almost every period of English literature, a three-
volume *History of Criticism* (1900–1904) and an exhaustive *History of
English Prosody from the Twelfth Century to the Present Day* (1906–10).
He revised Sir Walter Scott's 18-volume edition of the works of
John Dryden and coined the term 'Janeite' for a fan of Jane Austen.

Yet is for none of these great scholarly enterprises that he is
remembered but rather for a little book that he threw off when he
was already 75, *Notes on a Cellar-Book* (1920). It is for this sheaf of
reminiscences of the wines and spirits he had downed in the course
of his long life that he is still toasted by oenophiles everywhere.
('Oenophile', 'oenology' and other such terms are all of mid- to late-
Victorian invention, the wine cult seemingly a little later to revive
than the food cult.) Saintsbury's prose still permeates the copy of
wine merchants' catalogues and the columnists of the higher wine
journalism. Let us tiptoe down the steps into his cellar and sample
the inimitable atmosphere.

> . . . this was a red Hermitage of 1846. The Hermitage of the year
> before must have been made just before I was born; and I thought
> it very nice of the vines, where ancestors are said to have been of
> Shiraz stock imported by the crusaders, to have kept this produce
> till I was alive and ready for my first birthday present. For it was
> really a wonderful wine. When the last bottle of it was put on the
> table before I again broke up my household in London for a time,
> it was just forty years old. Now most red wines, if not all with the
> exception of Port, are either past their best, or have no best to

come to, at that age. And with all respect to the late Mr George Meredith and some other persons of less distinction, I think that even those who have forty years' old Port in their cellars had much better drink it. But my Hermitage showed not the slightest mark or presage of enfeeblement . . . it was the *manliest* French wine I ever drank; and age had softened and polished all that might have been rough in the manliness of its youth.[38]

Here already we have all the tricks of the wine buffer's style: the winsomeness – the vines give of their best in order to celebrate George Saintsbury's first birthday; the name-dropping – what did George Meredith do with his port, enough for us to know that Saintsbury dined with him (the book is dedicated to 'R.K., the best poet and taleteller of his generation', so probably Kipling was of the company too); the anthropomorphism, as though the Hermitage 1846 was a fellow diner.

The wine, he tells us, was 'uncompromisingly Gallic in its patriotism'. Its colour was 'browner than most of the Hermitages I have seen, but the brown was flooded with such a sanguine as altogether transfigured it. The wine was so full and complicated that it never seemed to come to a finish, and it possessed too that 'general "red wine" flavour which in some strange way is common to every vintage from Portugal to Hungary.' A wonderful piece of mystification, this. Why on earth wouldn't it have a red wine flavour? It's a red wine, for heaven's sake. But we are not finished yet. The actual wine is not the end of the performance:

I tried it with various glasses, for it is quite wonderful what whimsies the wine had as to the receptacle in which it liked to be drunk. The large, slightly pinched-in 'dock-glass' half filled, suited it as indeed it does almost any wine. But whether it was mere whimsy on my own part or not, I always thought it went best in some that I got in the early seventies from Salviati's, before they became given to gaudiness and rococo [chance here for G.S. to

sigh '*O tempora O mores*', which for once he does not take]. They
were glasses of about the ordinary claret size, but flat-bottomed
and with nearly straight sides, curly-stemmed, with a white but
rather cloudy body, an avanturine edge (very light) and deep blue
knobs, small and sparsely set, in one row below it. They were
good for all the great French red wines, but better for Burgundy
than for Claret, and better for Hermitage or Côte Rotie than for
Burgundy. Alas! The wine is gone, and with the wine went they,
though many years after it. [I didn't think we'd get away without
our 'Alas'].[39]

This is wine-writing, like the glasses, with knobs on. Horace and
Archestratus would have loved every word of it, including the bit
about the glasses. The Greeks had a huge array of cups for drinking
out of. One started the symposium with small cups, then progressed
to larger ones. Anacharsis, who coming from Scythia represented the
barbarian no-nonsense sort of chap, thought this very odd. Why
drink from small cups when you're empty and large cups when
you're full?[40] There are complaints too about the fashion for flatter
cups, for example, by Epigenes in his play *Heroine*: 'But the potters
don't make *kantharoi* nowadays, you poor chap, not those fat ones;
they make all these low-lying elegant things instead, as if it were the
cups themselves we were drinking rather than the wine.'[41]

Saintsbury's ideal symposium, like Grimod de la Reynière's banquets or Horace's, mixed in a good deal of literary talk with the
wine. Today, *Notes on a Cellar-Book* would fill several bumper editions
of *Pseud's Corner*. Echoes of the master are still to be heard, but for
more recent generations a more bracing tone was required.

It is quite a shock to go from Saintsbury's dithyramb on the
Hermitage 1846 to the character in the Kingsley Amis novel who
describes generic white burgundy as 'closely resembling a blend of
cold chalk soup and alum cordial with an additive or two to bring it
to the colour of children's pee'. Amis's little book *On Drink* (1972) is
designed as a corrective to the preciousness of the Saintsbury tradition:

Vintages – arrgh! Most of the crap talked about wine centres on these. 'The older the better' is another popular pseudo-rule. It does apply up to a point to château-bottled clarets, especially those known as classed growths. This is a precise technical term, not a piece of wine-snobs' jargon, but I cannot expound it here; consult your wine merchant or wine encyclopedia.[42]

But notice that Amis too lays claim to his share of the expertise, even if he is too busy being unpretentious to share much of it with the reader. Thus even modern writers who are dedicated to the demolition of pretension and bullshit feel that some basic knowledge of wine is the mark of a civilized person – or a good bloke, to put it in Amish. Amis is no less particular too about which glasses to use. A decent wine glass *must* be of plain glass so that you can see and appreciate the colour of the wine 'though a light floral or similar pattern on a basic plain-glass ground is acceptable'. A sherry glass, filled to the brim, should hold about 6 ounces and should have a stem to avoid hand-heating, but that stem need only be long enough to be held comfortably between thumb and forefinger. There must be short tumblers for the old-fashioned cocktail and long tumblers for the highball.[43] Travelling through Mexico, Amis insisted on carrying with him a sort of mobile cocktail bar containing tequila, gin, vodka and Campari; plus fruit juices, lemons, tomato juice, cucumber and Tabasco and various implements for making cocktails to his precise requirements when they stopped for elevenses.[44]

Like Amis, Auberon Waugh manages to write about wine while keeping Saintsbury's shade at bay, yet simultaneously displaying considerable knowledge lightly worn. Horace might have flinched at Waugh's descriptions of the wines that he is asked to taste for the *Spectator* Wine Club, just as Saintsbury would have recoiled from Amis's rude vocabulary, but Archestratus and Aristophanes would have recognized a mate. Greek gastronomes did not mince their words. On the question of whitebait, for example, according to

Athenaeus, Archestratus, the Daedalus of tasty dishes, says: 'All small fry, except the Athenian kind, are crap.'[45]

Here is a sample case of Waugh on wine:

I have yet to find a good Cahors (although everybody says they are to be found), but this wine has a rich and concentrated taste which I can only describe as *malty*: not in the way of malt whisky, but in the way of Radio Malt or Horlicks – malt extract before the brutes started adding cod-liver oil to it . . .

The thing about these Italian wines is that they come on like an express train or Manchester shop-girl, as you prefer, and will probably not need more than three months . . .

The Pichon Lalande from next door is even inkier and may end up twice the price, but this one looks like purple soup, tastes like Parrish's food with pepper, curry powder and blackcurrant jelly cubes, and seems all set to be a famous drink in ten years' time . . .

Vino Tesos Gran Reserva 1973 is the most Spanish of the three reds, with complicated Moorish undertones of jealousy and retribution. If you are prepared to believe, as I am, that Desdemona (like Dreyfus) was probably guilty, and Othello's suicide a great mistake, you will probably find it just your tipple. It is a heavy, expensive-tasting wine with enough tannin to save it from the toffee-apple, vanilla-flavoured sentimentality which is the first choice of this hairy, short-legged race.[46]

The rough banter does not disguise the fact that Waugh takes wine very seriously. I was myself pressed into service once or twice as a member of his tasting panel at his house in Somerset, and found it a surprisingly earnest business. Knowing little or nothing of wine and caring not much more, I found myself at a loss for words to describe the succession of to me indistinguishable clarets – I think they were clarets. I felt out of my element, like a Scythian asked to a symposium in downtown Athens.

The Un-godfather

If there is a single godfather of modern paganism in Britain, I would strongly advance the claims of Norman Douglas (1868–1952). His novels and essays, with the exception of *South Wind* (1917), never reached anything resembling a mass audience, but he had a huge influence on other writers who crossed his path including D.H. Lawrence, Graham Greene, Compton Mackenzie and Cyril Connolly. Douglas could do most things he set his hand to: he spoke half a dozen languages, played the piano beautifully, could identify any feature of the natural or man-made landscape at a glance. He was a trained zoologist who published several monographs on the flora and fauna of the Mediterranean. But what he was especially good at was doing exactly what he wanted. He was a voracious lover of both sexes and all ages – which, as he said, got him into trouble all his life. He was an uncompromising admirer of sensuality and believed in squeezing the last drop of pleasure out of life and to hell with what anybody else thought. He was particularly uncompromising in his love of the classical world and his loathing of Christianity. He admired, for example, the Emperor Tiberius, depicted as a monster of vice and cruelty by Tacitus and Suetonius. For Douglas, Tiberius possessed the supreme virtues: 'Common sense – that is the mark of Tiberius, and no wonder it was a feature offensive, almost unintelligible, to dreamers who yearned for things that are not, for things to come or things that have been.'[47] Christianity had destroyed our ability to take the world for what it was and to live at ease in the present moment.

> And the Greeks? The idea that we entered into the world tainted from birth, that feeling of duty unfulfilled which is rooted in the doctrine of sin and has hindered millions from enjoying life in a rational and plenary manner – all this was alien to their mode of thought. A healthy man is naturally blithe, and the so-called joy of

life of the ancient Greek is simply the appropriate reaction of the
body to its surroundings . . . The Greeks did not brood; a sane
mind broods over nothing; it insists on being distracted.[48]

And how better to be distracted than by seeking out the most exquisite sensations that the body offers, not merely those deliciously
offered by other bodies, but those afforded by the inescapable, every-
day business of eating and drinking.

What strikes one, above all, is the enormous amount of trouble
Douglas took to obtain the purest, most authentic tastes. During the
First World War he is in Rome, complaining bitterly of the horrible
wartime macaroni which is served up at meal after meal. Dining at a
restaurant on the Via Flaminia, 'one of the few restaurants in Rome
where nowadays a man is not in danger of being simultaneously
robbed, starved and poisoned', he wonders desperately 'where shall
a man still find those edible macaroni – those that were made in the
Golden Age out of pre-war flour? Such things are called trifles . . .
Give me the trifles of life, and keep the rest.'[49] Then he thinks of his
mysterious friend Mrs Nichol, who knows everything. He hurries
off to climb the ninety-three steps to her apartment at the top of an
old palace. She is playing cards and is not easily distracted by trifles.

'It is not a trifle,' he pleads. 'It is a matter of life and death . . . The
fact is, I am being assassinated by inches. Do you know of a place
where a man can get eatable macaroni nowadays? The old kind, I
mean, made out of pre-wartime flour.' Prompted by her partner, she
recalls the name of the place where she said something nice about
the white macaroni, it was called Soriano in Cimino. And there 60
miles away on the baking slope of an old volcano he finds Soriano:
'It was an unpleasantly warm day, but those macaroni – they atoned
for everything. So exquisite were they that I forthwith vowed to
return to Soriano, for their sake alone, ere the year should end. (I
kept my vow.)'[50]

A young English girl was bewitched by Douglas's obsessive quest
for perfection. Of all his admirers, none was more fervent or more

loyal than Elizabeth Gwynne who got to know Douglas at Antibes in the spring of 1940 when he was already 72 and she was only 27 and not yet married to Tony David, who was to give her the surname under which she became famous and not much else. Caustic and sceptical about most things in life, Elizabeth describes, with a schoolgirl's enthusiasm, how 'at the restaurant he would produce from his pocket a hunk of Parmesan cheese. "Ask Pascal to be so good as to grate this at our table. Poor stuff, my dear, that Gruyère they give you in France. Useless for macaroni." And a bunch of fresh basil for the sauce. "Tear the leaves, mind. Don't chop them. Spoils the flavour."'[51]

In the last year of his life, Douglas moved back to southern Italy, which he loved, to Capri, and Elizabeth would visit him there, her adoration undimmed:

Once during that last summer of his life, on Capri (he was then eighty-three), I took him a basket of figs from the market in the piazza. He asked me from which stall I had bought them. 'That one down nearest to the steps.'

'Not bad, my dear, not bad. Next time, you could try Graziella. I fancy you'll find her figs are sweeter; just wait a few days, if you can.'

He knew, who better, from which garden those figs came; he was familiar with the history of the trees, he knew their age and in what type of soil they grew; he knew by which tempests, blights, invasions, and plagues that particular property had or had not been affected during the past three hundred years; how many times it had changed hands, in what lawsuits the owners had been involved; that the son now grown up was a man less grasping than his neighbours and was consequently in less of a hurry to pick and sell his fruit before it ripened.[52]

Douglas was as downright in his denunciation of food he thought disgusting or inauthentic as he was in his appreciation of the real thing. His polemic against the fish soup they make in Naples deserves quoting at length, as it must be the most ferocious attack on any dish in world literature:

Take breath, gentle maiden; the while I explain to the patient reader the ingredients of the diabolical preparation known as *zuppa di pesce*. The *guarracino*, for instance, is a pitch-black marine monstrosity, one to two inches long, a mere blot, with an Old Red Sandstone profile and insufferable manners, whose sole recommendation is that its name is derived from *korakinos* (korax – a raven; but who can live on Greek roots?). As to the *scorfano*, its name is unquestionably onomatopoeic, to suggest the spitting-out of bones; the only difference from a culinary point of view, between the *scorfano* and a toad being that the latter has twice as much meat on it. The *aguglia*, again, is all tail and proboscis; the very nightmare of a fish – as thin as a lead pencil. Who would believe that for this miserable sea-worm with verdigris-tinted spine, which an ordinary person would thank you for not setting on his table, the inhabitants of Siren land fought like fiends; the blood of their noblest was shed in defence of privileges artfully wheedled out of Angevin and Aragonese kings defining the *ius quoddam pescandi vulgariter dictum sopra le aguglie*; that a certain tract of sea was known as the '*aguglie* water' and owned, up to the days of Murat, by a single family who defended it with guns and mantraps? And everybody knows the *totero* or squid, an animated ink-bag of perverse leanings, which swims backwards because all other creatures go forward and whose India-rubber flesh might be useful for deluding hunger on desert islands, since, like American gum, you can chew it for months, but never get it down.

These, and such as they, float about in a lukewarm brew of rancid oil and garlic, together with a few of last week's bread-crusts, decaying seashells and onion-peels, to give it an air of consistency.

This is the stuff for which Neapolitans sell their female relatives.[53]

Foodies from Archestratus onwards would stand up and cheer to hear this passage. Because they too believe in being 'passionate about food' – a slogan which adorns the window, and indeed the sandwich wrapper, of every branch of Pret A Manger.

The gospel of Elizabeth David conquered post-war Britain. In all social histories of the austerity age, she occupies an honoured place. Her early books, *Mediterranean Food* (1950), *French Country Cooking* (1951) and *Italian Food* (1954), brought the warm South to freezing, half-starved, wholly rationed post-war Britain. With their elegant prose and their atmospheric drawings by John Minton, her books imported a sense of style to the dining table, and eventually to the delicatessen and the restaurant. The essentials of her gospel were proper, authentic ingredients; simple recipes; and attention to detail – and that gospel derived directly from that pernickety old pagan Norman Douglas. He was the un-godfather of the modern age.

Domestic Gods and Goddesses

But how his un-godchildren have multiplied. There is now a restaurant column in every newspaper, which is not merely a consumer report but a fully fledged essay full of Douglas's enthusiasm, intolerance and *sprezzatura*. The sparkiest young journalists cut their teeth in the dining room, marking up or down every feature of the decor, the staff, the menu. Indeed, in many newspapers and magazines otherwise fairly devoid of wit, the restaurant column is where you will find the most brilliant, subversive, evocative writers: A.A. Gill, Craig Brown, Deborah Ross, Matthew Norman, Giles Coren. Several cooks who started out writing about food then graduated to stardom on television, such as Jennifer Paterson, Clarissa Dickson Wright, Nigella Lawson. Nigella's combination of voluptuous beauty and sensuous style of cooking on screen has won her the title of the Domestic Goddess, in itself a dazzling testimony to the social ascent of cooking. On the screen they compete with professional chefs who exhibit in an almost stylized way the characteristics of chefs down the ages: bad temper, vanity, jealous rivalry, obscene language. Celebrity chefs become millionaires and national figures, in the case of Jamie Oliver more trusted to give advice on nutrition in schools than government nutritionists.

Chefs are no longer mere craftsmen. Heston Blumenthal, proprietor-chef of the Fat Duck, the Thameside restaurant at Bray voted by his fellow chefs the Best Restaurant in the World in 2005, is a proponent of scientific approaches to cookery. He has his own research laboratory where he is photographed in a white gown peering at steaming retorts and crucibles conducting esoteric experiments in low-temperature cooking with the collaboration of scientists from four universities. Ferran Adrià, acclaimed as the best chef in the world, collaborates at his Costa Brava restaurant El Bulli with the artist Richard Hamilton and with the director of Tate Modern, who have together edited a sumptuous volume of homage to Adrià, including a catalogue raisonné of his dishes as if they were so many great works of art. Just as Balzac had envisaged, cooking has taken its place among the other -ologies and -onomies of art and science.

Young photographers now often choose to specialize in food photography, which has become an important branch of the photographic art. For not the least sensual element in food porn is the succulent snaps alongside the recipes: you can almost smell the *jus* dropping from the rack of lamb and feel like dipping your finger in the chocolate running off the profiteroles.

We should note here a piquant paradox. Despite this torrent of advice on how to cook, the shelves of fat cookbooks in the bookshops and the huge fortunes piled up by cookery writers – in the case of Delia Smith, enough to buy Norwich City Football Club – it is unlikely that people are in fact cooking at home more than they used to. Indeed, if you look at the rows of restaurants springing up along every street, credit crunch notwithstanding, people must be eating in a good deal less and eating out a lot more. Within walking distance of our house in Islington we can eat every kind of cuisine –

Mexican, Thai, French, Italian, Indian, Turkish, Ethiopian, Chinese, Japanese – and this was an area in which, even twenty years ago, the few restaurants that did dare to set up tended to close down within two or three months. Nor are those who eat at home all following the gospel of Norman Douglas and Elizabeth David, to judge by the piles of convenience foods in every supermarket. In other words, this is primarily a cultural rather than a practical phenomenon. Foodie heaven is located in the mind rather than the stomach.

What a *bouleversement* all this is from the days when it used to be regarded as 'common' in middle-class circles to discuss the food one was eating or indeed to talk about food at all. Now the upper bourgeoisie talk of little else. Looking back, we can see that the taboo on food talk was a watered-down secularized version of the Christian struggle to free oneself of fleshly appetites.

Today an articulate concern with food and drink is the mark of a civilized person. Someone who says, 'I'm afraid I'm totally uninterested in food,' is seen as the worst sort of killjoy and party-pooper.

A person who knows about food is regarded as knowing that much more about life. Gastronomy offers a key not just to the here and now but to the meaning of life – the healthy, blithe, this-worldly life set out for us by Nietzsche and Norman Douglas. If this seems a little fanciful, consider a curious fact.

The detective is the hero of modern literature. His or her powers of observation, reasoning and deduction offer the modern equivalent to the antique Oracle. The ace sleuth sees through deceitful appearances to the hidden truth. Frequently he curses himself for his initial blindness, for being so slow to see that truth when the rest of us are still baffled as to what it is that he has been blind to.

And it is remarkable how often one of the marks of the detective's supreme intelligence and discernment is his encyclopedic knowledge of food and drink. Rex Stout, the creator of the orchid-loving gargantuan Nero Wolfe, has even compiled a cookbook of his hero's recipes. Admirers have also produced a cookbook for Dorothy Sayers's languid sleuth, Lord Peter Wimsey.

Neither of these great men actually do the cooking. Wolfe is cooked for by his man Fritz, Wimsey by his man Bunter. Although not being housebound like Wolfe, Lord Peter enjoys the cooking in the pubs, clubs and restaurants that he happens upon in the course of his sleuthing. But both men are pernickety rhapsodists and capable of both extreme severity and unbridled enthusiasm in their judgements of food and wine, Wimsey for example going into ecstasies over a ham sandwich made from a Bradenham ham. Similar cookbooks have been misguidedly published in the name of other fictional heroes not notable for their cooking skills, such as Sherlock Holmes and James Bond. Agatha Christie's Hercule Poirot too is abnormally sensitive to what he eats and drinks. In the opening chapter of *Mrs McGinty's Dead* (1952), we are told that he was 'always a man who had taken his stomach seriously. He was reaping his reward in old age. Eating was not only a physical pleasure, it was also an intellectual research.' In modern mythology, profound expertise in matters of food and drink is a sign of intellectual genius as essential as the bulging forehead and the piercing eye. A further twist to this assumption that gastronomes are superior intelligences is John Lanchester's novel *The Debt to Pleasure* (1996), in which the narrator who turns out to be the villain is a gourmet of resplendent pretensions. What gives the book its delicious quality and led to it being translated into twenty languages is that the recipes are really more interesting than the murder plot. Here gastronomy reaches its highest peak yet. Eating and drinking have already risen to the same level as sex, now they compete with death. If and when we reach Valhalla, the gods and goddesses that we meet there will surely all be domestic ones.

Yet I cannot help feeling now and then a suspicion that there is something forced and unconvincing about the food cult. I am as ready as anyone to rhapsodize about the first new potatoes of the year, or the clean sweet crunch of a Worcester apple, or the salty tang of Morecambe Bay shrimps, or the sting of a good dry Martini or a glass of Chablis on a summer's evening. But can the business of eating and drinking, even more so the business of cooking and wine-making, really support such torrents of gush, such mountains of words and pictures, such a weight of expectation and reverence? In the elaborate rituals of foodism, its orgasmic oohs and ahs, its ceremonious finger-licking and napkin-wiping, there is an element not merely of pretentiousness (that we are willing to admit with a rueful chuckle) but of sheer make-believe. Somehow, it seems, we need to convince ourselves that Gordon Ramsay's pan-fried Grana Padano chicken represents an epiphany in our lives, or that St Teresa never knew ecstasy like that afforded by Jamie Oliver's roasted salmon with purple sprouting broccoli and anchovy-rosemary sauce. But the reality is that, time and again, a sour coulis of disappointment trickles in when the three-daisy meal is over and the terrifying bill has to be paid.

All too often when I am reading yet another food supplement in the Sunday papers or one of the absurdly ingredient-rich recipes in Apicius, I find myself not so much salivating with pleasure as trying to prevent my gorge from rising. For this temple is built so perilously above the sewer. If you pass the back door of the finest fish restaurant, the stench of rotting lobster and turbot will make the sturdiest gastronome begin to gag. '*Le goût du terroir*' at its most authentic comes dangerously close not just to the farmyard but to the latrine.

To be fair to the food writers, they are as savage in their criticisms as they are gushing in their praise. Adjectives such as 'insipid', 'rubbery', 'tasteless', 'greasy', 'stodgy' or even 'inedible' spatter their prose. 'My companion' who is brought along to share the feast will report herself unable to get through the *cassoulet à la mode de Toulouse* or the old-English treacle pudding. The more honest wine writers – those who are not literally in hock to the wine merchants who are supplying the booze – are equally ready to denounce stuff which they find undrinkable: the plonk which tastes of the antifreeze with which it was blended, the white wine that cuts your stomach like piano wire, the Sancerre which tastes not of gooseberries but of cat's piss.

The element of make-believe is made worse by the flummery that surrounds the whole performance. Dining at a smart restaurant is almost the only experience in modern life which deliberately attempts to re-enact the servilities of the ancien régime. The super-ciliousness of the maître d' is the nearest we come to encountering a duke's butler. Where else do we find footmen in full evening dress to take our coats, pull out our chair, fill our glass and reverently dole out our food? Where else does one fling cash on the table as one leaves, in the style of a *grand seigneur*? Modern eateries try to put you more at ease by dressing their staff in T-shirts and jeans, but the same elaborate courtesies are de rigueur. I have noticed that my socialist friends are just as demanding as any hedge funder when they sit down in a restaurant, as quick to complain if the service is slow and the food under- or overcooked. They show no discomfort at being waited on. Yet it is surely a peculiar new religion that insists on keeping a little corner of the feudal system alive.

In fact it's an odd sort of religion altogether that turns the cooker into an altar and excommunicates those who can't or won't bow down to it. Not-cooking becomes a sort of shameful deviance, revealing a mean-spirited approach to life. The suspicion cannot help dribbling into one's mind, drop by drop like olive oil into a mayo mix, that all this insistence is some sort of substitute for some-thing. Nigella Lawson – who is the only celebrity chef who includes modesty in her *batterie de cuisine* – confided to Julie Burchill, who had confessed that she herself did not cook, 'It's a thing I've noticed, that people like me who are obsessed with cooking and creating a home often didn't have the greatest home lives when they were young. We're trying to do it properly. Whereas people who had the real thing don't need it.'[54] This may be an unexpected explanation, but my own experience suggests that there is something in what she says. Burchill herself says, by contrast, that she had the happiest of child-hoods and has no hesitation in rudely denouncing food fanatics and telling them that they ought to 'feel sorry for yourselves that your inner life is so limited that you mistake feeding for faith and scoffing for sex'. If they can't stand the heat of the modern world, they should get back to the kitchen. But perhaps the real trouble is that the modern world is not warm enough. In a famous phrase coined by the historian Christopher Lasch, the family used to be described as 'a haven in a heartless world'. But if the heartlessness invades and undermines the family too, then perhaps the Aga may be the only place left to warm your hands.

Fasting and Feasting

There is a pocket cartoon by Osbert Lancaster in the old *Daily Express* which shows a stout naked woman standing on the bathroom scales and peering anxiously at the dial. At her side stands her husband who is in clerical garb. He is wagging his finger at his wife and admonishing her: 'Mildred, are we not in danger of undertaking our Lenten fast in the hope of material rather than spiritual benefits?' The cartoon must have been published in the late 1950s or early 1960s, just about the last moment in our history at which the point of the joke would strike home with a mass audience. For there were many more practising Christians in the population then, and quite a number of them did fast in one way or another. Even non-practising Christians and non-Christians would be vaguely aware of the notion that there were spiritual benefits to be had from abstaining from meat or alcohol or tobacco for a prescribed period. Quite a few would be aware too that this abstaining was carried out in memory of the forty days and nights that Jesus spent in the wilderness without food or drink.[55] That marathon fast was itself a fulfilling echo of the similar forty-day fasts recounted in the Old Testament: that of Moses before he received the Tablets of the Law on Mount Sinai[56] and that of Elijah before he went up to Mount Horeb where he had a vision of God.[57]

The Lenten fast is not the only one that is or was observed by Christians. Religious Jews at the time of Jesus normally fasted twice a week, on Mondays and Thursdays.[58] But the Apostles chose

Wednesday and Friday as their fasting days in memory of Judas'
betrayal of Jesus and the death of Jesus respectively. An ancient text
says: 'It is obvious, therefore, that not to fast on Wednesday or Friday,
except for grave reasons, is as if we have betrayed the Lord together
with the traitor and as if we have crucified him together with those
who crucified him.' These two days are still fasting days in the
Orthodox Church, although the less devout tend to observe them,
not by a complete fast but by eating one meal only, after 3 p.m., and
by abstaining from meat, fish, dairy products, eggs, wine and olive oil
at that meal. In the Latin Church, the Wednesday fast dropped away
in the Middle Ages, and even the Friday fast became laxer over the
centuries, until it became the no-meat, fish-only regime which lasted
into our own time.

These fasts are all what might be called 'mourning fasts'. The
abstainer honours and reflects on the memory of Jesus' Passion, his
own body at the same time being cleansed of the impurities of meat
and strong drink. There are other fasts, though, which prepare the
minds and bodies of the devout for the upcoming great festivals: the
Rogationtide fast before Ascension Day, the Advent fast before
Christmas; these have died out in the West, although again some of
them continue in the East.[59]

Western Christians have sometimes seemed rather envious of the
more tenacious asceticism of their Eastern brethren. Cardinal
Ratzinger, before he became Pope Benedict, declared that 'to fast
means to accept an essential element of Christian life. We need to
rediscover the corporeal aspect of faith: abstaining from food is one
of these aspects . . . and for this we must look for an example to our
brothers of the Eastern Orthodox Churches, great masters – still
today – of authentic Christian asceticism.'[60]

There remains only one type of fast which is widely observed by
Christians everywhere. That is the Eucharistic fast, based on St
Augustine's teaching that 'the Body of the Lord should enter the
mouth of the Christian before any other food'. Hence the tradition of
holding Communion services early in the morning before breakfast,

which made the fast easy to observe and gave the communicant what in secular terms would be called a buzz, as the mouthful of sweet wine was the first drink of the day. Chaplains at English public schools in the 1950s, normally suspicious of anything smacking of religious enthusiasm, did teach their pupils the importance of fasting before the Eucharist when preparing them for Confirmation, and for a time anyway the newly confirmed would abstain from the cornflakes and toast before early service.

The Orthodox Churches as usual took a sterner view and insisted that communicants should fast for three days beforehand, a rule still observed in Russia, Serbia and Bulgaria, though with the result that many members of the Orthodox Church receive the Sacrament very rarely, perhaps three or four times a year on great feast days.[61]

But, the Eucharistic fast apart, churches in the West, even the Catholic Church, have drifted away from fasting as a central discipline in the Christian life. Guidance from modern-day bishops at best includes fasting as part of a sober and godly life, along with not spending too much time and money on shopping and partying, and not watching too much television. Fasting becomes merely one aspect of that simplicity and moderation which make it easier for us to resist the temptations of this world and clear space in our minds for higher things. This modern attitude is but a pale reflection of the intense vision of the Desert Fathers. In early Christianity, fasting was a central, I am tempted to say the central, element in the quest to recapture what Peter Brown calls 'the unimaginable glory of Adam's first state'.[62] In Egypt and other parts of the Middle East where the Christians were multiplying, it was widely believed that the first sin of Adam and Eve was not lust but greed. The first of God's commandments that they had broken was, after all, to eat what they had been expressly forbidden to eat. From eating the fruit of the Tree of Knowledge, all other forms of greed – for money, sex and power – followed on inexorably. In a curious way, the Desert Fathers echoed in reverse the view both of Archestratus travelling the known world to satisfy 'his belly and the parts below his belly' and of the modern sensualist: food is like sex, and sex is like food – each as delicious or pernicious as the other.

Brown points out that the super-fasters of antiquity did not believe that their privations were damaging their bodies. On the contrary, they thought of the human body as a self-sufficient system, capable of running on its own heat. In its natural state – before the Fall – 'the body had acted like a finely tuned engine, capable of "idling" indefinitely'.[63] It was only the warped will of fallen men that had crammed the body with superfluous food, generating the surplus of energy which exploded into anger and lust. The whole cycle of ingestion, digestion and excretion seemed unnecessary to the early ascetics. Valentinus, the theologian of the second century AD, took it for granted that Jesus did not defecate. When St Anthony of Egypt emerged from his cell after twenty years, it was reported that he was not in the least wasted from lack of exercise or emaciated from lack of food but just as they had always known him; his body had maintained a perfect equilibrium throughout all his privations. Fasting clarified the body and reduced the temptation to wilful acts of every kind, conspicuously of course sexual acts.

'A prolonged fast,' Tessore tells us, 'takes us beyond our normal daily routine and into a different world. It is a mystical experience of leaving behind our normal selves to find a deeper, unfamiliar self.'[64] In its early stages, fasting is a process of suffering: tiredness, nausea, stomach cramps, headaches, causing lethargy, impatience and ill-temper. But rather as athletes talk of breaking through the pain barrier, after a day or two the cramps and the hunger begin to fall away and, Tessore, assures us, 'you begin to get a "taste" for this new "spiritual food". Only by trying it out for yourself can you experience the extreme fatigue and the inexpressible beauty of fasting.'[65]

To the modern secular mind, all this seems weird and even perverse. Yet in most civilizations throughout recorded history, fasting of this intensity and for similar reasons has been the rule, among the Confucians and the Aztecs, no less than among the Australian Aboriginals and most African peoples. In Buddhism and Hinduism, fasting occupies a central place, as it does among Jews and Muslims. In the Koran, fasting is one of the five pillars of the Islamic faith. Among orthodox Jews, the rituals of public and private fasting have remained unchanged since biblical times. The lists of foods forbidden in India and in the Taoist tradition have much in common with those forbidden by the Christian Churches – meat, fish, dairy, products, eggs, wine, oil.

Fasting is never an end in itself. It is no more and no less than an ascetic training regime (*askesis* means training) to enable us to lead a more Christian life. Like other forms of training, it is intended not to damage the body but rather to fortify it and to strengthen our powers of self-control. The purpose of mortification, Augustine tells us, is to extinguish desire, not to injure physical health, which is very wrong. In fact, the Fathers of the Church emphasize the medical advantages of fasting. St Basil tells us that fasting improves digestion and strengthens our physical resistance: 'Human bodies weighed down by continuous overeating easily fall prey to illness.' St John Chrysostom says that fasting is a medicine, but like other medicines we have to know how much and how long to take it for. In the second century AD, that wise old advice columnist, Clement of Alexandria, preaches the virtues of a simple, light diet for both body and mind; children develop better if their eating is controlled; the belching and snoring which come from eating and drinking too much disturb the calm clarity of the eye of the soul. Fasting was always seen as an aid to detoxing as well as to spiritual improvement, a view shared by the Prophet Mohammed.[66]

At first sight then, the religious traditions of fasting seem to have a good deal in common with modern dietary regimes. True, modern diets often seem weirder because they are so bewilderingly various, whereas the old religious regimes tend to follow a single pattern: a vegetarian or near-vegetarian diet, with minimal alcohol or no alcohol at all, and an avoidance of rich, heavy, and greasy foods. Modern dieticians, by contrast, may recommend high-protein, even meat-rich diets, or diets designed for drinking men, or virtually any other combination of food and drink – and still their books sell. Yet the majority today do recommend light, simple diets, low in meat and alcohol, and they emphasize the virtues of natural plain foods which have not been chemically tampered with or smothered in rich sauces. Does this suggest some kind of continuation by other means of the long tradition of fasting among the religions of the world?

Not really. There is a chasm between the two types of dietary discipline. Virtually none of the modern dieticians recommends intense fasting over anything but a very short period for the purpose of detoxing. On the contrary, they are more likely to issue serious warnings against the dangers of anorexia. In the modern canon, eating too little is as damaging as eating too much. 'Orthorexia' – eating the right things in the right quantities – is the ideal. Any deviation in either direction is denounced as medically dangerous. And it is taken for granted that medical criteria are the only ones that count.

An indecent excess of food and drink counts as one of the direst types of emergency that modern man can conceive of. In 2008, Alan Johnson, the British Secretary of State for Health, declared that Britain was in the grip of an obesity epidemic. 'In the UK two-thirds of adults and a third of children are already overweight or obese, and without action this could rise to almost nine in ten adults and two-thirds of children by 2050 . . . It was the scientists in their Foresight report who said that society is facing a public health problem that is comparable to climate change.'[67]

Since it is a firmly held orthodoxy in official circles that climate change is the single most serious problem facing mankind, we are to take it that fatness is an equally devastating threat. Leaving aside the absurd extrapolations from dubious statistics in the Foresight report, we may wonder exactly why we should take this epidemic so seriously. Because obesity threatens life expectancy? But life expectancy has continued to improve steadily while we have been getting steadily fatter. Because fat people are unhappier and feel worse than thin people? A questionable proposition on the evidence of one's own eyes and ears, and in any case the fatties still have the consolations of booze and grub, which on the non-medical pages of your newspaper are rated rather highly. Because their spiritual welfare is threatened by their obesity? No government minister would dare venture such a claim because government ministers don't do God. In any case, fat people have often been famous for their spirituality, for example, Thomas Aquinas and Søren Kierkegaard.

No, obesity is to be regarded as a menacing epidemic because and only because physical health and well-being are to be regarded not just as an end in themselves, but as the prime end of mankind. There is no ulterior motive, nothing beyond the imperative: thou shalt feel good about thy body.

Throughout the Christian era, doctors of the Church often doubled as medical doctors too, as did abbesses, such as the remarkable Hildegarde of Bingen. The medical advice they gave was sometimes rather sound by modern standards, sometimes eccentric or plain wrong. But when they talked about physical health in relation to fasting or anything else, its importance was secondary to spiritual welfare. They would have thought it ludicrous to place physical well-being, important though it was, at the summit of human endeavour, and so would the rabbis and imams who gave comparable advice to their congregations.

Our priorities are different. We take physical health desperately seriously. Sometimes one is tempted to think that it is the only thing we take seriously, because that is all we have. And in this ordering of priorities we can find two, and possibly only two, peoples in history who have thought and felt more or less the same as we do: the Greeks and the Romans.

It is no accident that the most enduring slogans for guidance on physical health, which, as we have seen, adorned the British version of Roman baths, should come from Latin and Greek: 'Mens sana in corpore sano'. A clean and healthy mind in a clean and healthy body. 'Meden agan'. Nothing in excess. 'Ariston men hudor'. Water is best. Such precepts of moderation and balance would be hard to extract from the Christian tradition, which often commends, by contrast, passionate and wholehearted commitment, devotion to excess and willingness not only to endure such sufferings as may come one's way in the line of duty but also actively to seek them out. We are instructed not simply to mourn and honour the sufferings of Jesus; we are to attempt, in our feeble way, to imitate them.

Such wilful going to meet suffering would strike the average Greek or Roman as slightly deranged behaviour. Naturally, it is one's duty to bear oneself bravely as a soldier and to endure the suffering of life without complaint. That stoical tradition long pre-dates the philosophical movement which we call Stoicism. But the idea that suffering has in itself a spiritual value which brings us closer to God – that is a thought which would strike the classical world as decidedly odd.

And so no fasting, or none really worth counting. *The Oxford Classical Dictionary* says bluntly that 'fasting (*nesteia*), in the sense of abstinence from all food for a stated time, such as a day, is very rare in classical religions, both Greek and Roman. There is, for example, no evidence whatever that anyone, priest or layman, was expected to come fasting to a sacral meal such as normally followed the killing of a victim.' Nothing then resembling a Eucharistic fast. There seem to have been a few atypical exceptions. The women conducting the rites of Demeter sometimes took no food. By contrast, the later mystery cults, which came from the East and became popular in Hellenistic times and under the Roman Empire, did demand ritual fasting. We shall have more to say later on about these Eastern cults and how sharply they differed from the established religions of Greece and Rome and what an important role they played in the transition to Christianity – a role which has often been underplayed, if not forcibly suppressed. But for the moment, let us stick to Greek and Roman religion in the strict sense.

Abstinence from food and drink for health reasons was common enough. Both Greece and Rome contained sworn vegetarians and food faddists of various kinds, for example those who forbade the eating of beans. Greek and Roman physicians from Hippocrates in the fifth century BC to Galen in the second century AD gave careful and detailed advice on how to follow a healthy and balanced diet. But by and large, fasting for spiritual reasons was alien to the classical world. As a regular discipline for sharpening the soul, it seems to have been virtually unknown.

The oil from the olive, the bread from the wheat, the wine from the vines – these were the gifts of the gods, of Demeter and Bacchus, which was only another way of saying the gifts of nature. It would be churlish to the point of sacrilege to refuse these gifts that lay ripening in the sun just beyond the garden wall. The sages of the Greek and Roman world sought out the orchard, not the desert. They would have recognized as a kindred soul the sight of Norman Douglas pottering up and down the terraces of Capri looking for the ripest figs. And they would have recognized too the north London housewife fingering the organic carrots in the farmers' market.

Who needed anything else, who needed anything more, especially when more seemed to mean less of the most precious delights of this life? If God's insistent demands included denying yourself the fruits that He had supposedly created, then was He really worth worshipping at all? We had no need of His help to resurrect the body. Was it really plausible that even if He did exist in some unknowable form, He actually cared about us or intervened on our behalf? These unsettling thoughts gathered pace as the nineteenth century wore on. But this was not the first time that men had thought these thoughts. So far we have been seeing how much our attitudes towards the flesh have in common with those of Athens and Rome in their heyday. Now we must compare our attitudes towards the spirit. We must turn from muscles to mindsets.

MIND

'God is dead.' It is a harsh and blunt sentence, and the crazy-brilliant philosopher meant it to be harsh and blunt. Friedrich Nietzsche wrote to shock. He hated to see the bland leading the blind. Which is why we remember what he said, even when we do not like it. But the bit after 'God is dead' is less well remembered. What Nietzsche went on to say was: 'But as the human race is constituted, there will perhaps be caves for millenniums yet, in which people will show his shadow.' Enlightened people would soon understand the uncomfortable truth, that God did not exist, but the great mass of stupid people would go on worshipping His flickering shadow, perhaps for thousands of years.

The metaphor of the cave-dweller watching the shadows cast on the wall is borrowed from the famous passage in Book VII of Plato's *Republic*, which describes ordinary people as living in caves of ignorance, bewitched by the flickering shadows cast by the fire of themselves and of the statues they have made to worship. Actually Nietzsche did not think much of Plato, still less of Plato's mentor Socrates.[1] He thought that philosophy started to go downhill when these two took control. But he was fond of the cave metaphor, as many other philosophers before and since Nietzsche have been fond. It is a consoling thought for philosophers that they alone understand the human condition.

All the same, the philosopher's position was still an exasperating one, because while he might have seen quite clearly and beyond a doubt that God did not exist, that there was no purpose, no deliberate design in the universe, only the necessities of nature, yet ordinary men and women would persist in these weak-minded illusions. 'For millenniums yet' they would go on believing in God and all the absurd legends and superstitions which He dragged in his wake.

Nietzsche was by no means the first to declare the indifference of the universe and the transience of man. The belief in divine purpose had received a severe blow half a century earlier. In his marvellous book *God's Funeral* (1999), A.N. Wilson describes the whole process from the first inklings to the final disillusionment. The first unmistakable clues came not from ourselves or our fellow mammals but from the rocks around us. A generation before Darwin, the palaeontologist Charles Lyell produced his *Principles of Geology* (1832–3). It was a crusher in every sense of the word. The fossils revealed in the epic upheavals and collapses of rock layers told a deeply unpalatable story: 'The inhabitants of the globe, like all other parts of it, are subject to change. It is not only the individual that perishes but whole species.' Tennyson read Lyell with mounting gloom and inserted into his long elegy *In Memoriam* the most brutal statement of Nature's indifference:

> From scarped cliff and quarried stone
> She cries, 'A thousand types are gone:
> I care for nothing, all shall go . . .'

In Tennyson's view, all the evidence pointed to the conclusion that Man was nothing but a fantasist,

> Who trusted God was love indeed
> And love Creation's final law,
> Though Nature, red in tooth and claw
> With ravine, shrieked against his creed.

This brilliant encapsulated statement of the facts was written at least ten years before the publication of Darwin's *Origin of Species*. It is still being echoed in books and on television one and a half centuries later by Darwin's most passionate devotee, Professor Richard Dawkins: 'The amount of suffering in the natural world is beyond all decent contemplation. During the minute that it takes me to say this, millions of animals are running for their lives, whimpering with fear. Thousands are dying from starvation or disease or feeling a parasite rasping away from within. For most animals the reality is struggling, suffering and death.'[2] Thomas Hobbes was right. Nasty, brutish and short – that's the state of nature for you.

All through the remaining years of the nineteenth century, intellectuals battled with the idea that man was a temporary resident in an unfeeling universe. Like Tennyson, the Prime Minister Arthur Balfour remained a believing and practising Christian, despite the grim picture he set out in his treatise *The Foundations of Belief* (1895), that Man's very existence was an accident, 'his story a brief and transitory episode in the life of one of the meanest of planets'. Man was destined to go down into the pit and all his thoughts would perish. Not the sort of upbeat message favoured by the Downing Street spin doctors of today.

Among intellectuals, and Balfour was an intellectual – our only twentieth-century prime minister to deserve that title – the tide of faith went out with startling speed, generating a vicious undertow that knocked the unwary off their feet. The melancholy long, withdrawing roar that Matthew Arnold heard on Dover Beach on his honeymoon in 1853 made even the devout shiver with apprehension. By 1910, Thomas Hardy felt able to pronounce the last rites in his extraordinary poem from which Wilson takes his title.

In that awkward, compelling way of his, Hardy describes a procession making its slow and painful way across a twilit plain. The mourners lament their folly in creating a God whom they could no longer keep alive. For two millennia we had believed, with varying degrees of certainty, that there was Someone watching over us, taking a personal interest in what we did or failed to do, forgiving our frailties which somehow made those frailties more glamorous although we pretended it didn't, lending purpose to our lives which did not end when we died because He still had plans for us although we were never quite as sure of those as we hoped. After we had gone wherever it was we went, He was still there to watch over the loved ones we had left behind, and so on for ever and ever. And now there was no one there. We were on our own. We did not come trailing clouds of glory from God who was our home. God had had a long funeral, but for huge numbers of us the funeral was now over.

Yet as Nietzsche had irritably prophesied, the whole rigmarole took a terrible long time to wind down. Unlike a travelling circus, the Big Top was not neatly dismantled and packed away overnight. The official guardians of the old faith refused to fold their tents and steal silently away. Hardy in his poem goes on to describe how, as the procession passes, it encounters bystanders in the background who will not accept that God really is dead. While the mourners wind on their way, they meet some people who claim to see upon the horizon 'a pale yet positive gleam low down behind', perhaps even a 'small light, swelling somewhat'. Hardy means here those revivals and revisions of the Christian faith which attempt to reach an accommodation with modernity. These watered-down versions of belief attempt to survive Darwin's hammer-blow by making their peace with natural science in general and evolutionary theory in particular.

Moreover, we have consoled ourselves with the thought that at least the morality that Christ taught us carries on regardless, as though its divine backing were still in force. We might be living in a post-Christian society, but at least it was a Christian post-Christian society. Our ideas of good and evil were still more or less the ones that Jesus taught us, and so our criteria for approval or disapproval continued to reflect those ideas. The ideals that seemed especially, in some cases uniquely, Christian continued to influence us, perhaps more than we knew, even if as usual we failed to live up to them:

loving-kindness, humility, chastity, contrition, forgiveness, indifference to material things. The Seven Deadly Sins might not provide an
exhaustive list of actions to be avoided, but they still had their uses.

Yet, as the pessimists had warned, this twilight could not last for
ever. Without being illuminated from above, this whole moral world
was bound to fade. Just as the lights had gone out on Christian
belief a century earlier, so the lights would dim on Christian values,
more slowly perhaps but nonetheless irreversibly. The Christian way
became a dim and shabby byway, followed only by those who were
themselves dim and shabby or those who took a perverse delight in
refusing to follow fashion.

Over the past few years something quite marked has happened. In
Britain at least, the old package has ceased to be available for a large
part of the population, like some obsolescent garments which can
only be found in small specialist shops. The well from which we
went on drawing our morals and our myths has finally run dry.
Millions of children in the new generation, those born at the turn of
the century, will grow up ignorant not merely of the basic Christian
doctrines but of the Christian stories and parables which illustrate
and enliven those doctrines. It is not simply that many children
already do not have a clue about the Incarnation or the Trinity, they
know nothing of Adam and Eve, or the Sermon on the Mount, or
Doubting Thomas. Even the basic story of the Nativity with all its
simple charm is fading. At Christmas 2007, it was widely reported
that only one in five schools was planning to stage a Nativity Play of
the traditional sort.[3] Instead, if schools put on a play at all around
Christmas, it would be a modern watered-down version with new
songs, new themes and new characters such as the Bossy King, the
Whoops-a-Daisy Angel and the Hoity-Toity Angel. The pretext
given by teachers for staging these cute little modern musicals in
preference to the traditional Nativity Play is that they do not wish to
offend the parents of the many non-Christian pupils in their classes.
Yet the leaders and congregations of most non-Christian faiths have
repeatedly said that they have no objection to the celebration of

Christmas and certainly not to Nativity Plays. Indeed, they would be surprised not to see such celebrations.

But we must note here an embarrassing, even shameful distinction. To put it bluntly, it is the poor who have been most brutally cut off from their religious heritage. That minority of children who attend fee-paying schools or church schools in nice areas are still taught the rudiments of the Christian faith. They grow up with some understanding of the spiritual history of their own country. But for the vast majority of children in poorer British families, many of whom would in a former generation have attended Sunday school or their local church, religion of any sort is a closed book.

There is a new inequality of ignorance creeping in across Europe. For in earlier times, the one sort of knowledge that did, on the whole, cross class boundaries was religious knowledge. Even the underclass, though wretched in material terms, was not totally cut off. In fact, universal church attendance was compulsory for centuries, and later on there were church schools and Sunday schools which the great majority of the poor did attend. But now paganism is most thoroughly entrenched among the industrial working class. For their teachers in state primary and comprehensive schools are, on average, the teachers most opposed to religion in any shape and the keenest to stamp out the last vestiges of religious myth and song from the school curriculum.

There is a deeper repugnance at work here. The only subject specifically prescribed in the 1944 Education Act is religious education. Yet a largely post-Christian teaching profession is unwilling to play any active part in propagating the Christian tradition. The kindly tolerance once extended by agnostics towards Christians and their myths and rituals has given way to a harsher intolerance and impatience. This new repugnance amounts to a kind of secular excommunication, in which practising Christians are no longer regarded as members of the congregation of modernity. They are written out of the script as weirdos and nutters, and many of the ills of society such as war and intolerance are attributed to their beliefs.

This anti-Christian repugnance is often expressed with astonishing violence. We shall examine it more closely later on. For the moment, we need only note it as a dramatic sign of how the terms of engagement have swung round. The loathing which once dared not speak its name is now the orthodoxy.

The question we are primarily concerned with here is: what has replaced the Christian world-view we knew and used to love and then could no longer believe in and grew ashamed of?

The answer to that question is a startling one, although perhaps it ought not to be, because when you come to dwell on what has happened, the outcome is logical enough. In fact, I don't think that we would have much difficulty in recognizing our whereabouts as Square One, if only we did not have this obsession that we are always heading into untrodden terrain. As a result, we are repeating ourselves without knowing it.[4]

For it is not simply our physical attitudes – towards the body, towards sex, towards eating and drinking – that have returned to the patterns of the Greeks and the Romans. Our mental attitudes have returned to Square One too, which is an even bigger surprise and, if we confronted it, would be an even sharper shock to our self-esteem, for we like to fancy that our ideas are all brilliant and new, that we have thought everything out for the first time. In this second part of our journey, we shall examine what goes on inside our heads, how we think about science and religion and superstition and conversation and politics and public life and art and nature. And we shall encounter similiarities with the attitudes of the Greeks and Romans which are even more striking than the ones we have already met in the bath, the gym, the bedroom and the kitchen.

V

SCIENCE

Back to Ionia

The cleverest boy at school was called Edward Hussey. He was streets ahead. The rest of us struggled to reach 60 per cent, 70 per cent if it was an easy paper. He never dipped below 90. Half an hour before the end of the allotted time, he would have put down his pen and be gazing straight ahead with his bright brown eyes, rather upright, hitching his gown over his bony shoulders for something to do. When we came to specialize, he won all the prizes for Greek and Latin one year, then to fill in time won all the prizes for history and mathematics the year after. At Oxford, his election to a fellowship at All Souls was a formality. We waited eagerly to see what he would do next.

I at least was taken aback when the first book he published was a decidedly slim volume on Greek philosophers, but not the Greek philosophers any of us had heard of such as Plato and Socrates. Edward's book was about the Presocratics, who preceded Socrates and the glory days of Athens and who perched, not in Athens or mainland Greece at all, but on various craggy Greek outposts on the coast of what is now Turkey. It seemed a perversely, inexplicably obscure choice of subject. Only now, forty years later, have I come to realize that the choice was just as brilliant as everything else that came out of Edward's head.

If you climb to the top tier of the amphitheatre, you can see the whole ancient city of Miletus spread out below you: the senate, the marketplace, the bath, the temple, and beyond them the delta of the River Maeander and the island of Lade and the wine-dark sea. But the buildings that you are seeing are the buildings of Roman Miletus – a decent place in its time, but nothing remarkable as Roman cities go. Of the far greater Greek Miletus that preceded it, you can see virtually nothing, except the low scrubby hills where it used to be.[1] For the old Greek city was burned to the ground by the Persians on the rampage after their thumping victory at the Battle of Lade in 494 BC. Greek Miletus was so thoroughly torched that even today archaeologists are not exactly sure where its boundaries lay. For most of the twentieth century, the Germans who were excavating the site scrabbled through olive groves and thorn bushes and rushy swamps looking for clues to the whereabouts of the intellectual centre of its time. Only in 1989 did they discover on the low eminence of Zeytintepe ('Olive Grove'), half a mile or so from the Roman town, the remains of the sacred precinct of Aphrodite. The archaeologists identified the place from Idyll XXVIII of Theocritus, where the poet looks forward to seeing this delightful spot, 'fresh and green among the tall soft reeds', as he sets sail from his native Syracuse to visit his friends in 'Miletus the delectable', the doctor Nicias and his wife to whom he will present the ivory distaff which accompanies the poem. That is pretty much all that was left: a few stones from the temple's foundations, some bits of pottery with 'APH' on them, and a couple of lines in a poem. All that was left of the city that the historian Herodotus describes as 'in full bloom and the glory of Ionia' in 500 BC, before the Persians came. They destroyed the sacred precinct of Aphrodite as thoroughly as the rest of the city. And what little remained was speedily hacked off and carried away by the locals for their own dwellings. The rest of the city was built anew by the world's first named town planner, Hippodamus, on the plain over to the north and east on a gridiron pattern – the first ever town planned on Manhattan lines. But Aphrodite's temple was rebuilt where it stood, among the tall soft reeds. And that was where, two centuries later, Theocritus came to know and love it.

As for the Maeander, which has given its name to a mazy motion, we have seen how the riverbed silted up over the years, so that by the fourth century AD Lade was no longer an island but a pimple in the middle distance and the coastline had advanced beyond the Miletus promontory, and those succulent grey mullet which greedy Archestratus came all the way to Miletus to buy had swum far away.

In its heyday, Miletus was the greatest city on the whole coast, greater even than Ephesus which a century or two later was said to be the greatest city in the known world. Miletus was a city of colonial settlers, refugees from mainland Greece. In the ninth century BC, invaders from the north, the Dorians, had swept down into ancient Ionia and the nimbler inhabitants had fled east across the Aegean to the coast of Asia Minor. Just as the exact location of Greek Miletus is still uncertain, so nobody is sure whereabouts in Greece the original Ionia was exactly, perhaps in Attica, possibly even in the Athens region. The origins of the Ionians were eclipsed by the splendour of the colonies that they established all along the coast of what is now western Turkey. Backed by the irresistible Milesian navy, the colonials in turn established more colonies all along the coasts and islands of the eastern Mediterranean, up to ninety of them according to some estimates. We may think of these secondary colonies as comparable in their effect to the opening up of the Midwest and far West by the citizens of the original thirteen British colonies in North America, adding to their wealth and power and enabling the new nation to overtake the mother country.

There was a physical energy and a mental freedom about the New Ionians. Their fizz dazzled old Greece, much as New York came to dazzle old Europe. The two clusters of Greeks remained strongly linked by race and language. All that distinguished the Ionians from other Greeks was that they spoke their own dialect, Ionic. After the Persians had conquered Ionia and suppressed the Ionian revolt with such brutality, a play entitled *The Fall of Miletus* was performed in Athens. The entire audience burst into tears and the playwright was fined 1,000 drachmae for making trouble. It was heart-rending to see the flower of Greek civilization cut down.

The achievements of the Ionians were already glorious, apart from the mere expansion of their political and military power. Homer himself is thought to have come from somewhere along that coast, Smyrna according to some, the island of Chios according to others. Those who believe that 'Homer' was in fact two or more poets also tend to believe that these multiple bards were Ionians of some description. But it is the explosion of scientific and philosophical thought two centuries later that startled the whole of ancient Greece as much as it has startled the most daring minds of our own time. Plato and Aristotle were just as impressed by the sheer originality, the dauntless open-mindedness of their predecessors as were Friedrich Nietzsche and Karl Popper 2,000 years later. There has been nothing like the Presocratics before or since. There was an uninhibited brio about them. '*Unbefangenheit*', was Nietzsche's word for them – literally

'uncaughtness', or dispassion, lack of prejudice, open-mindedness –
Gefängis means prison. All that we have left of most of them is a collection of quotations in other men's works, sometimes only a few
sentences. Their entire surviving works were first collected in a single
volume by two German scholars, H. Diels and W. Kranz, *Die
Fragmente der Vorsokratiker* (1903); these texts are easy to get hold of
today in a Penguin classic, *The First Philosophers*. Upon these fragments
and some later gossip about their lives and views we remain reliant.
Since it is often so difficult to establish their precise drift from these
brief, often cryptic, sometimes poetic fragments (for the Presocratics
were often poets as well as philosophers), it is harder still to estimate
exactly how far they influenced later philosophers and scientists and
how often they anticipate or foreshadow modern discoveries.[2]

What earns them their entry ticket is that open-mindedness,
their readiness to observe, to argue, to draw conclusions and offer
theories, and then to draw better conclusions and theories from
fresh arguments and fresh observations. They were rational, they
were empirical. Though they did not possess microscopes or computers or even telescopes, in a word, they were scientists. I will say
something about the six Presocratics whose fame has endured best:
Thales, Anaximander, Xenophanes, Anaxagoras, Democritus and
Heraclitus.

Thales of Miletus was regarded by Aristotle as the pioneer of natural philosophy and has been so regarded ever since. He also had a
remarkable reputation for practical expertise: he was a technocrat as
well as a philosopher. He is said to have predicted the solar eclipse of
585 BC, to have discovered the axiom that a triangle inscribed inside
a circle must be a right-angled triangle if one of its sides is the
diameter of the circle, and to have deduced a connection between
the Nile floods and the Etesian winds. He was said also to have
diverted the course of the River Halys to allow Croesus' army to
cross. When someone taunted him that, for all his brains, he was still
a poor man, he responded by getting control of all the olive presses
in Miletus, having made astronomical calculations that next year's

harvest would be a bumper one – the first example of a futures spec-
ulator and weather forecaster combined. He also calculated the
height of the Pyramids by measuring their shadow. As a political
guru, he pointed out to the citizens of the other Ionian cities that if
they were to have any hope of resisting the Persians they ought to
establish a single political assembly at their most centrally situated city
which was Teos – advice which the cities, proud of their traditions of
independence and self-government, paid no attention to.

In natural philosophy, he was famous for two theses: 'The magnet
has a soul' and 'Everything is water'. At first sight, these are rather
baffling axioms. Yet Professor Jonathan Barnes argues that between
them they mark the beginnings of Western science.[3] To put it simply,
what Thales means by the soul (*psyche*) is what we might call an 'ani-
mator' or a 'natural force'. Thales' magnet is the ancient equivalent
of the clockwork animals of the seventeenth century and of our
modern chess-playing computers. We know that they are not alive in
the sense that a rabbit is alive, but how are we to describe their self-
locomotion? The fact that an inorganic material object can possess a
force of its own compels us to look at the universe in a new way. The
claim that everything is water is a more fertile conjecture still. This
is the beginning of what is technically known as 'material monism',
the belief that the universe is all made of one stuff, the forerunner of
all those subsequent theories of atomism which the later Presocratics
in particular were to refine.

This strictly chemical analysis represents an even profounder break
with the past. For there are no gods in it. The composition of the
world is for Thales a strictly material this-worldly matter. Heavenly
beings do not intervene, nor is any part of it to be worshipped or
deified. His explanation is also oriented towards what was to prove
one of the abiding preoccupations of the Presocratics: how to
explain change. Of all the common constituents of the world, water
is not only one of the most prominent, it is also visibly and constantly in the process of changing between gaseous, liquid and solid
states. If you start from the assumption that water is the universal

substance, you are well on the way to seeing that universe as a process rather than an object – a leap which the late Presocratics were not slow to make.

Thales never wrote any treatise. But his fellow Milesian and younger contemporary, Anaximander of Miletus, was described as 'the first Greek whom we know to have produced a written account *Concerning Nature*', though its text has not survived. Karl Popper, the great twentieth-century philosopher of science, asserts that 'for Anaximander our own world, our own cosmic edifice, was only one of an infinity of worlds – an infinity without bounds in space and time. The system of worlds was eternal and so was space and time.'[4] Popper will not have it that, because many of Anaximander's theories, like other Presocratic theories, are in fact false, they cannot be described as scientific. On the contrary, he sees 'the most perfect possible continuity of thought between their theories and the later developments in physics'. They are the forerunners of Copernicus, Kepler and Galileo.

Anaximander has also been hailed as the first Darwinian. He argued that in the beginning men had to be born from creatures of a different sort. For other animals quickly manage to feed themselves but humans require a long period of nursing, and had their young been as they are now, they would never have survived.[5] Men's first parents were fish or fish-like creatures who retained their human off-spring in their bellies until they were able to fend for themselves. Nor were Anaximander's speculations confined to human beings: 'Anaximander says that the first animals were born in the moisture, surrounded by prickly barks; and that as they reached maturity they moved out on to the drier part where their bark split and they survived in a different form for a brief while.'[6]

Here we have, in embryo, evolution and the survival of the fittest. Animal species are not immutably fixed, and their development (metabiosis) is determined by the environment. Human beings are certainly not a distinct species created by God. They are part of nature. Of course, the exact process by which an animal species may metamorphose over countless generations is a long way from Anaximander's ken. But the idea of there being such a process is already lodged in the Presocratic mind.

Another account, given much later in the first century BC by the historian Diodorus Siculus, is almost certainly drawn from a sixth-century source. It carries the process on beyond the period of the evolution of *Homo sapiens* into our prehistory, and along lines which are still familiar to us. Animals developed out of the swamp and gradually evolved, some into winged creatures, some into swimmers, some into land mammals. Soon each kind of living thing was produced by sexual intercourse.

> Then the earth first of all became more firm as the fire from the sun shone down on it; and then, when the warmth caused the surface to rise as if by leavening, some portions of moisture gathered together in many places on the surface and swelled up. In these swellings there formed putrid substances enclosed in fine membranes, as is still observed to happen in swamps and marshy places wherever the ground has been chilled and the air with a rapid change of temperature suddenly becomes blazing hot. These parcels of moisture, then, were impregnated with life by the heat in the way described, and while this went on they absorbed nourishment in the night-time directly from the moisture that descended from the surrounding air, while by day they were made more solid by the heat. Finally, as the embryos attained their full growth, the membranes, shrivelled by heat, burst open, and there came forth animal forms of every kind . . .

Such is the account we receive of the first creation of everything, and they say that the first men to come into existence lived an unsettled and brutish life, going out to forage in ones and twos and eating the most agreeable of the plants and of the wild fruits. Attacks by wild beasts made them learn from expediency and come to one another's aid, and as they repeatedly gathered together from fear, they gradually came to know each other's features. Slowly they made articulate the utterances of their tongues, which at first were indistinct and unclear, and by making conventions among themselves about each object they taught themselves to use words to refer to everything. And because such groups formed all over the inhabited earth, not all men had the same language, because each group fixed its words arbitrarily. This is the reason why there are now all sorts of different languages, the first groups to form being the ancestors of all the different races of men.

Since no useful discoveries had yet been made, the first men had a hard life, without clothes or the use of fire or a settled habitation, and with no idea at all of the cultivation of plants for food.[7]

Thus it is physical processes and pressures that produce evolutionary mutations, and environmental hardships and necessities that generate social development – very much as we think today. This account, like that of Anaximander, describes the earth as drying out. Our next Presocratic, Xenophanes of Colophon, took a different view. Colophon was an inland city, just north of Ephesus and 50 or 60 miles north of Miletus. The city's territory extended eastward over the plain, good country for cavalry, and the city was famous for its horses. The sight of the Colophon cavalry coming over the hill was enough to settle any doubtful battle: hence the phrase, 'to put the colophon on it', as a clincher. This may be the origin of the word 'colophon' to describe the end-plate to a book (where publishers used to put the details they now put on the title-page), although *colophon* means 'summit' in Greek anyway and there is no need to bring on the cavalry to explain the derivation. The city was eventually spoilt by affluence. As many as a thousand of its citizens used to swan around the marketplace drenched in perfume and wearing purple robes that were worth their weight in silver. Colophon was destroyed in 299 BC by the tyrant Lysimachus and its population transferred to the great new city of Ephesus which he was founding. Of the old city of Colophon, nothing much is left.[8]

In fact pretty much all that survives of Colophon are the fragments of Xenophanes (580–470 BC), personally the most alluring of the Presocratics and most unflinching reason-addict of them all. He was a poet and satirist, he travelled widely, and clearly knew a lot about and was highly critical of his predecessors and contemporaries. Because he was so well read, there has been a tendency to write him down as an unoriginal mind. But the words attributed to him are so clear, so sweepingly confident and so sharp that his mind sounds unmistakably original to me.

Xenophanes had a theory of evolution too, which is just as remarkable as Anaximander's, though opposite in its prime assumption, viz. that the planet is getting wetter rather than drying up – the climate change debate already flourishing in the sixth century BC and on a rather grander scale than today. And he derives his theory from the kind of evidence that we think of as coming to scientific prominence only in the nineteenth century AD: shells and the imprints of fossils found in the mud, often amongst mountains miles from the sea.[9]

But what Xenophanes had to say about religion was more startling still:

But mortal men imagine that gods are begotten, and that they have human dress and speech and shape.

If oxen or horses or lions had hands to draw with and to make works of art as men do, then horses would draw the forms of gods like horses, oxen like oxen, and they would make their gods' bodies similar to the bodily shape that they themselves each had.

The Ethiopians say their gods are snub-nosed and black-skinned, the Thracians that they are blue-eyed and red-headed.[10]

In short, we invent our gods and make them up to suit our self-image. For Xenophanes, there is but one god, and he is 'in no way like mortal creatures either in bodily form or in the thought of his mind'. His god is entirely removed from us, inaccessible. And human beings have no more access to the truth than they have to God. In fact, Xenophanes' scepticism about whether we can ever attain certain knowledge is even more radical than his scepticism about the gods we invent for ourselves. All our so-called knowledge is a matter of conjections and refutations, as Popper argues in the introduction to his book of that title. As Xenophanes put it in verse:

> The gods did not reveal from the beginning,
> All things to us; but in the course of time,
> Through seeking, men find that which is the better.
> But as for certain truth, no man has known it, nor will he
>   know it; neither of the gods, nor yet of all the things of
>   which I speak. And even if by chance he were to utter
>   the final truth, he would himself not know it;
> For all is but a woven web of guesses.[11]

Xenophanes says in another fragment: 'These things, let us suppose, are like the truth [The Greek word is *eoikota*, "truth-like". Our nearest English equivalent is the rare word "verisimilar", which it would be a good idea to revive].'

Yet modern philosophers go on looking for bullet-proof sources of certain knowledge. Here in Xenophanes, two and a half millennia ago, we find the clear definition of the right way to go about things: to be sceptical about the possibility of attaining anything resembling certainty, but to be no less energetic and attentive to all the evidence that comes to hand.

Where Xenophanes is lucid and biting, Anaxagoras (500–428 BC) is a trickier thinker to get the hang of. He came from the small Ionian city of Clazomenae, 30 miles north of Colophon. He was 80 years younger than Xenophanes and so was born under Persian rule, which is presumably why he came to Athens and lived there for the next fifty years or more, becoming an intimate friend of Pericles. It was in Athens towards the end of his stay, perhaps in 430 BC, not in his native Ionia, that he was prosecuted for impiety (and perhaps also because of his friendship with Pericles). One of the grounds of the charge was that he had stated the sun to be a large rock glowing with heat. Pericles seems to have intervened to save him from a potential death sentence. And he then retired to the city of Lampsacus in the Dardanelles, where he died.

We do not need to delve too deep into the cosmology that Anaxagoras elaborated. For our present purposes, all we need to say is that he took several steps further towards a fully fledged system to explain the physical structure and development of the universe: the ultimate constituents of the world 'were unlimited both in number and in smallness – even smallness turns out to be unlimited'; nothing in the world is freshly created; new things are really rearrangements of the ultimate unchanging constituents of things; the deity who controls everything is quite separate from the cosmos, and this supreme power goes by the name of 'Mind' or 'nous'.[12]

It follows that these infinitely small components of the universe must be too tiny for us to observe. This microscopic structure of matter means that we have no access to the motions of the ultimate and determining mites that make up the universe.[13]

It was for the next generation of Presocratics to develop a fully worked out theory of atoms. Actually we have ceased to be strictly accurate in describing them as Presocratic, since the most prominent of them, Democritus of Abdera, was born at the same time as Socrates. Abdera was also the birthplace of Leucippus, the master of Democritus, of whom little is known except that he taught his pupil the elements of atomism. Abdera is a dim town on the northern shores of the Aegean, founded by refugees from old Ionia, like Elea in southern Italy – both cities being known for nothing except their philosophers.

What was new in the doctrine of Leucippus was not so much the atoms themselves. The 'atomon', literally 'not-cut thing', was indivisible and imperishable and uncreated – something like this as the ultimate constituent of matter had been suggested by other philosophers like Parmenides of Elea. What Democritus/Leucippus provided an answer to was: what separated these ultimate tiny bits from one another? The void was their answer. The two men of Abdera have between them worked out for the first time the idea of purely passive empty space. These atoms were unlimited in number, unchanging in shape, size and internal structure, and they moved for ever in a limitless void. How they came together, swarming and linking to form what we now call molecules, need not detain us.

What does need to be mentioned, though, is the consequence of this doctrine. For what the atomists had done was to remove everything 'mental' from the list of ultimate constituents. They could have said that each atom was or had a mind, something like Leibniz's 'windowless monads'. But they didn't – quite rightly, because if the atoms had been 'mentalized', it is hard to see how they could have remained unchanging. So atoms, space – that's all there was. Which leads pretty inexorably to the conclusion that what we call consciousness and perception must be secondary phenomena, somehow thrown off by the incessant rearrangements of the mindless atoms.[14]

The last representative of the Milesian tradition was, therefore, the first avowed materialist.

There remains one final philosopher, perhaps the best known to posterity. Certainly the two most famous sayings of Heraclitus of Ephesus have lasted into our own time: 'Everything flows, nothing stays still' and 'No man can step into the same river twice'. Aristotle tells us that the doctrine of Heraclitus was what we would naturally take it to be, 'that everything is in a state of becoming and flux, and that nothing has any firm existence, with the sole exception of one persisting thing beneath the changes'. Some modern scholars have argued that Heraclitus cannot have meant anything nearly so drastic and unsettling. But as Karl Popper fiercely counter-argues, if this theory was only 'a post-Heraclitean exaggeration',[15] why did Aristotle (and Plato too) think it wasn't? And if it wasn't Heraclitus who invented the flux theory, who was the unsung genius who did think of it?

The logical and sensible conclusion is to accept that Heraclitus was indeed that genius who first saw that:

> Everything is in flux and nothing is at rest. Everything is in flux, even the beams, the timber, the building material of which the world is made: earth and rocks, or the bronze of a cauldron – they are all in flux. The beams are rotting, the earth is washed away and blown away, the very rocks split and wither, the bronze cauldron turns into green patina or verdigris . . . Thus there are no solid bodies. Things are not really things, they are processes.[16]

Even those readers who know as little physics as I do must be able to see how the Presocratics bring us up to the threshold of modern physics, biology and philosophy. Their open-mindedness, their daring, their readiness to contemplate the most improbable possibility if it seemed likely to lead them closer to the truth – all this came from an attitude to life which was not restricted to science and philosophy but spilled over into the arts and into politics – the politics of the Great Generation of Athens and its epitome, Pericles. In the first volume of *The Open Society and its Enemies* (1945), Karl Popper invites us to listen first to the voice of Democritus and then to the voice of Pericles in his famous funeral oration, as relayed by Thucydides, the first great historian.

Democritus lived to the age of 90 or even 100, and achieved huge renown. In his lifetime he was known as 'Sophia' – 'Brains'. Posterity called him 'the laughing philosopher' – he wrote an essay on cheerfulness, as well as treatises on most branches of science and philosophy. A few fragments of his remarks on politics survive too:

> Not out of fear but out of a feeling of what is right should we abstain from doing wrong . . . Virtue is based, most of all, upon respecting the other man . . . Every man is a little world of his own . . . To be good means to do no wrong; and also, not to want to do wrong . . . it is good deeds, not words, that count . . . The

poverty of a democracy is better than the prosperity which allegedly goes with aristocracy or monarchy. Just as liberty is better than slavery . . . The wise man belongs to all countries, for the home of a great soul is the whole world.[17]

From these stray remarks you can sense the liberal temper of Democritus' mind, the mind of a true Ionian. We must remember that, after the suppression of the Ionian revolt, the cream of that coast went into a sort of double exile, back to the Greek mainland from which their ancestors had fled several centuries earlier. For sheer talent, there was probably never such a forced migration until the diaspora of those Jewish scientists and artists who managed to escape Hitler to end up in Cambridge or California. We have already encountered Democritus from Abdera, but there was also his fellow citizen Protagoras; in Athens too was Anaxagoras of Clazomenae who was Pericles' friend and was prosecuted on that absurd charge about the sun. There was Herodotus from Halicarnassus, further down the Turkish coast, the present-day port of Bodrum, an unreliable historian perhaps but an enthusiast for everything that Athens meant. It is to an audience of such open minds and liberal hearts that Pericles addressed what remains the most revered speech in human history, eclipsing in moral scope even Lincoln's Gettysburg Address. I believe that it reads even better if, instead of regarding it as the blueprint for future democracies, we look on it as the culmination of the Ionian tradition.

Our political system does not compete with institutions which are elsewhere in force. We do not copy our neighbours, but try to be an example. Our administration favours the many instead of the few: this is why it is called a democracy. The laws afford equal justice to all alike in their private disputes, but we do not ignore the claims of excellence. When a citizen distinguishes himself, then he will be called to serve the state, in preference to others, not as a matter of privilege, but as a reward of merit; and poverty is no bar . . . The freedom we enjoy extends also to ordinary life; we are not suspicious of one another, and do not nag our neighbour if he chooses to go his own way . . . But this freedom does not make us lawless. We are taught to respect the magistrates and the laws, and never to forget that we must protect the injured. And we are also taught to observe those unwritten laws whose sanction lies only in the universal feeling of what is right . . .

Our city is thrown open to the world; we never expel a foreigner . . . We are free to live exactly as we please, and yet we are always ready to face any danger . . . We love beauty without indulging in fancies, and although we try to improve our intellect, this does not weaken our will . . . To admit one's poverty is no disgrace with us; but we consider it disgraceful not to make an effort to avoid it. An Athenian citizen does not neglect public affairs when attending to his private business . . . We consider a man who takes no interest in the state not as harmless, but as useless; and *although only a few may originate a policy, we are all able to judge it.* We do not look upon discussion as a stumbling-block in the way of political action, but as an indispensable preliminary to acting wisely . . . We believe that happiness is the fruit of freedom and freedom that of valour, and we do not shrink from the dangers of war . . . To sum up, I claim that Athens is the School of Hellas, and that the individual Athenian grows up to develop a happy versatility, a readiness for emergencies, and self-reliance.[18]

It has taken us two millennia and more to recapture the importance of those words, just as it has taken us the same length of time to recapture the spirit of scientific enquiry which animated the first philosophers.

The Shutters Come Down

But even as Ionian thought reaches its high noon, the first shadows begin to fall. The open-mindedness begins to be clouded by dogma and political persecution. It is as though the most precious qualities of Ionian civilization do not travel well. The forced migrations from Asia Minor back to mainland Greece and Sicily expose Ionian science to suspicion and public hostility. We have already seen how, even in the heyday of Pericles, his protégé Anaxagoras was prosecuted partly for making the impious assertion, on the basis of a meteorite which had come to earth at Aegospotami in 467 BC, that the sun was merely a lump of hot rock. This was just as significant a prosecution as the trial of Galileo for asserting that the earth went round the sun. Yet it has not achieved such resonance in our minds, perhaps because it does not fit in with our general open-minded image of Greek thought.

Yet such a repressive, controlling attitude towards scientific enquiry was scarcely a novelty. The mathematician and religious thinker Pythagoras emigrated from his native Samos to Crotona on the heel of the Italian mainland in about 531 BC. There, long before the meteorite fell on Aegospotami, he established a kind of religious society in which the words of the master had absolute authority and free enquiry on fundamental questions was forbidden. This did not apparently prevent Pythagoras and his disciples from achieving advances in arithmetic, music and geometry, most famously the theorem attributed to him by Euclid. Eventually the school of Pythagoras became so unpopular that it was broken up and its members were killed or exiled (around 450 BC). While it had existed, its members had been bound not to reveal, or even to write down, the doctrines of their master – rules characteristic of a closed religious brotherhood, and the very opposite of a scientific tradition, for which publication and public dialogue are the breath of life. The evidence of what the Pythagoreans actually believed is scanty and derived mostly from late and unreliable sources, but what does seem to be the core of their doctrine is that the soul is a unity which is immune and immortal and lives through successive incarnations in human bodies or other animals and plants. It can escape from these various material tombs only by keeping itself pure from the pollution of the bodily passions and so rising to its true godlike state. The origins of this doctrine seem to be alien to anything in Greek tradition and are thought to have come from the shamans of the tribes on the steppes of Asia.

Several consequences follow from this belief. First, an ascetic lifestyle becomes the logical way to achieve the liberation of the soul. The Pythagoreans are thought to have been strict vegetarians, or at least to have abstained from taking animal, or even vegetable, life – presumably because one might be murdering a soul, though there are difficulties with this logic, if the soul is immortal. At any rate, the followers of Pythagoras are the advance guard for Christian fasting and asceticism.

At the same time, Pythagoras' doctrine of the soul reinserts a divine element into the material body. There is no question of the universe all being made of a single substance. On the contrary, the universe is to be seen as profoundly dual: matter and soul are not only distinct, the one perishable, the other immortal, but the immortal part is imprisoned within the perishable and irredeemably at odds with its polluting urges. The line of descent from the Pythagorean through Platonism and Neoplatonism to St Augustine and Christian thought is unmistakable. We are a long way from Ionia now.

Precisely how the doctrine of the soul was to evolve we can leave on one side, for the moment at least. Our concern here is: what follows from this doctrine for moral and political teaching in the secular world? Clearly the purifying of the soul must be the first concern for each of us. Nothing else can matter nearly as much, and so any measures which can help us to achieve this blessed state are fully justified, even if (or particularly if) they interfere with our liberties and leisure. The state has every right to interfere in our lives to help us along the right path. Indeed, it would be neglecting its duty if it did not do everything possible to guide us, just as the all-wise, all-seeing Guardians are to do in Plato's *Republic*. We are not to be left to our own devices and desires, for we should almost certainly be led astray. This view takes on a grimmer intensity in what Plato clearly intends to be his principal intellectual legacy, *The Laws*. There he states that everyone should follow his leader at all times and be taught never to dream of acting independently.[19]

Plato's defenders have argued that he was primarily thinking of the requirements for training soldiers. But Plato states clearly that these rules are to be applied in peacetime too, and in childhood; military training is not the exception; on the contrary, it is to provide the pattern for civilian life. Now because Plato is the starting-point of the philosophy curriculum, the father of Western philosophy if you like, his interpreters have gamely struggled to reconcile his stern totalitarian view with Christian and humanitarian values. Sir Ernest Barker in *Greek Political Theory* (1918) speaks of Plato seeking 'to replace selfishness and civil discord by harmony' and 'restoring the old harmony of the interests of the state to the individual'. But, as Barker admits elsewhere, this is to be achieved by suppressing the individual and subordinating all his interests to the interests of the state, in other words, by totalitarian methods. The truth is that Plato is an extremely dangerous guide.[20]

The perils of taking him too literally are most notorious in his treatment of Socrates, at once his hero and his nagging conscience. Almost all we know of Socrates comes through Plato, and it is impossible to estimate how much our view is distorted by this. What we can at least see for sure is that the two men are temperamental opposites: Socrates questioning, sceptical, distrustful of authority; Plato obsessed with the search for certainty and authority. The dialogues through which we see this extraordinary interplay leave us with a trail of unanswered, perhaps unanswerable questions, not least the question of what Socrates was actually put on trial for. We know it was for leading young men astray, but astray in which direction? We do know that Socrates' associates included the leadership of the Thirty Tyrants who overthrew Athenian democracy, including the irresistible Alcibiades and Plato's uncles, the ruthless Critias who led the junta and Charmides who became his lieutenant. Some claim that Socrates was a friendly critic of Athenian democracy, one who was trying at the same time to point out the defects of her existing institutions and to persuade the anti-democrats to understand the superiority of democratic dialogue. This may well be so, but seen through Plato's lens it is hard to be sure of exactly what we are seeing.

But whatever Socrates was or was not teaching young men – and whole volumes have been devoted to this question – what is clear is that his being put on trial for teaching philosophical or political doctrines was a sign that the closed-minded tendency in Athenian politics was at that moment dominant. Socrates had clearly committed some sort of thought crime, even if we cannot be entirely certain what sort.

In the Christian era too, there were periods when the closed-minded tendency was rampant – in the Spain of the Inquisition, for example, or the New England of the Puritan witch-hunters, or, in the political sphere, in the United States of the McCarthy period. In all such environments, we should note the sincere intense anxiety of the persecutors about the spiritual welfare of those they are persecuting. The Inquisitors would genuinely welcome an act of repentance; they have no itch to inflict punishment for its own sake, but only as a spur to contrition and example to others who might be enticed into heretical ways. But nobody who reads the Gospels with even the most negligent eye can be left in much doubt that such methods are far removed from the intention of Jesus, and of St Paul. We find no suggestion there that the state should control the hearts and minds of its citizens; Caesar is to have control only over the things that are Caesar's. The life of the heart and mind is free, answerable only to God. The presumption of free will is essential to Christianity as to the other great monotheistic religions.

But before the Christian era has even begun, we have already encountered the clash of mental temperaments which inspired Popper's famous distinction between the open and the closed society. On one side, he identifies the sceptical, open-minded, tolerant mindset which regards the search for certainty and absolute truth as misguided. On the other, he puts the dogmatic mindset which insists that we can have access to absolute truth, though it may be hidden either by deliberate human conspiracy or by impersonal forces, and that once we have uncovered that truth, its imperatives must be enforced. The sceptics range from Xenophanes and Socrates, through Montaigne and Erasmus to Russell and Popper himself; the truth-hunters begin with Pythagoras and Plato and end with Hegel and Marx, not to mention Lenin and Mao.

There is no simple progression over the past two millennia from closed to open (or indeed from open to closed). The two mindsets come and go throughout history, now one dominant, now the other. At memorable moments the two tendencies clash, as they did in fifth-century Athens. The open minds – Pericles, Socrates, Anaxagoras – came into conflict with their younger contemporaries who were to become the Thirty Tyrants – Critias and Charmides with Plato egging them on. These in their turn were defeated in battle and killed by Thrasybulus and the younger democrats. In the Christian era, the same culture that bred the Inquisition bred also the liberals of Renaissance culture, such as Erasmus and Montaigne. In Sir Thomas More, the two cultures mingle to produce an extraordinary combination of merciless persecutor and dauntless defender of freedom of conscience.

Nor is it the case that natural scientists are all on the side of scepticism, while clerics are all dogmatists. The search for absolute certainty has its inherent pitfalls, into which the most brilliant minds may fall, intoxicated by their discoveries. Scientists deny hotly that they too are vulnerable to the illusion of manifest truth, and that they inherit this illusion from the fathers of modern science, Bacon and Descartes, who both started out by doubting everything in order to end up with unshakeable, self-evident truths. In practice, though, we are always coming across scientists who are reluctant to think of their mental furniture as in any way provisional and of the accepted body of scientific knowledge as perpetually subject to falsification.

That body of knowledge has come to underpin a new secularist orthodoxy. This orthodoxy is as armoured with certainty as any of the old God-centred orthodoxies were in their heyday. The enormous practical achievements spanned by science and technology bring with them boundless prestige and unanswerable intellectual mastery. They also bring an ever-growing self-confidence, which now and then swells into a dogmatic and domineering intolerance.

It is only in the past ten years that we have witnessed a phenomenon not seen since the early centuries of the Roman Empire: a ferocious attack on God, not merely on the failings and fallacies of His priests and churches (all that was going on for large parts of the Middle Ages and the eighteenth century too) but on the idea of religious belief itself in any shape or form. Gone are the tact and respectful tiptoeing round the subject of old-style agnostics and atheists. It is only in our own time that we have seen the appearance on the scene of the anti-God-botherers.

VI

RELIGION
The Anti-God-Botherers

Nothing has been more startling in public debate at the start of the twenty-first century than the appearance on the scene of militant, proselytizing atheism as a force to be reckoned with. Religion, it was generally assumed, was quietly withering under the relentless erosion of science in general and evolutionary theory in particular, and interest in religious argument, whether pro or anti, was withering with it. Nobody, I think, prophesied the march of the anti-God-botherers. Certainly no publisher would have foreseen the huge and ongoing sales of such books as *The God Delusion* (2006), by Richard Dawkins, the geneticist and until recently Professor for the

Public Understanding of Science at Oxford, or *God Is Not Great* (2007) by Christopher Hitchens, the polemical essayist and former believer in the infallibility of Leon Trotsky. Philosophers too have rushed into the fray: the prolific A.C. Grayling and Daniel C. Dennett being well to the fore with their assault weapons, *Against All Gods* (2007) and *Breaking the Spell* (2007).

What explains atheism's sudden rise to the top of the charts, a phenomenon not seen since the time of Hume and Voltaire – indeed not even then, since the eighteenth-century sceptics had to cloak their core of disbelief under a non-specific sort of deism? Like all intellectual enthusiasms, the new atheism has taken on the character of a party or faction. Its *prominenti* cling together like footballers going into a huddle before the game. *The God Delusion* is heartily endorsed by famous writers such as Claire Tomalin and Ian McEwan and by Nobel Laureates such as Steven Weinberg and James Watson. Dennett, Grayling and Dawkins serve up puffs for *God Is Not Great*. And like most factions, this one likes to stick out its chest and proclaim that it can take on all-comers. Dawkins and Dennett suggest, half in jest, that their team should call themselves 'The Brights', which is going too far for Hitchens, who calls this 'a cringe-making proposal'.[1]

One of Dawkins's consciousness-raisers is 'atheist pride'. 'Being an atheist,' he says, 'is nothing to be apologetic about. On the contrary, it is something to be proud of, standing tall to face the far horizon, for atheism nearly always indicates a healthy independence of mind and, indeed, a healthy mind.'[2] The precedent of Gay Pride seems particularly auspicious to him: 'A good first step would be to build up a critical mass of those willing to "come out", thereby encouraging others to do so.'[3] It is the posture of humble submission common to most religions, especially to Abrahamic monotheisms, that Hitchens finds especially obnoxious. He abhors 'the guilty pleasures of subjection and abjection'.[4] In his polemic against Mother Teresa, *The Missionary Position* (1995), he looks forward to a greater day: 'If the baffled and fearful prehistory of our species ever comes to an end, and if we ever get off our knees . . . there will be no need for smoking altars and forbidding temples with which to honour the freethinking humanists who scorned to use the fear of death to coerce and flatter the poor.'[5] So no fatted calf for Bertrand Russell then, no incense for A.J. Ayer – except the incense of flattery of which he inhaled a fair quantity in his lifetime.

Throughout all these works, the assumption is implicit and sometimes explicit (especially in Grayling, the most cocksure in the coop) that these days only people who are thick and/or uneducated swallow the religious fairy tales which, in Hitchens's words, belong to the fearful childhood of our species.[6] Martin Amis, in *The Second Plane* (2008), says uncompromisingly that 'opposition to religion already occupies the high ground, intellectually and morally'. Faith may linger on among the lower orders for a generation or two, but it has no future worth talking about among serious people.

Why then talk about it at such obsessive length? If religion is hanging onto the ropes, groggy at the knees and virtually brain-dead, why insist on pummelling it into the ground and then stamping on its comatose semi-corpse? 'What we are witnessing is not the resurgence of religion but its death throes,' Grayling tells us.[7] There may appear to be a resurgence of religion, in the United States, in Latin America and in Eastern Europe, but this is in reality

a reaction to defeat, in a war that it cannot win even if it succeeds in a few battles on the way down. As before, the grinding of historical tectonic plates will be painful and protracted. But the outcome is not in doubt. As private observance, religion will of course survive among minorities; as a factor in public and international affairs it is having what might be its last characteristically bloody fling.[8]

All this brims with apparent self-confidence. Yet at other moments a note of anxiety creeps in. It is gasp-inducing, Grayling says, that more than 30 per cent of students at UK universities believe in

Intelligent Design. This 'is even more troubling as a symptom of a wider corrosion, the spread of a more virulent cancer of unreason, which is affecting not just the mental culture of our own country but the fate of the world itself'.[9] The religious education of children stirs passionate apprehension in the breasts of every anti-God-botherer. When asked in Dublin his views on the recent cases of sexual abuse by Catholic priests, Dawkins tells us: 'I replied that, horrible as sexual abuse no doubt was, the damage was arguably less than the long-term psychological damage inflicted by bringing the child up Catholic in the first place.'[10] Dawkins quotes with approval the psychologist Nicholas Humphrey's argument in his 1997 Amnesty lecture that the one exception to freedom of speech should be in the case of religious education for children. Parents had no god-given right to addle their children's brains with pernicious nonsense. In fact, society had a duty to protect children from it. As matters stand, I rather doubt whether most state schools in Britain need much instruction in keeping religion out of the classroom.

Dennett sets out to break the spell that religion continues to exert over simple folk, which may explain the cute, folksy tone that he adopts in appealing to them to join him. 'The spell that I say *must* be broken is the taboo against a forthright, scientific, no-holds-barred investigation of religion as one natural phenomenon among many.'[11] 'It is high time that we subject religion as a global phenomenon to the most intensive multi-disciplinary research we can muster, calling on the best minds on the planet. Why? Because religion is too important for us to remain ignorant about.'[12]

This sounds like an innocent, good-hearted appeal which any open-minded person would find hard to resist. Yet there are several odd features about it, or about the way in which Dennett and his colleagues embark on this grand investigation. Their treatment has a gappy, thin quality to it, often smeared with facetious, slapdash overpainting. Coming across a thesis of this poor quality in their own professional fields, in philosophy or the natural sciences, they would be horrified and contemptuous. Take, for example, this call of Dennett's for an intensive, multidisciplinary programme of research into religion in all its aspects. A reader arriving from Mars would assume that no such research had as yet been undertaken and that universities had maintained a respectful veto on the investigation of religion. In fact, of course, for at least a century and a half academics in Europe and the United States have undertaken every sort of rigorous enquiry into religion: into the archaeology of holy lands, into the history and semantics of sacred texts, into the sociology and anthropology of religion, into the rise and fall of sects and churches and schools of interpretation, into the statistics of religious observance. Far from religion remaining a forbidden region, the incoming tide of the human sciences swept across every sacred precinct with the same zest and curiosity as it swept across every secular area of life. Almost none of this material finds it way into Dennett, Dawkins and Hitchens. They behave like explorers claiming to be the first white men into some stretch of *terra incognita*, which later turns out to be quite well trodden and to contain several petrol stations and branches of McDonald's.

What seems especially strange, seeing that evolutionary theory is the big gun in their onslaught against religion, is that they are so little interested in the evolution of religion itself. A feature of human existence which has been so persistent across so many cultures for so many centuries surely deserves a careful explanation. Yet each of the anti-God-botherers devotes a mere handful of listless, uneasy pages to the topic. The only instance that really catches the interest of all three writers is the cargo cult, and in particular the cult on the island of Tauna, New Hebrides, which centres on the worship of a messianic figure called John Frum, derived from the arrival of American GIs during the Second World War.[13] It is a picturesque and charming cult, but it scarcely exhausts the variety of religious inspiration. Nor does it provide an overarching explanation for the rise of religions, which do not, on the whole, offer any obvious material benefits to their adherents. Rather the reverse, since many religions call for self-deprivation and self-sacrifice up to and including the supreme sacrifice of one's own life.

The archaelogist Colin Renfrew suggests that Christianity survived by a form of group selection because it fostered in-group
loyalty and so helped religious groups to survive at the expense of less
religious groups (the same explanation could obviously work for
other religions too). The American D.S.Wilson independently offers
a similar suggestion in his book *Darwin's Cathedral* (2002). And
Darwin himself, as it happens, offers a similar explanation in *The
Descent of Man*:

> When two tribes of primeval man, living in the same country,
> came into competition, if the one tribe included (other circum-
> stances being equal) a greater number of courageous, sympathetic,
> and faithful members, who were always ready to warn each other
> of danger, to aid and defend each other, this tribe would without
> doubt succeed best and conquer the other . . . Selfish and con-
> tentious people will not cohere, and without coherence nothing
> can be effected. A tribe possessing the above qualities in a high
> degree would spread and be victorious over other tribes: but in
> the course of time it would, judging from all past history, be in
> turn overcome by some other and still more highly-endowed
> tribe.[14]

Now this is, at the very least, an interesting theory which deserves
closer examination. Yet for once Dawkins turns aside, rather
brusquely, from his hero's words, and moves on to his own theory
which is that

> religious behaviour may be a misfiring, an unfortunate by-product
> of an underlying psychological propensity which in other cir-
> cumstances is, or once was, useful. On this view, the propensity
> that was naturally selected in our ancestors was not religion *per se*;
> it had some other benefit, and it only incidentally manifests itself
> as religious behaviour. We shall understand religious behaviour
> only after we have renamed it.[15]

Darwin's relatively benign explanation of how religions came to flourish is clearly repugnant to Dawkins. Religion can be accounted for only by *something having gone wrong* in the development of our species. Religion is the backfire from the defective exhaust system of the evolutionary motor, its noxious fumes farted out to pollute the landscape. Here, I think, the impartial observer would want to pause and speculate whether there isn't something a little too convenient about a system which is said to be firing correctly only when it produces results you approve of. This is not the only case in evolutionary science when an *ex post facto* rationalization muddies the plain record of what actually happened; where, as Professor Steven Rose has commented, the narrative takes on the quality of *The Just-So Stories*.

Nor will it do to move on hurriedly and resume denouncing, for the umpteenth time, the absurdity of the myths and legends with which organized religion is encrusted. For we have a duty to describe and account for the evolution not only of religion, with all its wickedness and superstition, but also of the kindly humanism which succeeded it in our hearts. Where did *that* come from? Well, the answer to this question is rather easier to establish, since the evolution of modern humanism in the West occurred not in some inaccessible period of prehistory but within the Christian Era. And there are particular features of the more amiable forms of the new humanism whose origins can be traced, certainly and exclusively, through the precepts of Christianity: the equal worth of every human being, the brotherhood of man, the principle of universal charity, the forgiveness of sins and the right to a fresh start in life. Some of these ideas can be found budding in pagan antiquity (in the Stoics, for example), but it is Christianity that gave them their central place in human life. There are certainly features in Christian morality which are absent from the new humanism, but there is not much in the new humanism which cannot be found in the teachings of Jesus and St Paul. It is, in fact, a pared-down, de-Godded version of those teachings, which is why on a great variety of practical, moral and political issues (not on all) humanists and Christians can happily collaborate without either regarding the other as freaks.

There is a singular reluctance in many anti-God-botherers to admit this simple and not discreditable fact: that humanism, at its best, is evolved out of the moral teachings of Christianity as well as of the ancient sages. As I am writing this, I have just been watching the 82-year-old Gore Vidal being interviewed by Melvyn Bragg on BBC2.[16] Vidal stubbornly asserts repeatedly that he hates lying and himself never tells lies and then, equally stubbornly and repeatedly, refuses to admit that he can think of a single thing for which Christianity in its entire history can take any credit at all. We are dealing here with an aversion so deep-rooted and passionate that it can, I think, be properly described as 'fundamentalist'. Dawkins and others fiercely resist this label because they maintain that their atheism is not a blind, stubborn conviction but a conclusion grounded in scientific evidence and open to correction at any time.

This would be admirable if it were true. But is it? Humanism has its passionate deep-rooted convictions too. There are things that Dennett, for example, would die for: 'I have sacred values – in the sense that I feel vaguely guilty even thinking about whether they are defensible and would *never* consider abandoning them (I like to think!) in the course of solving a moral dilemma. My sacred values are obvious and quite ecumenical: democracy, justice, life, love and truth (in alphabetical order).'[17] He goes on to say that he would be ready to question those beliefs, to decide which of them should give when they conflict. But then of course religious thinkers have to do that sort of examining and sorting of priorities too. There is nothing to suggest that the atheist's or agnostic's beliefs are any less capable of inspiring passions.

And indeed they do inspire passion. The anti-God-botherers spend dozens of pages listing the crimes, follies and cruelties committed in the name of God. 'Religion poisons everything,' Hitchens tells us over and over again, while tramping the world to bear witness to the horrors of sectarian conflict. Yet the major wars of the past two centuries, the conflicts that have killed millions, rather than hundreds or thousands, had little or nothing to do with organized religion. The Napoleonic Wars, the American Civil War, the Boer War, the Great War, the Second World War – all were fought in the name of non-religious purposes: the defence or acquisition of territory, the balance of power in the region, the deterring of aggression, the defence of democracy, racial justice. Often they were fought between co-religionists but not for one interpretation of their religion as against another. Lincoln and Churchill were not religious men. This is a point that goes entirely unmentioned by the anti-God-botherers, because they are unaware of how ingrained are their own faiths.

The slaughter on the Western Front was justified as the war to make the world 'safe for democracy', not safe for Christianity. Hitchens, to the consternation of his friends, was ready to support the invasion of Iraq in the name of democracy and human rights (although not to condone the prosecution of the post-war policy).

The anti-God-botherers do at least respond to their critics' accusations that the most horrible crimes of the twentieth century were committed by atheistic regimes led by atheistic brutes – Lenin, Hitler, Stalin, Mao, Pol Pot. They answer this indictment by arguing that these ideologies were in fact perverted forms of religion. But the perversion resided precisely in the fact that they subtracted from the potion that very feature that Dennett, Dawkins and Hitchens find most objectionable: the assumption of a personal God. They were perverted in the direction which scientific atheists would regard as desirable; moreover, their leaders and ideologists professed and actually possessed an immense admiration for modern science.

There is a reluctance in the anti-God-botherers to examine in any depth just what kind of a thing religion is. When Stephen Jay Gould proposed in *Rock of Ages* (1999) that religion and science should be considered as two 'non-overlapping *magisteria*' – two domains of concern and enquiry that can coexist peacefully as long as neither poaches on the other's special province – he was greeted with derision by his fellow scientists and philosophers. NOMA is 'implausible', according to Dennett,[18] 'bending over backwards to positively supine lengths', according to Dawkins.[19] Hitchens says that religion and science 'most certainly do not overlap, but this does not mean that they are not antagonistic'.[20]

What the anti–God–botherers cannot be bothered to contemplate is the possibility that religion (and indeed other cultural phenomena) might not be simply an alternative (and bogus) kind of science but a quite different sort of thing. Religion in all its forms is as much an activity, an allegiance, a practice as an attempted explanation of the universe.[21] The religious model of faith isn't so much cognitive as perceptual. Its insights are epiphanies, not falsifiable theories about the way the world is. The *AA Road Atlas* and the map of the human genome are alike in that they are descriptions of the physical world which can be shown to be true or false, or complete or incomplete. The Book of Common Prayer, by contrast, is made up largely of material which does not consist in verifiable propositions; there are exhortations and commandments, psalms of praise and celebration, prayers and confessions, creeds and homilies, rites and rubrics, blessings and lamentations, ceremonies of induction and remembrance. They simply are not utterances for which 'true' or 'false' would be an appropriate question to ask about them, any more than it would be appropriate to ask it about a Beatles song, or a council by-law, or a love letter, or an after–dinner toast.

It is also not often pointed out that the words used in this debate – truth, faith, belief – have taken on the meaning now most commonly used only in the last few centuries. Their derivations – *treu, fidelis,* be–lief (be–love) – belong in the realms of affection and allegiance rather than those of factual veracity. To this day we dimly understand the distinction between 'believing in' and 'believing that', between a loyalty to someone or something, which may be suffused with love, and an intellectual conviction that such–and–such is the case, which has nothing to do with emotional attachment.

I must have read getting on for 2,000 pages of polemic from the new militant atheists and only in a rather strange chapter in *Breaking the Spell* do I catch the faintest inkling that any of these fiery polemicists begins to grasp this distinction or that they are capable of registering the faintest interest in the *content* of religious experience, that is, in what it is like to be a member of any religious faith. Nor do we encounter any theologians or mystics in these pages, except where they are purporting to prove the existence of God. We hear nothing of Julian of Norwich, Dietrich Bonhoeffer, Meister Eckhart, John Henry Newman, Thomas à Kempis or Paul Tillich, to take a few names at random.

Rather than quote directly from any apologist for Christianity (or any other religion), Dennett invents his own 'Professor Faith', who protests that choosing religion is not like deciding whether or not to switch jobs or buy a car. When we 'see the light', it is not like suddenly figuring out a puzzle or getting a joke, it's like falling in love.[22]

All right, that will do to be going on with as a shorthand description. So what does Dennett make of this? Dennett is heartily in favour of love, he would not want to live in a world without love. 'I am inclined to think that nothing could matter more than what people love.'[23] That's a rather odd statement, isn't it? It seems that not love itself but whom or what we love is what counts. And indeed Dennett detects a snag in the ordinary concept of love. The trouble is that love is blind, and that is why love is not enough. 'Have you ever had to face the heart-wrenching problem of a dear friend who has fallen head over heels with somebody who is just not worthy of her love?'[24] So love is a good thing only if you love somebody who is worthy of your love.

But the whole point of love in most religions is that the object of love may be a miserable specimen. God loves us, we are told, despite the fact that we are miserable specimens, and we are to love our neighbours even though they may be miserable specimens too. The Catechism which all Christian children used to learn by heart sets out the two great duties of men: to love God, 'with all my heart, with all my mind, with all my soul, and with all my strength; and to love my

Neighbour as myself'. Humanists may say that this is an absurd impossible demand, and settle for the lower, less demanding command, 'to do to all men as I would they should do unto me'. This is an illuminating example, perhaps the most illuminating example, of how modern humanism adopts the demands of the Gospel after first draining them of passion. Hitchens tells us that 'many of the sayings and deeds of Jesus are innocuous, most especially the "beatitudes" which express such fanciful wish-thinking about the meek and the peacemakers'.[25] But the beatitudes are anything but innocuous. They call for a complete transvaluation of values in which the poor, humble and meek are to be regarded as blessed; nor is this wishful thinking, for in many religions the devout have carried the principle into practice.

Hitchens tells us that it is impossible to argue that religion causes people to behave in a more kindly or civilized manner. On the contrary, 'charity and relief work, while they may appeal to tender-hearted believers, are the inheritors of modernism and the Enlightenment'.[26] So how are we to account for all the hospitals and asylums and almshouses with which the pre-modern era was dotted? But then Hitchens is not too keen on ministering angels, at any period. His polemic against Mother Teresa is curiously counter-productive. Indeed, not having been a particular admirer of Mother Teresa before reading it, I found myself strangely respecting her by the end; the sins alleged against her, principally that of raising money from dodgy world leaders and being keen on saving souls at the expense of modern standards of clinical care, seemed fairly minor. They certainly do not justify Hitchens's slam-bang critique.

One cannot help noting here, as in the case of Gore Vidal, a determination not to allow religion a single credit mark, ever, under any circumstances. And it is hard to resist describing this determination as fanatical. The new atheists repeatedly declare their credentials as sceptics, their readiness to stand corrected by the evidence. Yet one often encounters a bombastic, sweeping tone, a hectoring impatience which makes for compelling polemic but poor science – science in the broadest sense of honest intellectual enquiry.

It is a running theme in the new atheism that religion ought not to receive the disproportionate respect which it still receives in our otherwise secular society. I find this complaint mystifying. In reality, you cannot open a newspaper without reading derisive articles about the Archbishop of Canterbury or the Pope and their particular stand-points, or about the iniquities of Islam and the vileness of its ayatollahs. These articles are often written by priests and devout Muslims about the shortcomings of their own faiths as currently practised. Many secular journalists can scarcely resist beginning every article on any faith-related matter 'Being an atheist myself'; it is in fact the atheists rather than the religionists who are most eager to bear public witness to their beliefs or non-beliefs. Far from being timidly respectful, the atheists wade in firing from the hip, spraying accusations in all directions. Cardinal Cormac Murphy O'Connor in a recent sermon warned of attempts to 'eliminate the Christian voice' from the public forum and plaintively enquired: 'Have you ever met anyone who believes what Richard Dawkins does not believe in? The God that is being rejected by such people is a God I don't believe in either.'[27]

And half-hidden behind the campaign to deny respect to religion, there lies a more far-reaching project: to deny not just respect but reverence to any person or text or patch of sand or lump of rock. In short, to eliminate the idea of the sacred. Holy turf needs to be paved over, Dennett proclaims, the Temple must not be rebuilt, there can be 'no untrumpable appeals to the "Sacred"'.[28] In the summer of 2007, the British Library held a marvellous exhibition with that very title, showing a vast selection of manuscripts, books and holy artefacts which have been sacred either to Jews, Christians or Muslims, ranging from the Dead Sea Scrolls to medieval Books of Hours. I have seldom visited a more touching or beautiful exhibition of man-made things. To Dennett, I imagine, the whole show would have been a pile of misbegotten rubbish.

The only acceptable theism is a new sort of pantheism which sheds an equal radiance over the whole earth and every creature on it, the sort of reverence and admiration for the structure of the universe as revealed by science which have become especially associated with the godlike figure of Albert Einstein.

Claiming to be 'a deeply religious non-believer', Einstein explains more precisely the quality of that admiration: 'I have never imputed to nature a purpose or a goal or anything that could be understood as anthropomorphic. What I see in nature is a magnificent structure that we can comprehend only very imperfectly and that must fill a thinking person with a feeling of humility. This is a genuinely religious feeling that has nothing to do with mysticism.'[29]

This is pretty much Dawkins's position too, and in another book, *Unweaving the Rainbow* (1998), he attempts to awaken our sluggish sense of wonder when we contemplate the endless complexity and variety of our universe. Keats complained that Newton had destroyed the rainbow by explaining it. Dawkins argues to the contrary that Blake and Keats and Yeats might have written still greater poetry if they had known more science.[30] D.H. Lawrence's poem about humming birds is almost wholly inaccurate scientifically, he says, and it would have been no less arresting and thought-provoking if Lawrence had had a couple of tutorials in evolution and taxonomy to get his facts straight.[31]

The new pantheism, Einstein's reverence, depends therefore on *understanding*. It does not depend on *mystery*. On the contrary, the more we understand about the structure and evolution of the universe, according to Dawkins, the more we shall wonder at it, and the more we ought to wonder at it. This position has the advantages of clarity and simplicity, but it is, I think, a more peculiar and demanding philosophy than it first seems.

The new pantheism offers first a psychological prediction: once you understand something of nature, you will be strongly inclined to revere it, that is the natural response. This is then amalgamated with an exhortation, almost a command: this reverence is not only natural, it is proper and desirable, and we new pantheists are going to wake you up, so that you experience the same joy and awe as we experience daily.

Now the sceptic may say, quite legitimately, in answer to the prediction: 'No I don't' and to the exhortation: 'No I won't'. It is quite possible and entirely defensible to find the evolutionary process depressing rather than exhilarating.[32] Some of Dawkins's readers have told him how troubled they were by his 'cold, bleak message'. How could he bear to get up in the mornings? You can find the same bleakness in the passages from *In Memoriam* and from A.J. Balfour which I have already quoted. Those passages depressed a lot of late Victorians too. Dawkins himself bounds along like a cheerful subaltern keeping up the troops' morale, but he can offer no plausible reason why nature *must* inspirit us. It is hard to see what reason there could be. And is there not something faintly saccharine in this relentless insistence that the universe is a wonderful place? Indeed, 'saccharine' is the *mot juste,* because it looks suspiciously like an ersatz sweetener to replace the forbidden sugar of religious faith.

It is a commonplace that David Attenborough's nature programmes are the best thing on television. I have enjoyed them along with everybody else, but I have never been able to suppress a faint unease while watching. The whole proceeding seems to contain an unpleasant voyeuristic streak, verging on the pornographic. This is brilliantly masked by the innocent quenchless enthusiasm and expertise of Attenborough himself. But isn't there something faintly repellent about a posse of cameramen training their sights on a python slowly swallowing an antelope or on a coot killing her surplus young – and then countless millions of us crowding round to watch the footage? In *Unweaving the Rainbow,* Dawkins devotes half a dozen pages to the strategies of the female cuckoo for invading the nests of the meadow pipit and the dunnock, throwing out their eggs and laying her own eggs there.[33] This passage, though certainly intriguing, evokes in me no sense of wonder but rather mild disgust.

As for those lovable, uxorious emperor penguins, do we keep on chuckling at their sweet ungainly antics quite so heartily when we see them finally arrive at the edge of the ice floe and start nudging each other until one of them falls into the Antarctic Ocean and becomes a sort of 'guinea penguin' to test if there are any predatory seals lurking? This unappealing ritual takes place after their heroic trudge across the ice in search of food. Even here one cannot help feeling that their genes have let them down. How much more convenient it would have been if natural selection had not downgraded their wings to impotent flippers.

Darwin himself showed unmistakable signs of distress when contemplating the cruelty arising out of the evolutionary process. The classic horror story for the Victorians was that of the ichneumon fly which lays its eggs on the body of a living caterpillar; when its larvae are hatched, they proceed to eat the caterpillar alive from the inside out. Modern scientists are almost gleeful in describing the ingenuity of this process. Not so Darwin. He wrote to a friend the year after publishing *Origin of Species*:

'I own that I cannot see as plainly as others do, and as I should wish to do, evidence of design and beneficence on all sides of us. There seems to me too much misery in the world. I cannot persuade myself that a beneficent and omnipotent God would have designedly created the Ichneumonidae with the express intention of their feeding within the living bodies of caterpillars, or that a cat should play with mice.' More passionately still, he had written a few years earlier to the great botanist Joseph Hooker: 'What a book a devil's chaplain might write on the clumsy, wasteful, blundering, low, and horribly cruel works of nature!'[34] (It is from this vivid exclamation that Dawkins borrows the title for his collection of essays, *A Devil's Chaplain* (2004), without apparently sharing his hero's sense of anguish.)

The new pantheism avoids the problem of evil by simply ignoring it and by concentrating on processes rather than outcomes; at times it comes perilously close to the optimum of Dr Pangloss, alias Leibniz: that everything is for the best in the best of all possible worlds. It was, you will recall, the Lisbon earthquake of 1755 which provoked Voltaire to write *Candide*, still the ultimate and unanswerable polemic against scientific optimism. Dawkins would no doubt indignantly deny this sly imputation and exhibit his credentials as a tireless fighter against cruelty and injustice, especially the cruelty and injustice generated by organized religion. In which case, why is *wonder* the proper posture in the face of a universe which never stops breaking eggs to make so many questionable omelettes?

In his ruminations on death and the end of religion in *Nothing to be Frightened of* (2008), Julian Barnes, brother of the Presocratic Jonathan, questions this sense of wonder:

> If what is out there comes from nothing, if all is unrolling mechanically according to a programme laid down by nobody, and if our perceptions of it are mere micro-moments of biochemical activity, the mere snap and crackle of a few synapses, then what does this sense of wonder amount to? Should we not be a little more suspicious of it? A dung beetle might well have a primitive sense of awe at the size of the mighty dung ball it is rolling. Is this wonder of ours merely a posher version?[35]

Barnes is not ill-disposed towards Dawkins, but he cannot help musing: '. . . just out of interest – it would be useful to know whether an atheist's sense of wonder at the universe is quantifiably as great as that of a believer'.[36] Might it not be a rather diluted compensatory version, a second-best consolation? And what exactly is this wonder *for*? What biological purpose does it serve?

It might, I suppose, be that this wonder pricks us on to examine and make sense of the universe, in our ancestors' case, for example, provoking them first to notice how knapped flints were useful for cutting things and then to begin to sharpen the flints themselves. But that sounds to me more like curiosity, which may be a fruitful quality but is quite different from reverence, for the nature of reverence is to revere things as they are and not for what you can make out of them.

There is a further difficulty. In rebutting the argument that the universe must have an Intelligent Designer, Dawkins points out,

quite energetically, how very unintelligently designed many key features of the world are, not excluding some of our own organs, such
as the human eye. The appendix, for example, has no known function and makes its presence felt only when it becomes infected. The
tonsils and the lymph glands do act as barriers against infection but
disastrously imperfect ones, being liable to infection themselves and
in the case of the lymph glands, to spread cancerous cells around the
body. Other body parts, such as the knee, were well adapted to earlier stages of evolution but are not so suited to our present upright
posture. *Homo sapiens* is not only a work in progress but one in
which quite a few wrong turnings have already been taken.

But if this is so, how can *wonder* be the appropriate reaction in
contemplating this suboptimal jumble? Irritation, or even despair,
would seem to be the more appropriate response. There is an enduring contradiction between the downgrading of the existing world
which is required to refute the Intelligent Designers and the upgrad-
ing required to comfort those who find evolutionary theory a
somewhat bleak theory of everything.

What I want to carry away from this controversy, though, is not
any kind of articulated theory about the new pantheism (for, as I
have said, it is rather poorly articulated). What I want to draw attention to is rather its *tone*: a blithe, upbeat, sometimes caustic, often
humorous tone. That tone is common to Dawkins, Dennett and
Hitchens and others of their un-faith. Where have we heard it
before?

Well, long ago on the Aegean is the answer. That sunny freedom
of spirit flickered briefly on the rocky headlands of the Ionian coast,
and then was extinguished. When Nietzsche and Norman Douglas
talk of 'the Greeks', it is the Ionians they are thinking of with their
restless, open minds, their lack of inhibitions, their caustic turn of
phrase, their readiness to make the most of the world they could
touch and see. Some of the Ionians too might have answered their
rulers as the mathematician Laplace answered Napoleon when he
asked why God did not appear in his calculations and Laplace replied:

'Sire, I had no need of that hypothesis.' This superb *bon mot* is quoted by Dawkins as well as by Hitchens and Grayling. Which prompts me to wonder why the anti-God-botherers do not more readily ransack the treasury of Ionian wisecracks, why they do not seem to think of themselves, literally, as Renaissance men, reviving the cool and bracing scepticism of the pre-Christian era. Is it perhaps because there is something ultimately a little sad in recognizing that, in their eyes, the last two millennia have been a mistake and we are essentially back where we started? It is, by contrast, a comfort to think that we are the heroic vanguard, for the first time shaking ourselves free of the old delusions and facing the future bathed in sunlight.

It is possible to claim that the Ionian men of science have been overvalued because all we have of them are fragments which we may have overinterpreted. No such downplaying is possible with Lucretius' huge and comprehensive didactic poem *De Rerum Natura*, *On the Nature of Things*. This amazing work summarizes all the science of the ancients, drawing out the logical conclusions of five centuries of Greek thought, from its Ionian beginnings, by way of the wisdom of Epicurus, whom Lucretius idolized. Almost nothing is known about Lucretius himself, but his poem can be reliably dated within a year or two. Lucretius is said to have died on 15 October 55 BC, the day that Virgil assumed the *toga virilis* (a kind of graduation ceremony). Cicero, writing a year later, makes it clear that both he and his brother had read the poem, which was left unfinished at Lucretius' death. As 55 BC was also the year in which Julius Caesar first invaded Britain, any cultivated lieutenant in the first Roman legions to stumble ashore on the Sussex coast could have introduced our woad-daubed ancestors to an entirely modern world-view. For that is what Lucretius offers us, in verse which is sometimes lyrical, sometimes bitingly scornful, sometimes noble and inspiring, but never less than crystal clear and logical.

Cicero was certainly not blind to the merits of Lucretius. He told his brother, 'the poems of Lucretius contain, as you say in your letter, many flashes of inspiration and also much poetic skill.' Yet he viewed the popularity of the Epicureans, from whom Lucretius learnt most of what he knew, with the darkest possible suspicion.[37] Cicero's objection was not that the teachings of Epicurus were untrue. It was that they were unwholesome and dangerous if taught to the masses.[38] It was all right for senators and professional philosophers to discuss amongst themselves such impious ideas as that the world was composed solely of atoms and that the gods did not interfere in the affairs of men. But these atheistic views, if they infected the plebs, would undermine the power and stability of Rome. Some modern scholars have swallowed the claim made by St Jerome, that bitter enemy of everything pagan, that Cicero actually prepared Lucretius' poem for publication. It is true that Cicero was well versed in Epicurean ideas, because his tutors had been followers of Epicurus, but nothing is less likely than that he should have helped the publication of *De Rerum Natura* in any way, because publishing the stuff was just what he so vehemently objected to. What the public needed was not scientific knowledge but moral instruction, backed up by the authority of the state religion. For Cicero agreed wholeheartedly with the cynical view that Polybius, the Greek historian of Rome, had put forward a century earlier: that officially propagated superstition was the foundation of Roman greatness. Inculcating belief in the gods and the afterlife was the only way to check the lawless passions of the masses.[39]

Cicero himself was quite open about this need to use religious awe to control the plebs. And he took it for granted that his readers, worldly-wise fellow members of the Roman elite, would agree with him. That was why it was so important that the priests should come from the officer class which produced Rome's statesmen and law-givers, for they would understand by instinct and training what the interests of the state required and adjust the verdict of the gods accordingly. The Stoic philosophers had taught the Roman ruling class to divide god-talk into three types: the poetic, which was for poets, the political, which was for the masses, and the natural, which was reserved for philosophers. Only the natural type was true. We call it science.

And the natural philosophy is what Lucretius shows us: a world which is governed entirely by the laws of nature; a universe which is infinite and composed of space and atoms, nothing else. When we die, the body rots and the soul perishes with the body. The world had a beginning and will have an end. Species evolve, as do human civilizations; both rise and fall and are extinguished. 'Everything is on the move. Everything is transformed by nature and formed into new paths.'[40]

There is a heroic story, though, and it is the story of man's self-liberation from ignorance and superstition. This story is epitomized by Epicurus, the teacher and hero of Lucretius, in whose honour the poem is composed. Epicurus, first of all men, smashed the locks of nature's doors. And we too can liberate ourselves. All life is a struggle in the dark. But by understanding nature, we can liberate ourselves from the baseless fears of children and work our way through to the light.[41] Don't worry, Lucretius assures us, you are not being led into a sinful path. On the contrary, it is the superstitious delusion that the gods intervene in human affairs which gives birth to sinful and impious actions. So many cruelties, such as the sacrifice of Iphigenia, are the consequence of religion. If men knew that their suffering was finite and ended with death, they would find the strength to resist the hocus-pocus and intimidation of the prophets. And what ghastly deities we invent for ourselves.

> Poor humanity, to saddle the gods with such responsibilities and throw in a vindictive temper! What griefs they hatched then for themselves, what festering sores for us, what tears for our posterity! This is not piety, this oft-repeated show of bowing a veiled head before a stone; this bustling to every altar; this kowtowing and prostration on the ground with palms outspread before the shrines of the gods; this deluging of altars with the blood of beasts; this heaping of vow on vow. True piety lies rather in the power to contemplate the universe with a quiet mind.[42]

Everything arises out of matter; 'nothing is ever created by divine power out of nothing . . . nature resolves everything into its component atoms and never reduces anything to nothing . . . all nature as it is in itself consists of two things – bodies and the vacant space in which the bodies are situated, and through which they move in different directions.' The number of different forms of atom is finite, but the number of any one form is infinite. Lucretius would not be in the least surprised to learn that in the early twentieth century physicists had narrowed the types of atoms down to three: positrons, neutrons and electrons. And of course this vast universe is indifferent to our concerns. Nor was it created by any agency, even a divine one: 'The universe was certainly not created for us by divine power; it is so full of imperfections' – a point taken up strongly by Dawkins. The idea that we ought to praise this piece of divine workmanship and regard it as eternal and immortal is sheer nonsense.[43]

The world is no more immortal than we are; since the elements of which it is composed 'all consist of matter that is neither birthless nor deathless, we must believe the same of the world as a whole'.[44] 'When we see the main component members of the world disintegrated and reborn, it is a fair inference that sky and earth too had their birthday and will have their day of doom.'[45] As for us, there is no need to repine. When we are dead, we shall not feel a thing. And what harm would it have done us to have remained uncreated? Dawkins has this thought too.

The gods are immune to our merits, and immune to anger. The earth has always been an insentient place. Nor does this unfeeling universe enjoy any kind of divinely ordered uniqueness. It is highly unlikely that our earth and sky are the only ones to have been created. If our world has been made through the spontaneous collision and congregation of atoms, why should there not be elsewhere other clusters of matter bringing forth life? There may well be life on other planets, so numerous are they and so vast the universe.[46] Again, Dawkins hazards the same guess as Lucretius.

But at the same time there is nothing arbitrary or capricious about the processes of creation (it is the gods on Mount Olympus who are capricious, not nature, which operates on strictly logical lines): 'Everything is created from specific needs and born of a specific mother and grows up true to type.' We may infer that this is determined by some specific necessity.

'It may also happen at times that children take after their grandparents, or recall the features of great-grandparents. This is because the parents' bodies often preserve a quantity of latent seeds, grouped in many combinations, which derive from an ancestral stock handed down from generation to generation.'[47] The idea of a genetic code is not far distant here. Nor is there anything outside nature in our minds or souls. Mind and spirit are both composed of matter. Mind and body both derive their vigour from their conjunction. Accordingly they sicken and die together.

Nor is there any refuge from these hard facts in a lofty scepticism which refuses to accept the possibility of knowledge. 'If anyone thinks that nothing is ever known, he does not know whether even this can be known.' Scepticism involves an infinite regress – how can you know that you cannot know that you can know?[48] At the end of the process it becomes impossible to open your mouth at all. Grayling could not have put it better.

Lucretius is always ready to say, when he has no hard evidence of the cause of some natural phenomenon, that he does not know the answer and that various causes are possible – about the eclipses of the sun and the moon for example. In offering his laborious explanation of magnetism, he says: 'In matters of this sort it is necessary to establish a number of facts before you can offer an explanation of them. This may mean approaching the problem by a very roundabout route.'[49] He is always open to correction and himself eager to correct unsound earlier theories. In short, just the sort of scientist Popper would recognize as a soulmate.

Obviously modern science would correct Lucretius on a great number of things. But his essential conceptions of the universe are not so different from those that prevail today. Nor is his heroic view of the triumph of human understanding, except that for him it happened 2,000 years earlier, with Epicurus and Democritus, rather than with Darwin and Einstein.

Classical scholars throughout the Christian era have attempted, quite successfully, to mute the subversive message of atheist poets and philosophers in the ancient world. They also managed to conceal quite how well-known in their day those ancient atheists and their doctrines were. It is usually only from their opponents, whether pagan or Christian, that we get some inkling of their presence in the debate. In the single surviving work of the Christian apologist Minucius Felix, the *Octavius* which dates from around AD 200, the pagan Caecilius (who believed in sticking to the old Roman gods who had served his forefathers pretty well) denounces those Greek atheists who had raged against the gods, such as Theodorus of Cyrene, Diagoras the Melian and Protagoras of Abdera who was expelled from Athens and had his writings burnt for his impious views. The pagan spokesman then goes on to denounce the Christians, with their 'old women's fables' about the afterlife, as far worse than the atheists, not least because they were gathered from the dregs of society, while the atheists were at least scholars and gentlemen. Caecilius is allowed plenty of airtime to develop his scorching critique, before Octavius has his say at twice the length and eventually converts Caecilius to the Christian faith. Octavius for his part argues that even the famous Greek sceptics, such as Epicurus and Xenophanes and the other Ionians, did at least believe in nature, which is rather like modern Christians trying to conscript Darwin and Einstein to their cause. It is quite clear from this lively dialogue that atheism still dared to speak its name quite loud and clear at this date. Non-believers had their role in the argument. The debate remained open. And Lucretius' views on religion could not be written off as those of a lone eccentric.

One simple device adopted by old-style classics masters was to translate '*religio*' as 'superstition', suggesting that Lucretius is talking only of the more absurd incrustations of religion and not of its vital doctrines. Indeed, it used to be the style in academe to present Lucretius as 'a rather lacklustre hack droning on about physics', to quote John Godwin's introduction to the Penguin edition of *De Rerum Natura, On the Nature of the Universe*. But it is clear from the text that Lucretius means his poem to be a life-changing experience for his readers, one which will liberate them for ever from the God delusion. He is in short the Richard Dawkins of 55 BC, or Dawkins is the Lucretius of AD 2000, though without the poetry of his pre-decessor which is by turns mordant, resonant and beautiful. Lucretius of course had no grasp of the genetic mechanics of evolution, any more than the supposed 'first Darwinian', Anaximander, five cen-turies earlier; but then Darwin too had little idea about how genes worked. Yet none of them would have been surprised by, or resist-ant to, the discoveries of modern genetics. The concept of minute variations over huge stretches of time is implicit in their sketches of evolutionary development. After being talked through the intricacies of DNA, they would all simply have said, 'Ah, so that's how it works then.'

The intellectual elite in the age of Lucretius and Cicero, just as in the century of Balfour and Dawkins, was agreed on at least a rough outline of how our world was created and how we ourselves came to exist. But that does not mean that everyone else, then or now, sub-scribed to the scientific consensus. On the contrary, the eclipse of a single God-centred explanation leaves an enormous empty space in people's lives. All sorts of other beliefs, therapies and rituals swarm in to replace the old religious orthodoxy. New gods appear on the scene, popular gods, deities created from below, not imposed from above. Then as now, a new age demands new cults.

VII

NEW AGE

Shopping in the Spiritual
Supermarket

Before he went to Geneva for the 1985 Summit, President Reagan had his favourite astrologer, Joan Quigley, draw up a horoscope for Mikhail Gorbachev (Pisces, if you're interested) for clues as to the Russian leader's likely behaviour. Quigley, from her San Francisco home, also advised Reagan on the exact moment at which he should sign the Intermediate Nuclear Forces Treaty in December 1987. It was Reagan's chief of staff, Donald Regan, who revealed in his memoirs that 'virtually every major move and decision the Reagans made during my time as White House chief of staff was cleared in advance with a woman in San Francisco who drew up horoscopes to make certain that the planets were in a favourable alignment for the enterprise'.[1] The revelation caused a furore. The press quickly identified Quigley, but found it hard to contact her because she had left San Francisco for a month's holiday in Europe in order to avoid the major earthquake in California which she had predicted for 5 May. Returning home on 7 May with the city undisturbed by the faintest tremor, she told reporters that 'she was confident any danger was past'.[2]

Quigley was not the only astrologer to advise a recent president. Richard Nixon listened to Jeane Dixon, whom he called 'the soothsayer', and when she predicted a terrorist attack on the United States, he ordered military preparations (no attack happened). She was famous for having predicted the assassination of John F. Kennedy, though at the time of the 1960 election she had predicted that Nixon would win. She also predicted that World War III would begin in 1958 and that the Russians would be the first nation to land a man on the moon. (Nancy Reagan, who was promiscuous in her choice of stargazers, consulted Dixon too.) Quigley got her first break after John Hinckley's assassination attempt on Reagan in 1981. Nancy asked Quigley if she could have foreseen and perhaps prevented the assassination attempt. Yes, said Quigley, if she had been looking, she would have known. Quigley and Dixon are only two of the dozens of astrologers whose columns have been syndicated in newspapers and radio shows all over the United States. Among the most syndicated (to 200 publications) were the columns of Joyce Jillson, a former actress, who became the official astrologer to 20th Century Fox, providing advice on the best opening dates for new movies. As in other fields of prophecy, she was able to take credit for the studio's successes, such as *Star Wars*; the failures were attributed to the poor quality of the films in question. She died before her last books, *Dog Astrology* and *Astrology for Cats,* could be published.

Nor are these astrological addictions confined to American conservatives. Francis Wheen points out in his splendid compendium of illusion that when the *Washington Post*'s famous reporter Sally Quinn declared that 'I have known since Reagan was elected that Ronnie and Nancy went to astrologers', she neglected to add that she and her husband Ben Bradlee, the *Post*'s editor in the great Watergate days, were private clients of the *Post*'s own resident astrologer, the wonderfully named Svetlana Godilla. Supposedly hard-headed businessmen are among the most profitable private clients for astrologers. A survey showed that 48 per cent of Wall Street stockholders used horoscopes when deciding what to buy or sell.[3] These days in Britain, even the supposedly serious newspapers, such as *The Times* and the *Observer*, have horoscopes.

And our own political leaders occasionally welcome help from occult forces. Cherie Blair, like Jeane Dixon a practising Roman Catholic, had a feng-shui expert in to rearrange the furniture in Downing Street. She also wore a magic pendant, known as a Bioelectric Shield, which had 'a matrix of specially cut quartz crystals that surround the wearer with a "cocoon of energy" to ward off evil forces'. Wheen tells us that Hillary Clinton put her on to the idea.[4] Later during her Downing Street years Cherie famously took up with the New Age guru and former topless model, Carole Caplin, who, among other things, introduced her to an 86-year-old dowser who treated her swollen ankles by swinging a crystal pendulum over them (I'm not sure whether the pendulum is the same as the Bioelectric Shield) and feeding her strawberry leaves grown within the electromagnetic field of the Neolithic circle he had built in his back garden.

Many of Carole Caplin's techniques find an echo in the treatments offered by the bearded healer of Belgrade, Dragan David Dabic, better known to the world as the indicted war criminal Radovan Karadzic. While on the run, Karadzic, a trained psychiatrist, built up

quite a practice by adding to his repertoires not only acupuncture
and homeopathy but also what he said were oriental therapies drawing on the life force and his patients' personal auras. He told them
that the plaited topknot which he had grown as part of his disguise
attracted different energies from the environment. He also sold neck-
laces which he called Vellbeing and which offered personal
protection against 'harmful radiation'. All this seems to have gone
down as well in Belgrade as it did in Downing Street.[5]

Dabic/Karadzic, like most New Age gurus, promiscuously chucks
into his cauldron a whole bunch of scientific as well as religious
jargon, reinforcing his credentials by claiming that his techniques are
based on an irresistible combination of knowledge and faith. Quigley
too, like most traditional astrologers, has asserted that hers is a true
science, related to astronomy, and one capable of achieving more
precise results these days, because of the discovery of new planets and
our greater knowledge of the stars generally. She does not claim
psychic powers. What she does claim is that: 'Not since the days of
the Roman emperors – and never in the history of the United States
Presidency – has an astrologer played such a significant role in the
national affairs of State.'[6]

About the Roman emperors at least, Quigley is perfectly accurate.
Under the Roman Empire, astrology exercised an absolute and
scarcely questioned authority over the minds of all citizens from the
lowest to the emperors themselves. Suetonius tells us that Tiberius
neglected the ancient gods because he believed only in fatalism, the
immutable course of events laid down by the stars. The Emperor
Otho marched against Vitellius, egged on by his astrologers and in
defiance of his old-style official clergy who warned him of bad
omens. Soon astrologers were consulted not only about public
events, like where and when to found a city or crown a ruler, but
also about marriages, journeys or moving house. Some people would
no longer even take a bath or change their clothes or manicure their
fingernails until the propitious moment. Learned men like the Stoic
philosophers took the underlying truths of astrology just as much for

granted as did Roman matrons who wanted to know whether the child they were carrying would be a boy or a girl. The Chaldeans who brought astrology to Rome from the banks of the Euphrates enjoyed the scholarly approval of no less a philosopher than Posidonius, the teacher of Cicero.

Why didn't the repeated failures of their prophecies discredit the astrologers? Well, then as now, the wizard would say that he had been given inaccurate information on which to base his calculations; or he would denounce other so-called astrologers as pitiful bunglers who had not had the training; or if hard-pressed he would confess that his own calculations had been inadequate, thus paradoxically boosting the claims of astrology to be an extremely difficult science.

The most essential principle of astrology is fatalism. You may believe in it passionately, or half-heartedly, or indulge it merely as a pastime, but in so far as you give it any belief, you are accepting that fate is in charge of human destiny. In the words of the Roman poet Manilius: '*Fata regunt orbem, certa stant omnia lege.*' The fates rule the world. That is why the Christian Church opposed astrology so fiercely and, for many centuries, so successfully. It had no objection to the claim that the motions of the heavens exercised an influence upon climate and vegetation, but it was intolerable when the astrologers claimed that they could accurately predict human behaviour as well as the weather and the prospects for the crops.

In getting rid of this part of stargazing, the Church experienced repeated difficulties. They had trouble persuading bridal couples to give up having their horoscopes cast before getting married. St Augustine noted ruefully how Christian converts continued to guide their life by astrologers' almanacs, charms and amulets.[7] But, by and large, the official suppression worked. Franz Cumont tells us that 'the Church succeeded in extirpating the learned astrology of the Latin world almost completely at the beginning of the Middle Ages. We do not know of one astrological treatise, or of one manuscript of the Carolingian period, but the ancient faith in the powers of the stars continued in secret and gained new strength when Europe came in

contact with Arabian science.'[8] In England, according to Keith
Thomas, there had been learned astrological authors in the Middle
Ages but few practitioners of the art, and their numbers dwindled, so
that when interest in astrology revived under the Tudors, it was necessary to resort to prognostications by foreign authors. Astrology as a
science rather than a collection of folk wisdom had pretty well died
out.

Science – that is the word that brings us up short and sticks in
our throats. Yet the second coming of astrology in the West was a
scientific advance, just as the first one had been too. Thomas calls
astrology 'probably the most ambitious attempt ever made to
reduce the baffling diversity of human affairs to some sort of intel-
ligible order'.[9] Astrology offered a genuine system of historical
explanation, and we can detect in it the germ of modern sociology,
as Auguste Comte, the founder of modern sociology, readily
acknowledged.[10]

The Chaldean astronomers really could foretell eclipses and the
transits of planets, and quite accurately too. And was not this fatalism
only another way of describing the regularities and necessities that
did in fact rule the universe? To that extent, astrology too really was
a science, even if a mistaken one, and its second coming liberated
natural science from the capricious will of the gods. Seen in this
light, it does not seem so strange that as a young man Isaac Newton
should have brought a book on astrology at Stourbridge fair or spent
so much of his later life in fruitless astrological speculations. It was a
false turning, but only a false turning from the right road.

But when we compare the present-day vogue for astrology with
the amazing grip it took on the Roman Empire, we must remember
that, then as now, astrology was not an isolated import.

To understand a little more about the Roman world into which
astrology intruded, with all its glittering appeal, we need to un-learn
a good deal of what most of us were taught at school about the history of religion in that world. We have, I think, a quite simple
picture of the gods on Mount Olympus receiving frigid tribute from

well-behaved Romans: these were carefully observed rituals and sac-
rificial offerings, some of them burnt, but for the most part they
were ceremonies with as little passion and commitment as the average village fete to raise funds for the Conservative Party with a
pig-roast as its highlight. The myths and legends which had grown
up around the gods and goddesses were full of charm and beauty and
had special local resonances for every Greek and Roman city and
island. They offered delicious material for poets and artists. But they
did not engage the heart and soul, as did the upstart religion that
blew in from the desert, with its enormous promises of spiritual salvation and a heavenly afterlife. Nor could the old gods offer the same
equality in Christ to the poor and the oppressed and the immigrants
that Jesus offered. Seen retrospectively in the light of this stark contrast, the eventual triumph of Christianity looks inevitable. It seems
obvious to us that for those seeking consolation and redemption, the
old gods can have offered no real competition, except to members of
the establishment who deplored change of any sort.

Yet the last years of the Roman Republic and the first centuries of
the Empire were really much more confused and unsettled in matters
of religion, for Christianity was the last rather than the first religion
to blow in from the East. From at least the third century BC onwards,
exotic, passionate, new faiths flowed into Rome and her empire
from all over what we now call the Middle East, from Phrygia in Asia
Minor, from Syria, from Egypt, from Persia. The new religions were
brought by itinerants and immigrant labour. From Syria, those
Chaldean fortune-tellers brought their barbarian gods – Baal of
Damascus and the Haadad of Baalbek whose immense temple was
considered the wonder of the world. It was all very well for Cato the
Elder to advise his fellow landlords to evict these wandering charla-
tans, but the squires of Latium, like English farmers today, were
desperate for anyone who was willing to work their fields. And
Syrian slaves had a good reputation, as did the Syrian merchants
who seemed to be everywhere.

Before we say a word about the nature of these cults, we should

remind ourselves of some of the key features of the old Roman religion (nearly 1,000 years old by this date), features which the new
cults lacked and for the lack of which they were treated with scorn
and suspicion by respectable Romans. First then, the old Roman
religion was intensely patriotic. It was focused on the *patria*. Its
prime object was that Rome should prosper in peace and win its
wars, and it was for that purpose above all that the gods were
invoked. As the Empire expanded, it was still the well-being of
Rome itself that was central. Although local cults were supported
and local deities amalgamated with or worshipped side by side with
Roman gods and goddesses (in the temple at Bath, for example, or
the temple of Mithras in the City of London) or occasionally
imported back to Rome by a process called *evocatio* – rather as a star
footballer might be transferred from an overseas club – Roman religion never purported to be in the least international. The new cults,
by contrast, professed no overwhelming allegiance to their countries
of origin and were easily exported to pretty well anywhere.[11]

The old Roman religion was not only intensely patriotic, it was
thoroughly civic. Its clergy were not a caste apart. On the contrary,
the *augures* and *pontifices*, despite their priestly titles and their religious
duties (reading the entrails of sacrificed animals, interpreting the flight
of birds and the utterances of oracles), were drawn from among the
leading senators, the very same men who dominated politics and the
law and who led Roman armies in battle. Young men from senatorial
families would get their first foot on the ladder by serving as augurs,
Julius Caesar, Pompey and Antony among them. And Romans were
proud of this. Cicero boasted that the system ensured 'that the most
eminent and illustrious citizens might ensure the maintenance of
religion by the proper administration of the state and the maintenance
of the state by the prudent interpretation of religion'. It would be
difficult in a single sentence to convey more potently the controlled,
cool-headed, this-worldly nature of Roman religion.

As the Empire expanded and the Emperor began to seem more
and more like a demigod, it is sometimes hard to distinguish Roman

religion from an Emperor cult supported by a few traditional deities. The temples were often dominated by statues of the Emperor and his family. Agrippa, when planning the Pantheon, had wished to set up a statue of his father-in-law Augustus there and name the building after him. When Augustus refused the honour, Agrippa put a statue of Caesar in the interior and statues of himself and Augustus in the porch. When Hadrian rebuilt the Pantheon in the marvellous shape we see today, he filled it with statues of the imperial family as well as of the gods, and he himself often held court there. Yet the most extraordinary passage in Hadrian's life happened not in Rome and had nothing to do with his family, but revolved around a boy of 18 or 19 of whom we know virtually nothing, except that he was beautiful and Hadrian fell in love with him.

The story of Antinous is one of the most bizarre episodes in Roman history. We should not lazily classify it with other examples of eccentric or debauched behaviour among emperors, for the story points forward to the great religious revolution that was coming. Antinous, supposedly a farmer's son from the Greek colony of Bithynia on the Black Sea, had often accompanied Hadrian on the Emperor's restless travels the length and breadth of his empire, which had taken him from Northumberland to the Upper Nile. It was during their expedition up the Nile on about 22 October AD 130 that Antinous was drowned. An accident? Suicide? Murder? The arguments about the manner of his death rage on two millennia later. But what is not in dispute is that the Emperor was shattered. The *Historia Augusta* says: 'He wept like a woman.' And in his grief he founded a whole new city, Antinoopolis, around the boy's temple or temple-tomb. It was a colossal project, three miles in circumference, with a main street a mile long, built on the gridiron pattern first used in the rebuilding of Miletus after the Persian destruction. There were temples, baths, immense gateways. Perhaps the most striking feature were the columns that lined the whole length of the main avenue, each column adorned with a sculpture of Antinous and his name inscribed on the entablature. No modern advertising agency could have devised more saturation coverage. Napoleon's surveyor Jomard gave a minute description of the remains, still formidable at that time to judge by his evocative engravings. Since then, alas, as at Miletus and at St Anne's Hydro, the locals have carted away every usable piece of stone, and all that remains is a sprawl of formless rubble.

No less remarkable was the swift expansion of the Antinous cult far beyond this obscure bend in the Nile. At least seventy cities all over the Empire scurried to build their own temples to honour a boy they had scarcely heard of and had certainly not seen: in Thessaloniki, at Lepcis Magna, at Luku in the eastern Peloponnese, in faraway Georgia. In Smyrna and dozens of other centres, coins were minted in memory of Antinous. Sculptures of him survive in vast quantities from East and West alike. Jomard counted 1,344 busts or statues of the marvellous boy in the two main streets of Antinoopolis alone.[12] In Athens, a new festival was established, the Antinoeia, which was still being celebrated 200 years later. Lamps, bowls and busts all bore the image of Antinous' lovely face. In death, the Emperor's toy boy had become not only an instant celebrity everywhere, he had become an instant god. He was the last non-imperial mortal to be deified, the only non-imperial head ever to appear on Roman coins.

Christian fathers everywhere in the Empire, in Carthage, Alexandria, Rome, Byzantium, Cyprus, Antioch and Bethlehem, all knew about Antinous, about his breathtaking beauty, about Hadrian's scandalous passion for him, and his even more scandalous declaring him to be a god. The trouble was that the cult of Antinous bore uncomfortable resemblances to the cult of Jesus, the immortal, self-sacrificing redeemer of Calvary. The pagan philosopher Celsus published an indictment of Christianity in about AD 176, where he argued that the honours paid to Jesus were 'no different from those paid to Hadrian's boy-favourite'. Christian apologists fiercely denied any such resemblance; again and again, they returned to the attack, Origen, Tertullian and Jerome all repeatedly denouncing Antinous as a public harlot and a corrupted Ganymede. None of them denied that he was beautiful. How could they? The sculptures present him as something like the Marlon Brando of *On the Waterfront*. Instead, they sometimes sought to distinguish the two saviours by presenting Jesus as positively ugly. The ferocity of their polemics shows how profound the impact of the Antinous cult had been, not merely on timeservers who wanted to suck up to Hadrian but on ordinary people.

As Royston Lambert points out in his brilliant *Beloved and God* (1984), Antinous, like Jesus, was an active god, helping and healing ordinary people. He was 'carrying out his work among the living', to quote the words on the obelisk which now stands in the Pincio Gardens in Rome. It was erected there by Pope Pius VII in 1822, the last year of a papacy that was wracked with humiliations, most of them at the hands of Napoleon who had dragged Pius to France to crown him Emperor only to snatch the crown from His Holiness's hands and crown himself. This obelisk is a strange thing, in the Egyptian style but with the hieroglyphs clumsily carved, probably by Roman craftsmen. It was just as well that they could not then decipher hieroglyphics properly (Jean-François Champollion first managed to translate the Rosetta Stone in that same year of 1822), for poor Pius would not care to have discovered that he had re-erected an obelisk that had been carved to honour an emperor's pagan catamite.[13]

Antinous was a god of change, not like the static gods of Rome. He suffered and died and, according to the obelisk, was raised again to life: 'The guardians of the gate of the underworld loosen their bolts and open their gates before him.' Because he had conquered death, he might help the rest of us to conquer death too. People wore Antinous medallions as protection against harm, and nailed pictures of him or labels bearing his name to the coffins of the dead.

Hadrian did not invent this remarkable cult all by himself. The Nile was a holy river to which the Egyptians owed their very survival, and it conferred sanctity and immortality not only on the drowned god Osiris, whose resurrection was celebrated each

October, but on anyone who drowned in its slippery mud. Victims of drowning might be honoured as gods themselves or identified with other gods, or venerated as martyrs. So it was the Egyptians who initially set Antinous on the road to godhood. But of course it took Hadrian's own superhuman status to broadcast the cult across the Empire.

It may seem surprising that a highly rational, intelligent and purposeful man like Hadrian should have listened so eagerly to the mysterious, deeply un-Roman pronouncements of Egyptian priests. Would his grief alone explain such a startling departure from Roman tradition as to make a god out of a mere boy who had no achievements to his name beyond a sultry, mesmerizing face and finely developed pectoral muscles? But the evidence suggests that Hadrian was and had been for some time in a strange mood: subject to fits of uncharacteristic brutality, notoriously against the Jews, and at the same time showing an equally uncharacteristic interest in the religions of the East. In company with Antinous, he seems to have participated in the Mysteries of Eleusis, which wrung out its devotees as thoroughly as any evangelical worship today. Plutarch describes the final moments of the initiation: 'Just before the end the terror is at its worst: there is shivering, trembling, cold sweat and fear. But the eyes perceive a wonderful light. Purer regions are reached and fields where there is singing and dancing; and sacred words and visions inspire a holy awe.' After being initiated, Hadrian, recently recovered from serious illness, felt 'reborn', according to an inscription on an official coin issued from Pergamon the year before the death of Antinous. And as Hadrian journeyed up the Nile, the Egyptian mysteries reinforced the Greek ones. With the astrologer priest Pancrates of Heliopolis, he saw spirits summoned from the underworld. At Hermopolis, the chief shrine of the god Thoth, the Egyptian equivalent of Hermes, the priests initiated him into their magic arts. In his heightened state of sensibility, the death of Antinous must have seemed a divinely ordained event, an Assumption of the beloved.

Even today the cult of Antinous still has its adherents. Hernestus Gill, the Priest of Antinous, circulates on his website *The Antinoopolis Gayzette*, which provides 'the latest news and views about Antinous the Gay God'. Much of this news is astrological, for the Star of Antinous rules all homosexuals, according to Gill, and its position in a natal chart says much about the astrological nature of a gay person. The star of Antinous was first seen in the skies either by Hadrian himself or by the astronomers of Hermopolis who assured him that this star, between the Eagle and the Zodiac in the Milky Way, was indeed a new one and must, according to the traditional belief about heroes, be the soul of Antinous blazing with eternal light. The grieving Hadrian seized on this explanation, and the word went out all over the Eastern Empire, so that the star appears next to the head of Antinous on coins from the Black Sea to the Mediterranean shore. Modern astronomers have deselected the star of Antinous and returned it to the constellation of the Eagle, but for adherents of the cult, it still burns bright in his memory. According to his high priest, its conjunction in your birth chart can mean all sorts of things, many of them rather grim and evocative of the fate of Antinous himself, such as 'a life of tribulations and broken relationships' (Moon in Square or Opposition), 'death by violence or suicide' (Mars in Square or Opposition), 'meteoric rise to fame and subsequent fall to obscurity' (Uranus in Conjunction); but on the plus side, if your Capricorn Natal Sun is conjunct with the star of Antinous, this indicates that 'your true genius lies in interior design or landscape architecture'.

Any such astrological indications would certainly have been lapped up in ancient Rome, but the hope of resurrection and redemption which the divine Antinous also offered was something new and, to conventional Roman citizens, unwelcome and puzzling. For, even in the earliest accounts of Roman religion, we can find no such hope of resurrection, few traces indeed of prophets or holy men, no explanation of creation or of man's relation to it, no discussion of the Four Last Things. So far as we can see too, the old Roman religion did not go in for daily worship. There was nothing in it which Jews or Christians would recognize as a requirement to lead a holy life, nor was there any expectation that religious experience might have the potential to change your life. Its ceremonies were not reserved for initiates like the rites of the Egyptian deities Isis and Serapis or those at Eleusis. Nor did they take place hugger-mugger, in what were little better than underground caverns, as did the blood-soaked rites of Mithras. Everything was public, out in the open. Sober Roman gentlemen such as Pliny, Seneca and Tacitus could be forgiven for regarding these upstart cults, priested often by ex-slaves, as belonging more to the realm of *superstitio* rather than true *religio*. And we may count them fortunate that they did not live to see the day, at the end of the fourth century AD, when the tables were turned, and Christianity was declared the true *religio* and the old religion downgraded to a mere *superstitio*.

Modern scholars are sometimes reluctant to call the new cults 'oriental', fearing to be denounced by Edward Said, even from the grave, as patronizing orientalists. Yet these cults did all come from the East, if mostly from the Near East, and there was undeniably something foreign, even exotic, in their practices and the passions those practices unleashed. One can imagine the apprehensive shivers from the villa as the senator heard in the distance the barbaric wailing of his slaves and freedmen at their worship, rather as a plantation owner in the Deep South might catch the singing of spirituals wafting across the lawn from the slave huts.

From Persia, according to Cumont though later scholars have disputed this, came the cult of Mithras, 'the invincible god', the tutelary deity of armies, worshipped in the first instance by soldiers who fought against Rome in the uplands of Anatolia and then by those who fought for Rome as her empire expanded further east. As the Romans marched towards the Euphrates, they became more intimately acquainted with the worship of Mazda and Zoroaster and Mithras the pure genius of light. Towards the end of the first century, the Mithras cult was spread by soldiers in the service of Rome along the entire length of the Empire's frontiers, leaving many traces in the

camps of the Danube and the Rhine, beside the stations along
Hadrian's Wall, by the walls of Londinium, and in other army posts
scattered along the edge of the Sahara and the mountains of northern
Spain. At the same time, Asiatic merchants were introducing the cult
to all the cities of the Empire along its commercial roads and waterways. Meanwhile, at the heart of the Empire, the oriental slaves
were everywhere, working as domestic servants and clerks as well as
in the fields and mines, and above all in the service of the Emperor
himself, where they supplied the need for a central bureaucracy to
administer the ever-growing dominion.

The Egyptian gods – Isis, Osiris, Serapis – for their part were
exported from the *serapeum* in the city of Alexandria, then at its peak
of power and splendour. Alexandrian merchants were among the first
exporters of Eastern religion to the Greek and Roman world. Temples
of Isis and Serapis sprang up along the coasts of Ionia and Sicily and
southern Italy. There was an Iseum at Pozzuoli in about 100 BC, and
at Pompeii too at the same date, adorned with beautiful frescoes.

In Rome itself, the authorities tried to check the influx of these
alien deities with their weird and passionate rites. Four times – in 59,
58, 53 and 48 BC – the Senate ordered their altars and statues to be
torn down, but to no avail. Augustus had a deep aversion to the gods
of his former enemies. If Antony and Cleopatra had defeated his
forces at the Battle of Actium, after all, Isis and Serapis would have
entered Rome in triumph. Augustus forbade any Alexandrian altars
to be erected in the sacred enclosure of the *pomerium*. Agrippa
extended this exclusion zone to 1,000 paces around the city. Tiberius
reinforced this edict and in AD 19 instituted the bloodiest persecution
yet of the priests of Isis.

Utterly futile. The worship of Isis and Serapis, like that of Mithras,
spread all over the Roman Empire. In the end, Rome had to cave in.
At that point, after all, Alexandria was still a more beautiful and
learned and better policed city than Rome. The mere Latins had to
translate her manuscripts, import her scholars and astronomers, and
her gods too.

After Tiberius died, Caligula erected the great temple of Isis Campensis on the Campus Martius just behind the Pantheon. His successors, the Flavians, the Antonines and the Severi, beautified that temple and built others – Caracalla's Iseum on the Quirinal Hill was said to be the most beautiful yet. We often remark on the amazing survival of the Pantheon as a Christian church, but we less often note that the Egyptian obelisk in the square in front of it, the Piazza Rotonda, comes from the temple of Isis Campensis, as does the obelisk that rides on the back of Bernini's dear little elephant in the Piazza della Minerva behind the Pantheon. There is a twin to the Rotonda obelisk mouldering in the garden of the Villa Celimontana on the Celian Hill. In the corner of the Piazza Venezia opposite Mussolini's wedding cake, there is a defaced female bust which is thought to be a figure of Isis from this same temple. Near the Pantheon again, off the Street of the Marble Foot, there is a colossal sandalled foot in marble, which from the style of the sandal is claimed to be a statue, perhaps of Serapis, from the same temple. Thus the goddess of Egypt still scatters her remains around modern Rome.[14]

The Mithraic religion too had its imperial imprimatur when Diocletian officially recognized Mithras as the protector of the reconstructed Empire. Thus all four of the principal variants of Eastern paganism had their day in the sun. And here and there amid the ruins of imperial Rome, we find these vestiges of pagan Rome. There were no fewer than six temples of Cybele, also known as Magna Mater, the Great Mother, within the *pomerium*, or sacred boundary of the city, along with ten shrines dedicated to the Syrian-Phoenician cults of the Sun and of Jupiter Dolichenus. There were thirteen temples dedicated to Isis and Serapis, and, by the end of the fourth century, some sixty Jewish and Christian catacombs outside the *pomerium*. And according to present estimates, Rome contained no fewer than thirty-five *mithraea*, or *spelaea* (caves) as they were originally called, for they were all built underground to commemorate the bringing of light to the upper world by Mithras.

As you leave the ticket office for the Baths of Caracalla, on your right you will probably miss the entrance to an inconspicuous underground building, discovered only in 1912, which is the largest *mithraeum* in Rome. Running down the middle of the gloomy long chamber, there is the characteristic trench where the new initiate used to cower while a bull was slaughtered overhead, so that he might be drenched in its blood. This rite, known as the *taurobolium*, was common to the cult of Cybele and the cult of Mithras. So even here in the Baths of Caracalla, in this purely secular complex dedicated to hygiene and relaxation, we find inconspicuously lurking right at the furthest edge of the precinct a temple of the more intense and other-worldly faith.

Deep under the earliest shrines of Christianity in Rome, there were temples dedicated to the worship of Mithras, many of which are only just coming to light, still half excavated and shown to the public rarely and with some embarrassment by the Church authorities.[15] The *mithraeum* under Santa Prisca occupies a building complex that had formerly been a palace of Trajan's. The remarkable thing about it, apart from the paintings and inscriptions on its walls, is that for two centuries it was divided by the thickness of a wall from an early Christian church. The same juxtaposition is to be found at San Clemente and at least one *mithraeum* in Ostia. The freedom of religious choice that gradually permeated Rome seems to have permitted these two faiths to coexist side by side, however much their claims might conflict. Since only men could be initiated into the Mithraic mysteries, is it conceivable that they might have allowed or encouraged their womenfolk to worship next door in the Christian shrine, where they would be more than welcome? But gender apart, it was the similarities between the cults that grated. On the walls of the *mithraeum* of Santa Prisca, there is a prayer to Mithras which sounds uncannily like Christian prayers to Jesus: 'And you saved us after having shed the eternal blood' (admittedly, in the Mithraic cult it was the bull's blood that was shed, not the hero's). And was not the sacred repast of Sol and Mithras with its exchange

of bread and water or wine, also depicted on these walls, just what
the Christian thunderer Tertullian called it, 'a diabolical imitation of
the Holy Eucharist'? No wonder this was the painting that the
Christians next door slashed most viciously when they officially triumphed and theirs was declared the one true faith at the end of the
fourth century. But it could have gone the other way. Only fifty years
earlier, the Apostate Emperor Julian had rebelled against his Christian
upbringing and attempted to reinstall paganism across the Empire.
The French historian Ernest Renan famously hazarded that 'if
Christianity had been stopped in its growth by some mortal malady,
the world would have been Mithraist'.

The best place I know to get a sense of the rich variety of religious
life in Rome is in the ruins of ancient Ostia. This delectable, not
much visited site with its cypresses and umbrella pines and cobbled
streets and lovely tawny ruins stretches for more than a mile along the
old course of the Tiber down to the former shoreline. The river silt
has pushed the sea several miles away, but Ostia still has the feeling of
a busy port, with its offices for shipping agents from all over the
Empire, its shops and warehouses, its public baths for merchants and
cart-drivers, and its temples and basilicas and synagogues (Ostia has
the earliest synagogue ruins found anywhere). And everywhere there
are temples of Mithras, next to baths and barracks and bakeries,
tacked on to private houses, under courtyards, fifteen of them uncovered so far, with paintings and mosaics and figures of Mithras slaying
the bull and his attendants Cautes and Cautopates, much of the work
amazingly bright when you sweep away the sand and the pine needles
which have protected them so long. Perhaps the most enchanting spot
in the whole of Ostia is the grassy triangle at the end of the lane when
you turn left off the main street. There grouped around a wild-flower
meadow stands the platform of a temple of the Phrygian goddess, the
Great Mother, under a canopy of umbrella pines, and across the
meadow the sanctuary of her shepherd lover the god Attis, guarded by
telamones (the male equivalent of caryatids) in the shape of fauns with
pipes and shepherd's crooks, and then next to the Attis shrine a

temple of Bellona, the Roman goddess of war. According to scholars, there is no better preserved sanctuary space in the whole Roman Empire; there can be none which is more numinous. Just up the lane there are temples dedicated to the usual Roman deities, Hercules and Neptune and Augustus; here we have a *campo santo* for the gods of the Near East. For at Ostia we see the ecumenical spirit in action – '*oecumenicus*' being used by both the Greeks and the Romans to mean 'belonging to the whole world', the word then falling into disuse before being revived in late Victorian times to refer to the idea of different religions coming together and talking to each other, something that had not been on the agenda since the fall of Rome.

It is in Ostia too that the Christian writer Minucius Felix has his civilized debate about religion with the pagan Caecilius and the Christian Octavius, as they walk through the city down to the seashore where they paddle in the gentle waves and watch the local boys playing ducks and drakes with the flat seashells. Their talk ranges over many things: how the climate in Britain, though lacking in sunshine, is warmed by the Gulf Stream; how the Romans easily adopt the gods of other peoples when they conquer them, so that 'what were formerly Egyptian rites are now Roman ones'; how the scepticism of Socrates and others is an easy cop-out; how oracles and auspices do occasionally turn out to be correct but only by accident. But what stays with one above all is the easy open temper of the talk – and the boys skimming their shells across the mild sea.

In the City of London, the traffic roaring down Queen Victoria Street takes no heed of the neatly reconstructed ground plan of our own Temple of Mithras, today perched on a platform above our heads but originally discovered in 1954 at a level 18 feet lower on the bank of one of the City's now hidden streams, the Wallbrook (the cult needed a flow of water, not least to wash away the bull's blood). It is a fair-sized building, some 60 feet by 25 feet, with a semicircular apse and brick-tile string courses running round the walls. Inside, there are twin aisles separated by sleeper walls each carrying seven stone columns, perhaps symbolizing the seven grades of initiation, and a raised altar. But it is the statues that were unearthed inside the temple and which are preserved in the Museum of London that take the breath away. Jocelyn Toynbee believes that 'the works of art from the Roman period from the Wallbrook temple constitute the richest, most impressive and varied series that any building or group of buildings so far excavated in Roman Britain has yielded.'[16] No *mithraeum* in Rome and only one in the entire Roman Empire (at Merida in Spain) can boast a richer set of marbles. It is clear, Professor Toynbee argues, that not only soldiers and labourers but also merchants and high-class government officials must have subscribed to the cult, for such works, many of them imported from Italy, to have adorned its temple.

But it is the figures of Mithras that catch the eye and stick in the memory. In his temple beside Wallbrook, where the church of St Stephen Wallbrook now stands, there were at least four statues of him, apart from a rondel relief of him slaying the bull. Just as there is no limit to the numbers of paintings and sculptures of the Madonna and the Crucifixion in a Catholic church, so the scene of Mithras slaying Taurus is endlessly repeated in the temples dedicated to him. There is, for example, the huge fragment, twice life-size, of his marble right hand gripping the cylindrical stone pommel of the knife into which a metal blade would have been inserted; then there is a limestone fragment of his left hand grabbing the fleshy upper lip of the bull; and, most unforgettably, there is the marble head of the god, which, for reasons of quality as well as scale, must belong to yet another, and far finer statue than the marble right hand.

It is the head of a young man with tousled locks and a floppy Phrygian cap worn casually on the back of his head, more of a fashion statement than a serious hat. His lips are full and sensuous and parted, as though in surprise. His eyes are staring but, like his whole head, not staring at the viewer but three-quarters twisted away, both himself transported and transporting his followers in this savage ecstatic moment as he plunges the knife in with his right hand and jerks the bull's head upright with his left hand inside its mouth.

It is the posture of a rock star reaching his climax on stage, that twisted torso and turned-away head drawing in the worshippers with a far more intense hypnotic attraction than if he had been making direct eye contact. Mithras and Mick Jagger, the god and the demigod, on the brink of getting that elusive ultimate satisfaction.

Like the Eastern religions of ancient Rome, our modern pop cults began without official stimulus or encouragement. To start with, they often met stern disapproval from the guardians of public morality. Like the Mithraists, their rites were first celebrated in underground caverns, most famously that of the Beatles in Liverpool. Then the cults grew until they staged vast festivals in the open air, at first held in tucked-away fields in the country rather than the normal sites of public celebration. They flourished because they proclaimed their subversion and offered a new world of intoxicating experience. They made mock of the stale old official religions, until the old religions had to beg for mercy and a kindly word. The demigods of the new cults were garlanded with official honours, MBEs and knighthoods, which they toyed with and sometimes tossed back to those who conferred them. And they conquered the world. Just as there is scarcely a remote pueblo or hill village that is unaware of Mick Jagger, so Mithras was a familiar cult figure to soldiers and the local natives in places as far afield as Austria and Slovenia and Caernarvon and Hadrian's Wall, where remains of no fewer than three *mithraea* have been discovered in recent years. The bull-slayer promised to take bored and lonely soldiers and wretched peasants out of themselves, to raise them to a state of ecstasy, *ek-stasis*. For those who kept to the old religions, *ekstasis* was an undesirable state. It meant losing your self-control, going doolally. For devotees of the new religions, it meant, well, ecstasy.

When Christianity appeared on the scene, the pagans compared their rite of *taurobolium* to Christian baptism, just as it was claimed that the Christians had copied their Passion rites at the vernal equinox from the rituals of the death and rebirth of Attis. The promoters of Christianity fiercely resisted the accusation that they had anything in common with the pagan cults. This was a New Gospel to wash away the sins of the world. It could not admit to sharing so much as a common origin with these idolatrous and pernicious heresies – which is why they have very largely been extirpated from Christian ecclesiastical history, to be replaced by a simpler story in which the old outworn Roman gods were replaced by Jesus. Later Christian theologians were willing enough to acknowledge philosophical debts to pre-Christian thinkers – to Plato and the Neoplatonists, to the humane and universal teachings of the Stoics. But to admit that they had anything in common with Baal and Cybele or Mithras and Isis and Zoroaster, that was unthinkable.

Yet if we confine ourselves, more modestly, to asking the question: How did Christianity come to be accepted at Rome?, then we shall find it unavoidable to examine the role played by the other religions that came from the East. What might be called a softening-up role. Christianity, when it arrived, seemed much less outlandish than it would have if the pagan cults had not been so celebrated by and integrated into the Roman Empire.

The first novel feature which the cults imported was monotheism, an idea unknown to classical antiquity. Originally Zeus seems to have been like a British prime minister, first among equals on Mount Olympus. Later on, he is described as the Supreme Governor of the Universe, but there are still other gods in the Pantheon, quarrelling, making love and striving for supremacy. In the oriental cults, by contrast, we can detect here and there a growing tendency to mark out a single god or goddess – the Great Mother, Baal, Mithra – as supreme. It seems, besides, to have been the personal wish of several emperors, from Claudius onwards, to encourage this tendency. Perhaps supreme power-holders tend to be more comfortable with a single deity in heaven who mirrors the uniqueness of their own position on earth, in much the same way that Henry Kissinger allegedly wanted to have a single telephone number to call when he wished to speak to Europe. The old, casual, sprawling religion of local deities, family cults, 'specialist' gods and goddesses – for love, medicine, war and so on – seemed inadequate, provincial, out of date. These convenient and appealing features of the old polytheism later resurfaced in Christianity in the cult of local and particular saints, but those were to be strictly licensed and subordinate cults. There was but one God.

The next imported feature, and the one which caused the early emperors most anxiety, was the strong appeal of the new cults to the poorer classes, especially to slaves and other immigrants. This was not simply because it was these same slaves and immigrants who had brought their native cults with them from their country of origin. It was also that the new cults had more to offer the poor. They were more passionate, more human. The gods of Greece and Rome enjoyed immortality and perpetual youth on Mount Olympus. The divinities of the East, by contrast, descended, suffered and died and then were reborn. Osiris, Attis and Adonis were mourned like mortals by wife and mother and mistress. And the believers too mourned for their deceased god and then exulted when he was reborn. Or if they were followers of the Persian faith, keeping watch over the sodden hills of Northumbria or manning the sand-blown forts at the edge of the Sahara, they joined in the passion of Mithras, condemned to create the world in suffering. There was nothing like this in the dignified, strait-laced old religion of Rome. There was a lot like it in Christianity.

And these consuming religious experiences were open to everyone. The oriental religions began as democratic and even revolutionary forces, turning out to be so strong that, in the end, the wiser emperors concluded 'if you can't beat 'em, join 'em' and co-opted the new cults into the Roman pantheon, restoring or building their temples all across the Empire, Antonius Pius, for example, restoring the great temple of Baalbek.

Fasting for prescribed periods, celebrating a daily service according to an unchanging liturgy, spending long periods in contemplative devotion, the priests of the Egyptian faith had a routine very like that which we see carried out to this day by their Christian counterparts.

All these elements combined to make Christianity seem more normal and more appealing. The traditional religion of Rome might be wholesomely civic and staunchly patriotic, but it did not engage the individual in the same way, offering no transformation of the individual soul. By contrast, Christianity was essentially passionate. It whispered, despite pagan mockery, the most intoxicating promises of salvation and immortality. It set itself above and apart from and, if need be, in opposition to governments, especially those of tyrants and oppressors.

In retrospect, it does not seem so odd that Christianity rose as the old religion fell into decline. Some modern scholars argue that the evidence for such a decline is unclear at best. Temples to the old gods were still being built or restored – Augustus boasted that he had restored eighty-two in his sixth year as consul alone.[17] The old rites were still being officially celebrated, both in a Rome that was growing and prospering and across an empire that was expanding at a dazzling rate, which was for pious Romans the acid test of religious success. Yet we cannot ignore the testimony of those same pious Romans who were convinced that the old standards had decayed and that a crasser, barbarian age had infiltrated its own impious values. After all, we can see today that our established churches have suffered and are continuing to suffer a precipitous loss of support, although their churches are being repaired at vast expense and fitted out with central heating and toilets. The present standing of the Church of England is, I fear, a little reminiscent of the state of the old cults in Rome in the last two centuries before the barbarians really did come.

But it is the consequential impact of the new cults upon Rome and the Empire which most concerns us here. And that impact can be summed up, quite simply, as *choice*. Under the old religion, local and particular cults were passed down from generation to generation, defined by the rites to be performed which were carefully taught to each batch of novices. Obligations were inherited. Now quite suddenly, within the lifespan of a couple of emperors, the market had opened up. At first it was mostly the lower orders who congregated around the new altars, many of them lonely and disoriented in the great city and eager to continue following the rites of their home countries. But soon these immigrant devotees were occupying high positions in the army and the imperial service. They were successful merchants and builders. They were major-domos whispering enticing new spiritual ideas into their mistresses' ears. By the time of the Antonine emperors in the second century AD – that period which Gibbon regarded as the summit of human felicity – Rome was a ferment of religious choice. You could believe in anything or nothing. You could put your trust in astrologers, snake-charmers, prophets and diviners and magicians; you could take your pick between half a dozen creation myths and several varieties of resurrection. Or if you belonged to the educated elite, you could read the poetry of Lucretius and subscribe to a strictly materialist description of the universe.

In short, this is a time when anything goes and the weirdest, most frenzied creations of the human mind jostle with the most beautiful visions, the most inspiring spiritual challenges and the most challenging lines of scientific enquiry. It is hard to think of any period quite like it, before or since – until our own time. For about 1500 years it was taken for granted that everyone in the nation had to worship the same god in the same way. This applied to kings and emperors as much as ordinary people. The rule was *cujus regio, ejus religio* – whoever the land belonged to, his was the religion of the country. This could work either way round. In the early centuries of Christianity, when the ruler or his wife or daughter was converted to the new faith, the rest of the population would be baptized in their wake. Conversely, the new ruler or his consort might themselves have to convert to the faith of the people in order to secure legitimacy and popularity. The most famous example was the Protestant Prince Henri of Navarre, who had to become a Catholic in order to become King of France and is said to have explained: 'Paris is well worth a Mass.' Those who belonged to other faiths, where they were tolerated at all, might be deprived of their civil rights, like

Catholics and Dissenters in England up to the middle of the nineteenth century. In even unluckier lands, such as the Spain of
Ferdinand and Isabella, forcible conversion of Jews and Moors was
the order of the day.

What scarcely anybody, throughout that long period, began to
envisage was that *competition* between different faiths and sects might
be tolerable, let alone healthy. The American Revolution and the
Constitution of the United States which it generated gave birth to
something quite new in the Christian era: legally guaranteed freedom of religion and ongoing competition for adherents between a
multiplicity of sects, all equally acceptable in the eyes of authority.[18]

What we are living through today is the second New Age, every
bit as free and giddy as the first. Can we identify the forces which
have unleashed this bewildering diversity? Are there any causes
which the two New Ages have in common? The first instinct in
both cases is to talk about a new freedom of spirit, a breaking down
of the old barriers and inhibitions. In particular, we notice how
people begin to talk of their lives as a personal journey. They themselves have to make the choices: which goal to choose, which route
to follow, which turning to take. Indeed, the making of the choices
rather than the actual choices they make is often the part which
makes them feel alive.

This is opposed to the traditional pattern – in the Roman
Republic as in Victorian Britain – in which life's satisfactions come
from fulfilling our duty. That tradition – everything which was com-
prised in the term '*romanitas*' – was not necessarily a pedestrian path.
You might, so to speak, overfulfil your duty by reaching heights of
courage, steadfastness and the love of country or of your neighbour,
but you were to achieve these things within the tramlines of the
good life as prescribed by tradition.

Yet all this is merely to describe the contrast between the two attitudes towards life. It does not begin to explain what triggers the
change from one to the other. We can find plenty of indicators
within the intellectual life of society to suggest when such a change

in the wind might be coming. But such intellectual changes may not touch the lives of ordinary people, or not until after a considerable time lag.

There is a more material change which may have an impact on the soul quite as intense as its impact on social and economic conditions. Both the Roman Empire and the end of the twentieth century were periods of rapid and non-stop globalization. I say non-stop because globalization is not a finite process like a glass slowly filling to the brim. It is, as Marx described in *The Communist Manifesto*, a restless, limitless, swirling surge. One year your T-shirts and trainers were being made in India and Pakistan, the next year they came from Thailand and Indonesia, now they are made in China.

Marx was writing 160 years ago, and that tremendous surge of globalization, fertilized by the political dominance of Free Trade principles, reached its peak in the years leading up to 1914. Indeed, there are economic historians who would argue that even today in terms of world trade we have scarcely recaptured that degree of globalization which was shattered by two world wars and the rise of protection.

Yet that surge in world trade seemed to make relatively little difference to the world of religion. Catholics and Protestants continued to squabble, Hindus and Muslims viewed each other with suspicion. But the mass of devotees stayed within their faiths, even if a handful might defect from one variant to another.

For this globalization of goods was not accompanied by a globalization of people. There was, it is true, large-scale emigration from Western Europe to North America and Australia and New Zealand. But these were mainly economic refugees who took their own faiths with them and preserved them as intact as they could within the new societies they were helping to build.

During the eighteenth and nineteenth centuries too, elite travellers reached the furthest bounds of the earth. Some of them took up residence in these realms that seemed so exotic to them. Lord Byron and Lady Mary Wortley Montagu and the explorer Richard

Burton dressed up in oriental costume. Painters like David Roberts, J.F. Lewis, the Daniels and George Chinnery sent their canvases of Egypt, India and China home to adorn the walls of London drawing rooms. But all this was mere cultural tourism. The objection to Edward Said's much contested polemic against the patronizing attitudes implicit in this 'orientalism' is not so much that his analysis is wrong as that it exaggerates the real impact of what was not much more than curiosity, a glancing by-product of the imperial age. What was remarkable about this imperialism in retrospect is how little rather than how much interpenetration of cultures it generated.

The immigration that happened at the end of the British Empire, in the twentieth century, was quite different. A desperate shortage of labour drove employers, both private and public, actively to recruit, or at least to accept workers from the West Indies, North and West Africa, and India and Pakistan on a scale never seen before and not foreseen at the time. In some cases, the recruitment was deliberate and official, as in the campaigns by the British NHS and London Transport to find nurses and bus drivers in the West Indies. In other cases, people just poured in from what came to be called the 'New Commonwealth' through the gaps in the immigration regulations to fill the gaps in the labour market, almost entirely at the bottom end of the market.

This intermingling from below parallels almost exactly what happened under the Roman Empire. Suddenly the streets were filled with foreign faces, black, brown or yellow, and within a few years entire public services seemed to be staffed by the new arrivals and whole areas inhabited almost exclusively by them. And in a few more years, their temples and mosques sprang up next to parish churches and the church bells alternated with the sound of the muezzin. Disused Anglican and Methodist churches were taken over by unfamiliar sects of charismatic and evangelical immigrants. Dying Church of England congregations were revived by enthusiastic singing, dancing and clapping fellow religionists from West Africa or the West Indies. Those passionate forms of celebration began to be

absorbed by English-born worshippers, and new liturgies imbued
with colour and vibrancy replaced the Book of Common Prayer. In
the United States, much the same consequences followed the immigration of blacks from the Southern States to New York and the
factories of Detroit and Chicago. Not only their exuberant forms of
worship but their Salvationist doctrines moved north with them;
black and white were born again together. This was by no means the
first Great Awakening in the history of American religion, but it was
perhaps the first in which the immigrant underclass showed the way.

These religious interminglings and regenerations bring other faiths
into the high street. At the same time, cheap travel permits religious
tourism on a scale not previously seen. The monasteries and ashrams
of Asia become accessible not simply as picturesque architectural
sites to be visited but as intense religious experiences to be sampled
and compared. Religious choice becomes available, not only in the
form of a once-for-all conversion but as an ongoing freedom that
operates, so to speak, all the way down. You can shop around, pick-
and-mix without further obligation, choosing to meditate according
to one tradition, do your physical exercises according to another,
decorate your house according to some quite different faith or philosophy. Yoga, Zen, feng-shui, astrology, t'ai chi are only the most
celebrated disciplines or fads that come to hand. Gurus and preachers of all sorts break free of the religious traditions which gave them
birth, to become independent celebrities. Of course, all religions
have thrown up charismatic preachers and teachers, celebrated rabbis
and imams. But in previous history these dazzling figures owed some
allegiance to the existing establishment of their faith and were subject to its disciplines. And when they broke irrevocably with that
establishment, they felt bound to found a new establishment with
new doctrines and disciplines often more stringent than the old
ones: for example, the founding of the ultra-orthodox sects of
Judaism, the new churches that Luther, Calvin and Wesley founded,
the irrevocable splits within Islam which led to new colleges and
theologies being instituted. But the gurus of today, whether deriving

from Christian or Hindu or Buddhist origins, often feel little need to found a full-scale new church with its own theological apparatus; they may insist on little beyond personal allegiance and financial contribution. They are in essence freelance operators, boutiques in the shopping mall, for this is an age where monolithic hierarchical institutions are out of fashion and the smart thing to do is to contract out your operations. It is not that the emphasis on authority has entirely disappeared. If 'religio' really does take its derivation from 'religio' – 'bind together' – then discipline and the authority that imposes discipline must be part of its essence. It is more that it is generally understood that authority is *replaceable*. So long as you are sampling the product, you are subject to its terms and conditions of use. But the only real enduring authority is your own sense of what is right and true; the individual conscience is ultimately supreme. Of course all religions ultimately depend on the assent of each believer, but in the days when religions were supported by temporal power, the penalties for a wayward conscience were severe – they still are in Islamist regimes. Even when legal penalties faded away, there were still social penalties for believing in the wrong God or no God at all. Only in New Ages such as the Roman Empire or our own are you genuinely free to believe in anything or nothing. G.K. Chesterton is often credited with the maxim that 'when people cease to believe in God, they will believe in anything'. But nobody has yet managed to find the source of that quotation and I doubt whether they will, since the thought seems too crude for that subtle thinker. It would be more accurate to say that 'when people cease to believe in a single God, they feel entitled to believe in anything, everything or nothing'. We are all shoppers in the spiritual supermarket, and we have the right to withdraw our custom whenever we fancy.

For non-belief is also a prominent feature of the New Age – and a logical one. For only in an age of total liberty or anarchy of belief is it a daily experience to see faiths jostling side by side, each claiming to possess a monopoly on the truth. In such an atmosphere, it is hardly surprising that many choose to echo the scepticism of

Xenophanes of Colophon. For the first time since the fall of Rome, there is open and unhampered competition between a myriad of faiths and no-faiths. One man's beliefs or non-beliefs are as good as another's. And the most exhilarating opportunity of all the opportunities that the spiritual supermarket offers is the opportunity to save yourself. And you can do this in the most dramatic way imaginable, by choosing to be reborn.

The Second Coming – Again

When Sarah Palin was plucked from an obscurity that was almost dazzling to be the Republican Party's nominee for Vice-President, elite commentators immediately denounced the choice as wholly unsuitable. The first objection was her lack of experience. She had held office for only two years as governor of the snowbound wastes and sparse populace of Alaska. The second objection was that her crass pro-business policies had accelerated the dismal process of melting those snowbound wastes. Her indifference to the ecological pieties was made all too visible by her willingness to pose for the cameras with her gun beside any passing moose she had just herself slaughtered and gralloched. The sporting bounce that had worked so well for Teddy Roosevelt a century earlier was now a blasphemy against the spirit of the age. But worst of all, and most predictable of all, was that this unspeakable hickette belonged to one of those weird churches which believe that a person can be born twice and that the end of the world is nigh – the word 'nigh' being now deployed only in connection with prophecies of this event. Such creatures from the backwoods ought to stay right there and not come into town and start plaguing decent modern folks.

Yet Mrs Palin's religious odyssey has been repeated by millions of Americans – South Americans as well as North. She received infant baptism into the Catholic Church. Then her mother began to take her and her siblings to the Wasilla Assembly of God, and at the age of 12 it was into that church that she was re-baptized, by total immersion in the waters of a lake during a family holiday. After being 'saved', as she called it, as do millions of others who have travelled that road, she embraced the typical practices of Pentecostal churches, such as the laying on of hands and speaking in tongues. She also heard many sermons from the Assembly of God's pastor, Ed Kalnins, declaring that the Latter Rain is beginning to fall. This doctrine asserts that the return of speaking in tongues and the new or refreshed Baptism of the Holy Spirit mark the 'Latter Rain' which will bring the Church's work to completion and herald the Second Coming of Jesus Christ. Several of the Old Testament prophets use the Latter Rain as a metaphor for the granting or withholding of God's favour, for example in Jeremiah 3:3: 'Therefore the showers have been withholden and there hath been no latter rain.'

That Second Coming remains imminent. Soon will come the Rapture in which true Christians will be caught up and taken away from earth to be with Jesus. This hope derives from St Paul's electrifying promise to the Thessalonians: 'For the Lord himself shall descend from heaven with a shout, with the voice of the archangel, and with the trump of God: and the dead in Christ shall rise first. Then we which are alive and remain shall be caught up ['*rapiemur*' in the Latin of the Vulgate] together with them in the clouds, to meet the Lord in the air: and so shall we ever be with the Lord.'[19] Pastor Kalnins hopes that the Rapture will take place within his lifetime: 'I'm looking at the window and I can see it's going to rain.' Trouble in the Middle East was one such indicator. 'Scripture specifically mentions oil instability as a sign of the Rapture.'[20] When Mrs Palin was elected to the Wasilla city council and later became mayor of the straggling little town, she switched her allegiance to the more mainstream Wasilla Bible Church, some claimed for political reasons, in order to seem less eccentric.

But her rebirthing stands. So does that of George W. Bush. In his New England youth, he was raised an Episcopalian. When his hellraising began to scare his family and himself, he was converted, partly by Billy Graham, pastor to Bush senior and many other post-war presidents. Down in Texas, Bush junior was reborn as a member of his wife's church, the United Methodists, who were growing as fast as the Episcopalians were declining.

Barack Obama was not brought up in a religious background. His mother was a secular intellectual who became an anthropologist: his father had decamped back to his native Kenya. His mother's parents, who did most of his bringing up, were of Baptist and Methodist stock but not themselves especially religious. As a social worker in Chicago, he says, 'I was drawn to the power of the African-American religious tradition to spur social change.' Being a young man on his own in a strange big city may have had something to do with it too. At all events, he began to attend the Trinity United Church of Christ on the South Side, and under the sulphurous tuition of the Revd. Jeremiah Wright eventually walked down the aisle to be baptized: 'Kneeling beneath that cross on the South Side of Chicago, I felt God's spirit beckoning me. I submitted myself to His will and dedicated myself to discovering His truth.'[21]

Here are three very different characters: a hockey mom from Alaska, a spoilt frat brat from the Ivy League by way of Texas, and a cool black dude who had made a remarkable journey from Hawaii to Harvard and eventually the White House by way of Indonesia and Kenya, and about that journey wrote the finest book ever composed by an American politician. In each of their lives, being born again was a central, momentous event – an event replicated in the lives of millions of Americans, both rich and poor. The sequence of Catholic baptism followed by re-baptism in one or other of the Pentecostal and Evangelical churches is shared by Sarah Palin with huge numbers across the barrios of Central and South America. It is a phenomenon both so dramatic on the individual level and so enormous in its collective impact that it is almost as startling how little discussed it still is in the mainstream media. If the reborn were a single nation, they would be a power to be reckoned with. Yet their emergence provokes little more than an embarrassed coughing fit from the secular elite.

There have been Great Awakenings in American religion before, just as there were all over Europe during the eighteenth and nineteenth centuries. There were earlier intimations of the Rapture too. In the 1840s, William Miller made several precise predictions that the world would end, first between 21 March 1843 and 21 March 1844, then after admitting a minor miscalculation, on 22 October 1844. The failure of these prophecies came to be known as the Great Disappointment. Millerites dispersed to found several new churches, the most famous and enduring of which was the Seventh-Day Adventist Church. Miller's debacle has not prevented twentieth-century Rapture enthusiasts from offering fresh dates for the ultimate blast-off, 1977, 1981, 1995, 2000 and 2011 being among the fancied years. A dark horse remains the prediction by Sir Isaac Newton, based upon his calculations from the Book of Daniel, that the Rapture could happen no earlier than 2060.

Such prophecies are uttered and listened to far below the radar of the national media. The Rapture only occasionally surfaces in mainstream popular culture, for instance in Johnny Cash's song 'The Man Comes Around', or Bob Dylan's 'When He Returns' from the 1979 album *Slow Train Coming*. In this number he quotes from I Corinthians 15:51–2: 'Behold I shew you a mystery; we shall not all sleep, but we shall all be changed, in a moment, in the twinkling of an eye, at the last trump.' Noel Gallagher twice refers to the Rapture on the Oasis album *Dig Out Your Soul*.

You will see no reviews in the mainstream media of books like Hal Lindsey's *The Late, Great Planet Earth* (1970), though they sell in their millions. Lindsey suggested that the final drama might play out in the 1980s, with the 1970s as the obligatory preceding epoch of the Antichrist, as prophesied both by Moses and by Jesus. The Antichrist was to rule over a ten-nation European confederacy, of which the then six-nation Common Market was the forerunner, though Lindsey stops short of fingering Jacques Delors as the Antichrist himself. In his later work, *The 1980s: Countdown to Armageddon*, Lindsey predicted that 'the decade of the 1980s could very well be the last decade of history as we know it'. The decade certainly did not bring Lindsey's sales to an end. By 1990, *The Late, Great Planet Earth* had sold 28 million copies.

How could it be that in an era which is totally dominated by the materialist world-view such thunderous and dizzy prophecies could take such a hold? Why do the churches which preach versions of such impending doom insist that we must be born again to be saved? And not just those churches only. Many Pentecostal and Evangelical churches which do not preach the Rapture still regard rebirth in the Lord as the best and only hope of salvation. Yet many if not most of their converts have already been baptized once. How could it be that the first washing in the Holy Spirit should be of so little effect, and why should the second washing work any better? Why should it be necessary in so many cases to move to a new church to be born again? After all, many of these new churches do not claim exclusive authority and are quite friendly to other churches, for it is a part of the process leading up to the Rapture that the churches shall be gathered together into one huge band of the Elect. Yet the rebirthing cannot help but be an implied criticism of the first baptism, just as much as it is a triumphant assertion of the possibility of salvation.

The outsider may sense a desperate air about this placing of the final bet just before the off. Certainly there is little here of the calmness of Pascal's famous wager. Pascal's argument is that you have nothing to lose by believing in God, because if God turns out not to exist you have lost nothing, and if He does exist you have gained eternal life. Such a laid-back calling of the odds would not go down well with a modern Pentecostal preacher. For the seeker after truth who finds the present time dry and arid without God, this is the final plunge.

What is not often pointed out, either by sceptics or by the mainstream churches, is that these beliefs, which seem so outlandish to the modern mind, have plenty of backing in the Bible. You do not need to twist or overplay the texts to derive scriptural warrant for interpreting them this way. In the New Testament, there are for example the passages from Corinthians and Thessalonians already quoted and several passages in the Gospels, notably Matthew 24:29-31. In the Old Testament, Daniel 9 has been used by Isaac Newton and many others to calculate how long we have to wait. Ezekiel 38 and other verses in Hosea, Micah, Isaiah and Deuteronomy, to name but a few, make prophecies which find reverberations in the New Testament and so back again, until the mind grows giddy with hope.

There is little doubt that the early Christians themselves, many of them struggling to survive in the Roman Empire, did look eagerly for the Second Coming. Perhaps with luck it would come in their own lifetimes. Had not Jesus told them to be on the alert and ready at all times? The strength of this belief is confirmed by the disappointment that was recorded when nothing happened. As early as AD 90, Clemens Romanus, the legendary third Bishop of Rome, wrote: 'We have heard these things [about the end of the world] even in the days of our fathers, and look, we have grown old and none of them has happened to us.'

From then on, the Church made the most strenuous efforts to bury the idea that there might be a physical Second Coming any time soon. On the whole, these efforts were successful. To proclaim the imminent end of the world became a heresy. The millennium was to be interpreted symbolically rather than in material terms, explained St Augustine in Book XX of *The City of God*.[22]

Augustine had when younger been something of a millennialist himself. And as so often, it is his change of heart and his personal odyssey which embody the Church's struggle to fix on a final position. Before Augustine, there were several Church Fathers who had had millennial leanings, such as Irenaeus and even the austere Tertullian. But by the time of Augustine and the fall of Rome two centuries later, these millenarian hopes and visions had been ironed out of the orthodoxy. For the succeeding centuries, the guardians of that orthodoxy had to argue that these dangerous texts did not mean what they appeared to mean.[23] When St Paul gave that spine-tingling prophecy to the Thessalonians, he had to be understood as speaking metaphorically. All the same, the message is so thrilling that you can forgive the people who first heard it for thinking differently.

Nearly 1,600 years after Augustine, the then Cardinal Ratzinger was equally scathing about the millenarians in his *Catechism of the Catholic Church*. He denounced the idea of an imminent physical Second Coming as 'the intrinsically perverse political form of a secular messianism'.[24] Like Augustine, Ratzinger maintains the sequence of events leading up to the Last Judgment (including the coming of the Antichrist), but pushes the whole process not only beyond our imperfect understanding but beyond history.

Secular rulers encouraged the Church's efforts to stamp out these millenarian hopes which were so unsettling to the populace, fomenting wild and unpredictable mobs. Throughout the Middle Ages, the Second Coming remained a potent threat to the civil peace and one which might break out at any time, especially in periods of famine or plague when the authorities, both civil and ecclesiastical, appeared to be losing their grip.[25]

And the dream is not dead today. Just as the second baptism is an implicit criticism of the first, so the revival of the Second Coming is an implied (and not only implied) denunciation of the established churches as empty husks which have lost the fresh vision of the early Church and which have no answer to offer to the arid materialism of the present time. The doctrine of the End-Times is not some erratic outbreak of hysteria but, within its own terms, a logical response to the times we live in and one which reflects both the present weakness of the mainstream churches and the daunting hegemony of the Darwinian orthodoxy.

At the same time, the world-view it represents takes us back to those early centuries of the Christian era in which the end of the world seemed so near that you could almost touch it. The Christians were by no means alone in thinking this way. The End of Days – *aharit ha-yamim* – appears several times in the core of Jewish scripture.[26] Comparable scenarios for the End-Times are to be found in both the Sunni and Shia variants of Islam. A common source may be found in the eschatology of the Zoroastrians, the oldest that we know of, current by 500 BC and thus a significant influence during the later Roman Republic and the early imperial era, first on Judaism while the Middle East was under the rule of the Achmaenid dynasty and then on the subsequently emerging Christianity and later Islam. Eschatology is 'the study of the last things', more specifically the four last things: death, judgment, heaven and hell. And Zoroaster provides a full-scale treatment of all four. In Zoroastrian myth, the world was destined to go downhill, the earth would become more barren, the crops would fail, men would become more debauched and deceitful: 'Honourable wealth will all go to those of perverted faith, a dark sky will make the whole sky night and it will rain a horrible rain.' There will be a great battle between the Righteous and the Wicked, followed by a final judgment and a punishment of the Wicked. After these cataclysmic purgations, the world will achieve perfection. Poverty, hunger, old age and death will all be abolished. There is a clear line of descent from this storyline to the Revelation of St John, and indeed to the modern forecasts of the Latter Rain.

In Rome at this period, we have seen a glaring contrast between the official religion, so this-worldly, so civic, so respectable, with its expensively maintained temples and its punctiliously observed ceremonies, and the unquenchable passion and outlandish promises of the new cults, in their hugger-mugger services in cellars or modest private houses. Included among those members of the elite observing the official pieties, we shall also find quite a few secularists who in their hearts are as sceptical as Lucretius but who believe in keeping up religious appearances for the sake of Rome.

All of which sounds not unlike the way that opinion divides in the Western world in the early twenty-first century. For millions of people, most of them outside the elites and below the radar of the official media, rebirthing is the last best answer to despair and disillusion, just as it was the first best answer 2,000 years ago. What goes around comes around. It is a Palin-drome which tells the same story if you read it back to front. And those who read it this way would agree with G.K. Chesterton: 'The Christian ideal has not been tried and found wanting; it has been found difficult and left untried.'[27] So why not try again, but do it properly this time?

Yet we must stress again that, now as in the Roman Empire, these are individual spiritual commitments and private faiths. They have nothing to do with the prevailing culture, the world of politics and commerce and the media. There the only faith is a vague belief in democracy and a rather more insistent belief in the necessity of dialogue. Indeed, the one commandment that may not be broken is 'Thou shalt engage in talks'.

VIII

DIALOGUE

From Plato to Paxman

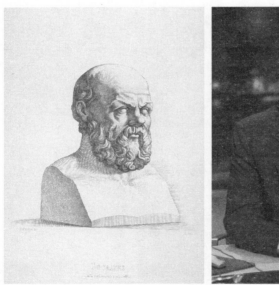

Has anything on television ever been more unsettling to the viewer than British Telecom's long-running series of advertisements in which the actor Bob Hoskins magically materializes in the middle of some startled family's living room and stands smirking in the background, oozing cockney menace, while the daughter dutifully telephones her mother in Australia or her sister in Sussex?

'It's good to talk,' Hoskins tells us confidingly. He does not need to add 'if you know what's good for you and don't want to end up sad and lonely and emotionally disturbed'. Never in human history has the importance of talking things out and over and through been quite so relentlessly hammered home by pastors and masters, teachers and therapists of every description. Dialogue is the shibboleth of our time. In the Bible the Ephraimites had their tongues cut off for failing to pronounce 'shibboleth' correctly. These days it would be a comparable misfortune to have your landline cut off or your mobile blocked.

This insistence on the importance of dialogue is intriguing and slightly mysterious. It is not, after all, as if people were reluctant to take Hoskins's advice and needed to be prodded, coaxed or bribed into talking to each other. On the contrary. The most abundant of all the fruits of affluence is conversation. On trains, on windswept street corners, in motor cars, on mountain tops, people of all ages clasp their mobile phones to their ears, desperate not to miss a second's talking time, however loud the traffic or biting the weather. The cheap phone call is the leveller of today, just as the cheap washing machine was the leveller of the 1960s.

The silent pub, like the silent Englishman, is as dead and gone as George Orwell's (or John Major's) little old lady cycling to Holy Communion. How quiet the milk bars and coffee bars of the teddy-boy era, how noisy the Frog-and-Firkins and Café Flos of today. You can still find country-house hotels as quiet as the grave, where the menu does most of the talking, but the typical smart restaurant in any British city now is designed to quadruple the noise, so that the conversation bounces off the shining floorboards up to the non-acoustic ceiling and back down on the glass table. Even bookshops now serve coffee, in the hope of provoking the odd *causerie*.

The 2008 report of Ofcom, the British communications regulator, recorded that in the previous year we spent an average of seven hours and nine minutes a day using an array of communications media: watching TV, surfing the net, using our mobiles and landlines

and sending text messages. The amount of time spent on our PCs
and laptops had quadrupled over the previous five years, the time
spent talking and texting on our mobiles had doubled. Nearly 60 billion text messages were sent in 2007 – up by an amazing 36 per cent
from the year before. There are now more mobile phones in circulation in the UK than there are people.

We believe, too, that talking really is good for our mental health.
From modest beginnings in Freud's Vienna, the talking cure has
conquered the world. If Freudian analysis seems too expensive and
too freaky, the Health Service will prescribe cognitive behavioural
therapy free of charge. There is also a vast array of licensed and unli-
censed therapists and counsellors who will offer to talk you through
every affliction that life throws up, bar a broken leg or a brain
tumour. Dialogue is the dominant cure for all forms of addiction –
drink and drugs, gambling and serial fornication, not to mention
doubt and despair. Now and then medication offers an alternative
which becomes fashionable for a time – Antabuse, methadone,
nicotine patches, lithium, Valium, Prozac – but the talking cure
always fights back. These chemical remedies, it is argued, do not
offer real cures; they are temporary dressings which mask the underlying cause, and that underlying cause can be got at only by
dialogue, either with a therapist or with your fellow sufferers. A cure
which is engendered by a course of one-to-one therapy, or by collective group work, is held to be more fundamental and likely to be
more lasting.

Now as a matter of fact, the benefits of conversation as opposed to
other means to health and happiness – medicine, cold baths, a skiing
holiday – are not by any means certain. The talking cure is just as fal-
lible as any other remedy for human misery.

In his remarkable little book *Conversation* (1999), the historian
Theodore Zeldin tells us:

> The kind of conversation I'm interested in is one which you start
> with a willingness to emerge a slightly different person. It is always

an experiment, whose results are never guaranteed. It involves risk. It's an adventure in which we agree to cook the world together and make it taste less bitter.[1]

In Zeldin's 'New Conversation', we are to desist from showing off and making jokes. Instead, we are to open up to one another. We need to develop models of 'how conversations develop equality'. There is no limit to the benefits of talking to each other in this new, open way. 'We could make our work a lot less boring and frustrating if we learned to talk differently.'[2]

These are huge claims. Yet one of the few concrete examples that Zeldin offers us of a conversation conducted in the proper spirit is not exactly encouraging:

> One of the most silent men I have known ended up committing suicide. When I was an undergraduate, the philosophy tutor of my college used to organise lunches in his rooms, inviting three or four students from different subjects. He brought us together for conversation, but he hardly ever spoke himself. And yet there was a wonderful warmth radiating from him, a gentleness, a modesty, which somehow made us talk, shy and ignorant though we were. We felt we had to respond to his kindness. I remember those stunted conversations as among the most moving I have ever had. Then one day he left a note outside his door, warning visitors that he had turned on the gas and that they would find him dead. Nobody knows why. Perhaps he felt he could not reach the impossibly high standards he set himself. But he knew how to bring people together. A conversation brings people and ideas together; and it's not disastrous if you keep silent while you watch ideas meeting.[3]

As it happens, Zeldin's college was also mine – Christ Church, Oxford – and so I imagine that the philosophy tutor he is talking about must be Michael Foster, whose suicide stunned the college during our time there. But the choice of this sad story to begin a chapter headed 'How conversation encourages the meeting of minds' strikes me as very odd. For what we all felt then was a sensation of collective failure. All the collegiate resources – friends at high table, the company of young and old (our company), the stimulation of the seminar, the solace of the cathedral (Foster was a wholehearted Christian) – had so utterly failed to remedy his despair. If his story teaches anything, it is a lesson about the limits of conversation. For conversation is no more an infallible remedy for melancholy than is offered by any other human pastime, such as work, sex or religion. Not every problem can be talked through and talked out. There will be days when nothing and no one can cheer you up.

In any case, the dominance of dialogue in our time does not always take the humane, modest form of a conversation in an Oxford don's rooms. In the broadcasting media, we are much more familiar with the interrogation, the verbal punch-up, the brusque that's-about-all-we've-got-time-for biff-bang of the *Today* programme or *Newsnight*. Nor is this phenomenon confined to the UK. In his splendidly quirky memoir, *To the Castle and Back* (2007), Václav Havel nicknames one of his least favourite TV interviewers Mr Please-be-brief. The pressure on producers to make public debate punchier, more confrontational, is unrelenting. The formula of programmes such as *Question Time* keeps altering over the years in the hope of sparking more fireworks. Instead of two or three spokesmen being given time to develop a point, the platform is uncomfortably crowded with half a dozen, who are in turn egged on, booed and baited by an audience selected, it seems, not so much for the balance of their opinions as for their irascibility.

The fashion for contestation is not just an accidental quirk of modern life. Nor is it a perverse, showing-off sort of thing, a fashionable variant of exhibitionism. It is built into the nature of modernity. Authority today is to be regarded as provisional, a temporary king who survives not by divine right but at our pleasure. At least that is the theory. In practice, we accept all sorts of authority because life is too short to contest everything. Agreement on practical arrangements is essential to civilized existence. So we agree that we should all drive on the same side of the road. We welcome standard sizes of electric plugs and computer layouts. Yet even these conveniences of daily life are open to challenge and improvement. Their dimensions and the rules governing their use are not to be thought of as god-given, because nothing is god-given.

The air we breathe is the air of Ionia. Everything can be challenged and queried and qualified and everyone has the right to engage in the conversation. That is what being a modern person means.

Yet within living memory things were quite different. Authority was an accepted and central element in both public and private life. Interviews on radio and TV were of a quite different timbre. It was regarded as a privilege for the viewers and listeners that the great man should condescend to appear. He would, as often as not, be asked what he would like to talk about. He could talk for as long as he wanted, and his remarks, however banal or disjointed, would be treated with unalloyed respect. I cannot think of any place where this tradition survives, except in the interviews with leading tenors and pianists, especially on Radio 3.

It has become unchallenged wisdom that all wisdom has to be challenged, vigorously and immediately. For half a century, the Reith Lectures on the radio offered a sequence of oases for reflective and sustained thought. From week to week, the listener would follow the speaker's argument and in the interval between broadcasts could brood on what the speaker had said. Now the speaker's time has been made substantially shorter in order to make room for a moderator, the sharp-tongued Sue Lawley, and an audience of selected questioners, who tend to ask the sort of banal questions that might be expected from the professions they are selected to represent. Any originality in the speaker's first thesis, far from being highlighted and refined, tends to be blurred and flattened.

This is not so surprising, because one of the things about dialogue is that it often has just such a tendency to blur and flatten fresh insights and new approaches. As the idea 'flows through' ('dialogue' means 'through-speech', not as one instinctively assumes 'two-speech', which is of course a duologue) the conversation, it risks having its sharp edges knocked off and being sandpapered down to a more generally acceptable shape.

That is, after all, often the deliberate purpose of dialogue in political or industrial disputes, to agree upon an acceptable package which preserves enough of each side's hopes and aspirations for the negotiators to be able to sell it to those whom they represent. The same is true in other types of dialogue which are set up in order to resolve conflict, between warring married couples, for example, or parties in a dispute over a will.

But many debates and dialogues are not like this. Often one conflicting insight or theory is truer, profounder, more relevant than its rival, and therefore it may be crucial that this side should be explored at length and should prevail, and not simply in a muted or neutered form but with all its original depth and force. For that to come about, it may be that you don't want anything resembling a dialogue. You want a lecture, a sermon, a speech, a book – some kind of medium in which a single voice speaks or sings, perhaps not for the four or five hours that Mr Gladstone and Fidel Castro regarded as the bare minimum to get their point across, but for long enough to sink in.

Besides, if we become so habituated to the to-and-fro of backchat, can we retain the power to listen properly to a sustained argument, that ability to read, mark and inwardly digest which used to be regarded as the heart of learning? May we not become hopelessly dialogged, mired in the fidgety habits and short attention spans of an interview culture?

Speech on television, and to some extent on radio too, has become reduced both in quantity and richness, so that when a character in a play or a public figure on a chat show talks at any length and with any complexity of thought or syntax, there is a faint feeling of embarrassment, as though the speaker has made a fool of

himself, revealed how pompous and pretentious he must be, broken
with the prevailing language-lite. I recently watched a play by David
Hare on BBC2. It is in itself a rare event to see a single play on TV,
a fact commented on with some asperity by Hare himself. The play,
My Zinc Bed (screened 27 August 2008), was to me a delight. The
characters, Jonathan Pryce as a Communist-turned-software-
millionaire, his wife a recovering alcoholic played by Uma Thurman
and Paddy Considine as a poet and another recovering alcoholic,
seemed to me utterly believable. They spoke, I thought, like people
of their sort do talk. Picture my astonishment when the next day the
TV critics, in a mixture of puzzlement and irritation, all dismissed
the play as hopelessly theatrical and the dialogue as stagy and unreal.
The intimate medium of television required, it was said, a less mannered and intricate form of language.[4] But why should this be?
Conversations between intimates do not, after all, have to be reduced
to the lowest common denominator. On the contrary, intimacy may
permit more profound and sustained explorations, just as Theodore
Zeldin describes his lunchtime conversations with Michael Foster.

Yet it has certainly become a fiercely held view among
programme-makers that both language and thought on television
must be as simple as possible and that utterances must be brief and
personalized in a warm, human-interest tone. In short, all dialogue
must resemble as closely as possible the format of an interview. Better
still, if as much as possible of the output actually *is* an interview.
Programmes about travel or archaeology or the arts, song-and-dance
shows, political programmes, quiz shows, comedy shows, sports coverage, in all of these as much airtime as plausible must be given over
to one person interviewing another. The actual singing and dancing
and hitting balls, the beauties of Beethoven and Salisbury Cathedral,
the speeches of statesmen and church leaders – all of these must
come second, feature as mere clips within an endless stream of
question-and-answer sessions, often of mind-splitting banality
because what the interviewees may be remarkable for is what they
do, not for what they have to say about it.

The word 'interview', in the sense of an organized conversation rather than simply a meeting – inter-viewing rather than verbal intercourse – dates back no further than the nineteenth century, when the specific sense of a meeting arranged between a politician and a journalist also became current. The *Oxford English Dictionary*'s first instance of the noun being used in this way is a pejorative one, from the New York *Nation* of 1867: 'The "interview", as at present managed, is generally the joint product of some humbug of a hack politician and another humbug of a newspaper reporter' – a definition which strikes a chord today.

If the word 'interview' is of recent origin, the high expectations we have of an interview are more recent still. These expectations are now so large that the interviewers themselves have become persons of huge consequence who will earn in their careers many millions, much more than half the people they will interview. Their techniques may be of various kinds – gentle and encouraging, smooth and oily, jokey and derisive, impatient and abrasive. But most of them share a determination to keep their subjects' answers brief and to make it clear to the viewers and listeners that this is very much a two-sided conversation, with the semi-comical result in the case of a taciturn interviewee that the questions may be longer than the answers, notoriously so in the case of James Naughtie of the *Today* programme. In the case of Brian Walden's TV interviews, his questioning was so subtle that quite often the words he suggested to his subjects became attributed to them as characteristic quotations; he suggested the phrase 'Victorian values' to Margaret Thatcher, for example, a phrase which she would never have used spontaneously herself, since 'values' is a term used primarily by leftish sociologists. For writers, an appearance on *Oprah Winfrey* or formerly *The Richard and Judy Show* can transform their financial fortunes, since the glow of interviewers' celebrity is transferable.

The authority of the interview has come to trump the authority of the interviewee's own unaided effusions – a speech, a lecture, an article, even a book. When some new politician or writer comes to prominence, a newspaper or magazine will proudly proclaim 'the first interview', as though it is the interview which is the really interesting thing which confirms Hawksbee's significance and will give the clue to the secret of his success, rather than anything that Hawksbee may have done, said or written, let alone what any professional critic may have had to say about his work. The interview will be blazoned across a full page, larded with animated photographs. By contrast, when the Prime Minister or the Leader of the Opposition submits an article under his own byline, it will usually be shunted to the bottom of the page or literally sidelined. In part, this is because the article will usually be written not by the man himself but by an underling in the great man's office. There is a chicken-and-egg effect here; these articles have come to be written by underlings, for it is understood how little prominence they will receive because the politician's supposed words have not been through the sacred mincer of the interview.

As for political speeches, which serious newspapers all used to report at length, now they will receive little or no coverage, unless some kind of story can be extracted from them. Except in the case of Budget speeches which contain concrete policy announcements, more space will be given to the Parliamentary Sketch which sets out, often with dollops of wit and charm, to convey the atmosphere and reactions in the Chamber, especially those of the punch-ups at Prime Minister's Questions.

TV news is, if anything, even more extreme in its avoidance of reporting political speeches *in extenso*. The screen will be dominated by our own correspondent, who will describe the contents of the speech in a couple of sentences, using most of his airtime to give his assessment of whether the speech has satisfied expectations, what its political consequences will be and what other TV networks thought of it. Indeed, this is what the anchorman asks for, Justin's or John's 'assessment'. Thus the news itself is blended into a series of interviews between anchorman and the man on the spot.

Among the purposes of the interview is to humanize the subject, to reveal his fads and foibles, to uncover the secrets of his family background, to recall his early setbacks and humiliations. These revelations may be fairly pedestrian; the famous *Paris Review* interviews with writers always ask the mundane questions that anyone might ask in casual conversation: do you write best in the morning or evening, do you use a pen or a typewriter (now PC), do you have a special room for writing in, have you ever suffered from writer's block? This process tenderizes the subject, makes him seem less daunting and angular, more like us. It is ultimately a reductive process from which it is insisted, quite sternly, that nobody can be exempt, however apparently impregnable or adamantine their personality, not Enoch Powell, or Mr Gladstone or President Coolidge. The most extreme measures have to be taken to evade the interviewer's embrace, so chummy and yet so vicelike, and the penalty of evasion is to be labelled a recluse, a weirdo, J.D. Salinger being a prime example.

To refuse to take part in a dialogue is to opt out of progress. For it is generally believed that 'the only way forward is through dialogue'. A solution which is the result of a solo effort is thought of as being 'imposed'. One person's answer is a 'diktat'. Real progress is made through a *process,* and that process involves people 'getting round a table' and getting down to 'serious talks'. We take this so much for granted now that we forget how, until quite recently, we accepted that in many situations a single voice had the authority to tell us what to do and to point out the correct path to wisdom and understanding.

In fact, to find a time when the elite believed that dialogue was the prime, the most direct, perhaps the only route to progress, we have to go way back, to long before the Renaissance or even the Christian era as a whole. Dialogue had its first heyday in the Greece of Socrates and Pericles. It flourished at the dawn of scientific and philosophical enquiry. And it was the registered midwife to those enquiries. Dialogue provided the best obstetric techniques for giving birth to the truth. The first intellectual jousts were oral, and they

were quick-fire affairs. The tempo was staccato, the rules of engagement as free as the most uninhibited modern interview. The tone
might be brutal, but it could also be lyrical and uplifting. Many of
the first philosophers, Plato and Xenophanes for example, were poets
too. And the intellectual enquiries flowed out of lyric and dramatic
poetry.

One of the earliest literary terms is '*stichomythia*': dialogue in alternate lines of verse in old Greek dramas. Thus the history of dialogue
in Western culture begins and ends with the one-liner. Far from
being a modern degenerate tendency, the sound bite represents a
return to the technique of the earliest recorded conversations.

A newcomer to those of Plato's dialogues in which Socrates plays
the starring role will be struck by the quick-fire, informal style. To
the modern reader, the conclusions that Socrates drives his inter-
locutors to acknowledge may seem commonsensical or they may
seem outlandish, but the style of the dialogue is startlingly, fetchingly
familiar to us.

First, the venue is casual, usually alfresco. Socrates tells us in the
Apology that he is in the habit of holding his seminars 'at the bankers'
counters in the marketplace'.[5] Socrates is in effect holding court at
the queue for the hole in the wall. In that same marketplace, Socrates
tells us later,[6] you can buy the writings of Anaxagoras 'for a drachma
at most'. Anaxagoras, as we have seen, was notorious for asserting
that the sun was nothing but a hot stone (and the moon a large lump
of earth). Socrates' point here is that these seditious teachings were
easily available a few hundred yards away 'in the orchestra', the circular space in front of the stage of the open-air theatre, where the
chorus danced during performances and which was a suitable spot
for bookstalls when the theatre was shut. Therefore it would be
absurd to blame Socrates alone for leading young men astray with
such heresies. In any case, he tells his friends in the *Phaedo*, the
account of his last hours on earth, that he used to be obsessed by natural science but now he has given up wearying his brain with such
enquiries because 'I am very far from supposing that I know the

explanation of any of these things.'[7] As he goes about the city talking to politicians and other public figures famous for their wisdom,
he reflects as he walks away that he is wiser than the other fellow if
only because he knows how little he knows.[8]

Socrates believes: 'God has specially appointed me to this city, as
though it were a large thoroughbred horse which because of its
great size is inclined to be lazy and needs the stimulation of some
stinging fly . . . all day long I never cease to settle here, there, and
everywhere, rousing, persuading, reproving every one of you.'[9] He
therefore advises the jury to spare his life, because they won't easily
find a replacement, and without a gadfly they will all go back to sleep
for the rest of their days.

The gadfly's role is a noble and necessary one which takes Socrates
buzzing all over the city. His ugly mug with its snub nose and shaggy
brows and staring eyes is known to everyone – one pictures him looking rather like Ernest Borgnine. He is a celebrity, guyed by
Aristophanes in *The Clouds* as a phoney guru who appears suspended in
a basket because his mind works better in the open air. He refers twice
to Aristophanes in the *Apology* as one of his accusers, but their conversation in Plato's symposium seems friendly enough. No doubt *The
Clouds* did Socrates' reputation some damage. They probably had one
of those prickly public friendships, like that between celebrities from
different fields who have teased each other on *Have I Got News for You*.

For all Socrates' protestations that he disdains the humbug of the
politician's oratory and his claims that it is possible to stay honest only
if one remains a private citizen, his *Apology* is certainly not without
rhetorical art. He reminds his audience that he has served his country in three great battles and at the age of 70 this is his first
appearance in a court of law. He says he will eschew the cheap sentimental trick of bringing his three sons into the court to plead for
his life; but his mentioning them at all is of course in itself a tug at
the heartstrings. Then right at the end of the *Apology*, he mentions
them again, beseeching the gentlemen of the jury to keep an eye on
them and if they are seen to be putting money or anything else

before goodness, then the city is to plague them and scold them just as it has plagued and scolded their father. In short, the *Apology* has plenty of deliberately tear-jerking moments which would go down well at the convention of any American political party.

In the *Phaedo*, Plato makes Socrates' warm and lovable nature even more palpable. When his friends go in to see him in his cell after his chains have been removed because this is the day he is due to die, his wife Xanthippe is already sitting there crying with their little boy on her knee and she has to be led away in hysterics, which doesn't quite fit with the conventional picture of her as a shrew not worthy of the great man.

Socrates then sits up on the bed and draws up his leg and massages the part which the chain has rubbed raw and launches into a discourse on the close connection between the pain of the fetter and the pleasure of having it removed. Phaedo, supposed author of the account of these final hours, describes Socrates' favourite trick of opening his eyes very wide and smiling, when a point made by his opponent strikes his interest. Socrates tells his friends what a charming fellow his prison officer has been and what good talks they have had together and how generous it is of him to shed tears for him at their parting – all this while the prison officer has gone out of the room to prepare the poison.

In the *Apology*, Socrates points out how many of his friends are present in the court: look, there is Crito, and over there my contemporary and neighbour, the father of this young man Critobulus, and young men and their brothers, including Plato himself and his brother – all have come to support their old friend, one of the most admired and loved figures on the Athens scene. Which makes it puzzling to the reader why the court should be so strongly determined to find him guilty and even more determined to condemn him to death rather than impose the sentence of banishment or fine which would have been open to them. It is a particular curiosity that the vote to find him guilty went 280–221; but the vote for the punishment was 360 for death and only 141 for a fine. So around 80 citizens who had thought him innocent also thought that if he was guilty he deserved the extreme penalty. Thus there was a majority of more than 5–2 in favour of the proposition that the sin he was accused of was extremely serious.

But what exactly was that sin? As we have said, this continues to be a vexing question. Socrates himself says that the indictment goes something like this: 'Socrates is guilty of corrupting the minds of the young and of believing in deities of his own invention instead of the gods recognised by the State.'[10] He makes short work of these charges in his characteristic bantering, thumping style of interrogation: how can he be corrupting the youth, since he makes no claim to knowing anything except how little he knows? Who among his fellow citizens would provide a better influence? Where can anyone show that he has created new gods or professed disbelief in the old ones?

None of which comes close to what one suspects must be the real objection: to the Socratic *method*, to its relentless critical debunking of all accepted pieties, so that the young men who flocked around the banking counters were being educated to believe in nothing at all, and to be incapable of piety of any sort.

In Socrates' dialogue with Euthyphro, which we assume to be a late conversation since Socrates mentions the indictment against him as already current, he torments his victim, a rather pompous but good-humoured character who is, bizarrely, prosecuting his own father for manslaughter. Why? Because he let a slave of his die through negligence and this was an impious thing to do. How does Euthyphro know it was impious? Because it was an act hateful to the gods. To which gods – all of them or only some (after all, the gods were famous for quarrelling)? And how does Euthyphro know? How exactly do our acts of piety benefit the gods in any case? And so on, on until Euthyphro retires baffled and the audience is left wondering how on earth, literally on earth, can there be any justification for attributing divine sanction for our acts. We can only hope to clear our heads and to achieve anything resembling justice by relentlessly examining our motives and our prejudices.

In our own day, something like this approach to education has captivated many educational theorists and alarmed traditionalists. Children educated in this critical tradition will be the first generation able to think freely for themselves, say the critical theorists. They will grow up unable to believe in anything, and will become rootless, discontented and cynical adults, say the traditionalists. True education does not consist in pumping children full of a mass of unexamined knowledge and prejudice, the critical theorists declare. On the contrary, without a deposit of knowledge and settled moral principles a human being is helpless, the traditionalists retort.

These are two extreme positions, neither of which is ever wholly realized in the classroom. In the real world, most education turns out to be a mixture of injecting facts and training in critical evaluation, a blend of information and scepticism. All I want to point out here is that the heart of the education debate in the twenty-first century is pretty much the same as the heart of the case *Socrates v. the city of Athens*.

But the spirit of Socrates lives on. One can imagine that bald, snub-nosed oddball whose ugliness was somehow part of his charm walking into the studio and dividing the audience into raucous opposing factions and then opening his eyes very wide and giving that terrible smile to see what havoc he had caused.

The dialogue is the key that opens up fortified intellectual positions and minds that are firmly closed. It is the dialogue that unsettles confidence, not just in a specific belief but in the belief that any belief can be beyond challenge. Only the dialogue brings into juxtaposition a speaker who is right and a speaker who is wrong and raises the possibility that we may not be able to tell which is which. Can laws and states and societies endure in such uncertainty?

These dizzying thoughts may begin to give us some clue why the bourgeoisie of Athens ultimately found Socrates intolerable – and why the dialogue form, after this brilliant flowering, went into a decline. The most striking indication of this is that Aristotle, who had been Plato's pupil for twenty years, so soon abandoned the dialogue. True, the handful of dialogues he wrote as a young man lack Plato's warmth and colour, so part of the reason might have been simply that he felt ill-equipped to carry on using the form. But it is clear too from the huge abundance of Aristotle's surviving work that he was basically a system-builder whose aim was to accumulate, analyse and organize data. It is he and not Plato who is the father of modern scientific discourse (not experiment), and the dialogue form was a distracting buzz which hindered clarity and precision of thought.

Great Romans like Cicero and Seneca continued to write dialogues on the Greek model, but these were more in the form of long, expository speeches, with the interlocutor little more than a formal presence. The dangers and benefits of a genuine intellectual debate mostly drained away. Dialogue as a literary form began to lose its intellectual drive, and the energies which had made it so seductive in Plato's hands began to be diverted into stage comedies and the narratives-with-speech which were recognized as the first novels, such as Apuleius' *The Golden Ass*.

In politics, though, the history of dialogue in Greece and Rome is rather different, more enduring and heroic but with a sadder ending. When Athens and Rome were republics, politics took place out of doors. Elections and debates, and decision-making too, took place under the blue skies of the Mediterranean and the Aegean: in Athens, first of all down below the Acropolis in the marketplace, the Agora, then later on higher up in the purpose-built amphitheatre on the hill opposite, the Pnyx (from *pyknos*, crowded, jam-packed). Here in the heyday of Athenian democracy the Ecclesia, or assembly, transacted all the business of the state by popular vote, which was also compulsory vote. For a quorum, 5,000 votes were needed, and Scythian archers chivvied laggard citizens up to the Pnyx from their shopping and gossiping in the marketplace. The Agora and the streets surrounding it were cordoned off by ropes daubed with wet red paint. Citizens found marked with the red paint forfeited their attendance money, a kind of decongestion charge. It is reckoned that the

Pnyx could hold as many as 10,000 citizens, a reasonable fraction of the total population, seeing that women and slaves and, for much of the period, the very poorest peasants were excluded.

To us, accustomed to virtually all political decisions being taken for us, not by us, either by unelected officials in inaccessible offices or by a handful of elected representatives in the Chambers at Westminster or in the local council chamber, all this mass participation seems breathtaking, almost unimaginable. We console ourselves with the thought that direct face-to-face democracy might be all very well in a small city state but would be wholly impractical in a modern nation state with its millions of people and hundreds of miles of territory. For us that sort of democracy can only be a utopian dream.

But then we must look to the other great example of classical democracy: the Roman Republic. This was no fleeting mayfly, but lasted roughly five centuries until Augustus defeated Antony at the Battle of Actium in 31 BC and instituted an empire which lasted even longer. As at Athens, Roman politics was carried on alfresco. Only the Senate had a roof, and the Senate was largely an advisory body which under the Republic never had the power to pass laws. Almost everything took place in the Forum, although some elections and committee meetings were held beyond the Pantheon, again in the open air, in the Circus Flaminius, part of the Campus Martius. As at Athens, the same space was used for all sorts of public activity: trading, money-changing, theatrical shows, criminal trials and civil suits, funeral orations and above all what were called *contiones,* informal meetings called by elected office-holders, such as the tribunes of the people, and attended by whoever happened to be around.

What strikes us about the Roman variant of democracy was its surprisingly casual style. Unlike in Athens, there was no official attempt to dragoon voters into turning up. True, in the last years, before the Republic's collapse, powerful men would hire their own claques to pack the Forum in order to get their favoured legislation through. Even the upright Cicero speaks of 'our people' standing up against the violence of the opposing mob. But attendance in all the political business was always voluntary.

It was this very casualness that helped the Republic to cope for so many years with what seems to us an insuperable and ever-growing problem: how could an empire of nearly a million people (according to the census of 70 BC), stretching from Lombardy to the toe of Italy, be governed from day to day by the same methods as had worked more or less when 'Rome' consisted only of the city itself and its sprawling suburbs? The solution that the Romans found was to ignore the problem. They simply carried on as before.[11]

Only those voters who were actually present in the Forum on the day were to have their votes counted. This was done by dividing them geographically into 35 *tribus*, the majority in each tribe or constituency to count as 1 vote in the final totting, so that the support of at least 18 *tribus* was needed for a *lex* to pass. In the 130s BC, a series of laws was pushed through by the tribunes to introduce the secret ballot, in order to remove the excessive influence of the *optimates*, the magnates, much to the disgust of Cicero who thought that the people needed some guidance from their betters. A *lex* was not simply a law as we understand the term, but any sort of executive decision: which of the consuls was to be sent to command the army in Gaul, how much free corn was to be distributed to the poor, how much to be spent on repairing the roads. It might seem that this system was grotesquely unfair to the more far-flung country constituencies, the *tribus rustici,* whose members could not hope to travel the hundreds of miles to Rome in time to record their vote in the Forum. But Rome was a city of immigrants, and in *The Crowd in Rome in the Late Republic* (1998) Professor Fergus Millar argues, in the absence of any contrary evidence, that these thousands of incomers still kept membership of their native *tribus*, however long it was since they had left Calabria or the Po valley.

Sometimes, it is true, as Cicero remarks, there was a very poor turn-out with barely 5 men per *tribus* bothering to cast their votes, but we may presume that these were usually uncontroversial measures of the sort which, in the absence of whipping, empty Chambers in any Parliament. For controversial stuff, you could expect a packed and noisy Forum.

Until recently, it was the academic fashion to concentrate on the class structures of Roman society and to uncover the ways in which the *optimates,* the families who usually provided the senators and consuls, managed to pull the strings and deploy their hangers-on, their *clientelae.* Classical scholars rather underplayed the crucial basic fact that in the end every law had to be approved by the people assembled in the Forum, that is, by every adult free male, including the sizeable number of freed slaves.

The Forum could accommodate as many as 20,000 people. Not surprisingly, such a huge crowd when packed into the confined space, some of them squeezed between the pillars of the surrounding colonnades and porticoes, others forced up the alleys leading down to it, could erupt into violent verbal and physical conflict, sometimes egged on by gangs hired by unscrupulous operators like Cicero's opponent Clodius. Alarming though these episodes might be, especially when they worsened during the latter years of the Republic, defenders of Roman democracy regarded open and uninhibited debate as its lifeblood.[12]

Cicero himself repeatedly deplored the way in which the mob could be swayed by sophistry and sentiment, not to mention bribery and intimidation. He tut-tutted about the occasionally perverse decisions coming out of the Forum. Yet he never ceased to believe that it was the people's right to choose. If candidates for office were simply chosen by rank, by whether they came from knightly or praetorian or consular families, liberty would be gone: 'Popular support will have been removed, voting extinguished; no competition, no freedom for the people to choose their magistrates, no need to wait for the result of the votes. There will be no more votes that come out against expectations, as so often happens now.'[13]

It was the statesman's role, while he was being buffeted by the storms of public opinion, to restrain and soothe the passions of the people. 'If we do not think honours of great account, then we need not serve the people. If we seek honours, we must not weary of supplicating the people.' An early rendition of 'If you can't stand the heat, stay out of the kitchen.'

To me, the most interesting feature of these debates was the practice by which the tribune of the people who was piloting the legislation through the Forum would 'produce' relevant public officials to answer questions in public, put both by himself and by the crowd. In fact, this is the first meaning of *'producere'* – to lead forward for interrogation. Everything had to be done in public. No law could be lodged secretly in the Treasury. The terms of every edict had to be written up on a white board in the Forum, the *album,* which Cicero tells us so many people crowded around that it was sometimes hard to get close enough to read it. In the same way, every public figure had to submit to a subpoena to give evidence before this Unselect Committee. Great men who misjudged the mood of the audience could be jeered at, just as they are today on *Question Time*, and with no more protection from the 'producer' than they can expect now from David Dimbleby. Cicero describes Pompey the Great returning to Rome from one of his triumphs and making a fool of himself in the Forum. He was brought forward by 'that most frivolous tribune Fufius', answered questions in an absurdly haughty style, and went on for hours.[14] The details of the controversy may elude us today, but what stays alive is the image of the arrogant young general, accustomed to having his commands jumped to, unwilling or unable to endear himself to the fractious mob. Shakespeare's *Coriolanus* tells just the same story. Coriolanus refuses to indulge in *'ambitio'*, the going around to gather support for his election, either in the Forum or in the constituencies. One cannot imagine him travelling out to the *tribus rustici* to make useful friends. Just as our whole modern idea of 'producing' a public show of any sort takes its origin from the politician being led forward to answer questions in the Forum, so our concept of 'ambition' derives ultimately from the arduous ambits that the would-be Roman politician had to make, often to the furthest corners of the Empire, if he hoped to clamber up the ladder of office: aedile, tribune, praetor, consul. In complete contrast to Coriolanus, Caesar was prepared to interrupt his military campaigning to spend the winter pressing the flesh in northern Italy to secure support for Mark Antony and himself.[15]

Roman politicians were running for office non-stop like American politicians today, constantly engaged in canvassing, bribing, laying on public entertainments (*ludi*) and making speeches. No one became a member of the Senate by right of birth, or without gaining some annual office that was filled by popular election. Even the priests and augurs were elected, and although it helped to be a son or nephew of a former consul or praetor to get elected, there were always candidates coming from obscure families. Cicero describes himself as a '*novus homo*', a new man in the sense that his family had held no public offices.

The key to Roman politics lies not in the structures of classes and clienteles but in the crowds swirling round the Forum, shopping and coffee-housing in between debating, quarrelling and voting. Until recently this incessant, casual politicking received less than its due academic attention, perhaps because it seemed rather vulgar and trivial to nineteenth- and early twentieth-century scholars who were accustomed to the dignified, distanced, largely private political practices of the elite in their own societies. We are, I think, more used these days to the hot breath of the crowd.

And when these democratic practices withered under the Empire, to be replaced by the rule of a single man and his court and his army, Romans knew what they had lost. For all its many faults, the Republic continued to be quietly mourned, all the time that the last vestiges of its elections and popular assemblies faded into inconsequentiality or extinction.

Of course, the new men who prospered under the Empire were often glad to see the back of the wearisome old rigmarole. On being appointed consul in AD 379 (no nonsense about election any more),

Ausonius of Bordeaux wrote a delighted thank-you letter to the Emperor Gratian:

> For my part, as consul by your gift, most august Emperor, I have not had to endure the horrors of the Campus Martius, or the voting, or the ballot boxes and the declaration of the count. I have not had to press people's hands, nor, confused by the rush of people greeting me, have I failed to reply with their right names to my friends or given them the wrong ones. I have not gone round the *tribus,* or flattered the committees, or had to tremble when the different classes were called to vote. I have not had to pay any deposits or made any deal with the returning officer. The Roman People, the Campus Martius, the order of knights, the rostrums in the Forum, the Cattle Pen [the enclosure in the Campus where the voting happened], the Senate, the Curia – for me, Gratian alone was all these things.[16]

Democracy was dead, and so was face-to-face dialogue with the people. Long live the Emperor!

The Christian evangelists who prospered under the later emperors did employ the dialogue device now and then, but they did so for a completely different purpose, to explain the truth of Christian doctrine in a vivid way, not to embark on anything resembling an intellectual adventure, let alone a free debate. Now and then, over the next millennium and a half, radical writers such as Hume and Schopenhauer did revive classical dialogue form, usually in order to undermine the conventional wisdom. The true Socrates would have approved these subversive initiatives. But in general the dialogue was dead or at any rate lying doggo. The preacher preached, the philosopher discoursed, the monarch pronounced, and that was that. There was not much answering back.[17]

I don't pretend that the *Today* programme is quite on a par with the *Crito* or the *Phaedo*, or that Plato and Jeremy Paxman deploy identical techniques. But the underlying assumption is the same:

that wisdom consists in challenging rather than believing and that there are few higher callings in life than asking questions.

And that being so, there can be no justification for restricting the debate to the high and mighty, to duly authorized persons. Professional journalists themselves are not to hog the role of questioners. Every newspaper columnist has to put his email address at the bottom of his column, so that any citizen, no matter what his level of education or degree of sanity, can join in. For the first time since fifth-century Athens, technology has made possible universal participation in public debate. Only slaves and people too poor to buy computers are left out of it. Blogging is, literally and unstoppably, a free-for-all.

The only limits to this non-stop challenging of authority are those imposed by health and safety: bloggers are not allowed to interrupt the work of brain surgeons and airline pilots. But outside the operating theatre and the cockpit they have licence to roam.

Now of course as in all redrawing of the conventional wisdom, the old humbug is displaced by a new sort of humbug. Politicians and journalists mostly pay lip-service to interactivity, regarding it as a harmless way of allowing voters and readers to let off steam. The promises of public consultation over the e-ways have often turned out to be little more than going through the motions. In many ways, twenty-first-century bureaucracy is more rather than less indifferent to public opinion. Nonetheless, dialogue continues to be the dogma of the day. It will not easily be dislodged, since that would require a new source of authority so powerful as to be beyond challenge. And there is not much sign of that on the horizon.

We have returned to the Romans in a highly specific way: the demand that public persons should make themselves *visible*. They must show themselves to us as and when we require. They must answer whatever questions we or our tribunes put to them and pretend to answer those questions with a good grace, no matter how trivial or intrusive they may think them. When Jonathan Ross asks David Cameron whether he has ever masturbated over a picture of Margaret

Thatcher, he is playing (some would say overplaying) the role played 2,000 years ago by 'that most frivolous tribune Fufius' needling the upwardly mobile Pompey. Modern technology has reproduced the conditions of pre-imperial Rome. The coming of television has made our leaders visible to whoever cares to switch on, just as the leaders of the Republic were visible to anyone who cared to stroll down to the Forum. And it is we who have the choice, not the great and would-be great men and women. For if they are to pursue their *ambitio,* they must allow themselves to be *productus* for our entertainment. Eloquence and *gravitas* may be optional, but dialogue is compulsory.

For those who remain unconvinced that something so basic to human life as conversation could ever have undergone any funda-mental change, I must end this chapter by mentioning another subject which undoubtedly does have a history: reading. After all, reading is dependent on writing, and we know there was a time before men had learnt how to make significant scratches on papyrus, stone and wood. In the history of reading, one of the key moments is when men first begin to read silently. The first account of some-one reading to himself without moving his lips, and doing so habitually, can be pretty accurately dated to AD 383, when St Augustine, then aged 29, came from North Africa as a young scholar and went to pay a call on the celebrated Ambrose, Bishop of Milan, who also happened to be a friend and adviser to Augustine's mother, Monica. In his *Confessions,* Augustine describes how impressed he was by Ambrose who spent much of his time alone in his cell read-ing: 'When he read, his eyes scanned the page and his heart sought out the meaning, but his voice was silent and his tongue still . . . Often when we came to visit him, we found him reading like this in silence, for he never read aloud.' In his *History of Reading,* Alberto Manguel quotes a few earlier examples of reading silently from the classical period, but these all seem either dubious or exceptional by reason of the context: for example, Julius Caesar standing next to his opponent Cato in the Senate in 63 BC and silently reading a billet-doux sent him from Cato's own sister.[18]

Thus habitual reading in silence seems to begin with contemplative intellectuals in the Christian era (Constantine had been
converted to Christianity on his deathbed only half a century before
Augustine met Ambrose). Until well into the Middle Ages, writers
assumed that their readers would hear rather than simply see their
texts, just as they would have spoken their words out loud as they
wrote them down. Punctuation was unnecessary if you were listening to rather than reading the text. It was the famous Irish scribes in
about the ninth century who began to split up sentences and mark
off the divisions with many of the punctuation marks we use today.
At about the same time, Manguel tells us, we come across the first
regulations ordering scribes to be silent in their *scriptoria*. So the history of silent reading takes place entirely within a Christian
environment, the practice being first noted by one of the four
Doctors of the Church observing another and the institution being
enshrined in libraries, first monastic then secular, inhabited entirely
by individuals engaged in solitary study and cocooned by their concentration from their fellow students.

Just as we can date our first encounter with silent reading, so I
think we can date our first definitive intimation of the impending
end of that tradition. The date was 9 October 2008, when Andy
Burnham, the Secretary of State for Culture, Media and Sport,
spelled out his vision of the library of the future in his speech to the
Libraries Association:

There's still a view in some quarters that libraries should be like
the galleries of old – solemn places patrolled by formidable staff.
Silence, it would appear, is a library's most valuable asset. But
learning is not all about quiet contemplation. I want to see
libraries full of life, rather than quiet and sombre. Attractive buildings exuding a sense of joy . . . Libraries should be the place where
real social networking happens – libraries as Facebook 3D;
libraries as OurSpace instead of MySpace. Look at the way book
clubs have taken off over the last few years – getting on for 10,000

clubs with 100,000 members according to estimates by the
Reading Agency. Libraries are the natural place to meet.

This reference to book clubs is almost the only mention of *books* in
Burnham's entire speech, and his approbation is reserved for what is
only an amiable extension of chat about them.

As politicians often do, Burnham is merely sanctifying what is fast
becoming standard practice. Many libraries have been abolishing
their strict rules of silence and their ban on mobile phones and have
been introducing computer games, in the hope of luring the young
back from internet chat rooms.[19] 'Private study', as it is now called
instead of simply 'reading', is on the way to becoming an eccentric
minority pastime in public libraries, and one which many librarians
who prefer the bustle of the internet café are disinclined to bestir
themselves to protect. The last sanctum of silence is on the skids, and
our public spaces are returning to the hubbub of the Forum and the
Agora.

It is in such public spaces that reputations are won and lost. In
former times, men could rise to eminence and power by working
most of their lives out of public view in a king's closet or a monk's
cell. But now making it depends, first and foremost, on being visible.
Even those who live by the written word, authors and commentators, now have to be physically seen by their publics, in
author-photographs, on television, at conferences and festivals.
Celebrity becomes a fleshly quality, all the more central in our culture for that reason.

IX

FAME

Let Me Through,
I'm a Celebrity

'We live in a celebrity culture.' It's not something we say with pride. In fact we may not wish to say it at all, although if pressed we would have to admit that the statement is true enough. And when we do say something along these lines, we say it with a rueful, puzzled, perhaps querulous tone in our voice. The cult of famousness seems to have crept up on us, without our intending it, yet making us complicit in its insidious advance, so that we become unable and finally unwilling to resist its treacly embrace. Celebrities are everywhere, filling the newspapers and television screens with endless repetitions of their image and the buzz of their chat. Some of them are famous for the old-fashioned reason of doing something, playing the violin or kicking a football or making jokes. Others are famous for being something, beautiful or odd-looking or even deformed or crippled. Others – and this is what really worries us – are simply famous for being famous. And they are all jumbled up together so that unless we are extremely alert, we cannot quite remember which is which. This jumbling is deliberate. It conveys to us that the famousness of these people is what is important about them. Modern fame shares the quality that Lord Melbourne approved of in the Order of the Garter: 'There's no damned merit about it.' Celebrity is a fluid, transferable, universal substance like 3-in-1 oil or WD-40, which can be squirted anywhere. The actor who played Baldrick in *Blackadder* is chosen to present the BBC's prime archaeology programme – and then goes on to host a guide to classical music on Classic FM. James Naughtie, the political interviewer on the *Today* programme, hosts the BBC Promenade Concerts and chairs the Booker judges. Alan Titchmarsh, the BBC's gardening expert, fronts a series on the architecture and landscape of Britain.

Better still to have celebrities shown trying their hand at some pursuit demanding a good deal of skill, one which they may have never attempted before and at which they are likely to be hopeless, or at best third-rate: conducting an orchestra, say, or training a sheep-dog. To the jaded viewer, seeing something done badly is more diverting than the tedious display of excellence. As the blasé Mr Mountchesney says in Disraeli's novel *Sybil* (1845): 'I rather like bad wine, one gets so bored with good wine.' I find myself quoting Regency bucks like the fictional Mountchesney and the real-life Lord Melbourne, because there is something of their style, a cynical and laid-back quality about the attitude of the modern public towards fame and those who achieve it. Talent shows used to be a minor supporting element in the TV and radio schedules. They were taken rather seriously by the competitors as a stepping stone to a career in music or comedy. But now the talent shows are the main event. The fact that the teenage singers are a little off key or over-weight is what catches the viewers' sympathy. And those who make it through to the final become celebrities for that achievement in itself, rather than for anything they may go on to do later. In the Fame Academy, graduation day may be the summit rather than the beginning.

To fill every available slot in the media, a steady flow of celebrities is required, constantly refreshed by new recruits, for there is no more damning criticism than 'It's just the same old faces'. Just as the material that would keep an old-style stand-up comedian in business for years is now consumed in a single show, so the clutch of celebs that used to feed the modest requirements of the media has to be reinforced at regular, ever-diminishing intervals. TV and the glossies have become insatiable in their appetite for fresh blood. They gulp celebrities down, chew them thoroughly and then spit out the remains, still hungry for the next meal.

All this puts a considerable strain on the viewer's attention. One has to remain on constant celebrity alert to have any hope of keep-ing up. For my own part, I long ago ceased to compete. Of the eight celebrities flailing their batons on *Maestro*, I was familiar with the names of only two, the actress Jane Asher and the former *Newsnight* presenter Peter Snow, although I thought I might have seen one of the others years ago in *Starsky & Hutch*, but I don't think he had a beard then.

It is not as if celebrity-spotting was confined to magazines designed for that purpose. Even the serious newspapers now carry several 'soft feature' pages which include interviews with celebrities describing their battles with alcohol or drugs, or their weight, or cancer, or divorce, or going bankrupt, or simply with the burden of fame (one way of winning that battle might be to stop giving interviews). Every

Friday, *The Times* runs in its *Times 2* magazine a two-page feature 'Celebrity Watch', in which Caitlin Moran records the ups and downs of celebrities over the course of the week, these being reflected in their standings in her chart. Many of these names are quite familiar, some from way back: HM the Queen, Hugh Hefner, Madonna, Wayne Rooney. But others have me beat. Who exactly are Agyness Deyn, Gene Simmons, Denise Richards, Kanye West, Lee McQueen, Sarah Silverman and Emma Griffiths, to name a random selection from 'Celebrity Watch' that I jotted down in the summer of 2008? And even if you can still identify them all now, how many can you be sure of remembering in a year's time?

Celebrity watching can scarcely be a pastime confined to low-brows, since *The Times* chooses to give it such regular prominence. When I worked on *The Times Literary Supplement*, of all the periodicals that came into the office the one that was most eagerly devoured and vanished soonest from the shelf was *Hello!*

Certain celebrities are, it seems, meant to suffer. They are destined to describe a tragic parabola from obscurity through glory to squalor, misery and humiliation. In the old-style pattern, they would start out as a hat-check girl in the Midwest, be discovered and soar effortlessly to stardom before paying the penalty of fame – drink, divorce, neglect. In some cases, there might be a comeback and then a second fall. In the case of Judy Garland and her daughter Liza Minnelli, the process seemed to be repeated over and over again. We may be seeing the same recurrence in the case of their more recent equivalents, Kate Moss, Britney Spears, Amy Winehouse and Pete Doherty.

Since modern fame is intrinsically democratic, the same parabola has to be described by celebrities who are famous simply for being famous, having become so by virtue of appearing on TV in quiz shows or reality shows, notably of the *Big Brother* type. Jade Goody's single achievement was to come fourth in *Big Brother* 3, yet in the 2006 *Sunday Times* survey of 'The Top 50 Names of the Moment' it is a picture of her, languorous, pouting and half-dressed, which occupies the centrefold.[1] This former dental nurse from Bermondsey was the daughter of an abusive heroin addict father and a one-armed lesbian mother, who herself became quite famous on the back of her daughter's rise to fame. Jade was indeed memorable not only because of her tough background but because of her raucous, down-to-earth, intensely self-aware personality, which led to a best-selling autobiography, a couple of her own TV shows and her own special perfume. 'Shh . . . Jade Goody' was launched by Superdrug in the summer of 2005 at a price of £19.95, and it became the store's third best-selling fragrance behind Kylie Minogue's and Victoria Beckham's. The history of perfume is itself an instructive example of the absorptive power of celebrity culture. At first, perfumes were made and marketed by specialists like the *parfumeurs du roy* described in Patrick Süskind's novel *Perfume* (1985). *Parfumeurs* were often agile immigrants like Juan Floris from Minorca who set up a shop in Jermyn Street in 1730 which is still in business there today. Then the territory was invaded by fashion designers like Christian Dior and Calvin Klein who saw a profitable way of extending the reach of their brand. Now cosmetics firms and their customers swoon before the irresistible musk of fame. 'Shh . . . Jade Goody' was temporarily removed from the shelves when Jade was accused of racism. She was already famous for her ignorance after saying that she thought Cambridge was in London and, after collapsing in the London Marathon, that 'I don't really understand miles.' Jade herself summed it up beautifully: 'I am famous for being famous. I'm famous for being a loser, really. I often get comments like that, and I totally agree with them. I'm not an amazing musician or a great writer, and a lot of people don't get noticed for these things any more because people like me come in and sort of bombard fame.'[2]

'Bombard fame' is a brilliant phrase. It should not be forgotten what an intense effort it requires to get selected for these shows in the first place. Judith Keppel became famous for being the first person to win a million pounds on *Who Wants to Be a Millionaire?* Her display of general knowledge was remarkable, but almost as remarkable was her willingness to spend hours and hundreds of pounds bombarding the TV networks' phones for a chance to be selected, in the confidence that she could win if only she could get on the show in the first place. Judith too had to describe, or have described for her, her two failed marriages and her brush with addiction. But at least she did not have to suffer the fate of Jade Goody, who in August 2008 went on an Indian version of *Big Brother* called *Bigg Boss* to be given while on air the surprise news from her doctor that she was suffering from cervical cancer. At around this time, a *heat* magazine poll reckoned her the twenty-fifth most influential person in the world.

But the announcement of Jade's illness was not the peak of her fame. In fact, as the cynics would say, it proved to be her astutest career move yet, though one which was of course not engineered by herself or even by her legendary PR man, Max Clifford. For the horror of that TV moment was palpable to the dullest imagination: 'How would I have felt if that had happened on screen to me or my mum?' Then, as the whole world now knows, the cancer turned out to have spread and was soon pronounced to be terminal. Jade's last days were played out in a blaze of mawkish coverage not surpassed by the impending deaths of kings or princesses. (The mourning for Princess Diana, the nearest parallel in modern times, was *post mortem*.) Jade was in the situation of those captured barbarian princesses who were carried in chains through the streets of Rome to execution or enslavement. They too were ridiculed for not being able to speak proper (they could only stammer 'B-ba-bar'), but their cruel fate eventually moved the gawping crowd to horror and pity.

A week before she died, the headline in the *Daily Mirror,* 'JADE'S LAST HOURS', was outstripped by the *Sun's* 'THE ANGELS ARE CALLING MUMMY'. When she actually died, on Mothering Sunday, the *Mirror* splashed 'MUMMY'S IN HEAVEN', while the *Sun* went for 'AT PEACE ON MOTHER'S DAY'. *OK! Magazine*, with an awkward deadline to meet, had its 'JADE GOODY OFFICIAL TRIBUTE ISSUE 1981–2009' on

the news-stands before she actually died. This issue featured the first
hint of Jade's possible resurrection with its World Exclusive, 'I WILL
COME BACK FROM HEAVEN TO LOOK AFTER MY BOYS'. Nor were the
broadsheets left behind. *The Times* had four pages on Jade, including
a full-page obituary, a full-page colour photo fronting *Times* 2, with
a two-page appreciation inside by the indispensable Caitlin Moran.
The *Guardian* had the same number of pages on Jade, quoting as did
all the papers the tributes from the Prime Minister, the Leader of the
Opposition and the Archbishop of Canterbury. These tributes and
obituaries all tended to take the line that Jade was an extraordinary
sort of modern heroine who from the most difficult beginnings had
made something of herself in the only way open to her, through
appearing on television, and who had captured the nation's affections. No more was heard from the crusty Jeremiahs who in these
same papers had denounced Jade and the network which spawned
her as epitomes of everything that was wrong with modern Britain –
ignorant, crass, foul-mouthed, morally chaotic. In some cases, it was
those same Jeremiahs who now detected in her dauntless, feisty per-
sona an example to be admired, not least because thousands of young
girls were inspired by her story to go and take cervical smear tests.
Her public dying had ennobled her. It even began to ennoble Max
Clifford, who announced that he too had been suffering from cancer
at the time. *Private Eye* claimed that Clifford had earned something
in the region of £200,000 from representing Jade.

Jade was certainly not the only *Big Brother* contestant whose life
was transformed by the experience of celebrity. Bart Spring in 't Veld
became the most famous man in the Netherlands when he won the
first ever version of *Big Brother* after consummating on screen his
affair with a beautiful housemate. He attracted shrieking crowds
wherever he went and was dragged from the stage whenever he
opened a club or a disco. He burnt his way through all his money,
slept with 130 women, took refuge in drink and drugs, then suffered
five nervous breakdowns. Now he says, 'I resented being famous just
for being famous, I was a false saint. I felt the whole country had

gone mad. I found the whole country had dumbed down. I had contempt for a society for which fame is an end in itself.'[3]

Andy Warhol, himself a manufacturer of celebrity as well as a keen analyst of it, famously declared that 'in the future everyone will be famous for fifteen minutes'. Later, he said that he had become bored with this line, and his new line was: 'In fifteen minutes everybody will be famous' – which is an equally subtle take on the modern age.

In his book *The Fame Formula: How Hollywood's Fixers, Fakers and Star Makers Created the Celebrity Industry* (2008), Mark Borkowski, himself a leading PR agent, says that, with the help of a good PR man, 'the first spike of fame will last fifteen months, not fifteen minutes'. But it needs cultivating. Fame, left unattended, goes into decline and those who wish to remain in the public consciousness must be prepared to pay for it.[4] Borkowski and some mathematical analysts conducted tests on a series of celebrities such as Paris Hilton, Nicole Kidman, Peter Mandelson and Jade Goody and also on several prominent brands such as Stella Artois, American Express and Adidas, measuring their appearance in print in the newspapers from 2000 onwards. And they came up with a formula for measuring the decline in fame:

$F(T) = B+P \left(\frac{1}{10} T + \frac{1}{2} T \right)$
where
F is the level of fame
T is the time, measured in three-monthly intervals, T = O is the peak of fame, T = 1 fame after three months etc.
B is base-level of fame, where the subject starts from, a large number for someone like George Clooney, zero for a new *Big Brother* contestant.
P is the increment of fame above the base-level.

According to Borkowski, this works out so that at T = 5, that is fifteen months later, almost 96 per cent of the fame-boost has been frittered away and the client is back to his or her base-level (and presumably needs to get a new agent). Then the client needs to reinvent herself – by having an affair with an England football manager, collapsing in the London Marathon or snorting something illegal again. Borkowski explains that the superheroes of the cinema have now been replaced by the supervictims, who, like the Greek gods, must fight against extraordinary odds to win and who, also like the Greek gods, are prone to the most human of foibles – pride, greed, envy, self-destruction – and are all the more adored for it.

This is a relatively innocent explanation. I'm not sure that it will do. There is so often a savage, exultant snarl about the media treatment of a fallen celebrity. If tabloid editors felt that their readers would not care for this approach, they would surely adopt a softer, more sympathetic treatment for such stories. No, the editors are convinced – and sales tend to suggest that they are right – that their readers too exult and snarl when they read those tales.

But I don't want to concentrate here on the savagery with which the media relish knocking down the idols they have built up. That may be a necessary consequence of humanizing the face of the idol. He or she must endure the hatred and contempt as well as the love and admiration which ordinary human beings experience.

What I want rather to note is the way that the modern media democratize and homogenize celebrity, so that all celebs are somehow equal and because they are equal, we do not think of them as really superior to the rest of us, merely more blessed by fortune. Being on a par with Jade Goody and Pete Doherty brings Daniel Barenboim and Seamus Heaney down closer to our level. The great goal of all celebrities, to shake hands with Nelson Mandela, puts them in the Mandela club, but it also enables us to touch Mandela at one remove. When the BBC TV *Ground Force* team did a makeover of Mandela's garden in South Africa, the programme seemed not very different from what it would have been if they had descended on our own little patch (Mandela's garden was quite a modest plot).

The heart of celebrity is *frequency* – '*celebriter*' in Latin means 'frequently', deriving from '*celeber*', 'much frequented, populous'. And that frequency is of course itself the work of the journalists who mediate the celebrity's creation. When they drool over the A-list, they are drooling because it is a list they themselves have helped to write. The celebrity journo often seems to show a special enthusiasm for those whose fame is more due to the frequency of their being mentioned than to anything they have actually done. These playthings of destiny can be toyed with, boosted or jeered at or dropped, whereas the leading goalscorer and the Nobel prizewinner are more immovable fixtures on the public scene.

In classical culture, especially in Roman culture, we find an obsession with fame equal to our own obsession – not just in the sense of admiration for and interest in famous people, but a fascination with the mechanics of fame. Poets and politicians and generals have always aspired to glory, but the business of getting it has been regarded in most cultures as a largely straightforward matter of solid achievement. By contrast, the Greeks and the Romans were intensely aware of the wayward, capricious aspects of fame and how artificial and falsely based it could be. For them, fame was a rather dubious goddess, Pheme or Ossa in Greek, Fama or Rumor in Latin, the spirit of rumour, gossip and report, and thus the source of both fame and infamy. The earliest of Greek poets, Hesiod, writes in *Works and Days*: 'Do as I tell you and keep away from the gossip of people. For Pheme is an evil thing by nature. She's a lightweight to pick up, oh very easy, but heavy to carry, and hard to put down again.' Virgil tells us that fame makes the small seem great and the great seem greater. Pheme is indifferent whether the rumours she spreads are good or evil, which may be why she is not allowed into heaven but dwells beneath the clouds and troubles the earth. People will do anything to achieve fame, run any risk, invest all their money, even sacrifice their lives. That is why fame, callous, amoral, fleeting though she is, runs the show, dictating what people should eat and drink and wear no less than whom they should admire. 'How many thousand

nobodies there are whom fame blows up to importance and author-
ity,' Andromache says in Euripides' play. Ovid's description in the
Metamorphoses of Fame's dwelling place makes it sound like the *Daily
Mail* newsroom on election night:

> At the world's centre lies a place between the lands and seas and
> regions of the sky, the limits of the threefold universe, whence all
> things everywhere, however far, are scanned and watched, and
> every voice and word reaches its listening ears. Here Fama dwells,
> her chosen home set on the highest peak constructed with a thou-
> sand apertures and countless entrances and never a door. It's open
> night and day and built throughout of echoing bronze; it all rever-
> berates, repeating voices, doubling what it hears. Inside, no peace,
> no silence anywhere, and yet no noise, but muted murmurings
> like waves one hears of some far-distant sea, or like a last late
> rumbling thunder-roll, when Jupiter (Zeus) has made the rain-
> clouds crash. Crowds throng its halls, a lightweight populace that
> comes and goes, and rumours everywhere, thousands, false mixed
> with true, roam to and fro, and words flit by, phrases all confused.
> Some pour their tattle into idle ears, some pass on what they've
> gathered, and as each gossip adds something new, the story grows.

We have already witnessed the single most astonishing example of
the manufacture of celebrity in ancient Rome: the canonization of
Antinous, an obscure page from Bithynia with nothing to his credit
but a lovely face and the adoration of the Emperor Hadrian. What
strikes us in retrospect is the speed and effectiveness of the Emperor's
spin doctors, given the long lines of communication in the
Empire. Within a year or two, there was scarcely a city that had not
built its temple to Antinous or issued its coins and medallions in his
memory. We have already seen how when a new star was seen in the
heavens, the astrologers of Hermopolis told the Emperor that this
must be the soul of Antinous blazing with light. Hadrian eagerly
accepted this interpretation and had it officially announced and

decreed, so that in the East, though not in the more sceptical West, the star of Antinous became a widely accepted article of faith and often appears on coins minted in his memory. The use of 'star' in its modern sense to mean a radiant public figure did not really come in until the mid-nineteenth century. But there is no doubt that in every sense Antinous was the first true star. Initially, like the modern TV celebrity, he seemed to be famous merely for being famous, but then as the cult grew, as we have seen, he began to have every sort of miracle-working power attributed to him.

Nowhere is the dodgy, ambiguous, manufactured nature of fame more systematically, and more flagrantly, on show than in that historical curiosity, the Roman triumph. We tend, I think, to imagine the triumph as a highly organized, codified affair, somewhere between a coronation procession and a Lord Mayor's Show. As with a state funeral in Britain, the Senate would unanimously decree a solemn tribute to a national hero according to ancient ritual. The victorious general would ride through the streets in a chariot wearing a laurel wreath and a purple toga, with a slave holding a golden crown over his head and whispering in his ear, 'Look behind you; remember, you are only a man.' In front of him would go the spoils of victory, all the loot of the kings and countries he had defeated, and the animals to be sacrificed and the captives in chains, the most important catches directly in front of him. Behind the general came his victorious soldiers, shouting the ritual cry '*Io triumpe*'. Well, none of that is untrue. But there is both more and less to the triumph than meets the dazzled eye, as Professor Mary Beard shows in her delightfully iconoclastic book *The Roman Triumph* (2007). First of all, and perhaps most important, triumphs were not as a rule spontaneously bestowed on the victorious general by a grateful Senate or people. Triumphs had to be claimed or demanded in a *supplicatio*. And this required a good deal of energetic campaigning, leaving aside the actual fighting. In his unsuccessful campaign to be awarded a triumph, Cicero claims that he wrote to every member of the Senate bar two – one an inveterate enemy and the other the ex-husband of his daughter – to persuade them to vote for his *supplicatio*. That would have meant around 600 letters. No would-be contestant on a TV quiz show can have put more effort into his application. Three of these letters survive, two addressed to former consuls in much the same terms: 'So I earnestly beg that you make sure that a decree is passed in the most honorific terms possible concerning my achievements, and as soon as possible too.'[5] Even if the Senate had refused your supplication, the triumph might not yet be a lost cause, for though it was the Senate that authorized the funds for the triumph, the people had the last word. After being refused by the Senate on political grounds, Servilius Priscus took his case to the people who enthusiastically endorsed it. Livy tells us the same was true of Valerius Publicola, fifty years earlier. It was always possible to go over the heads of the Senate and appeal directly to the people.

Cicero's military achievements in Cilicia were in truth not that impressive. Nor was Cicero a very willing soldier. He wrote to a cynical young comrade-in-arms, Marcus Caelius Rufus: 'If we could only get the balance right so that a war came along of just the right size for the strength of your forces and we achieved what was needed for glory and a triumph without facing the really dangerous and serious clash – that would be the dream ticket.'[6] Everyone was at it. In the next-door province of Syria, the fighting against the Parthians inspired all three provincial governors to claim a triumph. There was in any case a good deal of doubt hovering around the victory won by the Roman second in command, Caius Cassius Longinus (the same Cassius who conspired against Julius Caesar). Caelius claimed, wrongly as it turned out, that Cassius had made it all up. Another rumour had it that the invaders were not Parthians at all but Arabs in Parthian kit.

Lying about the number of casualties one had inflicted was so common that a law was passed penalizing generals who inflated the figures and compelling them to take a formal oath that their dispatches to the Senate had been accurate.[7] Almost as common were dirty tricks to scupper your rival's chances of securing a triumph instead of you. When Metellus Creticus was notching up victories against the pirates which threatened to overshadow his own, Pompey supposedly stole two of Metellus' prize captives to adorn his own triumph. Plutarch even claims that Pompey actually sent some of his own men to fight on the pirates' side.

Such accusations of exaggeration or outright fakery or foul play crop up repeatedly. Suetonius tells us that, to celebrate his triumph over the Germans, Caligula planned to dress up some Gauls to impersonate German prisoners. He chose the tallest Gauls to look good and specified the qualities he was seeking by coining the splendid new word '*axiothriambeutos*', 'worth leading in a triumphal procession', a souped-up version of 'photogenic'. These extras were to have their hair dyed red and learn German. Domitian is said to have raided his own palace furniture and plate to provide some impressive spoils of war. It was, after all, a major logistical undertaking to bring back all the way from Africa and Syria wagonloads of booty and to feed and water enough '*axiothriambeutos*' prisoners to make a decent show. Especial trouble was taken to look after celebrity prisoners, for as always celebrities need to be surrounded by celebrities. The great Augustus could not resist boasting in his autobiography, ghost-written perhaps as so many celebrity memoirs have been then and now, that: 'In my triumph nine monarchs or children of monarchs were led before my chariot.'[8]

The parading of these celebrity captives was liable to backfire. It might evoke pity rather than exultation or contempt, especially in the case of women and children. At Julius Caesar's triumph, the sight of the young Egyptian princess Arsinoe carried in chains on a cart moved the spectators to tears and prompted them to lament their own misfortunes, according to the historian Dio Cassius. Plutarch says that at the celebration of the victory of Paullus over King Perseus in 167 BC, it was the King's three children who captured the attention of the crowd, two boys and a girl too young to be aware of the scale of their misfortunes: 'The Romans fixed their gaze on the young ones and many ended up crying, and for all of them the spectacle turned out to be a mixture of pleasure and pain until the children had gone by.'[9] It all eerily recalls the crowds at the funeral of Princess Diana or Michael Jackson, or if you are looking for a live modern parallel, as we have seen, the last days of Jade Goody fit the profile perfectly.

But then almost anything about the triumph could backfire or break down. The axle of Caesar's chariot broke at his triumph and nearly chucked him out, and he had to wait for a replacement. An old actor dried at a key moment in the celebrations, and the parading of so many wild animals evoked nausea in some. Like circus proprietors of the old school, victorious generals always longed to have elephants in the show. As far back as the third century BC, these massive creatures had been brought back to Rome as part of the spoils of colonial conquest. But they were unpredictable performers, hard to yoke to the general's chariot. At one of Pompey's triumphs, the elephants were too big to go through the arch leading up to the Capitol and after two attempts had to be replaced by horses. In another of his triumphs, a group of twenty elephants assembled for the post-procession show tried to break out of the arena and began trumpeting pitifully to the crowd. Pompey's triumphs were memorably vulgar. His portrait made entirely of pearls evoked particular disgust from austere spirits like Pliny and Dionysius who deplored the competitive extravagance of these displays. In the old days, triumphant generals had been preceded only by a few sheep and cattle and a couple of cartloads of broken weapons.

But the image-makers had taken over.[10] Captives who were unavoidably absent, because of having been killed, would certainly be depicted on canvas. Mithradates and Tigranes were shown in Pompey's triumph as paintings. Caesar at his triumph displayed a series of canvases of the deaths of his various adversaries: Lucius Scipio throwing himself into the sea, Petreius shafting himself at dinner, Cato disembowelling himself like a wild animal. At the joint triumph of Vespasian and Titus, there was a mixed-media show: canvas scenes of the devastation of Judaea and the demolition of the

Jewish fortifications, and in front of them real-life captured Jewish generals acting out in frozen attitudes the moment of their capture.

Caesar's Egyptian triumph also featured a working model of the Lighthouse of Alexandria (one of the Seven Wonders of the Ancient World), complete with flames. Most memorably, his Pontic triumph was commemorated with a placard inscribed '*Veni, vidi, vici*'. This is recorded by Suetonius, though Plutarch tells us that Caesar first wrote 'I came, I saw, I conquered' in a letter from the battlefield. Caesar was a master of self-promotion as well as a military genius. And '*Veni, vidi, vici*' is the first, and in its terse alliterative punch perhaps the greatest, slogan of all time.

Octavian, later Augustus, had a 3-D model of Cleopatra at the moment of her death, lying on a couch complete with an asp or two. The poet Propertius claimed to have seen 'her arm bitten by the sacred snakes and her body drawing in the hidden poison that brought oblivion'. Well into the Renaissance and beyond, scholars tried to identify this or that marble sculpture as the model of Cleopatra that was carried in the procession, but the real thing may well have been no more than a rickety canvas prop. The ultimate in fakery was the triumph of Trajan in AD 117–18 to celebrate the Emperor's victory over the Parthians. Trajan himself was already dead; his place in the triumphal chariot was taken by a dummy.[11]

A triumph was well worth having. It put the stamp on celebrity and offered a way forward to power as consul or quasi-dictator. Which was why as one-man rule became entrenched, triumphs began to be reserved for the Emperor himself and members of his immediate family. Why allow an upstart rival to parade through the streets in a golden crown, putting in people's minds that here was a possible alternative to the incumbent?

For incurable exhibitionists, the triumph offered the most glorious opportunity for showing off that mankind had ever devised. Pompey's pearls and elephants might hover on the edge of high camp, the celebrations of some emperors toppled over right into it. Domitian's black dinner party, which was to be so slavishly copied by

Grimod in the eighteenth century and by Huysmans in the nineteenth, was part of the triumph celebrating the Emperor's victory
over the Dacians. This bizarre extravaganza was rivalled by Nero's
notorious tour of Greece, in which he was proclaimed the victor in
all the major Greek games. On his return, he rode through Italian
towns on white horses through specially made breaches in the city
walls, just as the old Greek warriors had done after their more
authentic victories. Nero wore the olive wreath of the Olympic
victor on his head. In front of his chariot, placards were carried, blazoning the details of all the athletic and artistic contests he had
triumphed in, together with the themes of his songs and plays – a
sort of mobile press pack. Behind him came his cheerleaders shouting that they were 'the soldiers at his triumph' – although no
hostilities at all had taken place in the entire trip. Animals were
slaughtered, the streets sprinkled with saffron; ribbons, sweets and
flocks of birds showered on the Emperor as he passed along the traditional triumphal route.

Scholars have puzzled over this over-the-top triumph-like ceremony. What was it all about, this triumph without a whisper of
actual military action? We, I think, can understand it more easily as
a high-camp spectacular which could have been devised by Sir Elton
John. The perfume that intoxicates both crowd and Emperor is not
simply the mixture of herbs and burnt offerings; it is the incense of
celebrity.

Surely at least this outrageous exhibitionism was tempered, just a
fraction, by that slave whispering in the ear of the triumphant one,
'Remember, you are only a man.' Alas, Mary Beard points out that,
for the greater part of the history of the triumph, 700 years or more,
we have no evidence of any slave in the chariot saying any such
thing. It is not until Tertullian in the second century AD that we hear
those words spoken by the second man in the chariot, and even he
does not tell us that the man was a slave. Besides, Tertullian was a
Christian writer, and he quotes the words in the context of a
Christian attack on the idea that the Roman Emperor was a god or

demigod. Did the slave in the chariot, if he was a slave, ever say those words? Or did Tertullian make them up – to be copied, more or less, by later writers?

What is clear is that a triumph was a triumph. It was not a Christian parable of humility, it was a machine for the manufacture of celebrity, a PR campaign with all the pretensions, over-the-top vulgarity and the absurd budget of a modern blockbuster film.

A Christian triumph, as Beard points out, would be a contradiction in terms. The victorious Christian general would go not to any pagan temple but to the nearest Christian cathedral and offer up a Te Deum – 'We praise thee, O God'. This is a tradition of thanksgiving that has continued into modern times. General de Gaulle gave thanks for victory in the Second World War with a Te Deum at Notre-Dame. The psalm used at thanksgiving services, No. 115, '*Non nobis, Domine*', makes the point more emphatically still: 'Not unto us, O Lord, not unto us but unto thy Name give the praise; for thy loving mercy and for thy truth's sake.'

It is no coincidence that the triumph should have gradually died out under the Christian emperors. The last memorable one seems to have been that granted to the general Belisarius after his victory over the Vandals in 534. But it is dubious whether even this much discussed celebration should count as a triumph in the old Roman style. Belisarius went on foot, not in a chariot and, instead of offering a sacrifice to Jupiter, both he and the captured Vandal king Golimer prostrated themselves before the Emperor Justinian. At the climax of the parade, Golimer had repeatedly muttered those scorching words from Ecclesiastes: 'Vanity of vanities, all is vanity' – not sentiments uttered at your average celebrity event. For the worship of celebrity is, in Christian eyes, no better than the worship of the Golden Calf.

Think of all those virtues which Christians especially prize and praise: modesty, humility, a sense of creatureliness and of gratitude to God for being created. These are precisely the qualities which are absent from the triumph, almost by definition. The Triumphant

One is himself, after all, being formally acclaimed as a demigod, or the next best thing. No less important in the Christian way of life is the cycle of guilt, remorse and contrition which engages the devout in a perpetual round of confession and repentance. This cycle is obligatory for the highest in society, up to and including the monarch, no less than for serfs and slaves. When a Christian victor hastens to make his confession to his Maker, he is acutely conscious that his most conspicuous sins, such as murder, torture and extortion, may be the very ones that got him where he is today.

By contrast, in a fame culture such as ours, any twinge of guilt feeling is to be suppressed. We are instructed to move on, not to look back or to indulge in the sort of introspection which might make us feel bad about ourselves. Expensive therapists and life coaches may be employed to help us keep at bay or get rid of any feelings of self-loathing or self-doubt. Our chariot's wheels are designed to roll forward smoothly, and its windows are not windows into our souls. They open outwards so that we can hear and acknowledge the plaudits of the crowd.

Many other faiths, and not just the Abrahamic ones, reserve an honoured place for the qualities of modesty and humility, because these are ways of expressing and revering our createdness. Conversely, the virtues that were honoured in classical pagan times bear a startling resemblance to those that are honoured today, especially in modern popular culture. The moral code of the tabloids is not much respected or examined. The style in which their villains are condemned and their heroes praised is too crass and lurid for sensitive souls to dwell on. Yet, if you do pause to think about it, the code of the tabloids is surprisingly like the code that ordinary Romans subscribed to: pride and courage are its prime virtues; cowardice and treachery are its most heinous sins; outrage, fury and indignation are manly and proper reactions; the desire for revenge and retribution is understandable and to be commended; offenders ought to be shamed as well as punished, publicly if possible, whether their offence be adultery, paedophilia, assault and battery or murder.

The values that are promoted today in the *Sun* or the *News of the World* would not have seemed out of place in imperial Rome or in any of the 'shame cultures' of earlier civilizations.

Thus it is no accident that secular modernity should generate a fame culture too, just as classical antiquity did, for fame and shame are two sides of the same coin. Where guilt and self-loathing are abhorred as obstacles to a proper thinking well of yourself, then fame and adulation become legitimate aims in life. One of the principal objections to Christianity made by its opponents, from Nietzsche onwards, is that it welcomes humiliation, suffering and failure. Christianity is, in the immortal words of Ted Turner, the founder of CNN, 'a religion for losers' (later, perhaps becoming aware how many of his network's subscribers also subscribed to that religion, he recanted the definition). We have already seen how the anti-God-botherers particularly dislike the religious postures of prostration and abjection. By contrast, they speak highly of pride and feeling good about your atheism or anything else about you. Pride, after all, is not alone among the Seven Deadly Sins created by medieval popes in having lost its old oomph: covetousness has been rebranded as retail therapy, sloth is downtime, lust is exploring your sexuality, anger is opening up your feelings, vanity is looking good because you're worth it and gluttony is the religion of foodies.

Rome had a class system, just as we still have a class system, though we like to pretend it isn't there. But for the Romans, as for us, celebrity trumps class, because class is dusty and dog-eared and ultimately bogus. Old money is no more to be revered than new money. The Romans too saw through the phoney claims to aristocratic descent. Cicero complains of the 'invented triumphs and too many consulships' with which leading families glamorized their pasts. Livy tells us that family histories are mostly bunk and that there are outright falsehoods to be found in the eulogistic inscriptions on the statues of the elite of the republic. Since nobody is to be somebody by right of heredity any more, we need the image-makers to make up our somebodies for us. And in the blazoning of celebrity Max

Clifford is our Garter King of Arms. For fame is the name of the ultimate game.

In societies like ours and those of ancient Greece and Rome, personal sanctity is unavailable or unregarded. Spiritual salvation is off the menu. All that we can aspire to is to be worshipped by our fellow men and women, if only for an agonizingly brief period. Fifteen minutes may not be long, but it is better than a lifetime of nothing.

X

ART

Museums Are Us

L ook again for a moment at the modern thirst for celebrity.
Where does this unabashed worship of fame come from? Who
started the fashion, who is its authenticating prophet? An artist, in
the shape of Andy Warhol. And where are the temples of this new
religion? In the art galleries and museums of the West, whose owners
and curators are the new high priests, the guardians and promoters of

artists like Picasso and Damien Hirst who themselves become millionaire celebrities on a once unimaginable scale. Yet we have to look back only a few years to a time when artists were supposedly averse to vulgar publicity and passing fashion, and devoted themselves to art away from the limelight and often in circumstances of hardship. Even if that shunning the limelight was always partly a legend, fame when it came to an artist was regarded as a by-product of the quality of his work, it was not the essence of his life. Something rather strange and unexpected has happened to the relationship between art and publicity. What lies behind this turn of events?

For millions of people, especially in Western Europe, religion is no way out. For them to proclaim that their life was centred around and justified by faith in a divine power would be an unthinkable sham. To subscribe to religious faith of any kind would be to live a lie. The ultimate dishonesty, in fact. This applies particularly to the more highly educated. Religious belief falls off sharply in the upper reaches of the educational scale. It is lower among university graduates and lower still, in fact barely visible, among Fellows of the Royal Society and Nobel prizewinners.

For the secular elite, religion is at best a historical curiosity, at worst 'a leader to darkness and death'. As we have seen, the active anti-God-botherers attribute to religion many if not most of the wicked acts of violence, cruelty and oppression that human beings have committed in the course of the history of the species. The most that they are prepared to concede to religious belief is that however absurd and misguided its creeds might be they did inspire great art. Handel and Bach and Beethoven wrote the Church's masses and oratorios, Raphael and Bellini painted the Madonnas for her altarpieces, Donatello and Riemenschneider carved her statues, and architects whose names we often do not know, at least until the age of Michelangelo and Palladio, built her cathedrals and churches. Art was one of the few real compensations, perhaps the only compensation, for what Richard Dawkins calls that 'misfiring' of our genes which poisoned the human mind for so many centuries.

But art was more. It was the highest expression of the human mind and spirit, at once a glorious celebration of and insight into the world and an exhilarating stretching of our limbs. Art was the best of us. We reached our intensest levels of being when creating or appreciating it. The artefacts that had been bequeathed to us deserved everything that we could lavish on them: preservation, scholarship, adoration and homage. We were bound too to pay homage to their creators. Once in a century the haphazard swirling of the gene pools threw up a Shakespeare or a Mozart whose existence justified our own. They were the true great men of history – almost all males so far, alas, but that would surely change. It was to the artists we should bow down, not to the popes who employed them.

So with a rapidity which in retrospect seems rather remarkable, we exchanged the art of religion for the religion of art. Within 100 years or so, the religious themes which had dominated art and literature for 1,000 years and more disappeared, at least from high art. Images of the Madonna and the Crucifixion were discontinued like any other obsolete brand of merchandise. Kitsch versions continued to be produced for the souvenir stalls outside the cathedral, but serious artists turned away from transcendental subjects. Instead, they began to depict the people and things that, in the heyday of religious art, had been relegated to the margins: the landscapes in the background, the pockmarked or pot-bellied donors kneeling in the wings, the equally unprepossessing figure of the artist himself who had formerly figured only as a face in the crowd. Already by the eighteenth century, when serious artists attempted religious subjects, the results tended to be emotionally false and hollow, little better than pastiches of the old devotional art.

We can discern the end of the old world and the beginning of the new in the famous clash between Frederick the Great of Prussia and Johann Sebastian Bach. The King had eventually lured the crusty old composer to Potsdam by putting pressure on Bach's son, Carl Philipp Emanuel, who was serving there as the King's keyboard maestro. The King was scornful of all religion and despised music that 'smells of the church'. For him, as for other cognoscenti of the Enlightenment, music ought to be 'natural' and 'delightful', a fitting accompaniment to the worldly pleasures of *galanterie*. Frederick demanded of Bach a 'musical diversion', something light and charming that could be played to entertain his court in the delicious pavilions of his pleasure palace, Sanssouci. What the devout Lutheran Bach gave or rather 'consecrated' to him – a heavy religious irony in the dedication – was a 'musical offering' of a rather different sort. If you read between the lines, which Frederick certainly could, being a capable flautist and composer, what Bach had written for him was something of a *memento mori*, full of melancholy and foreboding and drawing unashamedly on the techniques of the church music that the King abhorred (in his vast music library there was not a single *sonata da chiesa*). It was an ominous and contemptuous farewell from the old world to a new world in which paradoxically Bach was to be vener-ated more deeply than he could ever have been in his lifetime as a mere Leipzig organist. Of course the old man was famous, but artists were not yet gods, and Bach would have thought it a blasphemy to be treated as one.[1]

In this new world, artists were as ever, at least in part, responding to demand. Patrons wanted to see immortalized their woods and fields and houses, and the faces of themselves and their families. They did not wish to be reminded of a bleeding alien figure on a cross. At the same time, artists could work at their best only when confronting the real world around them and not when straining to express eternal verities that no longer meant much if anything to them. As ever, the artist created his own imaginative world within the tradition of the age, but now that tradition began to concentrate on the world his audience knew: the streets they walked in, the parks and theatres where they took their pleasure, even their kitchens and their bedrooms. What had once been slighted as 'genre painting' now became art's new subject.

Richard Wagner's essay 'Religion and Art' spelled out the sea change: 'One might say that where Religion becomes artificial, it is reserved for Art to save the spirit of Religion by recognising the figurative value of the mythic symbols which the former would have us believe in their literal sense.'[2] No honest man could believe in the literal truth of those old myths, but a great artist could make artistic truth out of them. Wagner, like Nietzsche and many of their contemporaries, was deeply influenced by Schopenhauer. And in another essay, he quotes Schopenhauer's thrilling judgement of the importance of art: 'Complete contentment, the truly acceptable state, never present themselves to us but in an image, in the Artwork, the Poem, in Music.'[3]

But what exactly was this wonderful stuff? Where did art come from, what ultimately lit its fuse? What gave art this unique, authentic, unfakable profundity? Religion was not, could not be its real inspiration, since religion was a wrong turning, a disastrous backfire in man's long journey. There must be some other deeper, truer source.

One answer that anxious intellectuals came up with is perhaps not so surprising. That new answer was that art somehow sprang from the customs and traditions and history of the people who produced it, in fact from their very souls and the souls of their forefathers. Art was, in its deepest, most unfathomable essence, a national thing.

It was the young Johann Wolfgang von Goethe (1749–1832), later to be celebrated as the wisest man in Europe, who in his hot youth expressed the answer most forcefully. Born in Frankfurt, he had gone up the Rhine to Strasbourg to complete his studies in law. There, aged 21, he discovered love, folk song and architecture. He also met the slightly older Johann Gottfried Herder who was in Strasbourg receiving treatment for his eyes. Goethe and the restless Herder collaborated on a volume of essays which they called *Von Deutscher Art und Kunst – Of Germanness and German Art*. Goethe's contribution was a hymn of praise to Erwin von (or de) Steinbach, one of the principal architects of Strasbourg Cathedral, whose soaring Gothic pinnacles Goethe perceived as essentially German (although the French liked to think of them as quintessentially

French). Herder's main contribution to the book was an essay in praise of folk song in general and in particular of the ballads of Ossian, the ancient Gaelic bard, which were sweeping Europe at the time. It was subsequently discovered that Ossian's works were largely but not wholly invented by James Macpherson, an upcoming young poet from Kingussie, who claimed merely to have translated them from the original. The discovery did little to dent the admiration of readers as diverse as Goethe himself, Napoleon and Matthew Arnold. How could ballads so simple and uplifting not be authentic?

A similar yearning for authenticity had led the English public to swallow the fake-medieval verse of the sixteen-year-old Thomas Chatterton as the genuine article. When Chatterton took arsenic in 1770, the year Goethe went to Strasbourg, he was still barely 18. Wordsworth famously wrote of him as 'the marvellous boy/ The sleepless soul that perished in his pride' and Keats dedicated *Endymion* to his memory, calling Chatterton 'the purest writer in the English language'. By 'pure', he meant that Chatterton, or rather his alter ego, the supposed fifteenth-century Bristol monk Thomas Rowley, had no French idioms or particles – ''tis genuine English idiom in English words'. What readers and writers wanted to recover was some pure essence of national spirit, uncontaminated by imports or artifices. The fact that what they rushed to admire so often turned out to be partly or wholly bogus or tarted up and heavily restored and interpolated did not faze them a bit.

Unavoidably then, the adjective 'national' crept in. Art and its national origins were from now on tightly bound up together. In one fatal splicing, art has become somehow intrinsic to the nation, and the nation has become intrinsic to art. The more intensely politicians in the nineteenth and twentieth centuries orated and agonized about the state of their particular nation, the worse their anxiety about the condition of the arts. Were the arts refreshing the nation's soul? Were they French, or German or English or Scottish enough, or were they infected by some enfeebling 'foreign flu' or 'cultural cringe'?

We shudder at the grisly record of Hitler and Stalin in relation to the arts, their ruthless determination to commandeer all art for their own vile ideologies and to punish all dissenters and mavericks. What could be more disgusting and absurd than the exhibition Goebbels had laid on in Munich in 1937 of Degenerate Art? And what a glorious snub that two million citizens came to see these great works by Chagall, Mondrian, Kandinsky, Klee and Kokoschka, three and a half times as many as visited the officially approved Grosse Deutsche Kunstausstellung round the corner. It was the rootless Jewish cosmopolitans and their allies who were creating the real art, while the pampered darlings of the Reich could produce only overblown kitsch: gigantic marble storm troopers and healthy, bosomy Fräuleins. In vain did the Führer himself lambast the critics for their craven kowtowing to the 'insane and inane monstrosities' of modernism in a speech to the official exhibition lasting more than an hour. Yet what he had to say about national tradition in the arts probably struck a chord with audiences far beyond the Nazi faithful: 'Art is not founded on time, but only on peoples. It is therefore imperative for the artist to erect a monument, not so much to a period, but to his people. For time is changeable, years come and go. Anything born of and thriving on a certain epoch alone would perish with it.'[4]

Even our own democratic regimes wanted to be proud of their artists and to show them off as emblems of their nation's special virtue. French critics wrote of the École de Paris as if no other art were worth writing about. Later in New York, the critics boosted their own abstract expressionists, not simply as the liveliest thing going but as exemplars of American freshness and raw frontier spirit. There was a line of descent from the nineteenth-century landscape painters who had brought back their enormous vistas from the dizzying emptiness of the American continent to the huge canvases of Jackson Pollock and Mark Rothko where you could lose yourself in the endless blurs and scribbles. Even in England, in our quiet way we saw something unrepeatably English in the romantic visions of Stanley Spencer, Paul Nash and Eric Ravilious. Here surely were the lineal descendants of Turner and Constable, of Samuel Palmer and William Blake.

Far from slinking into oblivion as the terrible events of the twentieth century discredited nation-mania, artistic patriotism actually continued to gain ground. As the century drew to a close, governments became more boosterish, pouring millions into projects intended to celebrate and broadcast the nation's artistic vibrancy. This reached its apogee with the immense emptiness of the Millennium Dome at Greenwich. No more spectacular conjunction of the pretensions of art and state can be imagined than the assembling of the glitterati of both realms on New Year's Eve 2000 to celebrate (inaccurately as pedants pointed out) the dawn of the Third Millennium after Christ. Britain was cool, the politicians told us – the last people qualified to say so, since even if Britain had been, they would have been the last to know. By now, it was a familiar sight to see the Minister 'for' (not 'of', 'for' suggesting a nurturing role far beyond the capacity of what we now knew as the DCMS) the Arts standing pluckily in the midst of pickled sections of shark or soiled underwear to proclaim that British art led the world in a peculiarly British way. No matter that half the conceits, provocations and paradoxes on show at exhibitions such as 'Sensation' had been thought of by Marcel Duchamp half a century or more before and had nothing particularly British about them. The creative spirit of the nation was expressed in its artists, and those artists had to be promoted to the outside world.

If they did not exist already, these collections needed buildings purpose-built to house them. Throughout the Renaissance and on through the seventeenth and eighteenth centuries, potentates and antiquarian magpies filled up the galleries of their palaces and their 'cabinets of curiosities'. These were essentially hoards for private delectation and for showing off to friends. It was not until the end of the seventeenth century that the glimmerings of a collection assembled and maintained primarily for the benefit of the public began to dawn.

First came Elias Ashmole's institution in Oxford, based partly on the collection in 'Tradescant's Ark', the huge assemblage of plants, scientific instruments and mineral specimens put together by the traveller-plantsmen Tradescant, father and son. The Ashmolean, opened in 1683, was really the first modern museum. The British Museum, founded on the collection of Sir Hans Sloane, came a century later, just after Louis XV had begun to show a selection of his collection in the galleries of the Palais du Luxembourg. The *Encyclopédie* (Vol. IX, 1765), in its article 'Louvre', outlined a scheme for turning the Louvre into an institution which would approximate to the Mouseion of Alexander the Great in Alexandria (in fact, a very different sort of institution, as we shall see). In Düsseldorf, the Hopfgartengalerie was already displaying pictures arranged by master and school. The gallery at Dresden could be visited on request by anyone, and already sported a two-volume catalogue with text in both French and German. In a famous passage in his intellectual autobiography, *Dichtung und Wahrheit* (1812–22), Goethe describes his trembling emotions on his first visit to the gallery:

> The impatiently awaited hour of opening arrived and my admira-
> tion exceeded all my expectations. That *salon* turning in on itself,
> magnificent and so well-kept, the freshly gilded frames, the well-
> waxed parquetry, the profound silence that reigned, created a
> solemn and unique impression, akin to the emotion experienced
> upon entering a House of God, and it deepened as one looked at
> the ornaments on exhibition which, as much as the temple that
> housed them, were objects of adoration consecrated to the holy
> ends of art.[5]

Here, as Germain Bazin puts it in his superb history, *The Museum Age* (1968), we have a new chapter in museology. No longer existing solely for the delight of refined amateurs, the museum becomes a public institution, an instrument of education and national celebra-tion, and a temple to human genius.

This movement to transform the private collections of rulers and plutocrats into institutions dedicated to the public good received a rude shove forward from the French Revolution. Thousands of works of art which belonged to the Church and had been expropriated, or to the King who had been executed or to the aristos who had fled were suddenly freed up. Some were sold off to pay the debts of the émigrés or of the new Republic, some were broken, melted down or burnt for reasons of politics or vengeance. But many passed into public collections under the guidance of the Committee of Public Instruction. This applied especially to those works which had been looted from the churches. The painter Alexandre Lenoir was made director of a depot set up in the Convent of the Petits Augustins on the Left Bank with the purpose of receiving works confiscated from the churches of Paris. Lenoir set off on a secular crusade to acquire all the medieval and Renaissance artefacts he could find, in order to prevent 'the disfigurement and complete destruction of masterpieces that formerly decorated the temples of fanatics, the palaces of tyrants and the houses of their accomplices'.[6] Out of these, Lenoir created a 'Muséum des monuments français', deployed in schools through the vast, empty rooms of the convent, which were ideal for the purpose and were to form the model for the museum of the future.

Lenoir was the forerunner of those energetic modern curators who are reluctant to leave the exhibits to speak for themselves. He wanted to weave a story out of them, to build them up into cultural tableaux. He conceived the idea of an Elysian Fields peopled with monuments, both genuine and faked-up, to the memory of famous Frenchmen such as Descartes, Molière and La Fontaine. For the monument to Héloise and Abelard, he supplemented the fragments of their original tomb with other ornaments he had ripped out of the Abbey of St Denis, which he regularly looted for the museum. When Lenoir's Muséum was later dismantled, the monument to Héloise and Abelard was transported to the new cemetery of Père-Lachaise where it can still be seen. Before the war, students in love used to go there and toss bouquets of violets on the monument. In a less sentimental age, they have stopped tossing violets. But the monument remains, a perfect demonstration of the modern itch to turn the past into a usable story, and to put it on display as an act of national piety and edification.

All over Europe and then later in the United States, similar things were beginning to happen. In northern Italy, Napoleon collected together the works of art he had looted during his rampage and put them on show in the old abbey church of Santa Maria di Brera in Milan. Though this ill-gotten collection was later transferred to a beautiful seventeenth-century palace in the city, the name of Brera stuck.[7]

From such beginnings, the nineteenth century secured – and deserved – the title of the Museum Age. Never were there so many works of art on the market, from looted churches and convents, from toppled monarchs, from smashed or disappeared grandees. Never before had there been so much new industrial money available to scoop up those works of art and build magnificent temples to house them, temples not only to the nation's genius but also to the munificence of the new plutocrats.

Nor was it simply a question of collecting works of art in the strict sense. There was a far wider spread of interests to be catered for. People wanted to know about the remotest past of their tribes and how their ancestors had lived. Every self-respecting nation had to have its own national archaeological museum. These were followed in the later years of the century by museums of 'folklore' – the term invented by the English antiquary William John Thoms (1803–85). This new impulse derived not only from a nostalgia for the simpler, more authentic life that our peasant ancestors had led. It was also driven by the same national curiosity, the urge to find out what was peculiar to *us* – not simply the pictures that our ancestors had painted and the pottery they had made but their rituals and myths and customs.[8]

Soon museums of everything were opening everywhere: of buses and railways and canals, of dresses and hats and fashion, of architecture and gardening and postage stamps, of surgery and scientific

instruments, of shells and slate and coal mines, of wine and lock-
smiths and perfume, and above all of places: towns and cities, coasts
and valleys and mountains. No locality was too small or dim to do
without its own museum to gather together the fragments of its
past.

And not only its past. The nation required a present and a future
too. And soon the impresarios of the Museum Age also began to col-
lect modern artefacts. While the Louvre was being turned from a
royal palace into one of the leading old-art museums of the world,
Louis XVIII established a gallery devoted to recent paintings in the
Luxembourg, which had before the Revolution been the first art
museum of any sort in Paris.[9]

At intervals throughout the later nineteenth century, other
European capitals also opened galleries of modern art: Munich in
1853, Berlin in 1876; the National Gallery of British Art, later
renamed the Tate, opened on Millbank in 1897, erected by Sir
Henry Tate the sugar king to house his contemporary paintings.

This completing of the story, from the flint axes and copper
bracelets of the prehistoric ages, through the paintings on wood and
wall and canvas of the Christian era to the collages and ready-mades
of the twentieth century, is an entirely logical process. If we are to
celebrate the human spirit in general and our own national spirit in
particular, we must do so from start to finish. There must be no
breaking off, no excluding or censoring.

But as the Museum Age prolonged itself and even gathered
strength through the later twentieth century and into the twenty-
first, several unexpected things became apparent. The first was that
often it turned out to be the building of the museum that was the
decisive act of homage to the past. Filling it with stuff was relegated
to a secondary operation. And as a consequence of this, the architect
of the museum itself became the focus of attention. Who now recalls
the architect of the Rijksmuseum or the Victoria and Albert? But in
the modern age, the museum architect is king, and the commission
for a museum, rather than for a palace or a Parliament building, let

alone for a church, puts him at the head of his profession. For these are our modern halls of fame, the true temples of our age.

Frank Lloyd Wright's Guggenheim Museum in New York, completed in 1959, was perhaps the pioneer. The huge cream rondels of its exterior, like so many Camembert cheese boxes piled on top of each other in inverse order of size, were startling enough, but the winding helter-skelter of its interior was more startling still. Few works of art stood a chance of standing up against the swirling signature of the architect. Another problem was that sometimes there was nothing much of merit available to put inside the museum, as for example at Tate Modern. The vast spaces of the turbine hall of the former Bankside Power Station dwarf the rather second-rate modern art huddled in relatively small hutches alongside it (the mediocre quality of the collection being due to the lack of interest in modernism of previous Tate Directors, notably Sir John Rothenstein).[10]

It is difficult in these vast and gleaming halls not to feel a certain diminishing of the exhibits themselves. This, I think, is not solely because they are on show in a place which is not quite suitable. Rather, they have somehow lost some of their power to move us. Not only have they been taken from their original setting, they have also been conscripted in the curator's ego trip. For the energetic modern curator is determined at all costs not to let his museum become a dusty, inert sort of institution where people come in only to get out of the rain. He is out to create a holistic experience for us. Yet the livelier his presentation, the cuter the way he slices up and repackages the past, the harder it becomes for us to concentrate on the actual works on display. The sassy, large-print caption boards and the chirpy audio guides will not leave us alone. Precisely because the past is so sauced and served up for us, we may not easily let our imaginations reach out to it and touch its frayed hem with the old hesitant reverence.

In these intrusive commentaries too, we often find a more disabling critique of the objects set out in front of us. For in interpreting them, the curator, perhaps only half-consciously, may begin to undermine our sense of their intrinsic value. These paintings and sculptures, even altarpieces and devotional pictures, cease to be simply things of beauty made by artists aspiring to the ideal. They are rather 'products designed to suit the tastes of a new consumer age'. 'Wealthy patrons commissioned these altarpieces in the hope of being pardoned for their notorious business practices.' 'These religious tablets were produced for the Continental market in standard sizes by the alabaster factories of Nottingham.' The objects are demystified, reduced to the material conditions of their production.

Just as the urge gathered pace to revere art and to build these enormous art-temples to freeze and capture it for our worship, so art objects began to leak the essence which had made them so totemic to us. We were fast losing touch with all the old myths and symbols. Only scholars still had at their fingertips the iconography which had furnished half the meaning of old art. At the same time, art had been 'commodified', to use the Marxists' cruel term. The most sublime paintings could now be described in terms of cash. In the new mass-market newspapers, those were in fact the only terms in which they could be described. A Titian Madonna now became 'a £10 million Old Master painting', for journalists were by training and instinct ill at ease with the idea of non-monetary aesthetic value and would not have dreamed of describing a stolen Rembrandt as 'beautiful' or 'glorious'.

The phrase 'the art world' was now employed to describe the business of buying and selling works of art, including the business of procuring them for museums, or sometimes of 'deaccessioning' them, that unlovely word for selling off surplus items, usually those which had been kept in store, out of public view.

It is a painful thought that the human race should turn out to have been through all this before. To degenerate once could be an unfortunate accident; to do so a second time suggests that we might be programmed that way. But the parallels here too with the experience of the Greeks and the Romans are too close for our comfort.

Our word 'museum' doesn't help us much here. For the word takes its origin in the Greek '*mouseion*' and the Latin '*museum*'. In the

classical period, 'mouseion' meant 'a learned academy', most famously
the one founded at Alexandria by the Ptolemies which contained
schools of astronomy, botany and zoology (with a wildlife park and
observatory), as well as faculties of literature and philosophy and an
enormous library. In the very earliest times, the mouseion might have
been a temple of the Muses in which the Muses were worshipped
and where statues and paintings to honour them might also be
found. But in the times of which we have proper record, it had
become something very like what we would call a university, not a
museum in our sense of the word.

Works of art were typically to be found elsewhere, in the temples
where they were admired and venerated with a mixture of religious
and aesthetic fervour. There is a delightful dialogue by the lively
sketchwriter Herodas which dates from about 270 BC and describes
two courtesans who come to make a sacrifice to Asklepios (Latin,
Aesculapius) in his temple on the island of Kos. After dutifully recit-
ing their prayers to the deities represented in the shrine, the two
women fall to admiring the statues there:

> *Coccale:* Ah what beautiful statues, my dear Cynno! What sculptor
> could have carved them, and who's the donor?
> *Cynno:* These are the offspring of Praxiteles. Don't you see the
> inscription on the base? It says the donor is Euthies, son of Prexon.
> *Coccale:* The gods bless them and Euthies too for such beautiful
> works of art. My dear, look at this child with her eye focused on
> the apple. Wouldn't you say she'll die if she can't have it? . . . And
> look at the child strangling the goose! If it wasn't made of stone,
> you'd say the child was on the point of talking . . .

Then they move on to the paintings in the temple (now presumably
lost, alas, like all painting of that date):

> *Coccale:* Look, Cynno, at these paintings! Athena herself must have
> painted these lovely things! My best respects to the goddess! That

child there, the naked one – if I pinch him, it will leave a mark, won't it? His flesh looks so warm and trembling . . .

Cynno: Yes, my dear, the hand of the master of Ephesus, the hand of Apelles, revealed truth at every stroke of the brush and one cannot say of him 'there goes an artist who favoured only certain subjects and shied away from others'. Whatever came into his fancy seemed to inspire him. Anyone who fails to go into ecstasy in front of any picture by Apelles I'd like to see hanged by the feet and beaten like a carpet.

Visitors to temples like the shrine of Asklepios on Kos were welcome if they paid an obol to the sacristan and paid their respects to the local deities. They were even more welcome if they made an offering of some desirable object in gold, silver or bronze. These donations would be recorded in an inventory, sometimes made of marble, and placed on show, with the larger statues being put in the forecourt, statuettes and other smaller ex-voto objects on shelves inside the temple, protected in cases if fragile. These inventories were reviewed at intervals, usually on a change of magistrate, and like a modern museum catalogue they provided extensive information about the object: what it was made of, its weight, the name of the god to whom it was dedicated, date of consecration and the donor's name and nationality. Sometimes, as at Athens and Delphi, the citizens would construct a small treasury near the temple to accommodate the overflow of such donations. There were already problems of conservation. The votive shields had to be coated with pitch to prevent rusting; the *Parthenon Athena*, one of the most famous works of Phidias, had vats of oil placed at its feet to act as humidifiers in the dry atmosphere. Surplus objects of little value were buried in offertory reservoirs; objects of precious metal thought to be of little aesthetic worth were sent to be melted down into ingots which helped to defray temple expenses – a practice which hard-pressed modern curators would love to be licensed to imitate.

In the earlier periods of Greek and Roman civilization, works of art were displayed in a religious setting, and their veneration was a mixture of religious and aesthetic feeling. But with the coming of the plutocrats and the emperors, the collections that they piled up, augmented by the loot of empire, began to migrate to secular settings, notably to their villas such as Hadrian's enormous complex at Tivoli. Hadrian here constructed replicas or pastiches of the buildings he had seen on his travels: the temples of Athens, the Serapeum and temple of Isis at Alexandria. These were adorned by copies of their finest sculptures, such as the caryatids on the Erechtheum on the Acropolis of Athens (it is from Hadrian's copies that we can establish details no longer visible on the originals). In building the funerary temple to Antinous (which probably lay unfinished at his own death), Hadrian employed a variety of Egyptian motifs. Here and elsewhere, the little Greek boy Antinous is portrayed as the Egyptian god Osiris in a pastiche of Egyptian sculpture. Roman sculptors were put to carving obelisks in the Egyptian manner, with clumsy Egyptian hieroglyphs spelling out a text that had been inadequately translated from a Greek original text. If as we now believe, the obelisk which today stands in the Pincio Gardens did start life in the Antinous temple at Tivoli, it would not have been out of place there, along with the other copies, pastiches and melanges of Greek, Egyptian and Roman styles and motifs. In fact, it is only the ruined state of the whole enormous complex that prevents us from seeing the element of high camp in it. In some senses, Hadrian's villa is nearer to Randolph Hearst's San Simeon or even a superior Disneyland than it is to Delphi or the Acropolis at Athens.

There was a vogue too for primitive work. Some Roman collectors boasted that they owned no art later than the time of Phidias. It was also expected that the finest treasures should be on public display. Like Queen Elizabeth II, the Emperor Nero was criticized for keeping so many of his works of art out of sight in his Golden House. And when Tiberius transferred to his sleeping quarters a celebrated sculpture by Lysippus which the virtuous Agrippa had kept on public show in front of his baths, there was such an outcry that Tiberius had

to put it back again. Sculptures were still on show in the temples at
Rome, most conspicuously at the foot of the Capitol in the temple
of Concord which had been rebuilt by Augustus. But sculpture was
just as likely to be visible under any plutocrat's portico or in the
public baths. The famous Laocoon Group was unearthed in the
Baths of Titus, the Farnese Bull in the Baths of Caracalla, having
been deposited there by Gaius Asinius Pollio, famous as the bene-
factor of Rome's first public library.

As a natural consequence, a vigorous art market began to flourish.
Market values of old paintings and sculpture rose steeply, while the
art actually produced by the Romans became increasingly derivative.
The art dealers clustered along the Via Sacra and in the colonnades
of the Saepta Julia. Collectors were ushered into luxurious premises
to view the merchandise. They became the targets of the satirists
Martial and Juvenal and of the moralists like Seneca for their
credulity and rapacity. The public sales became a fashionable resort
and the source of anecdotes like the one about the money-lender
who falls asleep during an auction and whose nodding is taken for
bidding, so that when he wakes up he finds himself with unwanted
goods to the value of 1.8 million sesterces. Pliny tells the tale of the
courtesan who buys a job lot of a candelabrum and a hideous,
hunchbacked slave whose master hoped to get rid of by pairing him
thus. She takes the hunchback as her lover, he inherits her fortune,
and in gratitude makes the candelabrum a god and founds a new
cult.

In imperial Rome just as in our own time, we can see the sacred
melting away under the blowtorch of Mammon. Some Romans
were uneasily aware of what was happening to them. There is a fas-
cinating passage in chapter XI of the *Satyricon* by Petronius Arbiter.
He was allegedly nicknamed Arbiter because he was Arbiter
Elegantiae, or style guru, to Nero, and the book, described by some
as the first surviving novel, dates from Nero's time. The lovesick
narrator, Encolpius, is wandering through the city and fetches up in
the colonnades of a picture gallery where he admires works by the

Greek painters of three or four centuries earlier, such as Protogenes and Apelles.

As he is admiring these old masters, a decrepit, ill-dressed old man with an interesting thought-worn face comes into the colonnade and says to Encolpius, 'Sir, I am a poet, and I trust of no mean genius, if these crowns mean anything. "Why then," you will ask, "are you so poorly clad?" Just because I am a genius. When did love of art ever make a man wealthy? . . . Men whose one idea is to pile up the cash cannot bear that others should have a nobler creed than they live by themselves. So they do down lovers of the arts at every opportunity, to put them in their proper place, below the moneybags.'

Encolpius asks the old man several questions about the paintings on display, about which the old man seems better informed than he is, and so he goes on to ask him why is the present age so decadent, why are the highest branches of art so utterly decayed, why does modern painting show not a trace of its former excellence.

'It is love of money that has caused the change,' the old man replies. 'In early days, when plain worth was still esteemed, the liberal arts flourished . . . But we, engrossed with wine and women, have not the spirit to appreciate the arts already discovered.' Money was now the only object of worship: 'What wonder then that painting is in decay when all, gods and men alike, find a big lump of gold a fairer sight than anything those crackbrained Greeks, Apelles and Phidias, ever wrought.'

Thus for the Romans too, the Museum Age was the age simultaneously of the veneration of art and of its degradation. At the very moment when men had most self-consciously separated art from the old gods and made it into a new god to serve their modern souls, it ceased to be able to support the weight of veneration. The old man's lament to Encolpius mirrors almost exactly the lament of the critic John Berger in his essay *Success and Failure of Picasso:* 'Picasso is now wealthier and more famous than any other artist who has ever lived.' But this does not mean that he is a freak. On the contrary: 'Picasso is *the* typical artist of the middle of the twentieth century because his is the success story *par excellence.*' For, 'Art, and especially "experimental" art, has now become a prestige symbol, taking the place, in the mythology of advertising, of limousine cars and ancestral homes. Art is now the *proof* of success . . . Today the living artist, however iconoclastic, has the chance of being treated like a king; only, since he is a king who is treated rather than who treats, he is a king who lost his throne.' Berger was writing in 1965, but all the trends he described have only intensified in the intervening forty years.

This uneasy mismatch did not survive the fall of Rome. As Bazin describes so well, the museum foundered and sank along with so many of the other institutions of antiquity. The marvellous capacity of the work of art to distract us from our mortality was incompatible with the new era. Now everything in human life was to be subject to the Last Judgment. Along with the bath and the gym and haute cuisine and the joy of sex, art disappeared as an independent force in human life.

It seems that now, at the beginning of the twenty-first century, art is back. For those who can no longer stomach religion, art is once again a potent consolation, for some the last consolation. The congregation at Tate Modern or MOMA is as devout as Goethe described the worshippers in Dresden two centuries ago. For it is *modern* art that attracts the largest and most reverent crowds and indeed regularly pulls the highest prices in the salerooms (except for the occasional rare old master which is not yet in a museum).

This is a puzzle, I think, for anyone who remembers the loathing and contempt with which, we are told, modernism was initially greeted. We need to answer a question which we do not care to ask: exactly why is modern art so popular? Why are there such long queues outside Tate Modern or MOMA, while you can often wander through the old-art galleries of Tate Britain or the Metropolitan Museum and meet only a few broken-down elderly characters such as Encolpius encountered in the colonnade? Even special exhibitions of old art may be received with indifference.

When I visited the Pompeo Batoni show at the National Gallery in the spring of 2008 – a dazzling exhibition of eighteenth-century swagger – I counted only five other people in the gallery. Such a thing could never happen to Picasso or Francis Bacon.

The conventional view is that the first reception of modern art was passionately hostile. Painters, writers and musicians who self-consciously set out to be modern, radically to change the face of their art, were met, not just with puzzlement but with rage and loathing.[11]

Some modernists, especially the writers, welcomed such reactions. It showed that they had drawn blood. The shock of the new ought to be violent, or it would not count as a proper break with the past. Part of modernism's thrust, especially modern writing's, was its critique of stale bourgeois convention and stale bourgeois life. If the bourgeoisie failed to recognize its ugly face in the mirror and did not do its best to smash the mirror, then the artist had failed. In any case, it was thought, much of modern art was simply too difficult for the 'booboisie', as the acerbic H.L. Mencken dubbed the poor saps. If they could not understand what Picasso was trying to do with his distorted anatomies and primitive masks, if they found Van Gogh's brushwork harsh and repellent, if they could not follow the plot of *Ulysses* or find anything resembling a tune in Stravinsky, this merely showed that art was now reserved for a minority: there was a new class of the intellectually and aesthetically superior.

This, curiously enough, was just what the bourgeoisie thought too, although they gave the minority ruder names. Both sides were at least agreed that modern art was not popular and never would be, because it was not intended to be. Such was the inescapable apartheid in artistic matters diagnosed on both sides of the divide.

But both sides turned out to be wrong. For the most part, the public was remarkably quick to adapt to new sights, sounds and sensations. The second post-Impressionist show created scarcely any stir, and it was not long before Stravinsky's *Firebird* became a staple of the repertoire and Cézanne, Picasso and Matisse began to be hailed as giants worthy to be ranked with the greatest of the old masters. Dublin has become Joycetown, and any educated person can recite portions of *The Waste Land* or at least recognize where they come from.

How can this be? Well, part of the answer is that we need to look back more closely at the initial reactions, which were rather more varied than the legend suggests. In the case of the Salon des Refusés, Ian Dunlop reminds us (*The Shock of the New*, 1972) that it was organized by the Emperor Napoleon III himself and that it was an enormous success. Like Goebbels's exhibition of Degenerate Art, it attracted far more visitors than the official Salon. If putting on such shows was a tactic to discredit the new spirit in painting, then it was something of an own goal.

According to Bloomsbury resident art critic, Clive Bell, the Grafton Gallery show too was 'a prodigious success. It set all England talking about contemporary painting, and sent the more alert not only to Paris but to museums and collections where they could have a look at primitive, oriental and savage art.'[12] The Armory show in New York the following year, starring Matisse, Duchamp and Cézanne, was a near universal success. Even the President, Teddy Roosevelt, turned up and wrote a characteristically rumbustious critique.

At all these shows, some came to scoff and fulminate; others suspended judgement or began to see that there might be something in this weird new stuff. But what strikes one in retrospect is not so much the mixture of reactions as the almost universal spirit of *curiosity*. Even those who had not yet themselves detected something stale and used-up in the existing traditions of art, music and literature had their interest sparked by novelty. There was a growing hunger for the new, shared to some extent even by those who did not always like it when they got it.

This neophilia was to work its way through the culture over the following decades, breaking down resistance wherever it was encountered, until newness came to trump every other card in the pack. And it was those artists who took novelty as their overriding purpose who became recognized as the heroes of modern art. Picasso was and is praised above all, not for the quality of this or that period of his multifarious work but for refusing to be pinned down, for never allowing himself to be trapped in any one style or preoccupation, for moving on. Fresh woods and pastures new were the only woods worth exploring and the only pastures worth browsing on.[13]

In the circumstances of modern art, it is an entirely logical development to put your artistic fate in the hands of chance, for only chance can be relied on to provide something new and unpredictable every time you spin the wheel, or rattle the dice or shake up the kaleidoscope. This principle, dignified by the epithet 'aleatory', has found a warm welcome in pretty well every art. The painter Gerhard Richter admits to being influenced by John Cage's practice of tossing coins to help him compose his music. The collages of Picasso and Schwitters eventually inspired writers like William Burroughs and B.S. Johnson to produce cut-up books in which the chapters and indeed the pages were bound together randomly. The photographer William Eggleston is famous for pointing his camera promiscuously around him without looking through the viewfinder. In fact, he has removed the viewfinder to avoid the temptation of trying to control the image. Deliberate composition is death. The poet Hugo Williams much admires the 'accidental' quality of Eggleston's photos, which he tries to imitate with his own camera and indeed in his own poetry: 'Eggleston's photos offer a shining example of what can happen when the ego is temporarily given the slip.' So-called 'bad' pictures can be better, fresher, more real.[14]

That is why, or partly why, modern art is not difficult at all. You can get the hang of it in the twinkling of an eye, because it is not marinated in forethought, or hidden allusion, or subtle philosophy. It buzzes at you, here, now, and then it flies off and that's the end of it.

On Monday, 13 September 2008, what was recognized as an epoch-making event took place at Sotheby's auction rooms. For the first time ever, a famous artist, in the shape of Damien Hirst, was to preside over the sale of his own work. The sale was a triumphant success: 56 lots sold for an average of a million pounds each, something unthinkable for a living artist until quite recently. Not surprisingly, at the post-sale press conference Sotheby's staff cheered Mr Hirst until they were hoarse. The highlight of the sale was *The Golden Calf*, a dead real animal with golden hooves and horns, suspended in formaldehyde in a vitrine with a gold-plated frame. This went for no less than £10.3 million, and it was of course the cream of Hirst's jest. Once again Mammon was being worshipped on the hoof, just as the Children of Israel had in chapter 32 of the Book of Exodus.

But the incense was being burnt not just to Mammon but also to the god of novelty, for *The Golden Calf*, like much of Hirst's work, really does give us a buzz. We have never seen anything like it. The trouble is that a buzz is all it gives us. Hirst's pickled calves and sharks are attention-grabbing pranks, depthless conceits, saucy ticklers. And that is just why we like them, because they catch our eye for a moment and that is all they demand of us. Hirst's master is Marcel Duchamp, just as Duchamp is also the master of Murakami and Jeff Koons and Jean-Michel Basquiat. For it was Duchamp who first taught the world to think that the true artist of our times makes gestures, not objects, rather as Jim Slater, the famous asset-stripper of the 1960s, taught his sharp young men that, when they took over manufacturing firms, their job was to make money not things. The artist created art by pointing at things, rather as God's pointing finger in Michelangelo's fresco creates Adam. But now the tables are turned: it is Adam's pointing finger which creates God, and art and everything else. In fact, if you look at the fresco again, it is indeed Adam's languidly extended index finger which seems to be the digit controlling the show.

The artist is a showman, not a craftsman. He shows us beauty and sanctifies wherever he points his finger and signs his name: on the cool white curves of a pissoir, on the spokes of a bicycle wheel. Once he teaches us how to see these things properly, they are as beautiful as any old-style landscape or Madonna. Like his two

brothers, Duchamp began as a painter, but he was not as good as
they were, and he could see that his muddy sub-Impressionist landscapes were going nowhere. So he decided to outflank his brothers,
and indeed the rest of the world, by the dazzling quality of his foot-
work. Marcel was always to be one up and one jump ahead, setting
up tricks and boobytraps for the panting public, until he finally
jumped out of the arena altogether and spent his last years playing
chess, the purest, the most unimpeachable, most perfectly pointless
of intellectual pursuits.

    If millionaires choose to shell out large sums of cash to the artist
for his gestures, who is he to complain? If museum curators decided
to spend half their budgets on restoring his fragile whimsies such as
Duchamp's *Bride Stripped Bare by her Bachelors* (nothing to the problems of conservation likely to be faced by those who have to cope
with those slices of decaying shark), why should he be expected to
discourage them? Any person, whether public official or private plutocrat, who devotes himself to collecting and preserving these things
is making a category mistake. These are not objects for permanent
veneration. They are fleeting performances with the life expectancy
of the mayfly.

    For all the pretentious verbiage usually to be found in the cata-
logue and the mystifying titles often given to the works, they do not,
cannot engage us at a deep level. Even those few painters of our time
who do seem to offer a vision of transcendence may, paradoxically,
do so only at first glance. The philosopher and composer Roger
Scruton found something profound and mysterious in Rothko's canvases when he first saw them as a lonely 17-year-old runaway. Half
a century later, he finds it hard to recapture the angelic visions he saw
then, and now wonders rather whether these canvases are not 'the
routine product of a mind set in melancholy repetitiveness, as empty
and uninspired as the pop art that Rothko (to his credit) was at the
time denouncing'.[15] Scruton's harsher judgement today may be the
disappointment of a disenchanted disciple. There is certainly more in
the sombre glow of Rothko's huge canvases than in Hirst's golden

calf and diamond-encrusted skull. Yet it is hard to quarrel with
Scruton's instinct – that there is simply less there to sustain the imag-
ination than we first thought. Even if Rothko is far superior to what
Robert Hughes denounces as 'the *fin-de-siècle* decadence' of the con-
temporary art scene, can he really feed the soul like Rembrandt or
Piero della Francesca?

It is hard to resist the conclusion that our situation is not so far
removed from that of the Romans in the first years of the Empire.
Just at the moment when we seek to find salvation through art, we
become uneasily aware that the art we are producing is unable to
bear the weight of our expectations. I do not mean that it is worthless. It is simply lightweight.

And in a sense, it is surprisingly modest too. For as often as not, it
points beyond and away from itself, to the world and our memories
and impressions of the world. Think of the work of Richard Long:
those annotated maps and arrangements of stones which retrace and
celebrate his long walks over hill and dale. By way of introduction to
his 2009 show at Tate Britain, Long tells us: 'I like the idea of
making something from nothing. In the mid-sixties I began to think
that the language and ambition of art was too formal and orthodox.
I felt it had barely engaged with the natural landscapes which cover
our planet, or used the experiences those places could offer.' Long's
works focus not so much on those landscapes as on his passage
through them: he photographs paths that he has trampled through
the wild, or stones which he has transported from one landmark to
another. Sometimes he simply records in large letters on a wall his
experiences on a walk. For instance, *Dartmoor Time* consists of notes
from a continuous walk of twenty-four hours, such as 'One and a
half hours of early morning mist – The split-second chirrup of a skylark – Holding a butterfly with a lifespan of one month – Climbing
over granite 350 million years old on Great Mis Tor – Eight hours of
moonlight – 55 miles.' Long thinks of his work as 'abstract art laid
down in the real spaces of the world' and claims that 'It is not romantic. I use the world as I find it.' I can only say that it seems intensely

romantic to me, but also intensely didactic in its desire to remind you of the world's vast and dazzling diversity. Come with me, and see the world.[16]

These works do have the power to affect us, but the way in which they affect us is not usually, as it was with the old masters, to draw us deeper into the work but rather to send us out of the gallery and force us to see and feel our physical surroundings afresh. That is certainly something worth doing, and worth calling by the name of art. But in itself art like this can offer us no salvation, no good reason for living. Art now is at best part of the supporting cast. What it does do is to point us back to the world, to heighten our awareness of rain, leaves and solitude. It points us back to the ground we stand on. And that pointing draws us on to our final strategy for recovering a purpose to life.

XI

NATURE

Darwin's Worms

The world is no more immortal than we are. Why should it be? Like us, it is composed of matter that is neither birthless nor deathless. 'So it is a fair inference that sky and earth too had their birthday and will have their day of doom.' As we have seen, Lucretius saw no reason to think that our world would go on for ever. And in our own era, we have tumbled to the same thought. For the first time since Lucretius, educated opinion believes that the world will one day come to an end, for strictly material, scientifically proven reasons. There will come a day when this planet is too hot or too cold to support life in general, or us in particular.

But we have added a twist. To most educated opinion now, it seems likely that we may be bringing that day nearer by our own actions. For the first time, we see ourselves as powerful enough to destroy our own planet – and our own species with it. If we go down before our natural time, it will be a case of assisted suicide rather than death by natural causes.

There is a curious coincidence here, one which nobody much cares to remark on. The finest scientific minds believe that we may be living in the End-Times, just as much as Sarah Palin and the backwoods fundamentalists believe it. This does not mean that the scientists and the backwoods people have the same reasons for thinking that the End of the World is just around the corner. But they do share the apprehension. What the majority of scientists fear is that the ecosystem which supports us is terrifyingly fragile and that the conditions which enabled this planet to bring forth life in the first place are precarious, unique and not to be repeated.

This has become an article of faith among respectable people. Their gospel is the 2001 report of the Intergovernmental Panel on Climate Change.[1] Most of the observed warming over the past fifty years, the IPCC concluded, is likely to have been due to the observed increase in the concentration of man-made greenhouse gases. It was mostly our fault. The IPCC's climate models project a further increase in world temperatures of between 2° and 11.5°F over the twenty-first century. This is if we take no significant action. Even if the levels of greenhouse gases are stabilized, global-warming sea levels and the incidence of violent weather events – floods, drought, tornadoes and tidal waves – are expected to continue increasing for centuries, perhaps for 1,000 years.

This overwhelming consensus among scientists across the world is supported by the vivid direct evidence in front of us: the melting of the Arctic ice, the retreat of the Alpine glaciers, the lengthening of the growing season in temperate regions, the change in the migration patterns of birds.

It has accordingly become a modern heresy to challenge this consensus. Climate-change deniers have been compared to Holocaust-deniers. This is a slick debating trick, because, apart from the enormity of the insult, the Holocaust is a confirmed historical event, whereas the most controversial part of the climate-change thesis lies in the future. Some of the few sceptics among scientists have been denied research funds and had their opportunities for employment or promotion blocked. Not since aspiring scholars were compelled to take Holy Orders, or at least conform to the articles of the Church, has mainstream academia insisted so rigorously on conformity to a set of beliefs.

Yet a scattering of sceptics have escaped the coop and put forward alternative explanations and offered contrary evidence. They point out, for example, that while the Arctic ice is undeniably melting, the icefields in the Antarctic are not. In places, they are thickening. In the past couple of years, some evidence of thinning at the edges has been found, but so far this is on a minor scale. Some glaciers are thickening too. In any case, over the first seven years of the twenty-first century there has been virtually no change in average world temperatures. Besides, historical variations in climate have been frequent and marked in the past, sometimes to be measured in centuries, with sub-variations lasting decades within those longer periods. Sceptics are especially fond of pointing out that the mild European climate in Roman times, known as the Roman Age Optimum, enabled the colonists to plant vines as far north as Yorkshire.[2]

An uncommitted layman might well conclude that though there must obviously be some relation between present CO_2 levels and future temperature levels, it doesn't yet seem certain or clear exactly what that relation might be. This does not mean that we should do nothing. There is a strong case for a third position, for what I would

call 'green scepticism'. As a precaution, we should make every effort
to minimize our carbon footprint and, in general, to tread upon the
earth more lightly. At the same time, we should continue to improve
our techniques for measuring and forecasting, while treating the
research findings we already have with proper scientific caution.

What strikes me is how few people take this genuinely sceptical
attitude, how ready – in fact eager – people are to believe the direst
predictions. It is as though the reports of global warming of the past
twenty years met and satisfied a pre-existing anxiety. They provided
a plausible narrative which would channel our fears for the planet
and a campaign which would concentrate our energies. Climate-
change sceptics describe this campaign as being 'like a new religion'.
Believers indignantly deny this description, asserting that their views
are strictly based on 'the science' and retorting that it is the deniers
who are the religious fanatics. Again, there is a case for a third position: yes, it *is* like a new religion, but that is not necessarily a bad
thing. For there is nothing ignoble in feeling a passionate devotion to
the well-being of our planet, even if our fears are sometimes irrational, just as a mother's fears for her children are sometimes
irrational.

Similar cataclysmic apprehensions were current in the 1960s, well
before global warming was discovered (or invented). There were anxieties whether the planet could go on supporting our teeming
billions, voiced in such works as Paul Ehrlich's *The Population Bomb*
(1968) and the first reports of the Club of Rome, *Limits to Growth*
(1972) and *Mankind at the Turning Point* (1974), arguing that there
were inescapable limits to economic growth. We were sucking the
world dry of raw materials and breeding far beyond our capacity to
feed ourselves. In the short-lived craze for global cooling, terrible
famines were expected as the cornfields of temperate regions iced
over, or flooded. A few years earlier, and perhaps even more influential than any of these wake-up calls to the human race, came Rachel
Carson's *Silent Spring* (1963). In this remarkable book were first voiced
all the anxieties that had been gathering for years beforehand: how

industrial agriculture was poisoning the land with its pesticides and fertilizers and turning the old landscape of copses and birdsong into featureless prairies. We were becoming estranged from the land which gave birth to us. In our arrogance, we were heading for a nemesis that we were too blind to foresee.

We had to fumble our way back towards a healthier way of existing before the damage we were doing to the planet became irreparable. We had to be scared back into sanity. If the preaching to the unconverted cut a few corners and minimized the uncertainties of the scientists' predictions, then this was in the best of causes. What looked like an inconvenient possibility, or at worst an inconvenient likelihood, had to be boosted as *An Inconvenient Truth*.[3]

The climate-change campaign (and the occasional ruthlessness of its tactics) is as much a symptom as a cause of a deeper and longer established impulse: the urge to re-earth ourselves.

There is a new goddess to be worshipped: Gaia, the old earth goddess but now dressed in the robes of modern science. In Greek mythology Gaia is the offspring of Chaos. Ouranos, Heaven, is both her child and her husband. It is the earth that gives birth to pretty much everything, including Kronos, Time, who is her youngest child. Gaia is the source. She is Mother Earth, 'Terra Mater'. Scholars surmised that, in the earliest forms of her cult and that of Tellus, her Roman equivalent, she represented simply the indwelling power or *mana* of the patch of earth which the worshippers tilled and lived on. But as far back as our records go, she is personified as a goddess, representing the earth in general. She can be seen as both the prime and ultimate deity, the alpha and omega of life.

In her modern reincarnation, she is the offspring of the many walks over the Downs taken in the late 1960s by two remarkable residents of the tiny south Wiltshire village of Bowerchalke: the scientist James Lovelock, and the novelist and future Nobel prizewinner William Golding, then working as a schoolmaster in Salisbury. Lovelock was at that time an independent operator, but he had previously worked for NASA on methods of detecting life on Mars.

This had led him to start thinking about the earth as a single organism, and to notice how self-regulating so many of its operations seemed to be, in a way that reminded him of the human body: how combinations of chemicals such as methane and oxygen persisted in stable concentrations in the earth's atmosphere, how the degree of saltiness in the sea remained stable too, how the surface temperature of the earth had remained remarkably constant when measured on a global scale, although the energy provided by the sun had increased by 25–30 per cent since life began on earth.[4] Might it not be then that the biosphere and the atmosphere and all the other chemical components of the earth formed a complex interacting system that somehow regulated itself, that the earth was in that sense a single living system and needed to be considered holistically?

Well, no, it most definitely might not, chorused leading Darwinians such as Stephen Jay Gould and Richard Dawkins. To them, this 'earth feedback hypothesis', as Lovelock originally called it, had too much damned intention about it. It was, to use the most accursed word in the Darwinists' dictionary, teleological. To assert that the system was operating with some deliberate purpose behind it was to smuggle in a variation on the discredited theory of Intelligent Design. And when Golding suggested making the hypothesis more vivid and popular by calling it 'the Gaia hypothesis', that was more intolerable still. The idea that the outcome of physical processes could resemble a person was not to be spoken of.

In fact, in its early years the hypothesis was not much spoken of at all. Aided by the microbiologist Lyn Margulis, Lovelock wrote several scientific papers which indicated that the hypothesis did have some predictive powers. But it was not until he published a more popular treatment, *Gaia: a New Look at Life on Earth*, in 1979, that the idea took root in popular consciousness. On the basis of this book, Gould and Dawkins were certainly entitled to criticize Lovelock for inventing the ultimate personality cult. In the very first paragraph of the book, the author asserts that 'the quest for Gaia is an attempt to find the largest living creature on earth'.

As time has gone on, the Gaia hypothesis has shifted and refined.[5] Weak and strong versions of the theory continue to be debated to this day. The most radical revision of the theory was provided by Lovelock himself in *The Revenge of Gaia* (2006), where he argues that human beings have shown no respect for Gaia and may have irreparably damaged her capacity for self-stabilization and self-renewal. By cutting down the rainforests, we are testing to destruction her ability to cope with the extra greenhouse gases. By warming the ocean, we are damaging the marine food chain. Gaia will do her best to prevent any runaway effects that wipe out life itself. Even so, the world population is likely to be mercilessly culled by floods, drought and famine. With these predictions, Lovelock has aligned himself with the direst predictions of the global warmers, though not without tossing in a rider that most of his green allies would regard as heretical: he now believes that nuclear power is the least bad and perhaps the only answer to the carbon problem. Gaia has been severely traumatized, and extreme measures will be needed to restore her health.

Notice how easily we slip into talking about 'her'. And I cannot help thinking again of Golding and Lovelock striding out over the high downs above Bowerchalke (Marleycombe Hill is nearly 700 feet above sea level), and looking back down at the gently swelling declivities all around and the meandering wetlands of the five small rivers that flow into Salisbury half a dozen miles away. My father used to make me recite their names in alphabetical order: the Avon, the Bourne, the Ebble, the Nadder and the Wylye. When the barley is the colour of pale honey on the chalk, there can be few places on earth where it is easier to think of the earth as a woman, nowhere more natural to imagine Gaia.

The landscape of the Wiltshire Downs has stirred many writers before Golding and Lovelock. William Cobbett on his *Rural Rides* (1830) described Norton Bavant, a few miles up the road on the water meadows of the Wylye, as 'one of the prettiest spots that my eyes ever beheld'. The same distance the other side of Salisbury,

William Hazlitt used to hole up for weeks at a time at Winterslow Hut (now the Pheasant Inn), partly to get away from his wife whose family owned property close by but also to allow his prickly temperament to be calmed by downland solitude.

Richard Jefferies (1848–87), the son of an unsuccessful small farmer in a village near Swindon, in his book *Wild Life in a Southern County* (1879), describes sitting on the top of a nearby Wiltshire down and observing in ever widening circles the fields and woods and animals and people below him. It is as though he fancied himself to be lolling in the navel of the world, Gaia's navel. The place he is sitting on is an ancient earthwork, Liddington Camp, from which there are huge views across the north Wiltshire plain. He reclines at the pleasant angle provided by the inner slope of the green fosse and listens to the sibilant 'sish, sish' of the wind rustling through the dry grass like the sound of the sea heard in a dream. The first time I read Jefferies's description, I felt an instant longing, almost a sense of obligation to go there myself.

Jefferies was famous for his descriptions not only of the natural world but also of the unremitting lives of agricultural workers (in, for example, *The Toilers of the Fields* (1892)). He caught the public too with his futuristic fantasy, *After London* (1885), in which the country reverts to nature after some unspecified catastrophe has depopulated England: fields are overrun by forest, domestic animals run wild, the hated London becomes a poisonous swamp, and the few survivors revert to a quasi-medieval way of life. This accidental Utopia did a lot to inspire William Morris's much better known Utopia *News from Nowhere* (1890). But Jefferies, though his short life was plagued by ill-health, was greatly admired, even loved, as was his successor as a country-writer and naturalist, W.H. Hudson, who insisted on being buried in the same churchyard in Sussex as Jefferies. Jefferies had retired to the south coast in the vain hope of rescuing his lungs.[6]

I used to love Hudson's tramps across the empty chalk counties of southern England, where he meets solitaries like himself, the shepherds and tinkers of the white highway. He had been brought up in

Argentina, and perhaps part of his strange freshness derived from his having come from another continent. In his account of a Wiltshire village, Burbage near Marlborough, he imagines putting himself in the place of the skylark rising from a field close by and singing from a considerable height above the road his human alter ego is tramping along. Like Jefferies, he imagines himself as both ranging over the whole chalkland landscape and being an integral part of it.[7] It is a thought borrowed from or at least shared with George Meredith, whom he quotes in the epigraph to another book.

> Once I was part of the music I heard
> On the boughs or sweet between earth and sky,
>   For joy of the beating of wings on high ·
> My heart shot into the breast of the bird.

The idea of shapeshifting, or metamorphosis, has never ceased to tickle the human imagination. Ovid's *Metamorphoses* were irresistible in their own day – lyrical, ironic, piquant – and they have proved immensely popular in all the languages into which they have since been translated. There seems to be an unfailing appeal about the idea of Daphne being transformed into a laurel, or Niobe turned into a frozen waterfall or Actaeon into a stag to be torn to pieces by his own hounds, and you cannot help noticing that in the twentieth century writers and film-makers have loved to play with such fancies more than ever. In Kafka's story *Die Verwandlung* (1915), Gregor Samsa wakes up to discover that he has been transformed into a beetle and is as a result horribly treated by one and all; David Garnett wrote *Lady into Fox* (1922), which does precisely what it says on the title. In his short stories, Saki loved to break down the species barrier: the oppressed small boy Conradin worships his polecat-ferret Sredni Vashtar as a god and prays to it to rid him of his oppressive guardian Mrs De Repp, and Sredni Vashtar obliges with his sharp little teeth. Saki's hero Clovis grants the wish of his silly hostess Mary Hampton and turns her into a she-wolf for an afternoon. The amazing cat

Tobermory is taught to speak and reports all the bitchy things the house party have been saying about each other. It is, I think, no accident that these stories tend to have been published around the time of the First World War when so many people lost their illusions about their fellow human beings. Morphing ridicules our human pretensions, undermines the conceit that we are separate from and superior to the rest of nature. It feeds the growing intimation that, on the contrary, nature might turn out to be our last best hope.

I was brought up in a small village in the middle of the Downs not unlike the one Hudson describes, although ours was 20 miles to the south. Our village had the same steep lane coming down off the hill between whitewashed cottages on raised banks and the same bare fields swelling up all around it. Our nearest landmark was Stonehenge and the whole country was humped and hollowed with barrows and earthworks. And I too responded strongly to both the Downs and the people who wrote about them. My bible was the Shell guide to Wiltshire, first compiled in 1935 by Robert Byron, the impetuous prince of travel writers, and then revised by John Piper in the 1960s, with its haunting black-and-white photographs of flint churches and sarsen stones. It was something to walk the chalky track southwards across the Downs to the high earthworks of Yarnbury Castle five miles away without seeing a single vehicle or human soul, and fancy oneself the successor to these old solitary wanderers.[8]

The popularity of English writing about the countryside is not so hard to explain. Ours was the first nation to experience industrialization and urbanization on a scale that seemed overwhelming. Accordingly we were the first nation to experience a sense of loss and of disconnection from our rural past. These country-writers shared that sense in their own lives, for in many cases they were as physically cut off from the countryside as the rest of us. What they made were, for the most part, *excursions* from the city. W.H. Hudson and his wife kept a lodging house in Kensington. Richard Jefferies spent many years of a life that was cut short by TB in Surbiton. Arthur Machen, whose full name was Arthur Machen Jones and who tinged with magic the Arthurian land of the Welsh Marches, was condemned to earn his crust as a London hack and had digs in St John's Wood.

What they sought in the countryside – and sought to recapture for their readers – was a double redemption. They set out to describe the unpolluted landscapes and uncorrupted working people who lived lives which were hard and unrelenting but which possessed a kind of truth and reality that the rest of us had lost. At the same time by these long walks and vibrant encounters they hoped themselves to share in something like that real life. As they walked the roads, and felt their limbs ache and tasted real hunger and thirst, and were drenched and frozen and worked up a glowing sweat, they too had rejoined the earth. They were back in Gaia's arms.

That tradition of country-writing has never faded. Between the wars, Adrian Bell's *Corduroy* (1930) was a best-seller. After the war, so was John Stewart Collis's *The Worm Forgives the Plough* (1939) and Ronald Blythe's *Akenfield* (1969). Every country bookshop is filled with the products of local historians and local presses, describing the neighbourhood as it used to be.

Some of these are unashamed exercises in nostalgia and given no more than a condescending glance by the metropolitan media. But, more recently, something has changed. Gaia has come to town. All eyes are upon her and everyone feels enormously protective towards her and wants a piece of her.

Consider first the startling growth in the number and strength of organizations dedicated to protecting 'the environment' – the new general term to describe Gaia's skin which only came into common use in the 1970s (the *OED Supplement* can find no use of the word in this exact sense earlier than 1956). At the end of the First World War, the National Trust had 700 members. By 1934 this had risen only to 3,400 and, as late as 1965 when Enterprise Neptune was launched, still no more than 157,881. Today it has just passed 3.5 million. Like the Royal Society for the Protection of Birds which has more than a million members, the Trust has now largely returned to its original purpose of acquiring for the nation those threatened patches of coastline and countryside in preference to the stately homes which were for a time its main focus. Friends of the Earth, founded in 1969, now has thriving and vocal groups of activists in seventy countries.

Most supporters of such organizations have hitherto done so from their armchairs and with their chequebooks and credit cards. With the great carbon panic there has come a call to arms. To do your bit for the environment, cash is no longer enough. Even from a fifth-floor flat or a suburban semi, it is possible, in fact imperative, to make a personal contribution: by abstaining from plastic bags, by recycling your old newspapers and empty bottles, by composting your garden waste, by growing your own vegetables and picking your own blackberries, by slashing your air miles and your food miles, by insulating your loft or installing a windmill on your roof, by walking or cycling instead of motoring and, if you must drive, by switching over to a hybrid or electric car. In seeking to convince voters that the Conservative Party was no longer the party of Gradgrinds and road hogs, the new party leader David Cameron lost no time in posing for a photocall in the Arctic to draw attention to the melting ice, changing the Party's hard-edged torch logo for a fuzzy tree, conspicuously cycling to the House of Commons and installing a windmill on his Notting Hill residence to associate himself with the cause of renewable energy. These stunts were mocked by some, admired by others, but nobody questioned their rationale. They were genuflections to the new conventional pieties, just as a newly elected leader in earlier ages would have lost no time in being seen attending Mass or matins.

We need to touch Gaia, to feel the knobbles on the organic carrots, to shake the earth off the locally grown potatoes. In every town and city now, the farmers' market attracts reverent crowds who hope by their attendance and their generous purchases of the overpriced merchandise to be shriven of their sins against the environment. At these farmers' markets there are none of the raucous cries of traditional street markets. Families troop round in that same hushed atmosphere of reverence that Goethe noticed in the art gallery at Dresden, and children who lay their sticky fingers on the fruit and veg are reproved as though they had fingered a Madonna. Self-sufficiency is the new path of sanctity. Like all attempts at spiritual improvements, this crusade too is open to mockery, as the original crusades were. But just as Don Quixote remained awkwardly heroic in his innocent folly, so in the television series *The Good Life* (1975) Richard Briers and Felicity Kendal were unmistakably on the side of the angels.

It is all very recent. After sailing round the waterways of England and Holland in a Dutch sailing barge, it was only in the mid-1950s that John Seymour (1914–2004) rented five acres of land near Orford in Suffolk and began his adventure in self-sufficiency, first described in *The Fat of the Land* (1961). Two years later, he moved to a farm near Newport, Pembrokeshire, from where he published *The Complete Book of Self-Sufficiency* (1976). This bible of the new movement also established the reputations of two young publishers, Richard Dorling and Peter Kindersley, the latter later becoming one of the new organic mega-farmers on his vast acres on the Berkshire Downs. Seymour remained a guru of the movement into extreme old age and never lost the fire in his belly. After he moved to Ireland (leaving behind a School for Self-Sufficiency in Pembrokeshire), he was taken to court at the age of 85 for damaging a genetically modified crop of sugar beet.

The campaign against GM crops represented a new and more passionate turn in the struggle to protect Gaia's purity. It was partly a return to the war against the old enemy, Big Pharma, with Monsanto represented as the most unscrupulous opponent and one who had forgotten nothing and learnt nothing from the earlier battles to ban its pesticides and fertilizers that were killing songbirds and spilling over into the lakes and rivers. It helped the campaigners that early trials of GM crops showed disappointing yields, but the argument was not ultimately about economics. Even if it could be shown that GM crops really could help to feed the hungry millions in poorer countries, the revulsion against any such tampering with nature would not be much softened.

'Self-sufficiency' is a rather inadequate word to describe the movement. It suggests an unadmitted selfishness, a wish to get away from the world and concentrate on your own well-being. But this is not how the new pilgrims see themselves. Like the old pilgrims, they view themselves not as going away from but rather as going towards the real world. They are not so much shunning contact but rather embracing Gaia, much as those who first worshipped the goddess must have seen themselves.

And the exemplars now held up for our admiration are those men and women who cast away their bourgeois inhibitions and their urban fearfulness and who plunge into Gaia's embrace. They are the ones who teach us what it is to live intensely. Even if we follow their experiences only at one remove, through books and TV programmes, we can hope to catch a little of their exhilaration and share vicariously in the rewards of living with Gaia.

Roger Deakin in his cult classic, *Waterlog: a swimmer's journey through Britain* (1999), describes his splashy odyssey across the country. Over several months in the late 1990s he swam in dozens of the rivers, lakes, llyns, lochs, streams and seas of England, Wales and Scotland. His aim was to acquire 'a frog's-eye view' of the country, to immerse himself in the element from which our remote ancestors clambered forth aeons ago.

There are other books about 'wild swimming' as it is now called, by Daniel Start and Kate Rew, for example, all dating back to the first recent book to take the swimmer as hero, Charles Sprawson's *Haunts of the Black Masseur* (1992). But these later works are rather more in the nature of recreational guides which tell you the places where you can best have a plunge. Only Deakin turns swimming anywhere any time into a natural part of life, even in his own muddy moat which is only a few yards long. His friend Robert Macfarlane in *The Wild Places* (2007) sets out to walk across moor and tor and beach and ridge, through beechwoods and salt marshes, to remind us how, even in the most densely populated country in the most densely populated continent, there are still wildernesses calling to us beyond the tarmac and the concrete. *The Wild Places* begins by recalling the extraordinary set-up at Deakin's Suffolk farmhouse, Walnut Tree Farm, and draws to a close by recalling Deakin's death there from a brain tumour in his early 60s, still full of the brio of a 25-year-old, the age at which he had bought the ruins of this Elizabethan farmhouse and 12 acres of surrounding meadow. The farmhouse was largely constructed of native wood – oak, chestnut and ash – and when the big easterlies blew, its timbers creaked and groaned, making sounds like a ship in a storm. Deakin kept the windows open to let air and animals circulate, so that the house seemed almost to breathe. Bats flitted in and out, swallows nested in the chimneys and starlings in the thatch. Through the summer months Deakin bathed in his midget moat, which was kept clean not by any chemical agent but by a colony of ramshorn snails.

When I first heard about Roger Deakin swimming his way across Britain, I thought there was something contrived and a bit sentimental about the project. The idea failed to catch my fancy and I failed to read the book. But then ten years later, we happened to be spending the first few days of the New Year in North Wales. Our friends took us walking in the Rhinog Mountains. It was a bright crisp day, blue skies above the ring of tawny peaks. There was hoar frost on the broken bracken stems and ice on the flagstones of the drovers' path over the pass leading ultimately to England, the so-called Roman Steps though they are more likely to be medieval. The steps were big flagstones taking a leisurely zizag across the heather and scree. They looked somehow arbitrary, designed more to show off the landscape than to find the quickest way to get cattle or sheep over the pass. They might have been put there by Richard Long to show where he had walked. And I later found that Long had walked in these parts, for in his Tate Britain show there is a colour photograph 'Snowdonia Stones 2006' showing a rocky bluff very like the one we were standing on in the midst of blue-green mountains very like these. On this bluff, Long has arranged a straggling group of dark, lichen-covered stones which from a distance look rather like one of those open-air congregations that John Wesley preached to. Whether in Snowdonia or on Salisbury Plain, you are never far from the trail of a writer or an artist. Ours must be the most intensely inscribed landscape on earth.

After we had slithered back down the steps, we turned up a winding grassy path along a mountain stream. The water was deliciously dappled in the midday sun. Below a little waterfall, the stream briefly widened into a winking pool. One after the other, each of us confessed to a sudden longing to strip off and jump in, although it was the beginning of January.

'This was where Deakin had his last swim,' Tanya said.

'No, really?'

I thought she was joking, or at least inventing a little. Even if Deakin had come to the Rhinogs, how could she know that this was the precise pool he had taken his final dip in? When I got home, I bought the book, and there was a whole chapter about his walking in the Rhinogs, and there it was, the pool below the waterfall, like a dream in an adventure story which becomes real.[9]

There was another thing which dispelled any doubt whether this really was the site of his last swim. Deakin describes coming across several strange little cave entrances half-blocked by turf and brambles. He crawls into one of them and finds a dark tunnel lined with slates. He is content to let the purpose of these tunnels remain a mystery to him. And there just a few yards above the lovely pool are the tunnels, exactly as he describes them. I get down on hands and knees and peer in but do not fancy crawling into the dripping muddy hole.

'They're manganese mines, for hardening iron. The railways used to mix in manganese to stop the rails breaking,' Henry said.

I wonder whether Deakin would have cared to know this fact or whether he would have been distressed that, even in this marvellous lost wilderness, nineteenth-century industry was burrowing away.

Perhaps he would have consoled himself with the thought of the miners coming up for air and splashing the mud off their sturdy white bodies in the gurgling pool he had just swum in.

That was not the end of my engagement with Deakin. In fact it was only the beginning. Over the next few days, some of the swims which I had myself taken over the years came back to me with an unexpected vividness: the time when we had walked up the Thames from Dorchester and it had been so hot that we had stripped off and waded in just below the bridge at Clifton Hampden and to our surprise the river had been so low that we could walk right across it; and another hot day years before when we had plunged into the muddy depths of Chantry Lake in Somerset, imagining that every time our toes stubbed on the stones they were crunching the crayfish which we had seen in the clearer water by the dam; another lake swim, on holiday in Ireland, off a landing stage in Lough Caragh on a golden morning with the crags of MacGillycuddy's Reeks all around and going back to a full Irish breakfast in a dining room full of businessmen in suits; and a day or two earlier, further down the Ring of Kerry, an impromptu dip in the encircled bay with its silky sands at Derrynane, the home of O'Connell the Liberator. The impromptu was the thing, the sudden unplanned instinct that there was nothing for it but to take to the water: after lunch on our honeymoon, on the Pilgrim's Road to Santiago, in a weedy stream by an ancient bridge outside a crumbling town called Sahagún. Because it was Spain and I hadn't shaved, I was fancying myself as Hemingway and Julia was horrified to discover that she had married a man who couldn't swim. Later, I could swim a little better, not much, when we paddled out from the beach at Corpus Christi in the Gulf of Mexico and floated on our backs and watched the pelicans flying low over us. But that was a place where people came to swim, and the most memorables bathes are those which have a thrill of the forbidden, like when my Oxford friend and I were fishing on a famous stretch of the Test and it was too hot for the fish and when we had finished the white wine we stripped down to our Y-fronts and drifted downstream in the duckweed, heedless of the trout we had failed to catch or the water bailiffs guarding the precious stream. I have written about that afternoon on the Test before, but I was not then aware why this spur-of-the-moment splash and the others which came after it were so memorable to me. But now I see that Deakin was right. The shock of the icy water breaks through the dull carapace of ordinary life and sharpens your sense of existing in a world which you suddenly feel intensely at one with, a moment normally unattainable, even undreamed of.

Other tree-huggers – not for the first time in history a derisive appellation coined by opponents can be worn as a badge of honour – have chosen different ways of embracing Gaia. By following birds through their seasons and their immigrations, for example. William Fiennes followed the snow geese in their vast peregrinations from their summers in the Canadian Arctic to their winters in the Gulf of Mexico (*The Snow Geese*, 2002). Mark Cocker, on a humbler mission, follows the deafening flocks of rooks and jackdaws which regularly pass over his house in Norfolk. He seeks out the roosts and studies the habits of these common but not commonplace birds in places as far apart as Cornwall and Dumfries, thus turning the whole of Britain into *Crow Country* (2007).

Or instead of going to the animal kingdom, you can bring it to you. If part of the mission is to break down the artificial separation between Man and Nature, then a lion or a tiger or a wolf should be welcome in the sitting room, just as a human being with binoculars feels at home in a rookery. The celebrated accounts of bringing up a cub from one of these feared species have several purposes beyond the intrinsic fascination of their unlikeliness: to make us feel more at home with nature, to understand that the big cats have their feelings too, to open the door of our fusty dwellings and let the world we are part of blow in. Mark Rowlands, an assistant professor of philosophy at the University of Alabama, in Tuscaloosa, bought off an advertisement a six-week-old wolf cub which he named Brenin. The moment he made the purchase, he began to adopt a kind of wolf's-eye view. He could remember his first sight of Brenin and the other cubs in a litter:

> But of the person who sold me Brenin, I can remember virtually nothing. Something had already started; a process that would become more and more pronounced as the years rolled on. I was already starting to tune out human beings. When you have a wolf, they take over your life in a way that a dog seldom does. And human company gradually becomes less and less significant for you.

They became inseparable for eleven years, eating together, running together, sleeping together. Brenin even sat in on his lectures. Rowlands claims that 'much of what I know about life and its meaning I learnt from him. What it is to be human; this I learnt from a wolf.'[10] Not so much an anthropomorphic outlook as a lycanthropic one in which the patient imagines himself to be a wolf.

Whether you are looking after a full-grown wolf or building your own farmhouse out of wood which you have cut and shaped yourself, one thing is clear: you are taking on a lot of work. Most of it will be heavy, exhausting and incessant labour. You will be stretching muscles that the rest of us hardly ever use. This work is not just an incidental burden of the process of getting close to Gaia. It is an essential part of the process. In physical work we are pumping the blood of our being. That is the sort of language that D.H. Lawrence might use, and in observing these awkward yet invigorating attempts to embrace Gaia, I cannot get Lawrence out of my mind, particularly his rhapsodies over the male body that had been hardened by manual labour – the miner in his bath in *Sons and Lovers* (1913), or Lady Chatterley coming upon Mellors outside his cottage, washing himself naked to the hips or hammering nails into a coop he has made or putting out food for his dog or coming down the ride with his gun under his arm, off to shoot vermin or nab a poacher – always working or resting from work, the muscles on his slim white body always tensing or slackening. The body *knows* best: as Nietzsche taught us, 'There is more rationality in thy body than in thy best wisdom. Write with blood, and thou wilt find that blood is spirit.' And the body is made for work, and the blood to be pumped and pumped hard.

In the last years of his life, Roger Deakin began to keep a journal, and in it he recorded sights and sounds of Suffolk: the single song thrush singing in the car park at Tesco's in Bury St Edmunds, the plum tree blossom lit up by the moonshine and at the same time by the lights of the American bombers returning to base from Iraq, the taste of young dandelion leaves, the noise of vetch-pods cracking open in the sun. What he recorded too, as an integral part of living close to the earth, were the joys of physical labour: of digging over the vegetable patch, of picking up the windfalls and of coppicing. He describes the exhilaration of starting up the tractor and trundling off into the woods with his billhook and chainsaw. As he is trimming and stripping off the hazel poles with his hook, 'My aim went awry and the sharp, glancing blade sliced straight through the leather glove and cut a choice fillet out of the ball of my thumb. The sudden sharp pain, the surprise and shock, then instant self-recrimination, are all still vivid enough. But what really struck home was the immediate and overwhelming realisation that this is what it feels like for the tree.'[11] As we hug Gaia closer, we can even get a glimmering of the tree's-eye view too.

In the Christian tradition, this intense appreciation of work is not often to be found. Christians work to live; they do not live to work, or rather the Lord's work is of a different, non-physical kind. The Sermon on the Mount exhorts us to take no thought for the morrow. 'The fowls sow not, nor do they reap, nor gather into barns; yet your heavenly father feedeth them.' More scandalous yet, we are invited to admire the lilies of the field who neither toil nor spin but who are arrayed more beautifully than Solomon in all his glory.[12] As far as humans go, we are told that the idle sister Mary who sits listening to Jesus has chosen the good and needful part, as opposed to the resentful Martha who is doing the dishes.[13] For Christians, physical labour may be a moral necessity; it is seldom presented as a spiritual fulfilment in itself. That would depend on the object of the work: tending the dying, for example, or building a church. More often, spiritual fulfilment is presented as an alternative to, or escape from physical toil: 'Come unto me all ye that labour and are heavy-laden, and I will refresh you.'[14]

This grudging attitude towards physical toil which pervades the New Testament is very different from the atmosphere of the Old Testament (and from the Judaism which is descended from it). The threat of scarcity and the hope of abundant harvests hang over the Children of Israel; good husbandry is applauded, bad husbandry denounced. After all, had not the Lord God put Adam into the Garden of Eden 'to dress it and keep it'?[15] At the end of Voltaire's *Candide* (1759), even the foolish Dr Pangloss recognizes that man was put on this earth to work. 'Keep working and don't argue,' says the unlucky old scholar, Martin, 'that's the only way to make life bearable.' Accordingly, the little group set about living off a smallholding, the women sewing and washing and making patisserie and the men tilling the earth and making the furniture. And every time Dr Pangloss starts blathering, Candide says, 'That's all very well, but we must cultivate our garden.'

Candide's attitude is intrinsic to the classical tradition from the earliest times. Hesiod is regarded by some as the earliest Greek poet we have anything left of, although others think he may have been roughly a contemporary of Homer or perhaps lived a little later. The consensus seems to be that the two of them flourished somewhere between 800 and 700 BC. In his long poem *Works and Days*, Hesiod preaches the need of every man to work for his living. The poem is addressed in part to his brother Perses with whom he has quarrelled over their inheritance from their father: 'Work, foolish Perses, the works which gods have appointed unto men, lest one day with wife and children in anguish of souls thou seekest livelihood among the neighbours and they turn away.'

As he takes the reader through the farmer's year, he describes how to fashion a plough and put together a wagon and the right moments to plough, sow and reap. Even in the nastier months of the year, Hesiod's description tingles with the compensating joys of farmwork. Wrap up well, he says, wear stout sandals and a felt cap that keeps your ears warm:

> For chill is the dawn at the onset of Boreas. And in the dawn a fruitful mist is stretched over the earth from starry heaven above the fields of happy men: a mist which drawing from the ever-flowing rivers is lifted high above the earth by the blowing of the wind, and anon turneth to rain toward eventide.[16]

In summer, though, when the artichoke comes into bloom and the chattering cicada pours forth his song, then, Hesiod says, give me the shade of a rock and Bibline wine and a milk cake, and some goat's milk and calf's flesh and I'll sit happily in the shade after lunch feeling the fresh westerly breeze on my face.

In Hesiod, at what is for us the dawn of poetry, we find this mixture of stern moral and agricultural advice mingled with the delights of being outdoors. He experiences – and makes us experience – the same tingle of anticipatory leisure as Roger Deakin does taking out his chainsaw or stripping off to plunge into his minuscule moat.

I think it must be because schoolmasters – and perhaps schoolboys too – are more interested in warfare and love songs that this tradition in classical literature has remained somewhat in the shadows, relegated to the second division of semi-technical manuals. It is certainly true that Cato the Elder's *De Agri Cultura*, in describing life on a farm in the Sabine Hills, does hand out a good deal of technical advice on everything from how to buy and manage an estate to the best grapes to plant, the best bedding for sheep and cattle, and the proper intervals between olive trees. He also includes several simple recipes – we have already quoted his recipe for *placenta* cake – and several medical tips, especially for digestive ailments and mostly involving cabbage leaves. He even tells you how to avoid a chafing bottom on a long journey: 'Keep a small branch of Pontic worm-wood under the anus.' (CLIX) It is in short a Mrs Beeton for farm managers. Yet in all his advice it is impossible not to sense that Cato, for all his greatness, has himself carried out all these tasks and taken much pleasure in their execution. His advice on how to plant and grow asparagus (CLXI), for example, radiates the experience of one who has raised and hoed his own beds, in just the way we do it today, and covered the shoots with straw in winter – or at any rate hired some itinerant Chaldean astrologers to do it for him.

De Agri Cultura was written about 160 BC, and it is just about the earliest surviving example of connected Latin prose. Indeed, Cato is said by Columella, a later writer on agriculture, to have been the first to teach the Romans to speak Latin. He was certainly not the last to write about agriculture. Columella's *De Re Rustica* was preceded by Marcus Terentius Varro's *Res Rusticae*. Varro (116–27 BC) was a politi-cian, admiral and antiquarian who lived to nearly 90 and claimed to have written 'seventy times seven books'. He seems to have copied a fair bit from Cato, just as Columella (AD 4–70) copied from Varro to produce his twelve volumes on the subject. So did Pliny the Elder (AD 23–79) for the relevant bits of his *Natural History*. There was, in short, a stream of agrilit on tap throughout Rome's heyday. And not all of it was in prose, unlike the works just mentioned. The boundary between what was appropriate for prose and what for poetry was less fixed then. And in his *Georgics* and *Eclogues,* Virgil (70–19 BC) carried on Hesiod's song: about the delights of rustic things and the sacred worth of the farmer's life. Virgil can be just as technical as any of the prose writers on agriculture, his advice on the correct construction of a plough coming more or less straight from Hesiod's book.[17]

Virgil in Books I and II of the *Georgics* starts with the growing of corn and vegetables. Book III discusses the rearing of cattle and other livestock, while the final Book IV deals with bees, asps and other insects. In his famous description of the life of bees, Virgil takes off into a famous pantheistic flight of fancy which celebrates the bees as, well, the be-all and end-all of life. The bees are seen as part of the mind of God and as deriving their vital force straight from heaven.[18] Within the same poem we find a bewildering range of expression: from technical advice, through practical observation of daily life, to romantic rhapsody and finally what is almost a religious hymn – but all of it tied to the work of the farmer. '*Georgic*' is only the Greek word for 'agricultural', though for some reason none of the poem's many translators has Englished its title as '*The Agriculturals*'.

Just as a technical treatise involving manure and cheese-making seemed to the ancients a suitable topic for poetry, so did the earthy incidents of rustic life. The *Idylls* of Theocritus (about 270 BC) alternate between celebrating the beauties of nature and reporting the antics of the labourers in unbuttoned terms. One Idyll is a dialogue between the cowherds Battus and Corydon who are driving their cattle up through an olive grove. Battus chases a cow out of a blackthorn thicket and gets a thorn in his ankle which Corydon pulls out, telling him not to go barefoot on the hill. 'Tell me, Corydon,' Battus asks, 'is the old man still screwing that little girl he fancied, the black-eyed one?' 'As ever,' Corydon replies. 'Only yesterday I caught him on the job down by the cattleshed.' More than 2,000 years before the cowpokes of Brokeback Mountain discovered sex, Theocritus' hill folk are very hard at it. Here we have a goatherd and a shepherd bickering.

> *Lacon:* Remind me, when did I learn any useful lesson from you?
> *Comatas:* When I buggered you, I taught you to moan and groan like
>   a nanny bleating when the billy shoves it in.
> *Lacon*: May you be buried no deeper than you bugger, poor cripple![19]

In Idyll Seven, the narrator and two of his friends have been invited to a harvest festival and set off to walk from the main town on the island of Kos to the farm where it is to be celebrated. The *Idylls'* translator, the poet Robert Wells, tells us that the topography of the walk is accurate and the route can still be followed today. Wells says that the landscape is 'not so much described as simply there when we happen to look', and so is the soft place to flop down among the fragrant reeds and freshcut vineleaves for the first drink on arrival at Phrasidamus' farm. In the thickets, the cicadas are keeping up their rasping chatter, there are larks and linnets overhead and plum trees bending low with the weight of their fruit, and 'the seal broken from the wine jars was four years old'. I can think of no more luscious harvest home in all literature.

Hesiod and Theocritus and Cato were earthed as naturally as Cato's asparagus. Even Jefferies, flopping down under the brim of his Wiltshire earthwork two millennia later, seems to us part of the scene he was born in. For us, the process of re-earthing is a more difficult and tortuous one. It is as though we had to be reinserted into the landscape, to superimpose our bodies on a scene that is fading even as we look at it.

We are much more in the position, several centuries later, of the Roman poet Horace, the son of an auctioneer and tax collector, who worked in the city as some sort of civil sevant before being rewarded with a farm in the Sabine Hills by Maecenas, the great patron of the arts and key adviser to the Emperor Augustus. Horace retired to the farm in his early 30s, much as a City banker today might cash in his share options and retire to a Wiltshire rectory where he grows roses and collects fine wines. Horace's *Odes* and *Epistles* sing the praises of a modest country life, free of all ambition: 'My one dear Sabine farm is bliss enough.'

Yet Horace's villa and his financial independence come from money earned in the city, by his father and by Maecenas as well as by himself. And as time goes by, he comes to depend more and more on commissions from Rome to celebrate this or that imperial triumph. In the *Epistles*, he asks eagerly for the latest news from town to provide fresh material. As he rhapsodizes about his crop of acorns and his hopes for the new vintage, we cannot help feeling that he sounds like a transplanted city slicker, a homeworking downshifter who looks out of the window now and then while he is rebooting his computer. Unlike the earlier Greek and Roman poets, he is not fully dug in.

Like any modern Nimby, Horace has nothing but scorn for the restless greed of the tycoons and property developers, who, blind to their impending death, order more and more marble to build on to their villas and push out their properties from the beaches of Baiae into the sea. But Horace too is an incomer, whose rural bliss depends on an uninterrupted view. And he speaks in *Epistles* 10 and 14 of building a house in a pleasant spot that was formerly farmed by five families. He teases his steward for longing to get back to the city, the shows and the baths. Horace claims that he himself finds city life disagreeable and is always impatient to return to the country. Yet it is clear that he still has plenty of business to conduct in Rome and that he needs to show his face there to maintain his public standing and his private income.

Like Horace, we have to go through a few contortions if we are to fit into the landscape, even half-convincingly. Deakin started in advertising – as a copywriter in Colman Prentis Varley, later a creative director – and then became an antiques dealer, then made radio and TV programmes for the BBC before he swam his way back to Gaia. His was an invented rather than an inherited life. Must the path back to nature for a modern person always have this chosen, artificial character?

There is perhaps one man who showed that a natural life might grow out of a modern life. In fact, his was the most modern life imaginable, for it was he who invented the age we are still living in.

As Charles Darwin reached his 70s, he needed a secretary. His son Francis, whose medical career had fizzled out, came back home to help. In carrying out experiments on his father's behalf, Francis yearned for the modern equipment that T.H. Huxley and his pupils were using in the Science Schools at South Kensington. But Darwin would have none of the newfangled high-tech stuff. At Down House, he continued to make do with his old collection of improvised gadgets and measuring devices. His seven-foot wooden measure was calibrated by the village carpenter. He measured tiny objects with a piece of card marked up, wrongly, from an old book.

He used his battered old chemical balance from his Shrewsbury days. He did most of his work in his old greenhouse or out in the garden.[20]

More and more, as he entered his 70s, he enjoyed the company of worms, believing that their intelligence was underrated. He spent much of his time thinking about them and devising experiments to test their powers. He tracked their trails across the damp paths to see how far they had travelled, dug for their burrows and counted the leaves with which they had lined their tiny snugs. At night, he and Francis would keep watch on their movements under the lime trees in the moonlight or in the darker fir trees with the aid of a hurricane lamp. Francis and his mother were deputed to play the bassoon and the piano to them, to see if they were sensitive to sound. Those worms which Darwin kept in pots he fed with tiny paper triangles or diamonds to see how they learnt to pull leaves into their burrows. These experiments were not very fruitful. 'I am becoming more doubtful about the intelligence of worms,' he wrote to Galton. 'The worst job is that they will do their work in such a slovenly manner when kept in pots.' As the experiments went on, he seemed to be slowing to the pace of his subjects. Sometimes when he got his gardener Henry Lettington to turn over the compost for him and he saw the wormholes in the dark earth, he thought he was glimpsing his own grave. But his life among worms was never anything but harmonious. Those who came to visit him at Down House (he had refused to follow the village in adding an 'e') remarked on the serenity of his last years. And the worms had their moment in the limelight. Darwin's last work, published in 1881, less than a year before his death, was *The Formation of Vegetable Mould Through the Action of Worms*. 'The subject may appear an insignificant one,' he wrote in the preface, but worms embodied the primary creed of his scientific life: 'small agencies and their accumulated effects'. The book sold faster and better than anything else he had written.

Beyond the purely scientific interest of the work, there was about the book a current of sympathy and even respect for the worms which must have caught the public affection. As that craggy figure bent down to inspect their progress across his lawn, his bushy beard and eyebrows sweeping the dew off the grass, the culminating perspective of his life's work seemed to be the worm's-eye view. He had hoped and expected to join the worms permanently in Downe churchyard alongside his brother Erasmus, but Galton and the other scientists were insistent that he be buried in the nave of Westminster Abbey, to celebrate the cause of evolution. And so he was. The greatest Englishman of his day had the last state funeral since Sir Isaac Newton's that was granted to a commoner who was neither a politician nor a general. He was not allowed to be consumed by those Kentish worms with whom he had so happily spent his final years.

We have seen the lark's-eye view and the frog's-eye view, and the wolf's and the tree's. Now finally Darwin showed us the worm's-eye view, which for him was the best view of all. From what better viewpoint could we inspect at the same time our ultimate origin and our all too immediate destination? Theocritus and Virgil – and perhaps old Cato too – would have liked the idea, I think. For that is the end of the enormous circle we have described. We have come back to earth.

XII

SCIPIO'S DREAM

It is a touching sight – the greatest of all natural scientists down on all fours following the worms. But before we leave him, it is irresistible to ask a little more about Charles Darwin himself. What made him the man he was? His sweetness, his modesty, his forgivingness, his consideration for others make him unique among Great Men. Most of them are monsters of selfishness. But Darwin really was the epitome of a Victorian Christian gentleman. And he never showed himself more so than in the way he behaved after he had abandoned belief in the Christian religion. He strove continually, both in his writings and in his public and private life, to give as little offence as possible to those who still believed, especially his wife Emma and other members of his family. He continued to subscribe to the village church at Downe. Nobody could have been less like the anti-God-botherers of his day or of ours. T.H. Huxley, 'Darwin's Bulldog', was never happier than when sinking his teeth into a fatuous bishop. Darwin himself was not like that at all. He fully understood the moral beauty of the religion he had been born into, even if he could no longer accept its scientific accuracy.

It would have seemed to him wrong, even wicked, to throw away the advances that Christianity had brought, merely because it could now be seen that the explanation the Bible gave of the origins and development of the universe did not correspond to the scientific evidence. The virtues that Christianity had invented and broadcast to the world – humility, modesty, repentance, sexual continence and fidelity – were an inalienable part of him. He would have regarded those virtues, I think, as *discoveries* to be valued no less than the discovery that the earth went round the sun. Seen in the light of Christianity, the upstanding virtues of classical times – courage, fortitude, pride, generosity – seemed inadequate and incomplete. Above all, the Christian sense of *createdness*, of our place in nature, stayed with him all his life, even if he himself taught us a new account of exactly how we came to be created.

It would be futile today to yearn for the return of an age of unquestioning faith. In any case, that is not what we want. Many, perhaps most, of us would shudder at the thought. Regimes based on such faiths have proved just as cruel in our times as in the Middle Ages; the Taliban and the ayatollahs can match the blackest deeds of the Inquisition. Yet we cannot pretend that the great one-God religions never existed, nor can we deny that they have permanently altered our moral horizons and our sense of who we are.

Can we, should we, hope to live like Charles Darwin, 'as if' Christianity were true in every sense except the scientific? To him this came naturally. For us, a century and more later, the suggestion is more troubling. We have taught ourselves to prize intellectual honesty above all things. The most important thing in life is to be authentic. How can it be right to live according to the commands of a fading myth that features a description of our creation which we know to be false? The whiskered sages of the late nineteenth and early twentieth centuries – Marx, Darwin, Nietzsche, Freud – taught us to *see through* those old fairy tales to the economic and social and psychological motives that lay behind them. Why, at this late stage, should we make any sort of effort to revive them?

There was another heavily whiskered philosopher of that era, much less famous but in his way just as interesting. Hans Vaihinger, who lived from 1852 to the year Hitler came to power, 1933, lived all his life in the leading French and German universities – Tübingen, Strasbourg, Halle – and devoted most of his career to untangling the philosophy of his immortal predecessor, Immanuel Kant of Königsberg (1724–1804). Vaihinger himself is remembered for a single book – *Die Philosophie des Als Ob, The Philosophy of 'As If'* – and even that book is in large part a clearer explanation of what Kant had said much more obscurely.

Vaihinger shows that what Kant is saying can be boiled down to something quite simple: 'All the nobler aspects of our life are based upon fictions.'[1] By 'fictions', Vaihinger and Kant mean ideas and entities which are not to be found anywhere in nature but which we ourselves have invented to help us along. We have to do this, because 'It is an error to suppose that an absolute truth, an absolute criterion of knowledge and behaviour can be discovered.' Because we cannot get at absolute truth, everything worth knowing, every moral and scientific rule is based, somehow and somewhere, upon an invented idea that we have dreamed up for ourselves, upon a fiction that we choose to take as true, upon an 'as if'.

This may be a simple idea, but at first sight it also seems a perverse, even wacky claim to make. Truth based upon fiction? This looks like one more instance of the propensity of philosophers to abandon common sense at the first opportunity. Surely reliable knowledge is based upon a quite different action programme, upon the principle of *verification*. We prove claims about the world to be true or untrue by testing them against the evidence. We construct hypotheses, and then we subject them to the most gruelling tests we can devise. As soon as we find one instance where the hypothesis turns out to be false, we toss that hypothesis in the bin, and try another one. That is how science works. No question of fiction at any stage. True or false – that's the only question, and verification is the only method.

But Vaihinger (following Kant) tells us that this is not how intellectual enquiry begins, or how it makes progress. Even the hardest sciences, such as mathematics, rely on fictional assumptions and abstractions which are not to be found in nature, such as 'infinity' or 'irrational numbers'. Geometry drains the physical world of substance and colour to fashion an abstract universe of points and lines and angles.

The fictions that we have come to rely on in daily life are too numerous to mention. By now, we take some of them so much for granted that we have ceased to be aware that they are fictions at all. The movies, for example. We do not nowadays think of film as a fictional convention. It is so much part of our life. Yet it demands quite a stretch of the imagination to accept that these flickering shadows cast on a flat surface can adequately represent reality, for many people today as potent a reality as the physical world. When the movies started at the end of the nineteenth century, they were greeted by a huge variety of reactions: delight, awe, suspicion, even terror in the case of the oncoming train in the early short film by the Lumière brothers, which allegedly caused the audience to scream, although the story is contested. The new medium was welcomed by some highbrows (Henry James loved going to the movies with his nieces) and dismissed by others as childish, suitable only for simple folk, to amuse them in penny arcades or as a new way of advertising goods; for the sceptics, its relationship to reality appeared about as distant as that of those shadows which the fire cast on the wall of Plato's cave. Indeed, Maxim Gorky in a famous article of 1896 described film as the Kingdom of Shadows. 'This is not life but the shadow of life,' he asserted:

> If you only knew how strange it felt. There were no sounds and no colours. Everything – earth, trees, people, water, air – was portrayed in a grey monotone: in a grey sky there were grey rays of sunlight; in grey faces, grey eyes, and the leaves of the trees were grey like ashes . . . Silently the ash-grey foliage of the trees swayed in the wind and the grey silhouettes of the people glided silently along the grey ground, as if condemned to eternal silence and cruelly punished by being deprived of all life's colours.

The young Fyodor Otsep, later to be a highly esteemed film director on both sides of the Atlantic, declared that 'we are dealing with a manifestation of delusion, a kind of hallucination'. It took time and technical development for people to 'get their eye in' and look at these moving pictures as if they were a perfectly normal way of perceiving reality, and to accept their conventions – the close-up, the jump cut, the loud swirling music – without a second thought. Sometimes in the cinema, I feel myself to be a throwback to those early days and find the images on the screen unbearably crude and unconvincing and I take refuge in looking around at the figures of the other people in the audience who seem infinitely more solid and interesting. I recollect with particular fondness from my childhood the Gaumont cinema in Salisbury which was decorated as a medieval jousting hall, so that when the film ceased to carry conviction, one could look at the 'real' decor of the movie-house instead. It is noticeable that when a scene in a film shows an audience watching a film, the secondary film seems pitifully unreal. In such a situation, we suddenly are made aware of the as-ifness of cinema.

In the social sciences, the need for usable fictions, is, if anything, even more inescapable. Take the dismal science of economics, and its most famous text, Adam Smith's *Wealth of Nations* (1776). This wonderful book assumes that all human actions are dictated by egoism. Men's motives and actions are described as if they are bargaining in a market, the sellers determined to obtain the best price, the buyers looking for the cheapest goods, all equally blind to anything except their own self-interest. Now Smith does not believe for a minute that human beings are really like that. In fact, he wrote another book, *The Theory of Moral Sentiments* (1759), which assumes precisely the opposite, that we are all drawn together by a shared sympathy which generates our acts of altruism and our habits of association. Neither 'the market' nor 'the sympathetic principle' is a full and accurate description of the world. In both cases, Adam Smith 'deliberately substitutes a fraction of reality for the complete range of causes and facts'.[2] He abstracts the elements that interest him and makes a model out of them.

At least there is such a thing as a market in the real world. When we say the word, we can think of a covered or open complex of booths or stalls with stallholders shouting their wares or chalking their prices on slates. Smith's fiction consists in pretending that all human society is a market and nothing but a market. But with some other mental fictions there is nothing in the real world that corresponds to the image we have cooked up. Take the idea of the 'social contract'. We are to imagine that thousands, perhaps hundreds of thousands of years ago, our ancestors clambered out of the primeval swamp where they had been living their solitary, nasty, brutish and short lives and came together to draw up a contract for their mutual protection and prospering. An absurdly improbable fiction for which there is not the slightest evidence. How could there be? How could these poor brutes communicate with one another? How could they have the faintest idea of what a contract was? Yet the Social Contract, dignified now with capital letters, forms the basis of the state in the theories of some of the greatest political philosophers in the Western tradition: Hobbes, Locke, Rousseau.

And it isn't dead yet. Perhaps the most influential political philosopher of the past forty years, John Rawls of Harvard (1921–2002),
constructed a new version, in which the old one is clearly recognizable. Rawls proposed that we conduct a 'thought experiment'. He
invited us to go back to what he called 'the Original Position'. Once
again our ancestors climb out of the primeval swamp to draw up a
contract for a civil society, but in Rawls's version they would be
negotiating behind 'a Veil of Ignorance' about the place that each
one of them would occupy in this new society. This, he said, would
lead them to construct a system which they would all be happy
with, even those who found themselves at the bottom of the heap. In
all likelihood, therefore, this new Social Contract would organize a
much more equal type of society. Now of course no such Veil of
Ignorance exists in the real world. We are well aware of our place in
the existing pecking order. And our ancestors would presumably
have been well aware of theirs. What Rawls has invented is a fruitful fantasy about the sort of society we would like to live in if we
were starting from scratch. The point of the fantasy is to teach us to
live (and to organize our political arrangements) *as if* we did live in
such a society where we were blind to our own interests.

What does Rawls's fiction remind us of? Surely it is the passage in
St Matthew's Gospel (chapter 25) when Jesus tells his disciples that
the Lord will curse and condemn to eternal fire those people who
gave him no meat when he was hungry and refused to clothe him
when he was naked or failed to visit him when he was sick or in
prison. When those people plaintively ask, 'Lord, when saw we
Thee hungry or thirsty or a stranger or sick or in prison and did not
minister unto Thee?' the Lord will reply, 'Inasmuch as ye did it not
to one of the least of these my brethren, ye did it not to me.' To help
or not to help any down-and-out person is to act *as if* we were
doing the same to the Lord himself. Kant employs a rather similar
fiction in his *Critique of Practical Reason* (1788): we ought always to act
as if the reasons for our actions were to be a universal law of nature.

All these fictions depend in turn on a greater fiction: the fiction that man is free. Scientifically speaking, we are not free at all: our actions are the outcomes of our genes, our upbringing, our previous fortunes and misfortunes, and of the precise circumstances and contexts in which we are acting. Yet Vaihinger (following Kant) says: 'Man must act, and his acts must be judged, *as if* he were free.'[3] And those, of course, are the presumptions upon we do in practice behave every day. As J.L. Austin, the great philosopher of ordinary language, once remarked to Isaiah Berlin, 'They all *talk* about determinism and *say* they believe in it, but I have never met a determinist in my life, I mean a man who really did believe in it as you and I believe that men are mortal. Have you?'[4]

Which leads us to our most ambitious invention yet, the invention of God. Kant argued that we had to invent God 'as the supreme head in a moral kingdom of purposes'. We needed a judge to whom we were accountable.[5] 'I believe in God' meant simply 'I act as if a God really existed'. It was not the theoretical belief that the Kingdom of God was coming which constituted religion; it was the endeavour to make it come. Religion was a practical undertaking. Kant came to regard the existence of God, in the ordinary sense of existence, as extremely improbable, if not impossible. Certainly he thought that the supposed 'proofs' of God's existence were worthless. It was difficult to see how there could be any such reliable proof that He existed (or did not exist).

But this did not make Kant think that religious belief ought therefore to be watered down into some misty pantheism, deprived of any superstitious decoration. On the contrary, he championed all those fantastical doctrines which so horrified the tidy Enlightenment mind: the Virgin Birth, the Atonement, the Last Judgment. For him, these passionate allegories provided the 'aesthetic machinery' to stir our moral impulses.[6] By acting as if these amazing things were true, we would live better, holier, more fulfilling lives.

And all sorts of people, both the extremely devout and the borderline agnostics, have found this 'as if' indispensable. That ironic old eighteenth-century sceptic, Denis Diderot, said (you can imagine his

weary sigh as he said it): 'After all, the shortest way home is to
behave as if the Old Man existed.' St Teresa of Avila, as you might
expect, went a lot further: her goal in life was to live 'as if nobody
existed except God and herself'.

Hans Vaihinger claims that 'many a statement made by the
founder of a religion was originally meant by him merely as a conscious fiction'[7] – but was then converted into a hard dogma by his
fanatical and literal-minded followers. He offers as an example the
famous dispute at Marburg in 1529 between the two Protestant
reformers, the German Martin Luther and the Swiss Ulrich Zwingli.
When Jesus said 'This is my body' and 'This is my blood', what did
the 'is' mean? Zwingli argued that Jesus was speaking in allegory:
'This bread is to be regarded *as if* it were my body; this wine is to be
regarded *as if* it were my blood'.[8] Luther, with his down-to-earth,
popular turn of mind, was extremely uneasy while Zwingli was talking. He tapped under the table impatiently with his finger, repeating
half-audibly, 'Is, is.' For Luther, Jesus's words were to be taken quite
literally, and anyone who disputed them deserved to be thumped.

Other philosophers before and after Kant had understood the
huge place that our inventions have played in our thoughts and in
such progress as we have made: in the eighteenth century, the French
psychologist the Abbé de Condillac; in the nineteenth, the English
utilitarian Jeremy Bentham and the visionary German Friedrich
Nietzsche and, above all, Arthur Schopenhauer, who regarded himself as Kant's only worthy successor. In his final chapter, Vaihinger
returns to Nietzsche. How well that tortured, brilliant soul understood that our illusions are vital to us, that we cannot live without the
'noble lie'. If only Nietzsche's career had not been cut short by
syphilis and insanity, he might have come round to the idea that God
is really still alive, after all. 'He would have justified the utility and the
necessity of religious fictions'.[9] For, in Nietzsche's own words, 'Our
greatness lies in the supreme illusion.'[10] It is a piquant fancy: the old
firebrand reconciled with the weakling Jesus whom he had so
despised, perhaps following his father and finding a late vocation as

Pastor Friedrich in some upland parish, staring at the mountains and glaring at his flock, in the last resort unable to get away from God.

The recognition that some of our illusions may be indispensable goes back to the early Christian Fathers and to Plato. And beyond Plato, back on the crags of Ionia, we find Xenophanes pointing out that we invent our gods to suit our own self-images. But Kant may be the first thinker to argue so thoroughly that we have to live and think by making things up, that fictions are our lifeblood and our most fruitful inheritance. We must get away from the assumption that fiction is invariably bad. For it is simply our way of describing the play of our minds. The word 'illusion', after all, comes from *illudo*, I play with something to amuse myself. Unfortunately, Kant did not express himself clearly enough to avoid being hopelessly misunderstood and as a result was claimed as a kindred spirit both by the atheists and by the orthodox religious. He had to wait a century for Hans Vaihinger to uncover what he really was on about and to explain that it is our fictions which tell us what we must do in the world. Contrary to the usual common-sense view of things, *invention is the mother of necessity.*

What would Immanuel Kant think of our present predicament if he were brought back to life and reinstalled as a professor at his old university of Königsberg? Well, in the first place, he would scarcely recognize the city, since it was flattened in the Second World War, then occupied by the Red Army and largely Russified under the new name of Kaliningrad. Today there is scarcely a German voice to be heard in what was once the Oxford of East Prussia.

As in the rest of the former Soviet Union, the city has seen atheism imposed by the state, then allowed to wither, to be followed by a revival of the old churches. Yet Kant might note, rather wearily, that after all these terrible upheavals and brutal chastenings, the old war of misunderstanding was still raging between the dogmatists and the atheists, each side as literal-minded as the other, neither able to understand God as a creation of the moral imagination, each insisting that its own views are unassailably true and that its opponents' are demonstrably false.

Kant might be more encouraged to see that the actual *practice* of religion corresponded more to his own view: that the point is to teach us to live and act *as if* God existed. He would find worshippers in the great religions still following the lines set out, for example, in the Anglican prayer of General Thanksgiving composed by Bishop Reynolds of Norwich in the seventeenth century: 'And we beseech thee, give us that due sense of all thy mercies, that our hearts may be unfeignedly thankful, and that we shew forth thy praise, not only with our lips, but in our lives; by giving up ourselves to the service, and by walking before thee in holiness and righteousness all our days.' The prime purpose of religion is not to offer a superior scientific account of the origins of the universe but to heighten our awareness of the divine, so that our actions are infused by a higher moral purpose.

But turning to the intellectual debates of our day, Kant would surely be puzzled by one thing which I have already touched on briefly. The dominant orthodoxy of our times is the theory of evolution, and Charles Darwin is its prophet. In 2009, the bicentenary year of his birth, that craggy bearded profile was to be seen everywhere, on banknotes and postage stamps, on bookstalls and TV programmes. Yet scarcely ever do we see that theory of evolution applied to religion itself. We have seen that Darwin himself had a few suggestions to offer, about how group religious loyalty might assist a tribe to survive better. But the leading evolutionists of our day appear to be so hostile to religion that they cannot bear to contemplate the possibility that God might ever have had His uses.

Yet all the monotheistic faiths are familiar with the idea of a religious tradition which develops over time and which needs to be reinterpreted to meet fresh circumstances and challenges. It stands to reason, literally, that we need to study the evolution of religion as we would study any other human practice if we want to gain a better understanding of man's search for the divine. Believers and unbelievers alike seem curiously reluctant to get down to the task, which is why Robert Wright's new book *The Evolution of God* made such a stir when it came out in 2008. Kant would undoubtedly have applauded this enterprise. He would have seen the evolutionary approach as the best possible way of showing the different ways in which men and women have chosen to live *as if* God existed.

I have said that living 'as if' does not come so naturally to us as it did to Darwin. But come to us it still does. Millions today still hold on to the old fictions, while being at least half-conscious that fictions is what they are. In fact, this is what so annoys the anti-God-botherers. Themselves glued to scientific dogmatism, they cannot tolerate the people who still prefer, almost instinctively, to live 'as if'.

In particular, 'as if' is very often the way parents want their children to be educated, for reasons they may not always analyse. It is remarkable, for example, that in the 1944 Education Act, which still dictates the basis of state schooling in Britain, the only subject prescribed as compulsory is 'religious education'. This clause was partly extracted by the Churches as a quid pro quo for bringing their schools into the state system. But it also reflected the wishes of MPs and their constituents. This did not mean that schools were to be judged by how many of their pupils were turned out as practising Christians (whereas schools *would* be judged by how successfully they taught their pupils to read and write). What it meant was that society agreed that education without some kind of religious understanding was a poor and shrivelled substitute for the real thing. Parents still wanted their children to be educated 'as if' there existed a universal, divinely ordained moral order.

Time has moved on, and one cannot honestly pretend that compulsory RE has done much to slow the fall in congregations and the decay of faith. So by every reasonable expectation, church schools should now be fading from the scene, or at least watering down the religious content in their curriculum, until it was as minuscule as the active ingredient in a homeopathic potion.

Nothing could be further from the truth. Existing church schools are proud of their religious commitment and have long waiting lists. Under the new name of 'faith schools', they are flourishing alongside so-called 'academies' which are being founded with the active encouragement of a New Labour government, most of whose members are not exactly noted for their religious zeal. Indeed, Tony Blair's personal religious enthusiasm was one of the things that made him unpopular within his own party. When Alastair Campbell, his Machiavellian director of communications, said, 'We don't do God,' he was rebuking his boss on behalf of the Party.

How then does it come about that, all of a sudden, even the secular educational world appears to be ready to 'do God' again?

First, we need to understand that the new religious schools really ought not to be described as 'faith schools'. Their purpose is not directly to inculcate the Christian faith, although their sponsors would obviously be delighted if that happened. The purpose is to educate their pupils in 'a Christian ethos'. Church of England state schools now commonly include 'an ethos statement' in their prospectus. For example, the primary school of St John's, Buckhurst Hill, Essex, tells prospective parents: 'Although we teach the six main world religions, we celebrate Christianity on a daily basis. Our assemblies reflect our rich and varied Christian heritage while drawing upon the beliefs and festivals of other cultures.'

'Ethos' is an interesting word to use in this connection. It is a relatively recent borrowing direct from ancient Greek (the first use of the word that the *OED Supplement* can find is in 1851). It comes from the same root as the much older word 'ethics' (first found in English at the end of the Middle Ages), only with a long 'e' in Greek as in English. For the Greeks, '*ethos*' meant as it does for us 'the moral spirit and atmosphere of a people or community', as opposed to the sterner demands of 'ethics', which we use to denote 'moral rules and principles'. I don't think it's a coincidence that it was the Victorians who felt the need for a looser word to describe moral atmosphere, for 'ethos' appears just at the moment when religious faith was beginning to wane and loosen.

In fact, if you want to know what a Christian ethos looks like, I can offer no better source than that classic mid-Victorian yarn, *Tom Brown's Schooldays*. The night before he sends his son Tom off to Rugby School, Squire Brown muses on what parting advice he should give his son: 'What is he sent to school for? Well, partly because he wanted so to go. If he'll only turn out a brave, helpful, truth-telling Englishman, and a gentleman, and a Christian, that's all I want.' What the Squire wants is for Tom to be brought up *as if* the Christian religion were true, and to act steadfastly on that assumption for the rest of his life. Which is pretty much why so many modern parents who are not themselves regular churchgoers try everything they know to get their children into a good church school.

They are fiercely denounced by the anti-God-botherers for their pains. Fiona Millar, Alastair Campbell's partner, managed to reduce one mother to tears in the television programme she made on the subject. What humbug, what deceit for parents to pretend a faith they do not genuinely believe in! How wicked to have their children brainwashed into accepting fairy tales! As we have seen, Richard Dawkins believes that sexual abuse by priests does less damage than 'the long-term psychological damage inflicted by bringing a child up Catholic in the first place'. Parents should no more be allowed to teach their children to believe in the literal truth of the Bible than to knock their teeth in or lock them up in a dungeon. When these ghastly parents claim to be 'only doing their best for their children', they are in reality trying to secure social advantages in life for them, by easing their way to better exam marks, posher friends and, in due course, better jobs.

Some kindlier atheists, such as Andrew Motion, the former Poet Laureate, do defend religious education on the grounds that without some grounding in our ancestral myths children will never be able to understand the great art and literature which are at the heart of our culture. That is true enough, but it is only a part of the underlying reason why parents go for church schools and not, I think, the most important part.

Though they would be embarrassed to put it in Squire Brown's hearty Victorian terms, they want their children to be educated in a Christian ethos, to be brought up in the belief that there is a moral and spiritual purpose to life, and that it is their duty to assist in that purpose. They want their children to be educated 'as if'.

Nor is this aspiration limited to parents who have enjoyed that sort of education themselves. Private education is one of the most widely shared aspirations amongst the less well off, and one of the first things they would spend their Lottery winnings on (of course another, and better solution, would be to make the same type and quality of education available within the state system). As she was dying, Jade Goody said, 'I know I'm ignorant but I'm going to make sure that my boys get the best education. I'm going to pay for their education for the rest of their lives because that'll give them the best chance in life.' By 'chance in life', she did not simply mean 'chance to make a lot of money'. After all, she herself managed to do that, despite suffering the worst start in life you can imagine. What she meant was something larger, such as a vision of the right way to lead one's life. A fortnight before she died, she had herself and her two sons baptized in the chapel of the Royal Marsden Hospital where she was being treated for cancer. At her funeral, thousands lined the route from Bermondsey, where she grew up, to the Anglican Church of St John, Buckhurst Hill, where she lived. The funeral service included a tribute from her former deputy headmaster. No one could have more clearly signalled than Jade Goody her determination to have her children brought up in the Christian tradition in the way advertised at her local C of E primary school. Though they might have expressed their aspirations for their children differently, Squire Brown and Jade Goody were siblings under the skin.

Why do so many people still feel this need? How is it that they can still subject their children, or themselves to this rigmarole? The anti-God-botherers would say, with something close to a sneer, that this is because they are looking for a source of solace and comfort, because they cannot face reality. On the contrary, they are making life tougher for themselves. They are placing demands on themselves and their children to live their lives according to a more demanding code, accepting (in theory anyway) the superiority of Christian virtues such as thrift, chastity, humility and self-denial. Doesn't sound like the easy option.

Let us look it at it from another angle. We have been arguing in this chapter that over the past century we have come back to earth with a bump. We have had the breath knocked out of us. And we have learnt instead to live something rather like the classical life. We take our pleasures easily, just as the Greeks and the Romans did. We keep our bodies in trim, washed and massaged and honed. We are twenty-four-hour gourmets, as discriminating and inventive in sex as in food and drink. We chatter and twitter and invent celebrities and cults for ourselves and shred them when we have had our fill of them. We are attracted by the idea of commitment, to people or to causes, but soon find that commitment conflicts with the demands of style, to stay loose, stay cool.

But there is something lacking. This isn't really the classical life, because it doesn't possess the underlying moral grandeur of life in Greek and Roman cities. By that I mean the patriotic seriousness that was part of being a citizen, the quality that came to be called *romanitas*, 'Roman-ness'. Ours is classical-lite, the sensuous, this-worldly way of living without the gravitas that underpinned it. And without that underpinning, there is something a little flat about it all. Even the stress which we sometimes complain about is scarcely heroic. And our moral challenges rather tend to lack grandeur. What could be more dispiriting than to be told that we still may not succeed in saving the planet, even if we do sort our garbage into the right bags or reuse our bathwater? And so some of us cannot help looking back enviously to the centuries when the poorest life trailed clouds of glory, and the smallest moment in our lives was a matter of eternal life or death.

What exactly was this *romanitas*? W.H. Auden became interested by the idea when he first came across it in a highly influential book of the war years, *Christianity and Classical Culture* by Charles Norris Cochrane, published in 1940 at a time when people wanted to know what it was that we were fighting for. It was in Cyril Connolly's *Horizon,* which itself set out to define our mission, that Auden reprinted just after the war an essay where he defined *romanitas*: 'The fundamental presupposition of *romanitas*, secular or sacred, is that virtue is prior to liberty, i.e., what matters most is that people should think and act rightly; of course it is preferable that they should do so consciously of their own free will, but if they cannot or will not, they must be made to, the majority by the spiritual pressure of education and tradition, the minority by physical coercion, for liberty to act wrongly is not liberty but licence.'[11] The opposite point of view, which Auden attributed, though not exclusively, to America and Americans (he was writing about Henry James), was that liberty came first. Freedom of choice was the basic human prerequisite without which virtue and vice were meaningless ideas. Choosing virtue was of course preferable, but even choosing vice was preferable to having virtue chosen for one.

Auden claimed that America had consciously rejected *romanitas,* while Europeans were still trying to preserve it. Sixty years later, though, *romanitas* looks to be in better shape in America than in Europe, certainly than in Britain. For the United States has kept her sense of patriotic mission, even if Americans differ fiercely about what that mission is.

The prime demand of *romanitas* was to perform your duties to Rome. The most conspicuous duty was, as it had been in most cities of ancient Greece, to do compulsory military service, often for a considerable period of your life. The citizen's first duty was to defend the city. We often forget how many great men of Athens and Rome fought in epic battles. Aeschylus took part in the Battle of Marathon, Sophocles held a command under Pericles in the expedition which suppressed the revolt of Samos, Socrates gained a reputation for bravery in the three battles he fought in, Horace joined Brutus's army and fought at the Battle of Philippi, Cicero fought in several campaigns (as we have seen, without securing the triumph he angled for). By contrast, in modern history the only period where military experience was widely shared by civilians was in the two world wars – these days an almost faded memory.

But *romanitas* included much more than answering the bugle call. The citizen's duties to the state covered every public and professional activity and aspect of life, demanding honesty, self-discipline, diligence, charity and fellowship at all times. Over the two centuries covering the lives of Cato and Cicero, and for many centuries after that, Romans were obsessed with preserving the moral qualities which they thought were responsible for their city's greatness and with beating back the encroaches of luxury, sensuality and greed (usually attributed to subversive foreign influences). The word '*romanitas*' is found solely in late Latin, suggesting that the Romans coined the word only when they felt that the quality was endangered by their own decadence. *Romanitas* did not come naturally. Cicero believed that it had to be constructed, and then conserved and reconstructed, not least against the threats posed by power maniacs like Julius Caesar and greedy plutocrats like Crassus.

Cicero has had a poor press from recent posterity. He is sometimes written off as an unscrupulous orator who merely recycled other people's ideas. But that is partly the point. He deliberately commended those rules of conduct and attitudes to life which had been forged out of experience and had stood the test of time. Nor did he believe that right conduct was simply a matter of following a set of instructions, a kind of beefed-up Highway Code. On the contrary, he believed that *romanitas* was effective only if it arose out of a moral vision of the universe.

Right at the end of what we assume was his masterwork, *On the Republic* (much of it is lost), we find a most extraordinary piece of visionary writing: 'Scipio's Dream'. It's a kind of moral science fiction. The famous general Scipio Africanus appears in a dream to his adoptive grandson, also called Scipio, and tells him that he too will have a glorious future and can earn immortality if he fulfils his duty to God and above all to Rome. Suddenly Scipio junior finds himself spinning through space with his grandfather, looking down on the city of Carthage which his grandfather tells him he is destined to destroy. The earth appears small and insignificant compared to the much larger stars they are whirling past. Scipio senior tells his grandson to stop gazing back at this piffling planet and instead turn his gaze to the heavens and listen to the sweet music of the spheres. He should forget about becoming famous, for his fame would be buried with him. Only if he treads the path of virtue and honour in life is his soul assured of immortality and a swift flight to its eternal home somewhere on the Milky Way. By contrast, those who have surrendered to lust and greed in life will be kept in a miserable state, hovering close to the earth and tossed about in torment for ages.

Cicero's extraordinary vision of immortality was hugely popular throughout the Middle Ages, more popular sometimes than the Church's version. Raphael painted Scipio's dream. Chaucer retells the whole story in his long poem 'The Parliament of Fowls' and refers to the space flight of the Scipios again in his own dream sequence, 'The House of Fame'. Mozart, at the age of 16, wrote a one-act opera, focusing on the interplanetary travel of the Scipios. Yet it remains the most amazing thing to find it at the end of a sober political treatise. Rather as if Karl Marx had finished off *Das Kapital* with a visionary poem by Alfred, Lord Tennyson.

Why does Cicero do this? Because he believes that moral codes and commands can carry conviction only if they derive from a universal moral order. At the end of all the sober examination of political arrangements and codes of moral conduct, we need to use our imaginations, to think outside ourselves, to invent a vision of what we might be, to weave our own destiny into the harmony of the spheres. For this supposedly prosy and derivative political operator was just as convinced as the author of the Book of Proverbs that 'without a vision the people perish'.[12] The Romans, Cicero believed, could live a life worth living only by living it as if there was a God who watched over them and judged their actions. *Romanitas* was not simply a recipe for hanging onto great-power status. It was a vision of life, not an idle fantasy but a compelling dream.

These days we catch that visionary gleam only now and then, and not for long: in Martin Luther King's speech when we see Mandela walking free. These are not simply high moments of life, they are glimpses of lost horizons. We have adopted some high principles from Athens and Rome: tolerance, and civility and equality and democracy. And we have picked up some agreeable habits. But we seem to have mislaid Scipio's dream. And the search parties are still out there looking for it.

EPILOGUE

LIDDINGTON CLUMP

I park the car on the verge of the B4192 with the white vans swooshing past over the Downs to Hungerford. The flint-strewn, muddy track leads straight up the hill to a clump of beech trees on the skyline. At the top I stop to catch my breath and look back down at the M4 coming round the brow and snaking past into the misty plain. The wind is fierce up here and blows the green beech leaves silvery. Just in front of the clump there is a Second World War block-house, ruined and covered with graffiti. That seems to be the only building for miles in any direction until you come to the beginning of Swindon's pale sprawl. Strangely, up here in this desolate spot, we are still within the town's boundaries. At 909 feet, this is the highest point in the borough, for all I know the highest point in any bor-ough in southern England. So this is a return to Swindon, though it doesn't feel like one.

The permissive path turns right off the Ridgeway towards the edge of the escarpment. And there before me is the outer ring of the great earthworks. Inside, the ditch is 20 feet deep, deeper perhaps in places, with nettles and cow parsley at the bottom and the odd windbitten hawthorn. On the sides of the chalky ramparts there are buttercups and daisies and patches of blowy white campion and a little blue flower which I don't recognize. The grass is wet, but the sun has come out and I fling myself down on the slope in homage to Richard Jefferies and see how right he was about the angle of the dyke nicely pillowing one's head and I listen to the lark singing overhead and look up squint-ing into the sun to see how he keeps station in the wind, as though the most important thing in life was not to be budged from that particu-lar patch of sky. And it is inexplicably satisfying to be lolling more or less where Jefferies used to loll more than a century ago. I too am in Gaia's arms. It feels almost like keeping an appointment.

There is a monument to Jefferies at the next hill fort along the ridge, Barbury Castle. It is a plain sarsen stone just below the big car park at Ridgeway Farm, where there are hundreds of punters enjoy-ing the fresh air. But it is here at lonely Liddington where there isn't anybody about that the gangling moony youth liked best to flop down and stare at the 40 miles of view. I remember he also said something about the way larks descend to earth in two stages, how they plummet 50 feet or so, then suddenly put out their wings to brake their fall and fly horizontally for a few yards, then land safely on the grass. I would like to see this for myself, but the lark above me stays where he is and keeps on singing.

Readers love Jefferies for his beautiful descriptions and explanations of how birds operate, why they fly in this formation or that or
no formation at all, nest in one place rather than another, roost here
rather than there. But there is nothing slushy about his attitudes to
nature, nothing in the least bit anthropomorphic. On the contrary,
he reminds us in *The Story of My Heart* (1883), perhaps his best-loved
book, that 'there is nothing human in the whole round of nature. All
nature, all the universe that we can see, is absolutely indifferent to us,
and except to us human life is of no more value than grass.'[1] This
Wiltshire farmer's son, almost entirely self-taught, despises the 'fatuous belief' in a Creator who interferes in human life. 'All things
happen by chance. I cease, therefore, to look for the traces of deity
in life, because no such traces exist.' Instead, he concludes that 'there
is an existence, a something higher than soul – higher, better and
more perfect than deity. Earnestly I pray to find this something
better than a god.'[2]

The odd thing is that, thinking the way he does and reared in the
age of Darwin as he was, he remains so hostile to Darwinism:
'Nothing is evolved, no evolution takes place, there is no record of
such an event.' It is not that he is unaware of Darwinian theory or of
what was then its weak point, the lack of corroborating evidence. He
just thinks it's all rubbish. 'The belief that the human mind was
evolved, in the process of unnumbered years, from a fragment of pal-
pitating slime through a thousand gradations, is a modern
superstition, and proceeds upon assumption alone.'[3]

So Jefferies worships neither God nor Charles Darwin, and he
loathes most of the Christian injunctions. He scorns chastity and self-
denial as 'pure folly'. Asceticism, he claims, 'has not improved the
form, or the physical well-being or the heart of any human being'.
What he believed in was the exact opposite: 'Give me life strong and
full as the brimming ocean.'[4] 'I believe, with all my heart, in the
blood and the flesh, and believe that it should be increased and made
more beautiful by every means. I believe . . . it to be a sacred duty,
incumbent upon every one, man and woman, to add to and

encourage their physical life, by exercise and in every manner'.[5] So for those who have no Downs to stride across, it's compulsory PE. He prays in particular for his own body: 'Let me be physically perfect, in shape, vigour and movement.'[6] All this springs from his love of the classical world which he had discovered entirely for himself. He fancies himself the heir of the ancient Greeks and Romans who possessed that true and natural appreciation of human beauty which we had lost.

Alas, 'nature has not given me a great frame'. However hard he rows or swims, however many tree trunks he splits with his beloved axe, his body does not respond and he puts on no muscle. Like other worshippers of physical health, like Nietzsche, like Lawrence, Jefferies was never destined to enjoy it himself. From an early age, his natural frailty was worsened by constant bouts of illness. In his 30s, married with two children to support on a hack's income, he developed an agonizing anal fistula which turned out to be tubercular. By the time he came to write *The Story of My Heart*, he was already ravaged by consumption and forced to decamp to the more bracing air of Worthing, where he died less than four years later, not yet 40.

Nevertheless, enfeebled though he was, it was in this period that he fully developed his sensuous pantheism. He claimed it had always been with him: 'I was not more than eighteen when an inner and esoteric meaning began to come to me from all the visible universe, and indefinable aspirations filled me. I found them in the grass fields, under the trees, on the hilltops, at sunrise, and in the night.'[7]

In the distance, just beyond the M4, I can see the shimmer of Coate Water where Jefferies sailed and swam as a boy and where he sets his children's stories about Bevis, that ingenious nature-loving lad whose exploits, in my experience, delighted schoolmasters more than schoolboys. In the Bevis books, Coate Water is an unspoilt Eden, referred to as 'the lake' or 'the mere', as if King Arthur might be rowed across it at any moment.

But what Coate Water was, and is in fact, is a municipal reservoir. It was constructed a few years before Jefferies's birth, in order to supply water to the nearby canal and the growing population of Swindon. The suburbs have now invaded the little hamlet of Coate, and Coate farmhouse where Jefferies was born shrinks beside the dual carriageway leading to the motorway. Even in his lifetime, the hum of urban life was never far away, the railway within earshot, and the main road too, and the townspeople coming out to stroll around the reservoir.

There was always in truth something a bit selective, even contrived about Jefferies's seductive vision. But then just like any other religion, pantheism needs to be capable of rising beyond the facts. Those hill forts where he sprawled so many delicious hours away were not romantic dreams but a chain of military strongpoints, an Iron Age Maginot Line, later to be exploited and enlarged by the Romans. Even after the Romans left, the forts continued to be fought from and over. Liddington is one of the oldest forts in Britain, dating back to the sixth century BC, but it has also has been suggested as the site of the Battle of Mount Badon where the Roman-British Celts defeated the invading Anglo-Saxons around AD 500, one of the last wins for the home team. According to the ninth-century *Historia Brittonum,* the Celts were led by King Arthur, but that is just as speculative as siting the battle here – hills outside places as far apart as Bath, Bridgend and Buxton have also been considered. If it's true, though, this camp was a military stronghold for 1,000 years and more. In civilian terms too, this was scarcely a remote or unpeopled area in Roman times. The north–south Roman roads from Cirencester to Old Sarum and Winchester and Silchester diverge below the hill and cross the pre-Roman Ridgeway running from west to east, just as the M4 crosses them today. This was the nearest thing in ancient Wessex to Spaghetti Junction. Today the downland is as much an area of intense military activity as it was in Roman times. The camps have spread across the landscape as fast as Swindon itself: Larkhill, Bulford, Knook, Warminster. As the sky begins to cloud over again, an old transport plane lumbers across the plain from RAF Lyneham – the base's huge curving sheds are visible over to the west.

I suddenly have a peculiar feeling that there is nothing left between then and now, that the intervening years have melted away and that the only permanent scars on the landscape are those cut by the Romans and by ourselves – their roads and camps, our motorways and air bases and blockhouses and factory blocks. Nothing in between.

As I begin to retrace my steps back to the car, the last lapwings of the year are flapping mournfully above the green shoots of corn. Darting below the lapwings there are a couple of the first swallows – winter and summer visitors crossing like holidaymakers on changeover day. Lapwings off to Norway, swallows back from Morocco, legionaries going home to Rome, riflemen off to Helmand Province, some back again in coffins, motorists to Membury Services – nothing but journeyings, blown by forces we do not control or understand. Jefferies's yearnings sound like whistling in the endless wind. Where exactly are we to find this 'something better than a god'?

Passing the beech clump, I need to take a leak. There is no other human being for miles around, but the old modesty drives me to walk over to the trees. Surprisingly, there is a neat little gateway in the fence and a path leading past the ruined blockhouse into the heart of the grove. I select one of the fine full-grown beeches to piss against out of the wind. As I am halfway through, I notice a small white object at the foot of the tree. Peering down at it, I can see that it is a plastic figure of the Virgin Mary, no more than 5 inches long.

A stab of horror overcomes me, though I try to pretend it hasn't. Why should I feel ashamed, I certainly didn't intend any sacrilege. In my mind's ear, I can hear old Prof Dennett saying in his folksy Yankee style, 'For Pete's sake, grow up, it's only a piece of plastic, nothing's sacred.' But I have got through life so far without pissing on the Virgin and I don't want to start now.

Then I see that there is also a little silver crucifix half-hidden in the wet grass by the tree, and pinned to the tree trunk there is a card covered in bedraggled cellophane saying: 'In Loving Memory of

Pearl, 1923–2006'. Below the card there is a more substantial-looking plate, brass perhaps, in memory of someone else but it's too tarnished to read the name. I walk on through the grove and every other tree has one or more little memorials on card wrapped in cellophane or brass or wood pinned or nailed to it: to Nan, to Bert and Mary, in memory of Doris who loved this place, to Betty: 'If flowers were people you'd be the one I'd pick.' And it seems this isn't only a place to remember the dead and not just for human beings either, because there is one saying: 'Martin and Claire married 13 October 2007' and another saying: 'In Memory of Whisper', which sounds more like a dog or perhaps a pony. Here in this windy corner under the moaning beeches, the old instinct to invent the sacred still survives, unquenched by the pitiless secular tide. People must have made this a holy place off their own bat, without any official opening or ground rules about who or what can be commemorated here and who if anyone is being prayed to. I have never been quite sure what a chapel of ease was, but this feels like one.

How long has it all been going on? The inscriptions which have a date on them are mostly from the past ten years, but earlier ones might have fallen down and mouldered away in the damp earth. Was Liddington Clump a sacred place in Richard Jefferies's day? If he doesn't mention it, is this because he disapproves? No, I don't think so. He loved the classical gods and goddesses and their sacred springs and groves (and when he was dying he started rereading the Gospels, though he never came back to the Church). He would have been pleased, in a patriotic sort of way, that north Wilts too had its own sacred grove. And so am I, though I still wish I hadn't relieved myself in it.

NOTES

INTRODUCTION

1 It is often argued in academic circles that the so-called 'Renaissance' between, say, 1400 and 1650 was the invention of nineteenth-century historians such as the Swiss Jakob Burckhardt. Even defenders of Burckhardt's masterwork, *The Civilization of the Italian Renaissance in Italy* (1860), defend it these days on the grounds that he wasn't really talking about the rebirth of Greek and Roman cultures but about the birth of the *modern*, based no less on the culture of the Middle Ages than on Greece and Rome.

2 'We can see from the buildings constructed by the Romans that, as emperor succeeded Emperor, the arts gradually declined . . . long before the invasion of Italy by the Goths the decline of sculpture was well under way . . . But what inflicted incomparably greater damage and loss on the arts than the things we have mentioned was the fervent enthusiasm of the new Christian religion.' (Georgio Vasari, *Lives of the Painters*, 1550)

3 Charles Perrault took the plots for his marvellous fairy stories not from antiquity but from French folk tradition. What was there in the tales of Greece and Rome that could match his 'Sleeping Beauty', 'Little Red Riding-Hood', 'Puss in Boots' and 'Cinderella'? How curious that this crucial battle for control of modern culture should have been fought by both sides using fairy tales for ammunition. On one side there were grasshoppers and ants; on the other, talking cats and kitchenmaids who turned into princesses. And how long the struggle for supremacy went on between the ancients and the moderns.

BODY

I THE BATH: *A Bigger Splash*

1 John Betjeman, in his little-known essay on the architecture of Swindon, says: 'There is very little architecture in Swindon and a great deal of building,' but he likes the railwaymen's cottages 'in the Georgian tradition of excellent ashlar, four-roomed houses with a fifth as wash-house built at the back. The lay-out looks a little cramped today. But in 1849 when the building on the Faringdon Road end of Emlyn Square was being completed, the effect must have been spacious and delightful.' These cottages were one of the earliest experiments in planned industrial building anywhere, and they look just as sweet and liveable-in today. They are said to have been designed by Sir Matthew Digby Wyatt, who helped Brunel build Paddington Station and became Secretary to the Great Exhibition of 1851, and he would have had no call to be ashamed of them if he did.

2 Not exactly a picturesque site, and yet the church greatly moved Betjeman:

> Whistles and passing trains disturb the services, engine smoke blackens the leaves and tombstones, and eats into the carved stonework of the steeple. But it is a strong church and though it is not much to look at, it is for me the most loved church in England. For not carved stones nor screen and beautiful altars, nor lofty arcades nor gilded canopies, but the priests who minister and the people who worship make a church strong. If ever I feel England is pagan, and that the poor old Church of England is tottering to its grave, I revisit St Mark's, Swindon.' (*First and Last Loves*, London, 1952, p. 186)

3 David Urquhart, *The Pillars of Hercules or A Narrative of Travels in Spain and Morocco in 1848*, London, 1850, Vol. II, pp. 38–50. For the history of the bath in classical and Ottoman times, see Fikret Yegül, *Baths and Bathing in Classical Antiquity*, London, 1992, and Garrett G. Fagan, *Bathing in Public in the Roman World,* Michigan, 1999; for the Christian era, see J. Zellinger, *Bad und Bäder in der altchristlicher Zeit,* Munich, 1928, and Albrecht Berger, *Das Bad in der byzantinischer Zeit,* Munich 1982. For the city of Bath, see Barry Cunliffe, *Roman Bath Discovered,* London, 1984, and other works by Cunliffe. For the Victorian revival, see Malcolm Shifrin's wonderful website victorianturkishbath.org and Richard Metcalf, *The Rise and Progress of Hydropathy in England and Scotland*, London, 1912.

4   . . . the patrons of the Russian bath are cast in an antique form.
       They have swelling buttocks and fatty breasts as yellow as butter-
       milk. They stand on thick pillar legs affected with a sort of creeping
       verdigris or blue-cheese mottling of the ankles. After steaming,
       these old fellows eat enormous snacks of bread and salt herring or
       large ovals of salami and dripping skirt-steak and they drink
       schnapps. They could knock down walls with their hard stout old-
       fashioned bellies. Things are very elementary here . . . Mickey who
       keeps the food concession fries slabs of meat and potato pancakes
       and, with enormous knives, he hacks up cabbages for coleslaw and
       he quarters grapefruits (to be eaten by hand). The stout old men
       mounting in their bed sheets from the blasting heat have a strong
       appetite. Below, Franush the attendant makes steam by sloshing
       water on the white-hot boulders. These lie in a pile like Roman
       ballistic ammunition. To keep his brains from baking Franush wears
       a wet felt hat with the brim torn off. Otherwise he is naked. He
       crawls up like a red salamander with a stick to lip the latch of the
       furnace, which is too hot to touch, and then on all fours, with tes-
       ticles swinging on a long sinew and the clean anus staring out, he
       backs away groping for the bucket. He pitches in the water and the
       boulders flash and sizzle. There may be no village in the Carpathians
       where such practices still prevail. (Saul Bellow, *Humboldt's Gift*,
       Penguin edition, London, 1976, pp. 78–9)

5   Fikret Yegül says firmly: 'In a world almost universally permeated
    with a sense of religiosity, baths and bathing seem definitely to belong
    in the secular sphere . . . the literary and archaeological record left by
    antiquity reveals nothing of a deeply religious content . . . Rather,
    baths represented quite the opposite idea: their luxurious interiors
    and their noisy, oily, sweaty, steamy atmosphere offered the individual
    a secular and sensual experience.' (*Baths and Bathing*, p. 124)

6   For more of all this, see the website www.discoverireland.com/wellness.

II THE GYM: *Bodies Beautiful*

1   Sisyphus was legendary for his cunning. In the *Iliad*, Homer describes
    him as the 'slyest of all men'. He was famous for encouraging naviga-
    tion and commerce, for building the city of Corinth and for
    originating the Isthmian Games. Despite these impressive achieve-
    ments, he was condemned to perform his hopeless labour through all
    eternity, because when Zeus sent Death to him, Sisyphus temporarily
    managed to fetter Death so that no one died. In other words, Sisyphus

was a multi-tasking fitness entrepreneur, dedicated to the postpone-
ment of death, the Fred Turok of his time.

2 *Tusculan Disputations XXXIII.*

3 E.G.Turner argues in *Greek Papyri*, Oxford, 1968, p. 84, that the gym
   had been '*the* educational institution of classical times in which pagan
   spiritual identity was deposited'. Accordingly, 'the collapse and disap-
   pearance of the gym, the focal point of Hellenism, more than any
   other event, brought in the Middle Ages'.

4 Romans 7:18, 23–4.

5 Quoted, David Newsome, *Godliness and Good Learning*, London,
   1961, p. 207. See also Norman Vance, *The Sinews of the Spirit*,
   Cambridge, 1985.

6 *Charles Kingsley*, F.E. Kingsley (ed.), *His Letters and Memories of His Life*,
   London, 1877, Vol. I, p. 249. See also Una Pope-Hennessy, *Canon
   Charles Kingsley*, London, 1948.

7 Kingsley did not particularly care for the name. But he wrote to the
   Revd. F.D. Maurice, his collaborator in the mission to bring Christian
   socialism to the poorer districts: 'I have to preach the divineness of the
   whole manhood and am content to be called a Muscular Christian or
   any other impertinence.' (*Letters and Memories*, Vol. II, p. 54)

8 *Macmillan's Magazine*, IX, January 1864, p. 216.

9 Pope-Hennessy, p. 39.

10 When John Keble told no one that he was leaving his college fellowship in order to get married, Newman commented to his friend
   Froude, 'which silence the said college puts down, I suspect, to a
   romantic delicacy and tenderness; a keener observer, however, might
   see in it an opinion that marriage is a very second-rate business'.
   (Quoted, Ian Ker, *John Henry Newman*, Oxford, 1988, pp. 120–21).
   When another Oxford friend Mark Pattison got married, Newman
   sighed, 'I see that M. P. is married! Sic transit Gloria.' (Frank M. Turner,
   John Henry Newman: The Challenge to Evangelical Religion, New Haven,
   2002, p. 428) When Mrs Keble died in great pain a month after her
   husband, Newman speculated that 'she was to be kept awhile as a
   penance for having kept Keble from being a Catholic'. (*Ibid.*, p. 428)

   Of his own natural bent towards celibacy, Newman said: 'Never, so
   be it, will I be other than God has found me. All my habits for years,
   my tendencies are all towards celibacy. I could not take that interest in
   this world which marriage requires. I am disgusted with this world. I
   have a repugnance to a clergyman's marrying.' (25 March 1840)

   For Newman all concupiscence had the nature of sin. His own
   mother had conceived him in sin. It was celibacy that was the holy
   state. In one of his *Sermons Bearing on Subjects of the Day* published in

1843 when he was still an Anglican vicar, he had lamented that 'the gross, carnal, unbelieving world is blind to the peculiar feelings, objects, hopes, fears, affections of religious people.' And for that reason, 'the wisdom of serpents is often needed by the religious.'

11   Quoted, *Apologia Pro Vita Sua*, ed. Martin J. Svaglic, Oxford, 1967, p. xxv.

12   Susan Chitty, *The Beast and the Monk: A Life of Charles Kingsley*, London, 1974, p. 8.

13   *Ibid.*, p. 81.

14   *Ibid.*, 24 July 1851. In her trail-blazing life of Kingsley, as well as these hitherto suppressed letters, Susan Chitty reproduces Kingsley's drawings of himself and Fanny swooning in ecstasy in the nude.

Chitty reproduces two other drawings Kingsley made of saints being tortured, which a Cambridge tutor said 'no pure man could have made or could allow himself to show or look at'. An assistant in the Manuscripts Room of the British Museum described the drawing of St Elizabeth of Hungary's mother being lynched as 'the most disgusting exhibition in the whole collection' and told Chitty that it ought to be kept under lock and key. To us today these drawings may seem pallid because Kingsley's draughtsmanship is so feeble. Only with difficulty can one make out that St Elizabeth's mother is having a burning torch rammed up her vagina, but Kingsley's letters still read scorching hot.

15   Friedrich Nietzsche, *The Gay Science*, tr. Thomas Common, London, 1924, v. 377.

16   *Ibid.*, v. 382.

17   Friedrich Nietzsche, *Thus Spake Zarathustra*, tr. Thomas Common, Edinburgh, 1906, pp. 28–9, 33.

18   John L. Tancock, *The Sculpture of Auguste Rodin*, Philadelphia, 1976; see also my Appendix: 'The Thinker and the Man of Sorrows', p. 415.

III THE BEDROOM: *It Is Not a Moral Issue*

1   *The Times,* 11 June 1963.

2   *The Times,* 9 April 2005.

3   *The Times,* 16 February 2008.

4   *Independent on Sunday,* 1 December 2002.

5   *Observer,* 6 January 2008.

6   *Ibid.*

7   *Daily Telegraph,* 28 January 2008.

8   John Updike, *Couples*, London, 1968, p. 91.

9   Paper read to the Memoir Club in 1922, quoted, Quentin Bell, *Virginia Woolf*, London, 1972, Vol. I, p. 124.

10 Quoted, Paul Delany, *The Neo-Pagans*, London, 1987, p. 160.

11 *Ibid.*, pp. 77–80.

12 *Ibid.*, p. 39.

13 Quoted, Michael Holroyd, *Lytton Strachey*, London, 1967, Vol. I, p. 73.

14 Quoted, Michael Barber, *The Captain,* 1996, p. 51.

15 Martha Nussbaum and John Sihvola, *The Sleep of Reason*, Chicago, 2002, pp. 3–4.

16 R.W. Inge in R. W. Livingstone (ed.), *The Legacy of Greece*, Oxford, 1921, pp. 28–31.

17 See, for example, Sir Kenneth Dover's trail-blazing *Greek Homosexuality*, London, 1978, and James Davidson, *The Greeks and Greek Love*, London, 2007. Also Robert Flacelière, *Love in Ancient Greece*, New York, 1962, and David M. Halperin, *One Hundred Years of Homosexuality*, London, 1990.

18 Nussbaum and Sihvola, p. 57.

19 *Ibid.*, p. 58.

20 Plutarch, *Life of Pericles*, 8, 8.

21 Matthew 5:28.

22 *L'Osservatore Romano,* English edition, 6 October 1980

23 Lucretius, *De Rerum Natura*, Book IV.

24 Aristotle, *Nicomachean Ethics,* VIII, 12, 7.

25 Quoted, Peter Brown, *The Body and Society*, London, 1988, p. 38.

26 Matthew 8:21, 22, Luke 9:59, 60, Matthew 19:12.

27 Brown, p. 242.

28 *Ibid.*, p. 335.

29 Matthew 19: 4–6.

30 Ephesians 5:25, 28.

31 Brown, pp. 412–13.

32 Augustine,*Confessions*, 8.11.26.

33 The passage in Ephesians concludes: 'This is a great mystery, but I speak concerning Christ and the church. Nevertheless let every one of you in particular so love his wife even as himself; and the wife see that she reverence her husband.' (v. 32, 33) At least that is what the Church of England's Authorised Version says. The New English Bible has: 'It is a great truth that is hidden here.' But what the Catholic Bible says is: 'This is a great sacrament.' The original Greek is '*to mysterion touto mega estin*', prompting Bishop Westcott in his commentary on Ephesians (1906, p. 87) to say in his lofty Anglican way: 'It is scarcely necessary to remark that this passage does not in any way support the opinion

that marriage is a sacrament, a conclusion which has been drawn from the rendering in the Vulgate' – so it is that crusty hermit St Jerome who translated the Bible into Latin to whom we owe the elevation of marriage alongside baptism and the Eucharist as one of the supreme moments of the Christian life. In fact, the most accurate rendering for modern ears would probably be 'secret', for the whole point of the Greek mysteries such as those at Eleusis was that the ceremonies were to be witnessed only by initiates who were sworn never to reveal their nature. The root of the word is *'muein'*, to close one's eyes or lips.

34 Calvin, *Institutions*, IV, xix, 34.

35 Jean Daniélou and Henri Marrou, *The Christian Centuries*, 1964, Vol. I, p. 176.

36 D.H. Lawrence, *Apropos of Lady Chatterley's Lover*, Phoenix edition *Lady Chatterley's Lover*, London, 1961, p. 26.

37 *Ibid.*, p. 28.

38 *Ibid.*, p. 31.

IV THE KITCHEN: *First Stuff Your Dormouse*

1 Plato, Epistle 7, *Gorgias* 518b.

2 Plato, *Republic*, 404d.

3 Frag 2, Athenaeus 278d, *Archestratus: The Life of Luxury,* tr. and ed. John Wilkins and Shaun Hill, Totnes, 1994, p. 36.

4 Frag 38, Athenaeus 116f, Wilkins and Hill, p. 93.

5 Athenaeus 457c-e, quoted, 'Archestratus Where and When?' Andrew Dalby in John Wilkins, David Harvey and Mike Dobson (eds.), *Food in Antiquity*, Exeter, 1995, p. 402.

6 Wilkins and Hill, p. 16.

7 Plautus, *Pseudolus*, I, 810ff, quoted, Barbara Flower and Elizabeth Rosenbaum, *Apicius: The Roman Cookery Book,* London, 1958, p. 19.

8 Frag 45, Athenaeus 311a, Wilkins and Hill, p. 82.

9 Frag 57, Athenaeus 399d, Wilkins and Hill, pp. 91–2.

10 Frag 35, Athenaeus 278a, Wilkins and Hill, p. 73.

11 Flower and Rosenbaum, p. 101.

12 *Ibid.*, p. 65.

13 Although Barbara Flower and Elizabeth Rosenbaum tried many of them and found them mostly palatable and one or two rather tasty.

14 Make *placenta* this way. 2 lbs of wheat flour from which you make the pastry base; 3 lbs of ordinary flour and 2 lbs of best husked grain flour for the *tracta* [a sort of flour cake]. Soak the grain flour in water. When it is quite soft, pour into a clean mortar and drain

well. Then knead it by hand. When it is thoroughly worked, add the 3 lbs of ordinary flour gradually. Make this dough into *tracta*. Place them in a wicker basket where they can dry out. When dry, brush them with a cloth soaked in oil. Heat up the hearth and the earthenware vessels thoroughly. Then moisten the 2 lbs of wheat flour, knead them and make a thin pastry base. Soak 14 lbs of mild, very fresh sheep's cheese in water. Macerate the cheese in the water, changing the water three times. Take the cheese out of the water gradually, squeezing it dry in the hands. When you have thoroughly dried all the cheese, knead it by hand in a clean mortar and blend it together as much as possible. Then take a clean flour sieve and make the cheese pass through the sieve into the mortar. Then add 4½ lbs of good honey. Mix this with the cheese very thoroughly. Then place the crust on a clean board 1 foot wide, over oiled bay leaves, and make the *placenta*. First place the single *tracta* over the whole pastry base, then cover it with the cheese and honey mixture. Place the individual *tracta* on top and then pull over the pastry crust. Then place the *placenta*, covered with a hot dish, and heap burning charcoal around and over it. See that you cook it thoroughly and gently. Uncover it for inspection two or three times. When it is cooked, remove it and spread with honey. This will make a half-peck *placenta*. (Cato the Elder, *De Agri Cultura*, 76, tr. Stephen Hill and Anthony Bryer, 'Byzantine Porridge' in *Food in Antiquity*, pp. 45–6)

15 Archestratus, Frag 4.
16 Frags 59–60, Athenaeus 296, Wilkins and Hill, p. 93. See also James Davidson, *Courtesans and Fishcakes*, London, 1997, p. 411.
17 Pliny, *Natural History*, 14: 20.
18 Horace, *Odes* 1.37, 3.14. *Epistles* I, 14. See also Oswyn Murray and Manuela Teçusan (eds.), *In Vino Veritas,* British School at Rome, London, 1995, and Jancis Robinson (ed.), *The Oxford Companion to Wine*, Oxford, 1994.
19 Cicero, *Brutus, 287*.
20 Pliny, *Natural History,* 14: 55–7.
21 Martial, *Epigrams,* 13.3.
22 Anthony Kenny, *Aquinas*, Oxford, 1980, p. 27.
23 Elizabeth David, *Is There a Nutmeg in the House?* London, 2000, p. 103.
24 Elizabeth David, *An Omelette and a Glass of Wine*, London, 1984, pp. 229–36.
25 David, *Nutmeg,* p. 250. Paul Johnson, *The Birth of the Modern*, London, 1991, p. 759.
26 *The Memoirs of Giacomo Casanova*, Vol. III, tr. Arthur Machen, London, 1952, p. 352.

27 J. Rives Childs, *Casanova*, London, 1989, p. 193.

28 Giles MacDonagh, *Brillat-Savarin: The Judge and his Stomach*, London, 1992, p. 301.

29 Balthazar Grimod de la Reynière, *Almanach des Gourmands*, Paris, 1803–12, Vol. I, p. xi.

30 *Ibid.*, pp. 272–3.

31 J.K. Huysmans, *Against Nature,* tr. Robert Baldick, Penguin Classics, London, 1959, p. 27.

32 Mary Beard, *The Roman Triumph*, Cambridge, MA, 2007, p. 257.

33 Giles MacDonagh, *A Palate in Revolution: Grimod de la Reynière and the Almanach des Gourmands,* London, 1987, p. 107.

34 MacDonagh, *Brillat-Savarin*, p. 151.

35 So memorable is Brillat-Savarin's style, 'like a bishop pronouncing the Mass', according to Balzac, that the maxim about the dessert without cheese finds its way into Flaubert's dictionary of clichés sixty years later. Under *Fromage*: '*Citer l'aphorisme de Brillat-Savarin. Un dessert sans fromage est une belle à qui il manque un oeil.*'
    Balzac speaks admiringly of the way this reactionary opponent of the jury system loves to coin new words – '*garrulité*', '*truffivore*', '*obésigène*' – and how Brillat makes us savour the delights of gastronomy all the more, by demonstrating the theory of it and in the process making all the other sciences into its tributaries: botany, zoology, chemistry, agriculture, anatomy, medicine and hygiene – all are valuable only for what they contribute to the supreme science of gastronomy.

36 Graham Robb, *Balzac*, London, 1994, p. 347.

37 Johnson, p. 109.

38 George Saintsbury, *Notes on a Cellar-Book*, London, 1920, pp. 5–6.

39 *Ibid.*, pp. 7–9.

40 Davidson, p. 63.

41 *Ibid.*, p. 64.

42 Kingsley Amis, *On Drink*, London, 1972, p. 61.

43 *Ibid.*, pp. 49–50.

44 Zachary Leader, *The Life of Kingsley Amis*, London, 2006, p. 601.

45 Frag 9, Athenaeus 285b, Wilkins and Hill, p. 45.

46 Auberon Waugh, *Spectator*, 23 April 1983; 2 July 1983; 17 September 1983.

47 Norman Douglas, *Siren Land,* Penguin edition, London, 1983, p. 47.

48 *Ibid.*, p. 151.

49 Norman Douglas, *Alone*, London, 1921, pp. 209–10.

50 *Ibid.*, pp. 211–12.

51 David, *An Omelette*, p. 122.

52 *Ibid.*, p. 123.

53 Douglas, *Siren Land,* pp. 103–4.
54 *Sunday Times,* 8 February 2009.
55 Luke 4:2.
56 Exodus 34:28.
57 I Kings 19:8.
58 Luke 188:12.
59 Dag Tessore, in his brilliant little book *Fasting* (2007), tells us that 'in modern secularised countries such as Greece, the discipline of fasting has remained virtually unchanged since the time of the Fathers of the Church, even though obviously only a small proportion of the population really adhere completely to those austere rules'. (p. 108)
60 *Ibid.,* p. 109.
61 *Ibid.,* p. 48.
62 Brown, p. 220.
63 *Ibid.,* p. 223.
64 Tessore, p. 75.
65 *Ibid.,* p. 78.
66 See Orhan Pamuk, *Istanbul: Memories and the City,* tr. Maureen Freely, London, 2005, pp. 166–7.
67 *Sunday Times,* 20 January 2008.

MIND

1 See Werner J. Dannhauser, *Nietzsche's View of Socrates,* New York, 1974.
2 *Guardian,* 5 August 2008.
3 *Daily Telegraph,* 3 December 2007.
4 We are, after all, well acquainted with the idea that what goes around comes around. In the ancient world too, the idea of the eternally recurring cycle was a familiar one, to the Egyptians, to the Persians and to the Greeks. Sometimes they believed in reincarnation too, sometimes not, but they were comfortable with the idea that the physical world's history was circular rather than linear. Empedocles of Sicily, an older contemporary of Socrates, believed that love and strife predominated alternately in the world's cycle. Zeno of Citium, the founder of the Stoics, believed that the universe underwent regular cycles of formation and destruction, a notion he may have picked up from Heraclitus, according to whom fire changed into water, then into earth, then earth changed into water and water back into fire again. These ideas beguiled nineteenth-century philosophers like Schopenhauer and Nietzsche, who popularized the

concept of eternal recurrence. The best we can do in this line seems to be to have invented Groundhog Day.

V SCIENCE: *Back to Ionia*

1 For the archaeology of Miletus, see *Milet I–III* (publication of the German excavations), Berlin 1906–36, now updated by their website *Ausgrabungen in Milet*. See also George E. Bean, *Aegean Turkey*, London, 1966.

2 For a deeper discussion of these devilishly tricky matters, see Edward Hussey, *The Presocratics*, London, 1972, and Jonathan Barnes's two-volume study *The Presocratic Philosophers*, London, 1979.

3 Barnes, Vol. I, pp. 5, 8.

4 Karl Popper, *Conjectures and Refutations*, London, 1963, p. 143.

5 Barnes, Vol. I, p. 20.

6 *Ibid.*, p. 22.

7 Diodorus Siculus I.7 and 8; Democritus, Frag 5.

8 Bean in *Aegean Turkey* says that the ruins of Colophon are 'scanty, difficult to find and unrewarding when found'.

9 Xenophanes thinks that a mixing of the earth with the sea is occurring and that in time it is being dissolved by the mist. He says he has the following proofs: shells are found in the middle of the land and in the mountains, and he says that on Syracuse in the stone quarries there have been found impressions of fish and of seals, and on Paros an impression of laurel in the depth of the rock, and in Malta prints of all sea creatures. And he says that this happened some time ago when everything was covered in mud, and that the impression dried in the mud. (Barnes, Vol. I, p. 21)

10 Xenophanes, Frags 4, 15, 16.

11 Barnes, Vol. I, pp. 25–6.

12 'If this is right,' Hussey concludes (p.140), 'Mind does not intervene in the working of the *kosmos* at any particular time, except perhaps at the beginning. The whole history of the *kosmos* from that beginning onwards was planned by it beforehand, and proceeds like a premeditated human action successfully carried out.'

13 'The quantity of the things that are separated out cannot be known either by reasoning or by practical measures.' (Hussey, p. 137)

14 It followed that the whole history of the universe was determined, if at all, by a 'meaningless' necessity inherent in the laws governing the collision and rebound of atoms, a force which was devoid of any inherent tendency to the better, or of any regard for the wishes and

requirements of such accidental by-products as conscious beings. (Hussey, p. 148)

15   Popper, p. 148.

16   *Ibid.*, p. 144.

17   Karl Popper, *The Open Society and its Enemies*, London, 1945, Vol. I, p. 185.

18   Popper's translation, *Ibid.*, pp. 186–7.

19   The greatest principle of all is that nobody, whether male or female, should ever be without a leader. Nor should the mind of anybody be habituated to letting him do anything at all on his own initiative, neither out of zeal, or even playfully. But in war and in the midst of peace – to his leader he shall direct his eye, and follow him faithfully. And even in the smallest matters he should stand under leadership. For example, he should get up, or move, or wash, or take his meals . . . only if he has been told to do so . . . In a word, he should teach his soul, by long habit, never to dream of acting independently, and to become utterly incapable of it. In this way the life of all will be spent in total community. There is no law, nor will there ever be one, which is superior to this, or better and more effective in ensuring salvation and victory in war. *And in times of peace, and from the earliest childhood on* should it be fostered – this habit of ruling others, and of being ruled by others. And every trace of anarchy should be utterly eradicated from *all the life of all the men,* and even of the wild beasts which are subject to men. (Quoted in Popper's own translation and italics, *Ibid.*, p. 103)

20   As Professor T.A. Sinclair points out:

        Plato's estimate of the human race is at once incredibly low and incredibly high: the flower of a country's men and women to have their lives and loves directed down to the last detail by a 'committee of experts', the majority to live the unthinking life of sheep. Between the wisdom of the few and the docility of the rest the human race has never been so exalted or so abased. His reputation has suffered as much from adulation as from attack. Blinded by his glory and bewitched by his poetry many see only what they wish to see and pass over the evil; others, infuriated by his inhumanity and his lordly affectation of knowledge, lose patience with the task of trying to understand him. But perhaps the strongest objection to the political theory of the Republic lies in the notion of an absolute government by a set of persons whose claim to superior wisdom and infallible knowledge must never be questioned. (*A History of Greek Political Thought*, London, 1951, p. 166)

VI RELIGION: *The Anti-God-Botherers*

1 Christopher Hitchens, *God Is Not Great: The Case Against Religion*, London, 2007, p. 51.
2 Richard Dawkins, *The God Delusion*, London, 2006, p. 26.
3 *Ibid.*, p. 27.
4 Hitchens, p. 283.
5 Christopher Hitchens, *The Missionary Position: Mother Teresa in Theory and Practice*, London, 1995.
6 Hitchens, *God Is Not Great,* p. 228.
7 A.C. Grayling, *Against All Gods*, London, 2007, p. 54. See also his *Refutation of Scepticism*, London, 1985.
8 *Ibid.*, p. 57.
9 *Ibid.*, p. 42.
10 Dawkins, p. 356.
11 Daniel C. Dennett, *Breaking the Spell: Religion as a Natural Phenomenon*, London, 2007, p. 17.
12 *Ibid.*, p. 14.
13 Dawkins, pp. 236–9; Dennett, pp. 99–100; Hitchens, *God Is Not Great*, p. 8.
14 Charles Darwin, *The Descent of Man and Selection in Relation to Sex*, 1871, Vol. I, p. 156, quoted, Dawkins, pp. 199–200.
15 Dawkins, p. 202.
16 BBC2, 18 May 2008.
17 Dennett, p. 23.
18 *Ibid.*, p. 30.
19 Dawkins, p. 78.
20 Hitchens, *God Is Not Great*, p. 282.
21 Joanna Collicut, co-author with Alister McGrath of *The Dawkins Delusion?* (2007), argues that 'we need to be clear that the superficially similar notions of "religious faith" and "belief in the existence of god(s)" are in fact profoundly different'. (*Guardian*, 31 May 2008)
22 Dennett, p. 250.
23 *Ibid.*, p. 253.
24 *Ibid.*, p. 254.
25 Hitchens, *The Missionary Position*, p. 117.
26 *Ibid.*, p. 192.
27 *Guardian*, 9 May 2008.
28 Dennett, pp. 335–6.
29 Quoted, Dawkins, p. 36.

30 Richard Dawkins, *Unweaving the Rainbow: Science, Delusion and the Appetite for Wonder*, London, 1998, p. 27.

31 *Ibid.*, p. 25.

32 Dawkins also quotes the beginning of *The Second Law* (1984) by his colleague Peter Atkins: 'We are the children of chaos, and the deep structure of change is decay. At root, there is only corruption, and the unstemmable tide of chaos. Gone is purpose; all that is left is direction. This is the bleakness we have to accept as we peer deeply and dispassionately into the heart of the Universe.' (*Unweaving the Rainbow*, p. xi)

Dawkins applauds this 'very proper purging of saccharine false purpose' and 'laudable tough-mindedness in the debunking of cosmic sentiment', but warns that they 'must not be confused with a loss of personal hope'. Why mustn't they?

33 Dawkins, *Unweaving the Rainbow*, pp. 245–52.

34 Letter to J.D. Hooker, 13 July 1856; 'Design and beneficence', quoted, Janet Browne, *Charles Darwin: The Power of Place*, London, 2002, p. 176.

35 Julian Barnes, *Nothing to be Frightened of*, London, 2008, p. 71.

36 *Ibid.*

37 Cicero lamented the Epicurean propaganda being disseminated by another fashionable enthusiast, Amafinius; 'by the publication of his works the crowd had its interest stirred, and they flocked to the teaching he advocated in preference to any other . . . After him came a number of supporters of the same system, who by their writing took all Italy by storm.' (*Tusculan Disputations*, IV, iii, 6–7)

38 'What followers of this school say and think is not unknown to anyone of even moderate learning . . . But I do not see why they should be read except in the circle of those who hold the same views and read their books to one another.' (*Tusculans*, II, ii, 5–7)

39 Polybius, *Histories*, VI, 56.

40 Lucretius, *De Rerum Natura*, Penguin Classics edition, *On the Nature of the Universe*, tr. R.E. Latham, London, 1951, p. 150.

41 When human life lay grovelling in all men's sight, crushed to the earth under the dead weight of superstition whose grim features loured menacingly upon mortals from the four quarters of the sky, a man of Greece was first to raise mortal eyes in defiance, first to stand erect and brave the challenge. Fables of the gods did not crush him, nor the lightning flash and growling menace of the sky. Rather, they quickened the keen courage of his heart, so that he, first of all men, longed to smash the constraining locks of nature's doors. The vital vigour of his mind prevailed. He ventured far out beyond the flaming ramparts of the world and voyaged in mind throughout infinity. Returning victorious, he proclaimed to us

what can be and what cannot: how the power of each thing is limited, and its boundary-stone sticks buried deep. Therefore
superstition in its turn lies crushed beneath his feet, and we by his
triumph are lifted level with the skies ... (*Ibid.*, pp. 11–12)

All life is a struggle in the dark. As children in blank darkness trem-
ble and start at everything, so we in broad daylight are oppressed at
times by fears as baseless as those horrors which children imagine
coming upon them in the dark. This dread and darkness of the
mind cannot be dispelled by the sunbeams, the shining shafts of day,
but only by an understanding of the outward form and inner work-
ings of nature. (*Ibid.*, p. 39)

42 *Ibid.*, p. 159.
43 *Ibid.*, pp. 133–4.
44 *Ibid.*, p. 134.
45 *Ibid.*, p. 135.
46 *Ibid.*, pp. 63–4.
47 *Ibid.*, pp. 126–7.
48 *Ibid.*, p. 107.
49 *Ibid.*, p. 190.

VII NEW AGE: *Shopping in the Spiritual Supermarket*

1 Donald Regan, *For the Record: From Wall Street to Washington*, San
Diego, 1988.
2 Francis Wheen, *How Mumbo-Jumbo Conquered the World*, London,
2004, p. 123.
3 *The Times*, 15 May 1988.
4 Wheen, p. 29.
5 *Guardian*, 23 July 2008.
6 Joan Quigley, *What Does Joan Say? My Seven Years as White House
Astrologer to Nancy and Ronald Reagan*, New York, 1990, quoted,
Wheen, p. 156.
7 Henry Chadwick, 'The Ascetic Ideal', in W.J. Sheils, ed., *Monks,
Hermits and the Ascetic Tradition*, Oxford, 1985, p. 9.
8 Franz Cumont, *The Oriental Religions in Roman Paganism*, London,
1911, p. 276; see also his *L'Egypte des astrologues*, Brussels, 1937.
9 Keith Thomas, *Religion and the Decline of Magic*, London, 1971, p. 340.
10 *Ibid.*, p. 387.
11 For a fuller account, see Mary Beard, John North and Simon Price,
Religions of Rome, Cambridge, 1998, Vol. I.

12 E. Jomard, *'Description d'Antinoe'*, ch. XV, *Description d'Egypte,* II, Paris, 1818. Also Royston Lambert, *Beloved and God: The Story of Hadrian and Antinous,* London, 1984, and Thorsten Opper, *Hadrian: Empire and Conflict,* London, 2008.

13 For a long time, the Pincio obelisk was thought, not unreasonably, to have been brought from Egypt, from Antinoopolis. But only nine years ago, the remains of the funerary temple of Antinous were discovered at Hadrian's Villa at Tivoli, just by the right of the entrance where Hadrian could see it from his bedroom window. Even after the recent excavations, those remains are vestigial – a couple of squares and a semicircle of stone on a stretch of dirty gravel – not only because of the depredations of later stone-gatherers but because the monument must have been left unfinished when Hadrian died. All the same, in the space between the footings of the two little temples and the half-dome which was to have covered the back of the monument, the exedra, you can see a base for the obelisk. And the fragmentary inscription on the obelisk itself (which had finally been deciphered in the 1970s) confirmed that this was indeed where it had stood: 'O Antinous! This deceased one, who rests in this tomb in the country estate of the Emperor of Rome.'

14 Other oriental cults too went through the same grudging but unavoidable process of acceptance. Under the Republic, the worship of the Great Mother, Cybele the goddess of the Phrygians, in central Turkey had been confined to foreigners. But Claudius allowed the cult of Cybele and Attis. Soon the holidays of these Phrygian deities were officially celebrated with even more pomp than in their home cities. It was Claudius who devised the cycle of holidays between 15 March and 27 March to celebrate the renewal of vegetation, personified in Attis who had been discovered by Cybele as a child left exposed on the banks of the Sangarius, the largest river of Phrygia. In the legend, Attis is dead to start with, and believers begin the festival by mourning and fasting. Then at his funeral, the devotees flagellate themselves and cut their flesh, accompanied by piercing ululations and the sound of flutes. There follows a vigil and then Attis awakes from his sleep of death, and the festival ends with wild celebrations and processions through the streets. A temple of Cybele was built in 204 BC on the high point of the Palatine Hill to guard the black stone sacred to the goddess, which had been brought from Pessinus in Phrygia to authenticate the temple's consecration, just as the obelisks had been brought from Egypt to adorn the Iseum Campense. There is not much left of the temple now, just a huge concrete platform and a few eroded column drums and pieces of cornice in grimy tufa, but it is a wonderful spot under a grove of ilexes with sweeping views of

Rome. Augustus and his consort Livia both chose to build their villas a couple of yards away.

As for the worship of Baal, the 14-year-old Emperor Heliogabalus, when elevated to the purple in AD 218, attempted to give this barbarian divinity precedence over all other gods. He too had a black stone brought all the way from Emesa in Syria to adorn his temple. This apparent attempt to introduce a new monotheism to replace the easy-going polytheism of old Rome was greeted with great indignation. But half a century later, the Emperor Aurelian attempted much the same thing, by creating a new supergod, *Sol Invictus*, the Invincible Sun. When Aurelian conquered the Egyptian stronghold of Palmyra, he transferred the images of Bel and Helion to his new temple.

15 In the beautiful church of San Clemente behind the Colosseum, the medieval upper church lies above a lower church that was mentioned by St Jerome in 392, and below *that* lies a *mithraeum* of two centuries earlier with an altar showing Mithras in his Phrygian cap sacrificing a bull to Apollo. The lower church had been discovered in 1857 by the energetic Father Mullooley, prior of the neighbouring convent of Irish Dominicans. Luckily for Mullooley's peace of mind, he did not find the temple and school of Mithras which lay beneath it and, in its fine state of preservation, demonstrates to this day that there was a thriving earlier cult on the site, adjoining, as was so often the case, a large, even palatial nobleman's residence. By the door of the San Clemente *mithraeum*, a modern notice triumphantly records that the temple was in use for 200 years until the proclamation of 'the one true faith' in AD 400. Under Santo Stefano Rotondo of the late fifth century, one of the oldest round churches in existence, a *mithraeum*, again two centuries earlier, was unearthed in 1973, next to a Roman barracks for the non-Italian troops, so many of whom were worshippers of Mithras. Together with the underground temple at the Baths of Caracalla, and the *mithraeum* under the church of Santa Prisca on the Aventine Hill, and the one under a former spaghetti factory opposite the Circus Maximus (now the costume warehouse for the Rome Opera) that makes five *mithraea* within a mile of each other, not to mention those not yet unearthed.

16 J.M.C. Toynbee, *The Roman Art Treasures from the Temple of Mithras*, London, 1986, p. 55. See also John D. Shepherd and N. Griffiths, *The Temple of Mithras, London*, London, 1998; and M.J.Vermaseren, *Mithras the Secret God*, London, 1963, and (with C.C. Van Essen) *The Excavations of the Mithraeum of Santa Prisca,* Leiden, 1965; and Franz Cumont, *The Mysteries of Mithras*, Dover Edition, New York, 1956. The largest fragment in the Museum of London is the lower half of the figure of Cautopates, the mythical bearer of darkness and death,

holding his long torch pointing diagonally downwards. He would have been accompanied by his lost twin, Cautes, who symbolized light and life and held his torch pointing to the sky. Then there is a head of the Egyptian god Serapis, a grizzled Neptune-like figure with his *modius,* the basket of corn symbolizing fertility, on his head.

Nor are the conventional Roman gods excluded. There is a beautiful, coolly classical head of Minerva, minus the metal helmet she would have worn. Minerva played a significant role in the Mithras cult, for it was her gift of wisdom that helped the initiate to attain immortality. And here in the heart of the City, a hundred yards from the grim walls of the Bank of England, we find also a small marble group featuring Mercury, the god of commerce, holding a moneybag. Beside him crouches a ram, another symbol of fertility, and also a tortoise. Mercury had invented the lyre by stretching four strings across the shell of a tortoise, and because of this the tortoise stands for happiness in the afterlife. Bernie Madoff could not have designed a better crest for himself than this little marble group. Later than the temple, perhaps dating from the fourth century, there is a figure of a drunken Bacchus with equally riotous figures of Pan and Silenus. Underneath, there is an inscription which reads '*HOMINIBUS VAGIS VITAM*' – 'Give life to wandering mortals'. Then in the marble altar rondel we see Mithras slaying the bull, surrounded by the twelve signs of the zodiac, Taurus of course being one of them.

The Temple of Mithras was not alone in the promiscuous welcome it gave both to the gods of the new religion and to the new science of astrology. Londinium was only a modest commercial centre and a garrison town tasked with guarding the river crossing that led from Colchester, which was then the Roman capital in Britain, back down to Kent and the Channel – and civilization. Yet all over the still only partially excavated remains of Londinium, archaeologists have found abundant evidence of how thoroughly the new cults had permeated this outpost of empire. In Smithfield and Billingsgate, over the river in Tooley Street, on the approach to old London Bridge, there are altars and votive figures and household ornaments, in clay and marble and bronze, of gods and goddesses from the other side of the Empire, figures of Isis and Attis and Serapis and Cybele and Venus and Diana and the mysterious Sabazios.

17 See Beard, North and Price, chapter 3.
18 As John Micklethwait and Adrian Wooldridge describe in *God is Back: How the Global Revival of Faith is Changing the World* (2009), the First Amendment set off a fierce competition between America's 'multiplicity of sects', with a succession of evangelising religions vying for people's attentions: the Methodists converted one eighth of the country within

a generation of the revolution. While Europe's state-sponsored religions shrivelled, America's free market kept faith alive.

19 1 Thessalonians 4:16–17.

20 *The Times*, 10 September 2008.

21 Barack Obama, 'My Spiritual Journey', *Time*, 16 October 2006.

22 All the things foretold in the Bible would come to pass, 'but how or in what order, human understanding cannot perfectly teach us, but only the experience of the events themselves'. Jesus 'does not speak of the second resurrection but of the first which now is' – a reference to Matthew 25: 'The hour is coming, and now is, when the dead shall hear the voice of God.' The millennium had already begun with the Nativity of Christ, and it was absurd anyway to imagine that thousands of saints were lolling about for thousands of years 'to enjoy a kind of Sabbath-rest during that period, a holy leisure after the labours of the six thousand years since Man was created', according to the millenarians, filling the intolerable interval until the Second Coming with 'immoderate carnal banquets'. Christ had come, and risen once, and that was enough to be going on with. There were whole sects of millenarians like the Montanists around Hierapolis, the modern Pamukkale in south-west Turkey, where the apostle Philip lived and died. In the century after the fall of Jerusalem, the Montanists, like many other Christians in Asia Minor, continued to believe that the earthly Messiah would come to them and come soon. In that region too travelled St John the Apostle, supposed author of the Book of Revelation, whose vision of the Apocalypse made the Second Coming so intoxicatingly vivid.

23 The Reformers almost all continued the anti-millenarian line ('amillenarian' is the technical term for their teaching). Cranmer's *Forty-Two Articles* of 1553 included Article 41: '*Of Heretics called Millenarii:* They that go about to renew the fable of Heretics called *Millenarii* be repugnant to Holy Scripture and cast themselves headlong into a Jewish dotage.' This article and two others relating to the heretical teaching of the Anabaptists were omitted from the Articles passed by Convocation after the death of Queen Mary, leaving the Church of England with the Thirty-Nine Articles it has stuck with.

24 In Ratzinger's words: 'The Antichrist's deception already begins to take shape in the world every time the claim is made to realise within history that messianic hope which can only be realised beyond history through the eschatological judgment. The Church has rejected even modified forms of falsification of the kingdom to come under the name "millenarianism", especially the intrinsically perverse political form of a secular messianism.' (*Catechism of the Catholic Church*, 1995, p. 194)

25 See Norman Cohn's marvellous book *The Pursuit of the Millennium*, Oxford, 1970.

26 The Talmud states that this world as we know it will exist for only 6,000 years. During the End-Times, the scattered Jewish exiles will be gathered in to Israel, all Israel's enemies will be defeated, and the land of Israel will be transformed from a desert into a garden, the Temple will be rebuilt, the dead will rise again, and the Messiah will become the King of Israel – a fairly comprehensive wish list.

27 G.K. Chesterton, *What's Wrong with the World*, London, 1910, chapter 5.

VIII DIALOGUE: *From Plato to Paxman*

1 Theodore Zeldin, *Conversation*, Londoon, 1999, p. 3.

2 *Ibid.*, p. 50.

3 *Ibid.*, p. 84.

4 Lucy Mangan in the *Guardian* (28 August 2008) confessed:
   I can't work out if it is a depressing testament to the debasing effects of the junk-television diet we habitually follow that the heightened language of *My Zinc Bed* – unashamedly writerly writing – felt like an affectation and distraction, or if it is simply a sign that the intimate medium of television does indeed require a less mannered form of language, lest it overwhelm rather than serve the piece.

5 *The Last Days of Socrates*, Penguin edition, London, 1959, p. 45.

6 *Ibid.*, p. 57.

7 *Ibid.*, pp. 153–4.

8 *Ibid.*, p. 50.

9 *Ibid.*, pp. 62–3.

10 *Ibid.*, p. 54.

11 'The institutions of the enormously expanded Roman *res publicae* remained exactly those of the original nuclear city-state.' Fergus Millar, *The Crowd in Rome in the Late Republic*, Michigan, 1998, p. 21.

12 Cicero recounts how an earlier Mark Antony, not to be confused with Julius Caesar's defender, had argued this line while acting as defence counsel in a trial some time in the 90s BC: 'I surveyed all the successive phases of our republic and concluded that, even though all the examples of civil discord had been an affliction, some nonetheless had been just and practically necessary . . . Without dissension among the nobles, the kings could not have been driven from this state; nor the tribunes of the people created; nor the power of the consuls so often limited by popular vote; nor the precious right of summoning granted to the people.' (my version, as are the following four excerpts,

but see Millar, p. 218). Or as Nye Bevan might have said: our liberties didn't fall into our laps, we had to fight for them.

13 Millar, p. 173.

14 Quoted, Millar, p. 116.

15 As Hirtius describes in *De Bello Gallico*:

> Having arranged his winter quarters, Caesar set out, as fast as he could, for northern Italy in order to woo the towns and colonies to which he had commended Mark Antony for the post of augur. Caesar strove to exert his influence, both with pleasure on behalf of a man who had such close ties to him and whom he had sent on a little earlier to start campaigning and also with anger against the small group who were out to destroy Antony and so shatter Caesar's influence. Even though he heard en route that Antony had actually been elected augur, he still felt compelled to visit these towns and colonies, to thank them for having offered him their support and for staying loyal to Antony. He could also take the opportunity to build up his own election campaign for the following year. (See Millar, p. 189)

16 Millar, p. 199.

17 The thesis that the growing dominance of Christianity helped to extinguish the dialogue form is supported in Simon Goldhill, ed., *The End of Dialogue in Antiquity*, Cambridge, 2009, published too late to be considered here, but see *TLS* review, 18–25 December 2009.

18 Alberto Manguel, *A History of Reading*, New York, 1996, ch. 2.

19 Fiona Hamilton for *The Times* tested the new approach in a library in Whitechapel and found the noise inside the premises almost as loud as out in the street. Nobody batted an eyelid when she conducted a fifteen-minute interview in the middle of the library and her BlackBerry rang out at full volume. (*The Times*, 19 September 2008)

IX FAME: *Let Me Through, I'm a Celebrity*

1   *Sunday Times*, 8 October 2006

2   *Ibid.*

3   *The Times*, 5 September 2008.

4   Quoted, *Guardian*, 28 July 2008.

5   Mary Beard, *The Roman Triumph*, Cambridge, MA, 2007, pp. 191–2.

6   *Ibid.*, p. 188.

7   *Ibid.*, p. 210.

8   *Ibid.*, p. 120.

9   *Ibid.*, p. 137.

10 As Beard puts it: 'Ancient authors focus not only on the plunder and

the spectacular image in the procession; they return repeatedly to how the display was staged as if *representation itself* – its conventions, contrivances, and paradoxes – was a central part of the show. The triumph is, in other words, construed as being a ceremony of image *making* as much as it is one of images.' (Beard, p. 181)

11   With all the potential snags and mishaps, it is not surprising that some generals did not seek to secure a triumph. When a sycophantic senator suggested that Tiberius should celebrate a triumph on returning to Rome from Campania, the Emperor replied that 'he was not so lacking in glory that, after subduing the fiercest nations, and after receiving or declining so many triumphs in his youth, he would now at his age seek an empty honour merely for a trip in the country'. (Beard, p. 271) Augustus boasted of turning down additional triumphs. Agrippa twice refused one. Vespasian, exhausted by the long procession of his triumph, quipped that 'I've got my comeuppance for being so stupid as to long for a triumph in my old age.' Septimius Severus declined one on the grounds that he could not stand up in his chariot because of his arthritis. Marcus Fabius Vibulanus refused a triumph that was spontaneously offered him by the Senate because his fellow consul and his own brother had been killed in the fighting: 'He would not accept laurel blighted with grief.'

X ART: *Museums Are Us*

1   See James R. Gaines, *Evening in the Palace of Reason*, London, 2005.
2   Richard Wagner, *Bayreuther Blätter*, October 1880, in *Prose Works*, tr. William Ashton Ellis, London, 1897, Vol. VI, p. 213.
3   *Ibid.*, p. 261.
4   Ian Dunlop, *The Shock of the New*, London, 1972, p. 246.
5   Germain Bazin, *The Museum Age,* tr. Jan van Nuis Cahill, London, 1968, p. 160.
6   *Ibid.*, p. 173.
7   In Genoa and Venice too, looted works of art were deposited in convents. Similar institutions were established on Napoleon's orders in most of the great provincial cities of France. Even during the Restoration, the religious works of art did not return to the churches they came from. Instead, they became part of the nation's story, torn from their context, deconsecrated, educational tools rather than objects of veneration.
8   Within this enterprise there was, scarcely disguised, a desire to claim as large a slice of the past as possible for our own people. Stockholm's

Nordiska Museet, opened in 1873 by the Pan-Scandinavian fanatic, Dr Artur Hazelius, envisioned a Nordic civilization that had once stretched from Lapland to the Alps. His museum included a reconstructed Lapp village, peopled by men and women in regional costume plying their old crafts. In winter, a family of genuine Lapps came to live in one of the Lapp huts. The whole thing was intended as 'a microcosm of Sweden' (Bazin, p. 237). Similar folk museums were soon to be found all over Europe and the United States.

9   As Bazin points out (p. 216), it was with some generosity that the King included five large paintings by David, who voted for the death of Louis XVI but who was now to be forgiven by reason of his genius, that quality which now outranked the lineage of dukes and princes.

10   These conversion projects can be almost as remarkable as the new-build museums. Just as the first public museums tended to be converted convents, so today there is scarcely any large building which is not liable to be converted into a museum as soon as its original purpose falters or disappears. In Paris, the Gare d'Orsay becomes the city's Impressionist gallery. In London, the medieval church of St Mary, next door to Lambeth Palace, is turned into a museum of garden history. In Leamington Spa, as we have seen, the delightful Turkish baths are now part of the town's museum and art gallery.

Often the premises are less suited to the purpose than were the large bare spaces of the convent refectories and dormitories. The aisles and platforms of old churches and railway stations make it difficult to hang exhibits or show them satisfactorily. Some uncomfortable ghost of their former purpose obstinately clings to them. Though they are much adulated, I find these places somehow out of kilter. But nobody would dream of asserting that the conversion was a mistake, for the establishing of a museum is an unimpeachable enterprise, the one act of homage that in our sceptical time does not attract derision.

11   John Ruskin famously wrote of Whistler's *Nocturne in Black and Gold*: 'I have seen, and heard, much of Cockney impudence before now; but never expected to hear a coxcomb ask two hundred guineas for flinging a pot of paint in the public's face.' (*Fors Clavigera*, letter lxxix) The Impressionists were not allowed to exhibit at the official Salon but were relegated to a specially organized Salon des Refusés. When Roger Fry's first show of post-Impressionist art at the Grafton Gallery held its press day on 5 November 1912, the critic Robert Ross claimed that this was an appropriate day 'for revealing the existence of

a plot to destroy the whole fabric of European painting'. (Dunlop, p. 120) Ross was supposed to be a supporter of the avant-garde – he became, after all, remembered as Oscar Wilde's loyal friend Robbie. Yet he regarded the paintings of Cézanne, Gauguin and Van Gogh as a danger to public health: 'If the movement is spreading, it should be treated like the rat plague in Suffolk. The sources of the infection (e.g. the pictures) ought to be destroyed.' (Dunlop, p. 142) The poet Wilfred Scawen Blunt was no less virulent: the paintings at the Grafton Gallery were 'works of vileness and impotent stupidity, a pornographic show'. (Dunlop, p. 120) Similar, if less violent, spasms of revulsion erupted at the International Surrealist Exhibition at the New Burlington Galleries in 1936 and, after the war, at the first London shows of the American Abstract Expressionists.

12   The attendance was a record for the gallery; the sales were more than satisfactory; the Yorkshire Penny Bank, which held the Grafton in mortgage, made a pretty penny. Clive Bell, 'How England Met Modern Art', *Art News,* October 1950.

13   Gerhard Richter, regarded by some as the Picasso of the twenty-first century, says: 'I have no programme, no style, no direction . . . I pursue no objectives, no system, no tendency . . . I'm what you might call a passive painter . . . chance does the work much better than I ever could.' (*Sunday Telegraph*, 28 September 2008)

14   *The Times Literary Supplement*, 5 September 2008.

15   *The Times*, 26 September 2008.

16   Or take the works, rather less celebrated, of Mark Boyle and his family. In the 1960s, Boyle set out on what he described as a mission 'to include everything in a single work. In the end the only medium in which it will be possible to say everything will be reality.' The Boyles started by making assemblages from the debris of bomb sites, then still plentiful in London. This was merely carrying on the tradition of Schwitters and Picasso. It came to seem too arty, too deliberately composed. Accordingly they devised a method to select random sites for 'a journey to the surface of the earth'. They would blindfold themselves, and throw darts at a map, and then travel to the site indicated by the dart and throw a T-square into the air and make an exact reproduction, usually about 6 foot square, of the patch of ground where the T-square landed – a pavement, a gutter, a potato field. Thirty years later, you can still find artists doing much the same thing, for example, Stefanie Bushler's *Puddles* (2006, exhibited Berlin, 2008), which reproduces in earth, stone and epoxy resin the dark, winking mystery of a muddy puddle.

XI NATURE: *Darwin's Worms*

1 Four vols., Cambridge, 2001.
2 The Roman Age Optimum was followed by the Dark Ages Cold
   Period, known as the Migration Period Pessimum. In the climatic
   sense, the Dark Ages really were dark. Tree-ring data suggest a rapid
   cooling from the fall of Rome down to the end of the first millennium AD. Agriculture retreated, forests advanced, bogs grew, lake
   levels rose. This in turn was succeeded by the Medieval Warm Period
   lasting from about the tenth century to the fourteenth century. De-
   icing in the North Atlantic enabled the Vikings to colonize
   Greenland, and agriculture advanced again. During this period, temperatures, at least in Europe, may have been only a touch cooler than
   they are today. Then came the Little Ice Age from about 1400 to
   1850. Since then we have been warming up again, although even
   according to the IPCC consensus by an average of less than 2°F. A run
   of lower average temperatures in the late 1960s and early 1970s led to
   a temporary panic that the world was actually cooling down once
   more. There was even talk of another Little Ice Age somewhere on
   the horizon, from leading climate scientists, such as Cesare Emiliani,
   the founder of palaeoceanography, and Hubert Lamb, after whom the
   Climate Research Unit at the University of East Anglia is named.
   Our present panic may be more securely based on the evidence, but
   that evidence too is drawn primarily from a very short run of years.
      The controversial Richard Lindzen, professor of atmospheric sci-
   ence at MIT, himself a contributor to some of the research on which
   the IPCC's conclusions are based, argues that the IPCC's 'Summary for
   Policymakers' overeggs the certainty of the research findings, and varies
   crucially from the draft summary prepared by the scientists themselves.
   The 'Summary' claims that greenhouse gases are responsible for 'most
   of the observed global warming over the past fifty years', while the
   IPCC Report itself more cautiously suggested only that greenhouse
   gases were 'a substantial contributor' to the warming. Lindzen argues
   also that there are methodological flaws in deducing from the modest
   rise in actual mean global temperatures that we are in for a terrifying
   jump in temperatures over the course of this century. These uncertainties do not of course undermine the case for reducing our carbon
   emissions for other reasons as well as the threat of global warming,
   notably the pressing need to reduce the acidification of the oceans.
3 Gore's 2006 film of that title won two Oscars, though when a Kent
   school governor brought a High Court ruling on whether the film

should be banned from secondary schools, Mr Justice Burton (who had no quarrel with Gore's central thesis that climate change was happening and was being driven by man-made emissions), found nine scientific errors or unsupported assertions, such as Gore's claim that the melting of the ice in Greenland or West Antarctica would cause a rise in the sea level of up to 20 feet 'in the near future'.

4   This concept of *homeostasis*, the maintenance of stability by self-regulating mechanisms within a body, seems itself to be fairly recent. The earliest reference to the word that the *OED Supplement* can find dates back no further than 1926. There it is still spelled in the etymologically correct form of *homoeostasis* (staying the same). It was there applied to such phenomena as the way the body maintains the same temperature despite external shocks. Thus the Gaia hypothesis can be seen simply as an extension on the grand scale of processes that are quite familiar to us in our own bodies.

5   Margulis, in particular, has been careful to get rid of the more extreme claims made for it. There was, she declared, no special tendency of biospheres to preserve their current inhabitants, still less to make them comfortable. Lovelock himself protested that 'nowhere in our writings do we express the idea that planetary self-regulation is purposeful, or involves foresight or planning by the biota'.

6   Henry Williamson, author of *Tarka the Otter* (1927), discovered this fact by accident on a pilgrimage to the grave of Jefferies, whom he regarded as 'irregularly the greatest writer in English literature after Shakespeare'.

7   W.H. Hudson, *A Traveller in Little Things*, London, 1921, p. 83.

8   I could have gone the same distance in the other direction to 'Imber on the Down, five miles from any town', if the Army had not closed the track for their tank ranges and demolished the village except for the church. The trails of the tanks left white scars on the rolling landscape. It was easy enough to think of them like scars on a person. The militarization of the Plain was scarcely a novelty by my time. As far back as 1909, W.H. Hudson was recording how many local people loathed the sight of the camps and the everlasting booming of guns and thought that the War Office had desecrated 'the wild ancient charm of the land'. (W.H. Hudson, *Afoot in England*, London, 1909, p. 242) For me, all this was part of the charm. The rumbling of the tanks was a reminder of the heroic past, of the preparations for D-Day and the invasion force passing through our village on the way to Southampton and me being held up by my father to watch the King come to review them, though I cannot honestly remember this but only the thrill of being told it later.

9   I took the left fork and followed a delightful little rushing brook
        about four feet wide that ran steeply over a series of waterfalls

between two and ten feet high. It ran along a south-facing stone wall that acted as a sounding board for its song, a continuous chord composed of the deep notes made by the spouting of water into stone hollows and the descants of the shallower rapids. Thus serenaded, I cooled off in a pool below a waterfall, so shaped that I could lie facing the morning sun with the cascade on my shoulders. By angling myself further back, I could get the full, icy force of the water over the back of my head, a sensation more often associated with warm water and the hairdresser's chair, and utterly exhilarating.' (Roger Deakin, *Waterlog: a swimmer's journey through Britain*, Vintage edition, London, 2000, p. 93)

10 *Daily Telegraph Magazine*, 8 November 2008.
11 *Guardian Weekend*, 25 October 2008.
12 Matthew 6:26–34.
13 Luke 10:38–42. Later efforts were made to upgrade the values of domestic service. For example, in George Herbert's poem. 'The Elixir', better known as the hymn 'Teach Me, My God And King':

> A servant with this clause
> Makes drudgerie divine:
> Who sweeps a room, as for thy laws,
> Makes that and th'action fine.

Herbert was an Anglican priest and a gentleman who sought, out of kindness, to gild the un-lily-like lives of the labouring poor. Yet even in his words one senses something of an uphill struggle. The essential damage had been done long before.

14 Matthew 11:28.
15 Genesis 2:15.
16 Translated by A.W. Mair, 1908.
17   The elm tree in the grove
       While yet a sapling small must be constrained
       By pressure strong to take the curving line
       Of the plough's handle; joined to this the pole
       Stretches eight feet in front; there is the pair
       Of earth-boards, and the share-beam fitted well
       With double-timbered back. Cut for the yoke
       A linden light, and from a beech tree tall
       Wood for the staff which at the base controls
       The turning of the plough. Long time each piece
       Should hang in hearth-smoke for good seasoning.
       (Virgil, *Georgics*, Book I, lines 167–77, tr. T.C. Williams, 1915)

18   These acts and powers observing, some declare
          That bees have portion in the mind of God
          And life from heaven derive; that God pervades
          All lands, the ocean's plain, th'abyss of heaven,
          And that from him flocks, cattle, princely men,
          All breeds of creatures wild, receive at birth
          Each his frail, vital breath; that whence they came
          All turn again, dissolving; so that death
          Is nowhere found, but vital essences
          Upsoaring in the vast, o'er-vaulted sky
          Move unextinguished through the starry throng.
          (*Ibid.*, Book IV, lines 222–33)
19   Theocritus, *The Idylls*, tr. Robert Wells, London, 1988, see pp. 13–14.
20   Janet Browne, *Charles Darwin: The Power of Place*, London, 2002,
     chapter 12.

XII SCIPIO'S DREAM

1   Hans Vaihinger, *The Philosophy of 'As If'*, tr. C.K. Ogden, London,
    1924, p. 24.
2   *Ibid.*, p. 20.
3   *Ibid.*, p. 258.
4   Quoted, *Oxford Revisited,* Justin Cartwright, London, 2008, p. 17.
5   Vaihinger, p. 302.
6   *Ibid.*, p. 320.
7   *Ibid.*, p. 264.
8   *Ibid.*, p. 265.
9   *Ibid.*, p. 362.
10   *Ibid.*, p. 344.
11   W.H. Auden, 'The American Scene', reprinted in *The Dyer's Hand*,
     London, 1963, p. 318.
12   Proverbs 29:18.

EPILOGUE: LIDDINGTON CLUMP

1   Richard Jefferies, *The Story of My Heart*, Totnes, 2002, p. 50.
2   *Ibid.*, p. 55.
3   *Ibid.*, p. 89.
4   *Ibid.*, p. 107.
5   *Ibid.*, p. 124.
6   *Ibid.*, pp. 81–2.
7   *Ibid.*, p. 122.

APPENDIX
THE THINKER AND THE
MAN OF SORROWS

The original conception of *The Thinker* formed part of Rodin's massive project for *The Gates of Hell*, to adorn the entrance of the Musée d'Art which was to be built on the site of what in fact became the Gare d'Orsay (which in modern times has come full circle to the first intention of placing an art museum on the site). The figure in the middle of the work was, as we have seen, originally intended to represent the poet Dante. Rodin himself described the evolution of the figure:

> *The Thinker* has a story. In the days long gone by, I conceived the idea of *The Gates of Hell*. Before the door, seated on a rock, Dante, thinking of the plan of his poem. Behind him Ugolino, Francesca, Paolo, all the characters of the *Divine Comedy*. This project was not realised. Thin, ascetic, Dante in his straight robe separated from the whole would have been without meaning. Guided by my first inspiration I conceived another thinker, a naked man, seated upon a rock, his feet drawn under him, his fist against his teeth, he dreams. The fertile thought slowly elaborates itself within his brain. He is no longer dreamer, he is creator.' (Quoted, Albert E. Elsen, *Rodin's Thinker and the Dilemmas of Modern Public Sculpture*, Yale, 1985, p. 43)

As Professor Elsen says: '*The Thinker* has served more purposes than any other modern sculpture, confirming what Rodin's admirers considered was his ability to render a timeless universal symbol.' Not merely are the twenty bronze casts of the piece scattered around the public spaces of Europe and America, replicas are to be found standing before many an art museum and philosophy department. *The Thinker* often figures in advertisements for electrical and electronic equipment and courses to improve one's brainpower, not to mention in cartoons, where the familiar pose is adapted for all sorts of comic purposes. And among modern artists too this revival of the heavy-limbed muscular ideal reverberated for a long time in, for example, the work of Brancusi, Maillol, Léger and Picasso. In the forecourt of the British Library squats Eduardo Paolozzi's monumental bronze of Sir Isaac Newton seated, bending forward with his dividers. Paolozzi calls the figure *Newton after Blake*, and indeed the effortful pose is copied from Blake's painting, but the sheer muscular bulk of the figure is unthinkable without the example of *Le Penseur*.

Where did Rodin derive this extraordinary idea, so novel in its conception and yet evoking such an immediate sympathetic response from his own times? Rodin was an intensely thoughtful artist who consciously drew much from the great sculptors of the past whom he had studied closely not only in the museums of Paris but also in his years in Brussels, Florence and Rome. Elsen tells us (p. 19) that 'the pose of the upper thighs and torso of *The Thinker* is unthinkable without the *Belvedere Torso*', the sculpture attributed to Apollonius of Athens and now in the Vatican Museum. The *Belvedere Torso* was a favourite model of Michelangelo, who was Rodin's supreme hero. And it is Michelangelo that art historians tend to identify as *The Thinker*'s principal source, in the figure of Jeremiah in the Sistine Chapel and especially in the statue of Lorenzo de' Medici, Duke of Urbino, in the Medici Chapel in San Lorenzo, Florence. The young duke, armoured and helmeted, sits in a negligent pose with knees apart and ankles together, the back of his right hand resting lightly on his knee, the fingers of the other hand playing with his upper lip. He is pensive, certainly – the statue is known as *Il Pensieroso*, but you can see the muscles rippling beneath the breastplate.

So, yes, there are quite a few similarities. And yet somehow the *tone* of the two sculptures differs, I think rather crucially. Elsen tells us that 'statues of seated male figures had been made many times before and invariably the subject sits with back erect, head up and the face fully visible. This arrangement imparts a sense of dignity through good posture and mental alertness.' A sense, too, in the case of Lorenzo de' Medici, of being on top of things rather effortlessly, an air of lordship. It is true too of Michelangelo's statue of Moses in San Piero in Vincoli in Rome, which has also been mentioned as a possible source for *Le Penseur*, although Moses sits in a much more dominant, almost aggressive posture.

There is something heavy, effortful, engaged, about *Le Penseur* which the Michelangelos altogether lack. I am reminded rather of a quite different series of works from the other side of the Alps. At almost exactly the same time as Michelangelo finished *Il Pensieroso* – the mid-1520s – the south German sculptor Hans Leinberger finished his limewood statue of *Christ Resting* (now in the Bode Museum in Berlin). This work too is said to be influenced by the *Belvedere Torso* (Geneviève Bresc-Bautier in *Sculpture from Antiquity to the Present Day*, eds. Georges Duby and Jean-Luc Duval, Cologne, 2002, p. 659), but the result is entirely different.

The statue shows Jesus at the moment on the Mount of Olives when he and three disciples – Peter, James and John – reach a place called Gethsemane and he tells them to sit down while he prays, 'and he began to be sorrowful and very heavy' and prays, 'O my Father, if it be possible, let this cup pass from me: nevertheless not as I will but as thou wilt.' (Matthew 26:37–39, also Mark 14:32–35 and Luke 22:39–44). Jesus is shown here at his maximum moment of vulnerability and weakness, his maximum moment of being human except for that moment on the Cross when he complains that God has forsaken him. His head is cast down, his knees splayed apart in an attitude which suggests despair and fatigue rather than the elegant negligence of *Il Pensieroso*. His right elbow rests on his knee, his cheek is sunk into his right hand, while his left arm rests on his thigh with the hand flopping inertly downwards, its index finger pointing to the ground in a reversal of its pointing to the sky in the blessing. The whole figure suggests abject exhaustion, a man at the end of his tether.

Leinberger was one of the leading sculptors in this period in south Germany where the last flowering of Gothic religious feeling encounters the first confident vibrations of the high Renaissance. But this particular sculpture follows closely the conventions of this scene in the life of Jesus, conventions which were already more than a century old and were to last almost two more centuries. All over Burgundy and southern Germany there are statues of *Christus in der Rast* or *Christus in Elend* (*Christ Resting* or *Christ in Wretchedness* – both terms are used for the same figure). In Leinberger's native district of Dachau (a region which in later history was to give terrible cause to deepen Christ's wretchedness), there are at least ten such statues still to be found. Each follows closely the same dispositions of the limbs, even when the local parish carver could not match the technique and expressive quality of Leinberger.

When my elder son saw a late-seventeenth-century version of 'Christ on the Mount of Olives' (another name often given in English to this figure), he instantly said, 'Now I see where Rodin got his ideas from.' The bent back, the splayed knees, the head resting on the hand, the elbow on the knee, the contained, self-absorbed nature of the whole immediately suggests Rodin's *Thinker*. And I cannot resist the thought that Rodin who was so attentive to his forerunners and so ready to learn from them had somewhere in his travels seen one or more such figures and absorbed their potential into his creative mind. For he was just as open to the great Gothic sculptors as to their classical successors. Yet of course the figures are significantly different. I don't mean just that Rodin has the right elbow awkwardly thrust across to rest upon the left knee rather than, more naturally, on the right one. The whole purpose of Rodin's enterprise is to suggest the ability to dominate and make sense of the world, to show man as master of nature. What we see is coiled strength rather than that confessed weakness which was exposed to the night air on the Mount of Olives. As a young man, Rodin had briefly joined a Catholic order. *Le Penseur* is a very un-Catholic piece of work.

ILLUSTRATIONS

INDEX